# Jeep 4x4
## Performance Handbook

Jim Allen

MBI Publishing Company

## Dedication
To my wife Linda—always my major source of inspiration.

## Acknowledgments
To all of those gearheads, professional and shade tree, who shared trade secrets, tidbits of information, and most importantly, their precious time. I owe them for the good stuff in this book: John Ambrose, Tom Anderson, Brad Bricker, Fred Coldwell, Tony Curless, Don Dolezal, Donna Fox, Pat Gremillion, Shawn Gregory, Gage Hartman, Mark Hinkley, Ron Hix, Richard Imholdt, Jim Jackson, Bill Long, Jim McGean, Dave McNurlen, Greg Moser, Harold Off, Chris Overacker, John Partridge, Mark Pearson, Ranch Pratt, Bob Riegel, Rick Rimmer, Bob Ritzman, Mike Rossi, Joe Schaff, Ed Shaffer, Rob Shehan, Dave Shelton, John Sloan, Joel Snider, John Stark, Flint Stevens, Tom Telford, Jim Wagner, Darryn Wallace, Steve Watson, John White, Willie Worthy, Chris Wood, and Tom Wood.

First published in 1998 by MBI Publishing Company, 729 Prospect Avenue, PO Box 1, Osceola, WI 54020-0001 USA

© Jim Allen, 1998

All rights reserved. With the exception of quoting brief passages for the purpose of review no part of this publication may be reproduced without prior written permission from the Publisher.

The information in this book is true and complete to the best of our knowledge. All recommendations are made without any guarantee on the part of the author or Publisher, who also disclaim any liability incurred in connection with the use of this data or specific details.

We recognize that some words, model names and designations, for example, mentioned herein are the property of the trademark holder. We use them for identification purposes only. This is not an official publication.

MBI Publishing Company books are also available at discounts in bulk quantity for industrial or sales-promotional use. For details write to Special Sales Manager at Motorbooks International Wholesalers & Distributors, 729 Prospect Avenue, Osceola, WI 54020-0001 USA.

Allen, Jim.
    Jeep 4x4 performance handbook/Jim Allen.
       p. cm.
    Includes index.
    ISBN 0-7603-0470-X (pbk.: alk. paper)
    1. Jeep automobile—Performance. 2. Jeep automobile—Customizing. I. Title.
TL215.J44A39          1998
629.222—dc21          98-35041

**On the front cover:** With a few intelligent modifications, your Jeep can be scaling walls like this one with ease. Jim Allen

**On the back cover:** Like their smaller, shorter counterparts, Cherokees and Grand Cherokees can and do serve as competent off-road rigs. Jim Allen

Printed in the United States of America

# CONTENTS

Acknowledgments                                                    2

Introduction                                                       4

Chapter 1    **GETTING STARTED**                                   6
             The Whole Jeep

Chapter 2    **TIRES AND WHEELS**                                  11
             Footprints in the Sand

Chapter 3    **SUSPENSION AND STEERING**                           27
             Long Legs

Chapter 4    **AXLES, GEARING AND DRIVESHAFTS**                    60
             Power to the Ground

Chapter 5    **TRANSFER CASE, OVERDRIVE AND SPLITTERS**            82
             Torque Splitting

Chapter 6    **TRANSMISSION**                                      93
             Multiplying Torque

Chapter 7    **WINCHES AND RECOVERY GEAR**                         104
             Inertially Challenged

Chapter 8    **CHASSIS, BODY AND INTERIOR**                        115
             Skin and Bones

Chapter 9    **BRAKES**                                            129
             Whoa Nellie!

Chapter 10   **ENGINE AND ENGINE SWAPS**                           139
             Go-Power

Chapter 11   **ELECTRICAL SYSTEM**                                 165
             Zap Rap

Chapter 12   **SAFETY ITEMS**                                      177
             Stayin' Alive

             **Appendix 1    Sources**                             185
             **Appendix 2    Bibliography**                        191
             **Index**                                             192

# INTRODUCTION

Welcome to the world of high-performance Jeeping. If you're reading this, you fit into one of two categories.

Are you the inveterate tinkerer; that person for whom the project will never end as long as there is life? Is that never-ending mechanical journey more fun than the arrival? If so, you are the true gearhead and 90-weight runs in your veins.

You could also be a person who wants something more or different from a Jeep. You could be looking for a single step or a few steps that will take you closer toward a performance goal, whatever it may be. You might be looking for a few closely considered options or a blueprint for a complete makeover.

First off, this is not a "How-To" book. It's more of a "What-To," or to be more precise, a "How-To-Know-What-To" book. I won't show you how to install the parts you choose, but I will show you how to make the choices. This is the more important part of the deal, I think. The accessory world is full of ad hype, misinformation, myths, and outright bovine scat. To survive a Jeep buildup with your fortune intact, you need a BS detector, and this book is it!

*Jeep Performance Handbook* is written for all Jeeps, and I hope that you can walk away with some fresh ideas, whether you drive a CJ, a Grand Cherokee, or a Forward Control. Because the Universal type Jeep (CJ, YJ, TJ) is the most popular platform for buildups, there is a definite bias in that direction, but my goal was to give all Jeep owners something to take home. For that matter, many of the principles you will read apply to nearly any 4x4.

Bang-for-buck is a recurring theme here. It's not so much what a part or modification does, but how much it does for the money you spend. Embarking on a big Jeep buildup is not for the faint of heart or the light of wallet. To get what you want from your Jeep, spend your money wisely on the things you need. Trendy is fine, as long as it delivers performance at a price you're willing to pay.

You'll see a lot of product photos in this book that were kindly supplied by assorted manufacturers. They're used mainly to illustrate points or to show options, not as free ads. I chose photos of high quality products that get the job done, but there wasn't room for everything. You'll no doubt continue to search for other high-performance components. I hope you will be able to spot a good product by the time you are done here.

Every effort was made to present the facts accurately. Designs, manufacturers, and parts numbers may change, but the laws of physics won't. The basic stuff in this book is useful today and should remain so as long as there are Jeeps. I have also tried to keep most of my opinions out of this book, but I will admit that there is a slant toward moderation—toward identifying what you need to get the job done. In slanting the book this way, I have left out some of the most radical and super hard-core Jeeping stuff. The people who are into that realm probably won't need this book!

This is not exactly a beginner's book, nor is it for engineers. I have assumed some basic technical knowledge on your part, and also that you have a manual handy on your particular Jeep model. There are definitions for most of the technical terms used, and don't feel bad if one slips by you here or there. The technical stuff comes mostly from the mouths of the experts in the field, to whom I am eternally grateful for the meeting of the minds.

Even in a book like this, there isn't room for everything. No doubt, you will have some burning question not answered by this book. Apologies in advance. I've tried to address the recurring questions and problems I encounter in my life as a writer for a variety of 4x4-oriented magazines.

Finally, there are more than a few mathematical formulas in here. Don't grind your teeth about it the way you may have done in math class years ago. Just get a basic calculator and work 'em out. Overall, they're pretty easy stuff. Hey, my brain goes to four-wheel drive for anything tougher than 2+2. If I can do this stuff, so can you. Enjoy!

—*Jim Allen*

## Jeep Model Abbreviations

| Code | Corresponding Models |
|------|----------------------|
| C-101 | 1966–73 Jeepster. |
| CJ | The standard production Civilian Jeeps, 1945–86, to include CJ-2A, CJ-3A, CJ-3B, CJ-5,CJ-6, CJ-7, CJ-8. |
| FC | The Forward Control Jeeps, 1957–65, to include FC-150, FC-170, and FC-170DRW (dual rear wheels). The M-series military FC are also referred to in this category. |
| MJ | The XJ base Comanche pickup. |
| PU | The 1946–65 Willys-style pickups. |
| SJ | The post Kaiser-Jeep "Big Jeeps," the 1971–92Wagoneers, Cherokee, and 1971–87J-seriespickups. |
| SJ(G) | The 1963–70 Kaiser-Jeep "Gladiator" pick ups and Wagoneers. |
| SW | The 1949–65 Willys-style Station Wagon. |
| TJ | The 1996 and up coil sprung Wrangler. |
| YJ | The 1987–95 leaf sprung Wrangler. |
| XJ | The 1984 and up midsized Cherokee. |
| ZJ | The 1993 and up Grand Cherokee. |
| 715 | Rounds up the military Gladiators, M-715, M-725, M-729. |

The key to building the Jeep of your dreams is carefully determining what you really need. Your Jeep can be modified to master tough terrain with surprisingly few alterations.

# Chapter 1

# GETTING STARTED
## The Whole Jeep

The first lesson to learn in a Jeep buildup is that you have to think beyond just one part. If one snazzy gizmo becomes the whole focus of your mechanical lust, take a step back and evaluate the big picture. Changing one part may have an effect on something else, and that part will affect another, and so on.

The trick is to get an idea of just what you want the

Jeep to do, following all the threads that lead from that goal and then integrating the modifications required to create a "whole Jeep." For the purposes of definition, we'll call a "whole Jeep" one that is assembled so that the modifications enhance rather than fight each other. The whole vehicle is balanced in strength and ability according to the uses you plan.

This 1947 CJ-2A is powered by a 2.3-liter Ford four-cylinder that relies on light vehicle weight (2,600 pounds ) and low gearing to get the job done. The 1975 Pinto mill is slightly warmed and backed up by a Ford T-18 four-speed that feeds though a Mustang Turbo clutch. A Dana 20 with Dana 18 gears splits torque to a pair of Dana 44s with Detroit Lockers and 5.38 gears. At 100 horsepower, the Ford engine has enough grunt to turn 36/12.50-15 Super Swampers. Steve Regula owns this "Fighting Flatfender."

## What Do You Need?

If you are starting from scratch, this may be the hardest question to answer. People who have built a Jeep and four-wheeled it already have a pretty good idea of what they need. If you are just starting out in the Jeep game, your brain is probably full of the ad jargon from aftermarket suppliers and the advice of well-meaning experts. The advice is often good, but filtered through that person's experience.

To learn what you need, start off easy. Take your stock rig out and learn to use it. Properly driven, a bone-stock Jeep is a formidable machine but very forgiving of a new owner. It'll take you far enough into the tough stuff to get you well and truly scared the first few times out. Taking an off-highway training course and joining a Jeep club are two ways to learn to use your Jeep with good effect and may even save you a few repair bills as you learn.

With experience comes confidence. Confidence inspires greater challenges and finally, one day, you may find that you have outgrown your Jeep, at least in OEM trim. Along the way, you will have learned your personal tastes and will have some idea of "the right stuff" your Jeep requires to take you there. You may find that it's perfectly adequate in stock form, though there are some goodies that you should consider from a safety standpoint.

Jeeps are remarkably adaptable machines. Throughout their history, the folks who tinker with them have wondered if the engineers didn't have certain aftermarket modifications in mind. In recent years, Jeep engineers have acknowledged that many owners will be playing with their masterpieces and may even engineer a few shortcuts for them. Chrysler Corporation regularly tests the better aftermarket parts from a variety of manufacturers and uses the R&D from countless Jeepers on the trail to improve their product.

To finally answer the "what do you need" question, I'll say that when you get right down to the core of it, there are only two things you need in a four-wheel drive: traction and clearance. Yep, it's really that simple. If you want to improve trail performance, make improvements in those two areas and you're set. Well, it's simple in word but not always in deed.

## The Compromise

It's a plain fact: the further you go into the high-performance trail machine realm, the further you get away from docile, mild-mannered street performance. There is no doubt that Jeep now engineers its vehicles to be docile (and safe) on the street and is willing to sacrifice some

Powered by a 1988 TBI Chevy 350, this 1969 Jeepster has more than enough grunt for any situation. The 350 hands off to a TH-400 trans and Dana 300 T-case. The axles are both Dana 44 units with 3.73 gears. The rear axle carries a Detroit Locker and the front mounts an ARB Air Locker. The suspension utilizes a 4-inch lift on custom Alcan springs. This rig, owned by Lyle and Leona Schrader, is a head turner that's drivable in every venue.

raw trail performance in the process. In the olden days, when 4x4s were primarily marketed for commercial use, the primary emphasis was on their ability to do a job. Raw trail performance and comfort were often sacrificed to haul a load or run a pump. In the beginning, Jeeps saw little recreational use. Still, in most ways—stock to stock—the Jeeps of today can outperform the Jeeps of yesterday, on the trail and certainly on the street.

Modern engineering has closed the gap between street and trail performance but there still exists a line beyond which you lose in one area or the other. Your first decision is where that particular line is going to be for you. Most 4x4s spend 90-plus percent of their time on the street. Many are used as basic transport. Where do you fit here and what are you willing to trade?

Some trail machines can leave your jaw hanging in wonder at their performance in the dirt, but for

This 1974 J-10 was built from the ground up to go fast and fly. It's powered by a well-massaged four-barrel AMC 401 thumper. A TH-400 transmission hands off to a Quadra-Trac T-case and a pair of 4.10:1 geared wide-track Dana 44s that have been structurally enhanced with welded-on trusses. The suspension is soft and supple to absorb terrain taken at speed. The passengers are protected by a built-in cage system that's integrated into the chassis. Chris Overacker built this hi-po prerunner, drawing on his Baja racing background.

day-to-day, back-and-forth-to-work driving, daily beatings would be preferable. There are many levels between tame and extreme, but what do you lose in the transition from a street-biased machine to an extreme four-wheeler? It varies somewhat from Jeep type to Jeep type, and it occurs on two levels: human comfort and drivability.

On the comfort side, a highly modified Grand Cherokee would retain more plushness than a stripped CJ. It's very possible to retain comfort items on a built-up machine—even one built up to extreme standards—but most people don't. Items like air conditioning, power seats, fancy stereos, and power windows all add weight and complexity. The weight costs trail performance and requires stronger and heavier drivetrain and suspension components. Most extreme rigs are lean and mean and, by nature, uncomfortable. The majority of even the toughest extreme Jeepers would rather take a beating than drive their rig on a long freeway trip. They claim that you recover from the beating faster!

On the drivability side, the discussion gets a little more serious. Once you decide to pursue trail performance, you will have to give up many of your carefree street shenanigans. Going back to our traction and clearance discussion, the typical buildup will include a moderate to high lift, tall and fat tires, a locker, and low gears. All of these items detract from performance on the street.

Suspension and tire changes affect handling to varying degrees, depending on the vehicle. Short wheelbase Jeeps are the most affected, but in extreme configuration, these modifications limit the handling of any vehicle—no more fast, sweeping turns or abrupt freeway lane changes! The tall suspension raises the center of gravity, and because the suspension geometry has changed, the Jeep doesn't handle the same, or as well, as it did before. The huge tires grip the road and won't let go. Instead of breaking loose and skidding, the extra traction combines with the high center of gravity to flip the vehicle over much more easily if you lose control.

In less critical situations, you will find that the big tires follow every groove and react to every pebble on the road, making constant steering corrections a new way of life that you ignore at your peril. A moment's inattention can land you in the ditch. A loose, trail-worn suspension can multiply this effect. Mud tread tires, common and popular for good reason on trail rigs, are marginal performers compared to street tires on icy or rain-slicked roads. They require a much slower pace under these conditions. They also generate a substantial whine on highways, which can give you a headache if you're driving alone, or make you hoarse if you have a passenger. The low gearing needed for trail work can limit your freeway speeds. Some trail rigs can't even safely reach the national speed limit. The engine screams at a high rpm and you can watch the fuel gauge drop as you drive. The extra noise adds to driver fatigue.

Certain types of automatic locking differentials can bark the tires and grab in turns. They can also affect cornering to a certain degree, by locking and unlocking with throttle release or application. Some of them are downright unpredictable in icy conditions.

Well, I've painted a pretty gloomy picture, haven't I? That was the plan. An extreme rig is a conscious choice. Compromises should be made with full knowledge of the benefits and the pitfalls. A real four-wheeler will not build a trail monster, drive it like a Ferrari, crash and burn, and then expect to sue someone for his or her choices.

The moral of all this is that you have to adjust your driving style to suit the vehicle and its level of modification. This is commonsense stuff for people with good judgment but it needs to be said anyway. Take it to heart and mind. Don't let your ego dictate your driving style or your level of modifications, especially if you are carrying special cargo, e.g., your family!

OK, you've endured the pulpit area of this book (the only one, by the way), from which a little preaching was done. 'Nuff said.

## Extreme Rigs

If you decide on an extreme buildup, the odds are good that you will trailer your rig. A Jeep atop a car trailer, towed by a motor home or camper, makes for an ideal vacation machine. You have the comforts of your home away from home, and a Jeep you can haul to any locale around the country. Your family can enjoy a vacation campsite even if they don't put the gnarly wheeling at the top of the list, as you do. The other benefit is that if the Jeep breaks, as it will someday if you are into the high-adrenaline realm of four-wheeling, you will have the means to get the carcass home without sweating on-site repairs.

## The Dual-Purpose Machine

This is where most people fit in and is the primary focus of this book. Dual-purpose owners usually drive to and from their trail excursions, exercising care and judgment in trail choices so they can drive back. The level of modifications is kept to those that don't greatly affect day-to-day uses, at least where it counts. Rigs like this can be very capable and, with a skilled driver, give the Big Dogs a serious run for the money.

The Jeep Sport Utes also fit here, like Wagoneers, Cherokees, and Grand Cherokees. Just a few carefully chosen modifications can put these rigs pretty high up on the trail performance food chain. The downside is that they are more vulnerable to cosmetic damage than a bobtail CJ, YJ, or TJ.

## Bang for the Buck

Most of us don't have unlimited funds, so modifi-

cations must be chosen carefully to bring a good result for the money spent. We'll get into the details of that later on, but the most common mistake is buying something on the basis of popularity instead of need. Also, the order in which you buy things should be considered. If you buy the stereo before the differential guard and crack open your diff housing, the mirror is the only place you can go to point the finger.

One of the big questions is whether to do the work yourself. Labor prices being what they are today, you can save a lot of dinero doing the work yourself. The big question is whether you and your toolbox are up to it.

Out on the trail, you will run into folks who can build a Jeep out of a pile of rust flakes and a bottle of 90-weight, with just a hammer and a Crescent wrench. These folks will make everything sound easy and give all lesser gearheads an inferiority complex. Again, don't let your ego dictate your choices. Be very honest and calculating with these choices, but pay attention to what the master gearheads say.

If you are a novice wrencher, your first step is to get the service manual for your Jeep and start tackling some of the maintenance chores. Perhaps you can even do some of the easier modifications. Be patient and deliberate in your work and leave the timeclock out of the garage. You will have a learning curve, so be kind to

With TBI-injected, 383-cid Chevy power, this CJ-7 scores nearly a thousand on the ramp, tackles every tough trail, and is a comfortable street runner. It uses a TH-700R4 trans, Dana 300 T-case, Currie-built 9-inch axles with 4.86 gears, a Detroit Locker in back, and an ARB Air Locker up front. The cushy interior includes a full cage and racing harnesses. The front suspension features extra-long National springs, reversed shackles, and dual shocks in a custom hoop set. The rear also uses supple Nationals. Doug Engel owns this rig built by Stage West.

Comfort and trail prowess combine in this 1993 Grand Cherokee. The lift works out to about 5 inches, but the axle mounts were relocated to maintain pinion angle and caster. The engine is a massaged 4.0-liter six that pumps out about 230 horsepower. This runs through a stock four-speed auto to an NV-242 T-case modified with a 4-to-1 low-range kit and Currie tailshaft kit. The stock front Dana 30 and rear Dana 35 axles were retained, with the addition of 4.56 gears, ARB air lockers, and custom alloy axle shafts. Billy Vickers pilots this rig.

yourself. Eventually, your toolbox and experience level will grow and peak to suit your own comfort level.

When you go shopping for products, remember the apples and oranges adage. Unless you are looking at nearly identical products, don't shop on the basis of price alone. Look first at *what* you get, *then* check the price and compare it to the other items that fit into the same general category. Remember, you get what you pay for!

## Jeeps and the Family

Jeeping and Jeep buildups can be like a drug, and without trying to sound sexist, most of the addicts are men. OK men, while your wife and family may tolerate your addiction, they may come to despise your Jeep as something that steals you away. The Jeep game becomes a true joy when you can share it with the whole family. So, how do you go about making that happen?

1. What's more important? If the Jeep comes between you and your family and it can't be resolved, the Jeep's outta there!
2. Don't act unilaterally. Coming home with $5,000 worth of parts that you bought without discussion with your wife could make life real tough. Talk the parts needs over first and be patient in answering the inevitable "why do we need this again" questions.
3. Don't spend the family fortune.
4. Let your Jeep become the family pet. Perhaps it will take on a name that all of you like.
5. When it comes down to the buildup, let everyone

have a say in some of the choices. If your wife likes red seats, get red seats!
6. Encourage and let anyone help who wants to, even if it slows you down, but don't force anyone to "put in hours" on the job.
7. Balance the time spent on the Jeep with family time. If the wife takes a moment to recognize your face when you come in from the garage, it's a good sign that you've been out there too long.

## What To Do First?

Some of this depends on the vehicle and its particular pluses and minuses. In my not-so-humble opinion, the chapters in this book represent a good order, with the exception of the recovery and safety items. They should obviously come first, to include a winch, other recovery gear (jack, snatch strap, etc.), fire extinguisher, and cargo tie downs.

No matter how capable your Jeep becomes, it will always be susceptible to getting stuck or catching fire. Cargo tie downs will not only prevent cargo from rattling and shifting, but in the event of an accident (it could happen on the highway too), it prevents loose objects from becoming potentially lethal projectiles.

This book will help you build for specific terrain. Some of your choices will be dictated by the type of terrain you generally traverse near where you live or where you commonly travel. While it's possible to build a fairly universal machine, the needs of an all-out, down-south, gumbo-mud Jeep and a Rocky Mountain high-ridge rock-runner are completely different.

*Chapter 2*

# TIRES & WHEELS
## Footprints in the Sand

### Tires

A set of sticky tires may be the most cost-effective performance mod you can make to your Jeep. A taller tire by itself offers more clearance under the differentials and chassis. A wider tire, or a change in tread pattern, can give you more traction. Sounds great, but it isn't always as simple as picking out a tire and jamming it on. Bigger is often better when it comes to tires, but bigger may not always fit.

Here we get into our "whole Jeep" concept again. You want the tires to work with everything else. In order to fit that really huge tire, how much articulation, ride quality or safety is it going to cost you? While an incremental increase in tire size on a stock rig could easily give you a healthy performance boost with few fitting problems, a jump to monster tires could bring on some oversized headaches. It may be worth it or not. It all depends on what you need.

### *Radial vs. Bias Ply*

This is getting to be a pretty dated discussion but since there are still some bias-ply tires out there, it's somewhat relevant. A bias-ply tire has belts of rubber-impregnated fabric that overlap each other diagonally from bead to bead. This was the industry standard for much of the pneumatic tire's long history. The bias tire has very tough and stiff sidewalls. A variation is the belted bias ply, which features several additional belts of material around the circumference of the tire. The belted bias tire came in response to the European radial. Most off-road and street tires today are radials, but there remains at least one good bias tire for four-wheeling. Interco's Bogger and Swamper bias-ply tires are renowned for good service and performance at a great price.

The radial tire, which emerged in the 1950s and became popular in the 1970s, has gradually taken over the tire world. The radial tire has overlapping belts that run straight from bead to bead, with more belts that run around the circumference. It typically wears longer than a bias ply, supplies better traction, and runs cooler.

The radial tire is very flexible in the sidewall area and offers a good ride and better conformation to rough ground than does the average bias tire. This equates to better traction in the dirt. The bias-ply tire is generally known for tougher sidewalls but advances in radial tire technology have gradually narrowed the gap. BFG's "Tri-Gard" has set the standard for tough sidewall design in a radial tire.

### *Tread Design*

Here we get into a can of worms because there are as many opinions on this topic as there are four-wheelers. As far as tread designs go, you have to pick your poison and stick with it. Or, buy more than one set of tires! Four basic tread types are available with a few subclasses. They are generally biased toward stellar performance in one area, but a careful choice will give you a tire that will be great for your particular environment

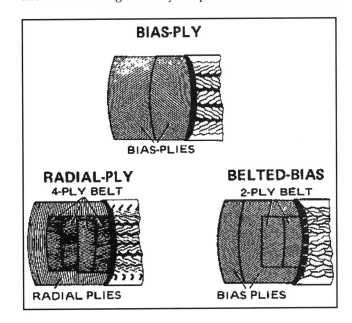

11

but generally OK when you stray from it.

## Highway Tread

This your ordinary passenger car tire and is designed with the needs of the pavement in mind. Potentially useful in sand and certain types of rocks because of a nonaggressive tread, they are often seen in LT sizes built for 4x2 trucks. Beyond this, they are essentially useless on the trail. There is no real advantage to having them unless your Jeep is strictly a boulevard cruiser. A subclass would be *all-season* tires, which are tires that are specially designed to perform better in inclement weather. These are potentially more useful to the 4x4 owner but still not worth many words.

Highway Tread.

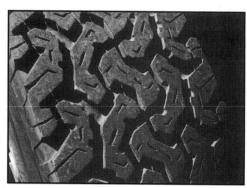
All Terrain Tread.

Mud Tread.

## All Terrain Tread

Even though BF Goodrich makes a tire of this name, the term has come to represent a tire that is designed to perform well in a variety of off-highway conditions. It is a fairly recent innovation that has closed the street/trail performance gap. The closed tread design is usually quiet on the highway, though noisier than a street tire, and performs well in rocks, sand, and on the highway. They are generally decent rain, snow, and ice tires also. As you would guess, they tend to load up in mud but some of the AT designs are surprisingly good in the goo. An AT tire would be outstanding for a rig that is biased toward highway performance with minimal effect on trail performance.

## Mud Tread

Mud tires come in a variety of styles, from the old bias-ply mudders that give new meaning to the term road noise, to modern radial mud designs that are surprisingly quiet (this is relative, of course) and docile in

other elements. As a rule, the radial MT designs are the weapon of choice for most four-wheelers. Their aggressive good looks play a part, but beyond their obvious attributes in soft stuff, they are generally outstanding in rocks of all types and good in deep snow. The flexible radial MTs can also be very good in sand, despite their apparent liabilities of being an aggressive tread design. The MT is at its worst in rain and especially ice. Some MTs can be downright dangerous in ice and should be avoided for use in icy conditions.

## Snow Tires

A 4x4 is a natural for snow country, so a few words on snow treads are in order. Contrary to old myths, a good snow tire is not an open-lugged design like a mud tire. It is moderately open, so that it can clean itself, but close enough to compress the snow inside the tread and use its cohesion to supply traction. Snow tires also use sipes and kerfs (see page 21, Tire Glossary) to aid in ice and wet traction situations. Often, the rubber compound is changed in a snow tire to offer better ice traction. Some snow tires are studded, though studs are not legal in every state. The metal studs dig into the ice for traction. There are M&S rated tires of many types that are essentially standard tires reengineered to pass the Department of Transportation's (DOT's) mud and snow requirements, and then there are all-out, full-gonzo winter tires, like the Bridgestone Blizzak. The M&S designs have some potential use as a pseudo AT, but the dedicated snow tires, especially studded tires, tend to wear quickly on dry roads.

## *Fenderwell Clearance*

The first step in a tire upgrade is to determine how much room you have for the tire in the fenderwell. Not only must the clearance be sufficient with the Jeep at rest, it must accommodate maximum up- and down-

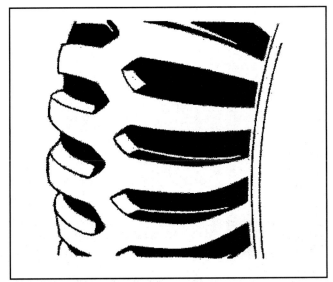

One of the original mud treads. The nondirectional tire (called the "All Service" in civvy years) was pioneered in World War II, proving itself capable. It's not as effective on wet streets, but it continues to be popular in some circles and is still in production.

travel and side to side tire movement caused by steering and cornering.

If you plan a mild tire upgrade, you may find it easier than you think. A little research on your part can yield what other tire options were available for your rig. In the case of a Wrangler YJ, the books show these units could be fitted with 235/75R-15 tires but 30x9.50 and 31x10.50s were optional. That means that any one of the three should fit with no clearance problems, bearing in mind that each manufacturer's sizing is slightly different. I have given you a little help and done most of the research for you. The commonly available tire options are listed on page 24. It should cover the mild upgrades.

If you are going for the larger-sized tires, the wicket gets stickier. In these cases, a suspension lift, body lift, fender trimming, or any combination of the three might be required to fit the tires, and in some cases, minor rubbing in noncritical areas might have to be tolerated. In other cases, a reduction in suspension travel is the price of the big tires. We'll deal with these issues in the appropriate sections.

Many tire shops will test fit tires for you and a little playing around with floor jacks can show you what fits and what hits. Many 4x4 shops use a 20 degree ramp (see chapter 3) for testing and fun. This can be a useful tool for tire fitting, because you can "freeze frame" the vehicle at full articulation and carefully observe the clearance, or lack thereof.

Another option is to attend one of the larger 4x4 events and test a set of tires. That's right! Many of the tire manufacturers are bringing semitrucks full of tires mounted on common rims to the larger events, like the Easter Jeep Safari and All-4-Fun Week. You can sign up and test-drive the tires for a day on the trail. This not only gives you a good idea on fit, but you can try out the specific brand and tread design that interest you.

### Tires and Gearing

A change of tire size changes your overall gear ratio. With a Jeep that has "high" gears (numerically low, such as 3.07, 3.31, 3.54), the effect on acceleration from a radical tire swap can be like starting in second gear. The effect of going from a 28-inch tall tire to a 30-inch tall tire is like trading 3.54 gears in for 3.31s. More radical changes produce more radical gearing changes.

From the other perspective, going from a 30-inch to a 33-inch tire is like swapping 4.56 gears for 4.10s, and this could be advantageous in the highway cruising department. The moral here is that if you figure out what diameter tire you want, you can pick a gear ratio that gives you the best off-roading gearing (see chapter 4 for more info), combined with a livable highway cruising rpm.

The "gearhead math" on page 25 gives you some formulas on figuring the effect of a tire swap. If you just want to get back where you were overall, use the equivalent ratio formula. If you want to go a notch or two lower to enhance trail performance, you can calculate the effect on rpms at cruising speed by using the first formula.

Since many transmissions have an overdrive 4th or 5th gear, calculate both for the overdrive top gear and for the 1:1 gear that precedes it. This will give you the flat-ground cruising rpm in top gear that lets the engine lug a little under a light load on the flats. You'll also get your "power" gear for passing or climbing hills where you can let the engine rev a bit.

Many vehicles are "overgeared" from the factory in an effort to increase fuel economy. This may work with the OE dinky donut tires, but if you install some real *zapatos,* it can begin to have the opposite effect. An engine turning a few hundred rpms more than stock may actually deliver better mileage because it doesn't need quite as much open throttle to maintain speed, especially if there is wind or a slight hill. The engine is most efficient (read economical) when at or near the torque peak. If they are run far above or below that, economy will suffer.

# Air Up!

An onboard compressor is a necessity for a frequent off-roader. Most trails require airing down to some degree, and there isn't always a gas station waiting at the end for airing up. Compressors start with cheap discount store models that take half a lifetime to fill a tire and wear out in a short time. Quality goes up from there, and price typically increases with pump speed and durability.

Air conditioning compressors can be converted to become air compressors. They can crank out 5–7 cubic feet per minute and will run air tools. If you do not have A/C on your rig but the engine still has brackets, like this one did, it's a bolt-on. The compressor is controlled by the A/C electric clutch. Slick and efficient, though the A/C compressors tend to wear out faster used this way. You need to fit the intake side with an air filter, and an intake oiler (similar to those used for air tools) helps with longevity by keeping the cylinders lubed.

This Pacific Scientific compressor is the king of the 12-volt compressors. Several models are available, but this unit has a 1/3 horsepower motor (draws 26 amps) and pumps out 1.75 cubic feet per minute at 20 psi. Currie and others market this compressor with installation kits.

If you have room, a small air tank can maintain air volume and shorten tire fillups by a large amount. This five-gallon tank from Sun Performance can mount on the chassis or under the hood. Some creative welders will use bumpers, frame sections, and even nerf bars to hold air.

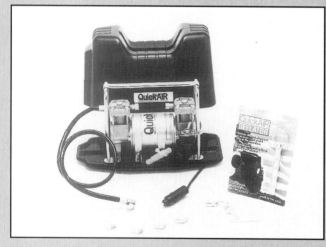

The QuickAir twin-cylinder unit from Sun Performance puts out 1.06 cubic feet per minute at 20 psi and draws 7 amps. This is the portable model, but a similar unit with mounting brackets is also available.

Right: You can use high-pressure tubing and air fittings to provide air stations wherever it is convenient. Then, a small hose will reach to the nearby tires.

Gearing has an effect on engine durability as well as fuel mileage. Running your engine down the freeway at 4,500 rpms for long distances will have a bad effect on economy and engine life, but you might be surprised to learn that lugging an engine under heavy loads can be as bad or worse. Part of the engine's lubrication comes from the splash effect, which is reduced at low speed. Generally, low rpm loads are fairly light and of short duration, so it isn't a problem. When you are cruising down the freeway in top gear at 1,200 rpms, however, rolling and wind resistance will give the engine a very heavy load and without the splash effect, it may be inadequately lubricated for that load. Tall gears and low revs contributed to the rash of cam failures in GM engines of the late 1970s and early 1980s.

### Speedometer Correction

Speedo correction will likely be necessary with a tire swap. One correction method is to determine overall ratio with the setup you built and look for a new speedo drive gear. By looking though the gearing choices in your era of Jeep and working out effective ratios with your tire swap and a selection of gear ratios, you may find an equivalent ratio that corresponds to a ratio that was actually offered with your Jeep's original tire. You could then order the speedo drive gear for that application and be set. Otherwise, a speedometer shop can recalibrate or install a corrective gearing device in your speedo cable.

### Tire Tuning Street Pressure

Learning to manipulate tire pressure in different situations, on and off the road, gives you a great tool for Jeep performance. It goes further than just airing down when you hit the trail. The correct pressure on the street ensures long tire life, a good ride, and predictable handling. On the trail, maximum traction and floatation are ensured.

Pressure too high on the street can cause extraordinary wear in the center of the tread and a rough ride. Too low, and heat buildup will kill the tire quickly or wear it out prematurely. Low pressure can also cause handling problems.

Dealing with street pressure first, you will find that most people look on the sidewall of the tire and note that it says "Max Press. - 35 psi" (or whatever). Automatically, they pump in 35 psi and spend the next few years complaining about ride quality and tire wear.

The max pressure listed on the sidewall is for a maximum load. If the tires are rated for 2,000 pounds each,

then the only reason you have for using max pressure is if your Jeep weighs or is carrying enough weight to gross out at 8,000 pounds. Jeep gives you a street tire pressure on the tire inflation sticker and in the owners' manuals, but unless you are using the same tires, these recommendations may be useless. There is a method for determining the ideal tire pressure for a given tire, vehicle, and load.

1. Set them at maximum pressure listed on the sidewall of the tire.
2. Make a mark across the tread using chalk or a crayon.
3. Drive forward in a straight line for a short distance. Do not turn under any circumstances, or you'll invalidate the test. (That's why an unoccupied parking lot is best.)
4. Look at the tread and see which part of the mark is worn off.

If the mark is worn off in the center but not at the edges, then the inflation is too high. Drop the pressure a few pounds and do steps 2–4 over and over until the mark wears off evenly across all the tread. At that pressure, you are near the ideal pressure for that tire at that load. Watch carefully! An underinflated tire will scuff the chalk, and that's why you start from the high pressure and work down.

You will find that front and rear loading is entirely different. With the engine up front, it is usually the heaviest part of an unloaded rig. If you fill your rig up with your normal camping load, or a simulation, you can find the ideal pressure for your loaded-for-bear setup.

Final tuning will be done seat-of-the-pants, adding and subtracting pressure until you like it best. Especially for light Jeeps, you will find the difference in ride quality at the lower pressures quite amazing. You may also be amazed at how much less pressure you need on a light rig.

The relationship between tire pressure, temperature, and atmospheric pressure is interesting. Even the change in seasons will bring a need for tire pressure adjustments. A 10 degree drop in ambient temperature will drop your cold pressure approximately 1 psi. This 10 degree/1 psi relationship follows into the pressure differences between the hot, running-down-the-road temperature and the cold, at-rest temperature. Also, most tires lose about 1 psi per month due to the porosity of the rubber or slight rim leaks.

Tire pressure will increase slightly with altitude due

Currie offers a whiz-bang deflater that works very quickly by unscrewing the valve core and holding it while you let the air out. When the correct pressure is reached, you screw the core back in and head off.

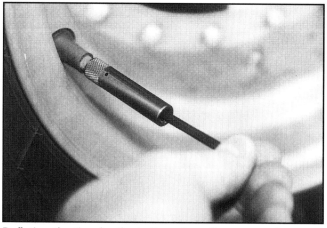

Deflating the tires for the trail can be a time-consuming process by normal means. Oasis Off-Road has come out with an easy means of doing that with these adjustable automatic deflaters. First you decide how low you want to go and preset your deflater with the Allen wrench. On the trail, you simply screw them on and drive off, as your tires automatically deflate to the proper pressure.

to the lower atmospheric pressure. Usually, it's only a few pounds but if you happen to check your street pressure in Leadville, Colorado, at 10,000 feet, you'll find its a few pounds higher than it was below sea level at Mojave, California.

### Tire Tuning—The Trail

Most experienced Jeepers drop their pressure as soon as they hit the trail. There are many good reasons for doing so, not the least of which is a smoother ride on a rough surface. Since travel is much slower in the dirt, heat buildup problems and handling are not an issue. If you are a "Baja Racer" type, obviously your tire pressure will need to be higher.

Another reason to air down is to increase traction. Traction is a situation that pits engine torque (multiplied by the drivetrain) against the tractive ability of tires to maintain a grip on whatever ground surface is being encountered. When the applied torque exceeds the traction available, the tire slips. Much of this has to do with the type of ground, but it also depends on the tires.

Tread design and ground type aside, much of the tire's ability to grip depends on ground pressure and the contact patch. Ground pressure is a formula involving the tire's contact patch (the patch of tire rubber actually on the ground) and the amount of weight on that patch. More weight on the same patch increases the psi being applied to the ground. By increasing the contact patch at the same weight, the ground psi decreases, and vice versa.

The contact patch varies according to the size of the tire and the air pressure in the tire (less air equates to a bigger patch). A bigger patch (whether from a bigger tire or lower air pressure) offers a bigger surface to grip the ground. Seldom is the ground perfectly flat, so by airing down, you are also allowing the tire to conform or wrap itself around various imperfections that might lift an aired-up tire and allow it to lose traction.

You can tune your Jeep, via air pressure adjustments, to best suit the terrain at hand. John Williams at Oasis Off-Road Manufacturing has come up with a formula (see page 26) that's a good starting point. After that, experience is the best teacher. By taking *your* Jeep and *your* tires through various terrain and at various pressures, you can determine what's best for your particular combination.

On the trail, you will see light rigs with fat tires down to 5–8 psi, medium rigs at 8–10, and heavy rigs at 10–15. How low you can actually go depends on the tire and rim designs. You want to avoid airing down to the point where you roll the tires off the rim. Some rims are better at clinching the tire, just as some tire beads are better at clinching the rim.

Remember also that when you air down, you are effectively decreasing your ground clearance several inches by reducing the working diameter of the tire. This has the added good effect of lowering your gear ratio slightly. On the minus side, you are making the sidewalls of the tire more vulnerable to damage, so you will need to avoid spinning the tires in loose rocks or slamming them into sharp objects. Also, with less air, you will find that the tires are more prone to allowing dirt and crud into the bead area, and this later causes small leaks.

Also, remember that there is a point of diminished returns to airing down. If the ground pressure is minimized beyond a certain level in certain types of terrain, you can actually decrease traction. This point is seldom reached except on the lightest rigs with the largest tires.

Airing down also gives you a bigger contact patch that increases floatation. When you are dealing with sand, snow (sometimes), and mud (sometimes), you want to float above the soft stuff rather than sink into it. The lower your ground pressure, the more the weight of your vehicle is spread over a larger patch of ground. The difference is amazing. You may struggle to cross one soft patch, air down, and drive the rest with impunity. You may also find yourself stopped in the quagmire with high pressure in the tires, air down, and drive out.

### A Final Word on Tires

Your tire choices, it is hoped, are a bit easier now. One last bit of advice is not to get so involved with trick and cool terminology or ongoing trends that you forget the Jeep parts shopper's basic credo—"the mostest for the leastest." Once you know the type of tire you need, look at what you are getting for the money and remember that if one tire is so much cheaper than the others, there is probably a good reason.

### Tire Repairs

The tires are the single most vulnerable part of your Jeep out on the trail. With sharp rocks, jagged logs, and even man-made hazards, the trail is littered with potential tire killers. Careful driving and tough tires are giant steps in the right direction, but if you 'wheel long enough, sooner or later you are going to hear the sound of escaping air. "Well, there's always the spare," you point out. True, but there may come a time when the jagged cleaver of fate swings in your direction and you hear escaping air twice on one trail. Then what?

The sad fact is that most trail damage is of the major kind, usually torn sidewalls. Tire repair kits are available that can permanently fix some tire damage as well as could be done in a tire shop. With some ingenuity, they can temporarily repair major damage that will be enough to hold air for a slow run back to civilization.

An alternative is to break the tire down, using tire tools that can be found in catalogs such as J. C. Whitney, and put a patch over the cut. This requires a fresh patch and vulcanizing compound. You may want to add a tube for more security. In some cases, a large tear can be stitched closed with fishing line or even wire and a patch applied to hold air.

If you attend any of the major off-road events around the county, look for the tire manufacturers "tire test" stands. They keep popular sizes and types of tires mounted on common rims and you can test them for a day. This is useful both for a general feel, and to try out various sizes for fit.

These "bubblegum and bailing wire" repairs should be your get-back-to-civilization fixes only. You are reasonably safe at low speeds on the trail, but don't consider the tire safe for a high speed jaunt back to the house. Get to a tire shop ASAP and replace the tire. This can be a life or death deal!

### Tire Chains—For More Than Just Snow

No tire can equal the mobility that tire chains offer on icy roads. Some snow tires, including those with studs, can come close, but the steel links of a set of chains will offer better grip on ice than anything else. You know this already. What you may not know is that chains can also be ideal for muddy conditions. Depending on your locale, chains can be an important addition to your Jeeping arsenal.

There are two basic types of chains of interest to the Jeepin' crowd, pattern and ladder type. (Cable chains and those cheeseball plastic paddle deals are strictly Geo Metro stuff!) Of the two, the ladder type chains are the most common. As the name implies, ladder chains use lengths of chain that cross the tread from sidewall to sidewall. Pattern chains resemble a chain "net" over the tire.

Each chain type has advantages. The ladder chain delivers the best forward traction, while the pattern chains are best in high-speed situations (relative, of course) and turns. For off-highway work, ladder chains are the most common and popular, as well as the least expensive.

The composition and design of the chain links determine traction and durability. Decent chains are made of carbon steel that is sometimes surface hardened. Better chains are built from a nickel-manganese alloy that is also surface hardened.

The chain links themselves come in several variations, including standard and twisted link, square link, reinforced, and v-bar reinforced. The standard link is just that, a fairly standard-looking chain link. The twisted links include a quarter-turn twist that makes them a little more flexible and grippy. Square link chains, as the name implies, offer sharper gripping edges with which to bite into the ice. Reinforced links use a bar welded across the link for strength and grip. V-bar reinforced link use a v-shaped bars for even more traction.

There are chains specifically designed for mud, usually of the ladder type. The links are larger than snow chains by a considerable margin. Snow chains can be used effectively in mud, but mud chains are usually too rough to be used in snow or ice on paved surfaces.

Tire chains generally have a fairly short life. The two keys to extending chain life are to keep the speed

Studded tires are a good compromise for winter areas. They are not as grippy on ice as chains, but are better than most snow tires. Mud tires need the most help on ice, and few accept studs. Studs are not legal in all areas.

Pattern chains are best for high speed work and cornering. This set is reinforced (note the bars welded across the links). These links are also square, which makes them more grippy than the round type.

down and keep the chains tight. At 30 miles per hour or less, 100 percent of the designed chain life will occur. Upping the speed just 20 miles per hour brings the chain life to a mere 30 percent of design. The same pattern applies to loose chains. A chain loosened one link from tight will drop to 50 percent of normal service at 30 miles per hour. The trick is to install 'em tight, but without the rubber tighteners, drive a quarter-mile, and check for tightness again before installing the tighteners.

## Wheels

Choosing a wheel seems like a no-brainer and subject more to looks and taste than anything else. Not so! While looks are a part of the choice, function must be the first consideration. There are thousands of cosmetic choices, but only a few functional ones. They boil down to size (dictated mostly by the tire size), offset, and material.

The best material for the wheels of a 4x4 is another of those hotly debated topics that has very good arguments on all sides. The two common materials are steel and aluminum alloy, but you can't compare them directly because they have different methods of construction. Let's deal with each one singly. Bear in mind that I'll deal only with the functional aspects and will not presume to dictate style or looks.

### Steel Wheels

In OE applications, a steel wheel consists of a stamped steel center with a rolled steel outer rim that are welded together. In the old days with tube tires,

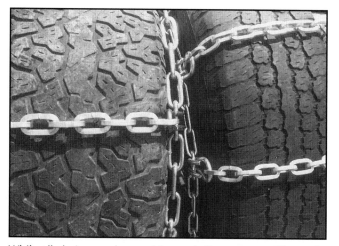

While all chains can be used in mud, there are specific mud chains. The mud links on the left are larger than the snow links on the right. Mud chains are usually too harsh for use on highway snow.

they were riveted. This setup is strong, easily repaired, and cheap. There's nothing wrong with using a stock wheel if it will fit the new tire you plan to use. The steel wheel can be repainted over and over when the rigors of off-roading make it unsightly. Aftermarket manufacturers build steel wheels in a similar fashion, but sometimes they use better and stronger materials and make them in sizes that better fit the larger tires.

The disadvantages to steel wheels are mostly in the performance area. A vehicle equipped with a light alloy wheel will accelerate noticeably faster and stop more quickly than a vehicle equipped with ordinary steel wheels. Since this is mostly on-road, fast-moving stuff, a dedicated four-wheeler might not consider it overly important.

A steel wheel will bend much more easily than an aluminum wheel, but unlike some alloys, it will merely bend and not break. Some opponents of steel point out that the heavy weight of a steel wheel can contribute to broken drivetrain parts, due to the extra inertia generated by the weight. This may be an issue in a rig where torque input and tire size are already at the maximum for that axle. Also, a neglected steel wheel can rust and weaken in time. Steel wheels are generally the least expensive wheels on the market.

### One-Piece Cast Alloys

This is the most common type of alloy wheel. A cast-aluminum alloy wheel can weigh a third or more less than an OE-style steel wheel and half as much as some heavy-duty steel wheels. This can result in some noticeable performance increases, as discussed in the steel wheel section. Cast-aluminum wheels are very robust, and they resist bending much better than steel or some other alloy wheel types.

The disadvantage to a cast alloy wheel is that when overstressed, it may break instead of bend. In truth, wheel breakage in cast alloy is uncommon and reserved for the most violent encounters. If damaged, cast wheels are more difficult and expensive to repair. Like all alloy wheels, they can get scratched or dinged in the rigors of trail running and are not easily made presentable again. They do not generally corrode to the point of being unserviceable. Cast-aluminum wheels come in a variety of price ranges, but are most often the second-most expensive alloy wheel type.

### Two-Piece Alloy Wheels

Also known as modular wheels. Generally, these are made with a cast center to which a spun aluminum rim is attached via welding or rivets. This makes for a very lightweight wheel. For that reason they are popular for street vehicles but less so with 4x4s. The spun aluminum rim bends easily and doesn't generally hold up well in the hard off-pavement environment. It is difficult to repair. It is the least expensive alloy wheel type and is very common.

### Forged Aluminum Alloy Wheels

These are the brutes of the alloy wheel realm. They are far stronger than steel and are stronger and lighter than cast aluminum. They will also bend rather than break and can be more easily repaired. They are the most expensive type of wheel to buy, but are the hands-down best if cost is no object.

### Wheel Size and Offset

These elements are dictated primarily by the tires and the vehicle. In general, the rim diameter will stay the same during a tire swap, but the rim width is dic-

Wheels are mostly a matter of taste. Here are a few popular ones from American Racing, from basic painted steel to chrome steel, to cast alloy. Most experts recommend staying away from two-piece alloy, or modular styles (not shown), because they tend to be more fragile. Also not shown are forged aluminum alloy, which are acknowledged as the strongest, and most expensive, wheel.

tated by the size of tire being installed. For each tire, the manufacturer will list a rim width range. It's best to stay within this recommendation, though many four-wheelers prefer to stay on the narrow size of the rec-ommendation. Some folks even want to go narrower or wider than recommended, for their own reasons.

The narrower rim lets the sidewall bulge out a bit. This tends to protect the rim from damage. The nar-rower rim also helps keep the tire beads in place at low pressures. The downside is that the tire is somewhat less flexible in this situation and may deliver less traction.

The wider rim allows the tire to flex more and spread out a little better for traction. At low pressures, the tendency to roll off the rim is increased. A wide rim combined with very low pressures makes the use of a beadlock device almost a necessity.

Wheel offset, or back-spacing, is a critical dimen-sion. These are two common terms used when dis-cussing the orientation of the wheel rim (where the tire mounts) to the mounting flange (where it bolts to the hub). The centerline is the dead center of the rim. The mounting flange may or may not be on the centerline. If the centerline is offset to the outside (away from the axle), the mounting flange moves to the inside and the wheel has negative offset. If the centerline is to the inside, it's called positive offset. Backspacing is the distance from the inside of the rim to the mounting flange.

### Beadlocks

These devices physically lock the tire to the rim so it can be run at extremely low pressures. Are they nec-essary? To the diehard gear grinder who runs the Big Dog trails in a specially prepped rig, perhaps. The aver-age 'wheeler in a dual-purpose machine would proba-bly find them an unnecessary expense. Some specialty wheels come with beadlocks, but most often, you have them attached by a wheel repair outfit. The cost of doing this is fairly high, so the best advice is to do without until you have proven the need.

### Choosing the Right Wheel

The first step is to determine the backspace needed. The stock wheels can give you an indicator of where the factory had things set up. If you need to, lay the wheel face down and measure the backspace with a straightedge across the rim and measure down to the mounting flange.

The OEM designs the wheel so that the load is placed evenly over the wheel bearings. Altering these

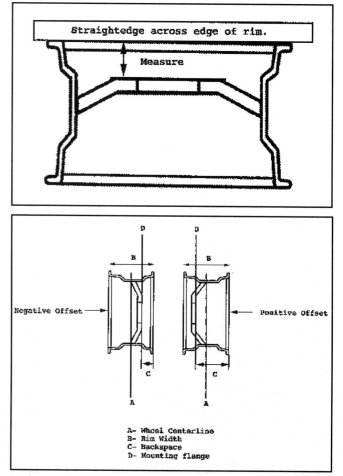

A- Wheel Centerline
B- Rim Width
C- Backspace
D- Mounting flange

Backspacing is a very important consideration. Stay as close as you can to the OE backspace. If you increase rim width, add the width to both sides of the wheel to keep the centerline of the wheel on the original spot. If you do not, turning radius is affected, as well as wheel bearing life and steering effort.

dimensions radically can cause premature bearing wear, unwelcome changes in steering geometry that increase your turning radius, steering effort, and load on the ball-joints or king pins. If you need a wider tire, what can you do to minimize the bad effects?

The ideal is to keep the centerline location in the same spot as designed. If you are using stock rims with larger tires, it's usually only a small problem. Ditto for an aftermarket wheel of generally the same dimen-sions. Changing from a very narrow rim to a much wider rim is when the problems start

The best option is to increase rim width by adding the extra width equally on each side to keep the cen-terline in more or less the stock location. If the OE rim was 7 inches, for example, with a 5 1/2-inch backspace, going to an 8-inch rim with a 6-inch backspace would keep the centerline exactly to stock specs. Interference

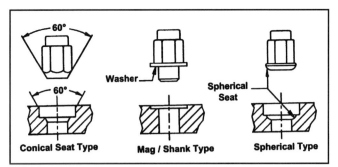

Don't find out the hard way that your lug nuts don't fit your fancy new wheels. This illustration shows the three most common types. *Courtesy American Racing*

between inner fenders, springs, and whatever may make this impossible, so you just have to do the best you can. You may even have to limit your tire size to what will fit without a major compromise.

The next item is to find a wheel that is rated for the load you will carry. DOT requires the maximum load to be shown on aftermarket wheels. That rating, times four, is your maximum permissible vehicle weight. It doesn't hurt to go a little beyond what you need to cover you in the event of a little exuberance or a really tough situation.

# Wheel and Tire Terms and Tables

## Section 1: Tire Glossary

*Aspect Ratio:* The ratio between the tire's section height (the height of the sidewall) and its section width (the width of the tire, sidewall to sidewall). A tire with a 6-inch sidewall and a 10-inch section width would be a 60 series tire. Expressed as a percentage, aspect ratio influences the tire's profile, or the distance between the tread and the rim. Lower profile tires have a lower aspect ratio.

*Bead:* The area that mates the tire to the wheel. This area is a critical part of the tire's construction and consists of a hoop of high tensile steel wires to which the belts are attached. This anchors the belts as well as providing a firm grip on the rim.

*Bead Seat:* This is the smooth face on the bead area of the tire that seals against the rim to hold air.

*Belts:* Rubberized woven fabric that runs around the circumference of the tire under the tread. Polyester and steel in combination is the most common construction material these days, but many experts regard Kevlar (or Aramid fiber) as the best.

*Casing:* The body of the tire built up from cords and belts of material. Also known as the "carcass."

*Compound:* The mixture of material that is the "rubber" part of the tire. There are five basic ingredients: rubber, carbon black, plastisizers, a curing ingredient, and an ozone retardant.

*Contact Patch:* The tire "footprint," the tread material that actually contacts the ground.

*Cord:* The stranded material incorporated into the belts and plies that are made into the casing of the tires.

*Crown:* The center of the tire tread.

*Deflection:* The amount the tire "gives" under load. Essentially, the difference between its free and unloaded radius and its fully loaded radius.

*Directional Stability:* The ability (or lack thereof) of a tire to maintain a straight line rather than following irregularities in the road.

*Gum:* The industry word for the "rubber" that makes up the tread and soft parts of the tire.

*Hoop Strength:* The inherent strength of the material in the belt to hold its circular shape.

*Hydroplaning:* A condition that occurs when the tire floats above water encountered due to speed or tread design and loses traction. The tire actually rides up on the water like a speedboat on a lake, losing contact with the road surface.

*Kerf:* A cut or slit built into the tire and used for traction. A kerf is similar to a sipe, but is molded into the tire rather than cut in. Kerfs enhance wet and icy traction.

*Liner:* A fairly thin layer of dense rubber on the inside of tubeless tires designed to hold air.

*Plies:* The layers of corded material that provide the structural "building blocks" of tire construction.

*Rollover:* When the tire gives in to the G-forces of hard cornering. The inside edge of the tire tread may lift and the sidewall may actually contact the road. In extreme conditions, it may pop the bead and suddenly deflate the tire.

*Rubber:* A common term for the material of the tires. In the old days, this was actually rubber from the rubber tree, but now it's a synthetic material derived from petroleum products. Also known as "gum."

*Section Width:* The sidewall-to-sidewall width of the tire. Not to be confused with tread width.

*Shoulder:* The area of a tire where the tread joins the sidewall.

*Siping:* Slits or cuts in the tread blocks that allow the blocks to move and grip. Sipes can be built into the tire by the manufacturer or added later. Siping usually enhances the wet and icy performance of the tire.

*Void Ratio:* The ratio of open areas in a tire tread vs. the parts that actually contact the ground.

## Section 2: Reading the Sidewall

There are three basic tire designations seen on Jeep 4x4s: metric sizes, floatation tires, and numeric tires. They are all a little different, but they all share performance and construction information that is embossed on the sidewall near the bead. Not all the info is required on all the tires. The metrics generally have the most information. Here is a mix of what you will see on most modern tires.

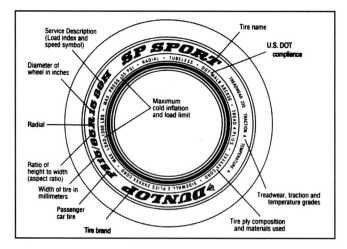

*Tubeless:* Most tires in use today are tubeless with the exception of those used in certain heavy-duty applications. Many of the old-time bias-ply tires ran tubes and these tires are still on the market. Some older rigs use wheels (with rim riveted to the center) that require a tube-type tire, but for most light-duty applications tubeless is the way to go. Note that putting a tube in a tubeless tire can cause it to run hotter.

*Treadwear:* Many tires have a treadwear rating that is an indicator of their ability to last. Rubber compounds, tread depth, and general construction contribute to this rating. Sixty is the lowest rating and the numbers climb in 20-point increments to the highest number, 500. This test is only an indicator of wear, and because the actual DOT test does not simulate a real world scenario, this is a controversial rating. Generally, if you see a tire with a nice deep tread and a low treadwear number, it probably has a very sticky rubber compound that would offer good traction but poor wear characteristics.

*Traction:* This is an indicator of the tire's wet pavement traction performance. The ratings run from "A," the best, to "C," the worst.

*M&S:* If it's on the tire, it means that it has been approved by the DOT for mud and snow use. It's kind of a given for a 4x4 tire, but the rating will get you past a chain stop where they are allowing only chained-up rigs or M&S rated tires.

*Temperature:* This shows the tire's ability to tolerate and dissipate heat. The ratings run from "A," the highest, to "C," the lowest.

*Load Range:* A rather archaic system that is mostly seen on the light truck rated tires. In the old days, tires were rated by the number of plies built into the tire carcass, four-ply, six-ply, etc., and more plies meant more capacity. Nowadays, they can get more capacity with fewer plies, so a true four-ply tire can be rated as six-ply. You will see it expressed as a "six-ply rating," or as load ranges running from A to E, which correspond to the ply rating. Here is how it works out:

| Load Range | Ply Rating |
|---|---|
| A | 2-ply |
| B | 4-ply |
| C | 6-ply |
| D | 8-ply |
| E | 10-ply |

*Max Load:* A more useful way of expressing "load range" because it gives you the maximum load capacity of the tire in kilograms and pounds and the maximum rated pressure. Buying a tire that is rated for grossly more than your rig can carry may be a waste of money. Also, if each tire is rated for 3,000 pounds at 35 psi and your rig weights 3,300 pounds, running full pressure is needlessly tough on the kidneys.

*Speed Rating:* The ability of a tire to endure the heat and force of continuous high speed work. Not usually an issue with Jeepers, but a good indicator of general robustness. The speed ratings apply mostly to metric tires. An unrated passenger car tire is actually required by DOT to endure a continuous speed of 85 miles per hour. Here are some speed ratings seen on 4x4 tires:

Q= 99 miles per hour
S= 112 miles per hour
T= 118 miles per hour
U= 124 miles per hour
H= 130 miles per hour

*Metric Tire Details:* The metric tire sizes have been used in Europe for many years but were adopted here in the late 1970s and early 1980s. They have all but taken over the passenger car realms and dominate the light truck market. The tires are measured in millimeters (except for rim diameter) and a typical light truck tire might read LT235/75R-15. Breaking it down:

LT = The tire type, in this case Light Truck (P = Passenger car, ST = Trailer).

235 = Section Width in millimeters. The distance between the sidewalls but not the tread width.

75 = The aspect ratio, or the height from the rim to the tread expressed as a percentage of the section width. In this example, 75 percent of the 235-millimeter section width would be a 223.25-millimeter section, or sidewall, height.

R = Radial tire.

15 = The rim diameter in inches, believe it or not.

*Figuring Metric Tire Diameters:* Knowing the mounted height of a tire is important to figuring overall gear ratios and engine rpms. The metric numbers don't make that easy but there is a formula for figuring the height of a metric tire. Bear in mind that the actual mounted height might be somewhat different than the formula shows. The tire manufacturer can supply very detailed specs on its tires.

$$\text{Tire Diameter} = 2 \times \frac{\text{section width} \times \text{aspect ratio}}{2{,}540} + \text{rim diameter}$$

In the case of our 235/75R-15, the formula would look like this:

$$28.88 = 2 \times \frac{235 \times 75}{2{,}540} + 15$$

Light truck metric tires commonly come in 70, 75, 80, and 85 aspect ratios. A 235/85R-16 (31.7 inches) and a 265/75R-16 (31.6 inches) are nearly the same height but the 265 is about an inch and a half wider. You can convert millimeters to inches by dividing by 25.4.

*Floatation and Light Truck Sizes:* Next up are floatation tires. These are built, regulated, and sized to a different DOT standard. Unlike the metric tires, floatation tires are meant solely for light truck use and are a little more robust in their construction. You will also find that the tread depth is often a little more than a comparable metric sized tire. Floatation tires are usually rated for capacity by the A–E method and/or the actual capacity in pounds at a given maximum psi.

Figuring out tire size designations is easy on floatation tires. Take a 31/10.50R-15 tire, for example:

31 = The designated mounted height in inches. This may not be its actual height, however. A Dunlop 33/12.50R-15 Mud Rover tire has a mounted height of 32.8 inches while a 35/12.50R-15 version is 34.1 inches. Go figure. Read the actual mounted height specs from the tire manufacturer. Very few are precise in their rated diameter.

10.50 = The designated section width (sidewall to sidewall) of the tire. Not to be confused with tread width. A Dunlop 31/10.50R-15 has an actual section width of 10.6 inches (more than designated) and a tread width of 8.1 inches.

R = Radial construction.

15 = Rim diameter in inches.

You may still see some light truck tires that use designations such as 7.50-16. This is the oldest style of tire sizing, and the "7.50" is the section width and the "16" the rim diameter. You will also see the load range A–E to signify load capacity or even the older "six-ply rated" designation.

## What Fits—What Doesn't

The first thing to remember is that this is a *guide* to maximum tire sizes for Jeeps. There are too many variables to cover every possible combination of tire and vehicle. For example, one brand of 33x12.50 might have a 33-inch mounted height and a 13-inch cross section, while another might be only 32.1 inches tall and have a 12.50-inch cross section. Lifts are also somewhat variable, and other suspension mods may complicate the issue. Some of the most extreme sizes are not listed. For these tires, you're on your own, though the manufacturers should have some recommendations regarding vehicles and uses.

### TIRE FITMENT GUIDE

| Vehicle | Setup 1 | Setup 2 | Setup 3 | Setup 4 |
|---|---|---|---|---|
| 1942–68 MB, CJ2A, CJ3A, CJ3B | 30x9.50 | 7.50-16 (1)<br>31x10.50 (1)<br>32x11.50 (2.5) | | |
| 1954–86 CJ5, 6, 7, 8 | 7.50-16<br>31x10.50 | 32x11.50 (2.5)<br>33x12.50 (3) | 33x12.50 (2.5) | 33x9.50 [1]<br>33x12.50 (2.5) [1]<br>35x12.50 (4) [3] |
| 1987–95 Wrangler YJ | 31x10.50 | 32x11.50 (2.5)<br>33x9.50 (3) | | 33x12.50 (3) [1]<br>35x12.50 (4) [1] |
| 1996–up Wrangler TJ | 31x10.50 | 32x11.50 (2) | | 33x12.50 (3) [1] |
| 1984–up Cherokee XJ | 30x9.50 | 31x10.50 (2.5) | 32x11.50 (2.5) | 33x12.50 (3) [1] |
| 1963–91 Wagoneer SJ | 30x9.50 | 32x11.50 (3)<br>33x12.50 (4) | 31x10.50<br>32x12.50 (3) | |
| 1974–86 J-Series PU, Cherokee Chief (wide track only) | 32x11.50 | 33x9.50 (1.5)<br>33x12.50 (3) | 33x9.50 | 35x12.50 (4) [1]<br>38.5x15 (4) [3] |
| 1993–up Grand Cherokee | 30x9.50 | 32x11.50 (2-3) | 33x12.50 (4) | |

### Key
Setup 1 = Stock vehicle, maximum tire size that can be fitted.
Setup 2 = With a lift. Approximate suspension lift required is shown in parentheses.
Setup 3 = Combination of suspension lift required, in parentheses, and fender trimming or metalwork may be required.
Setup 4 = Combination of suspension lift, in parentheses, and body lift, in brackets, required. May also require fender trimming.

## Jeep Tire Options - 1941–1997

A wide variety of tires were available for Jeeps over the years. For the older rigs, many of these sizes are no longer easily available.

| Vehicle | Std/(Optional) |
|---|---|
| 1942–45 MB | 6.00-16/(7.00-16) |
| 1947–53 CJ2A, CJ 3A | 6.00-16/(7.00-15) |
| 1953–64 CJ3B | 6.00-16/(7.00-15) |
| 1947–65 Willys PU | 7.00-16/(9.00-13 sand) |
| 1949–65 Willys SW | 6.50-15/(7.00-15, 7.60-15) |
| 1957–65 FC-150 | 7.00-15/(6.50-15, 7.60-15) |
| 1957–60 FC-170 | 7.00-16/ (7.50-16) |
| 1959–65 FC-170DRW | 7.00-16/(7.50-16) |
| 1963–87 SJ PU, half-ton(1) | 7.10-15/(8.15-15, 8.55-15, H78-15, 225/75R-15, 235/75R-16) |
| three-quarter and one-ton | 7.00-15/(7.00-16, 7.50-16, 8.00-16.5, 9.00-16.5, 9.50-16.5) |
| 1976–87 Honcho, wide track | 9.00x15/(10.00x15) |
| 1963–91 SJ Wagoneer* | 7.10-15/(7.75-15, 8.45-15, F78-15, HR78-15, 225/75R-15, 235/75R-15) |

| Vehicle | Std/(Optional) |
|---|---|
| 1976–83 Cherokee Chief | 10.00x15 |
| 1984–98 Cherokee XJ* | 195/75R-15/(215/75R-15, 225/75R-15) |
| 1967–73 Jeepster C-101 | 7.35-15/(6.00-16, F78-15, 8.45-15, H78-15) |
| 1954–68 CJ-5, CJ-6 | 6.00-16/(7.00-15, 7.35-15, 8.45-15) |
| 1969–71 CJ-5, CJ-6 | 6.00-16/(7.00-16, 7.35-15, 8.55-15, G70-15, H78-15) |
| 1972–75 CJ-5, CJ-6 | E78-15/(F78-15, H78-15, 6.00-16, 7.36-15) |
| 1976–83 CJ-5, CJ-7, CJ-8 | F78-15/(H78-15, HR78-15, 9.00-15, L78-15, 10.00-15) |
| 1984–86 CJ-7, CJ-8 | 205/75R-15/(215/75R-15, 235/75R-15) |
| 1987–96 YJ | 215/75R-15/(225/75R-15, 29x9.50-15, 30x9.50R-15, 31x10.50R-15) |
| 1997–98 TJ | 205/75R-15/(215/75R-15, 225/75R-15, 30x9.50R-15) |
| 1993–98 Grand Cherokee ZJ | 225/75R-15/(245/75R-15, 225/70R-16) |

*Many tire options and changes for these trucks. List shows only the highlights.

---

## EFFECTIVE GEAR RATIO

To obtain the "effective" gear ratio: $\frac{\text{old tire diameter}}{\text{new tire diameter}} \times \text{original ratio} = \text{effective ratio of new combination}$

To obtain engine rpm at a given speed: $\frac{\text{mph} \times \text{total gear ratio} \times 336}{\text{tire diameter (inches)}} = \text{engine rpm}$

To obtain equivalent ratios: $\frac{\text{new tire diameter}}{\text{old tire diameter}} \times \text{old ratio} = \text{new ratio}$

Speedometer correction (tire swap only): $\frac{\text{new tire diameter}}{\text{old tire diameter}} \times \text{indicated mph} = \text{actual mph}$

Speedometer correction (tire and gear swap):

indicated speed in mph or kmph $\times \frac{\text{new tire dia.}}{\text{old tire dia.}} \times \frac{\text{old gear ratio}}{\text{new gear ratio}} = \text{actual speed}$

To find final drive ratio (in OD): OD gear ratio x axle ratio = final drive ratio

---

## Tire Load vs. Inflation

Each tire is rated differently by its manufacturer for maximum load at a given maximum inflation, but this chart will give you a general idea of how much weight a given size tire will carry at a lower inflation. This chart was compiled from Tire & Wheel Association Charts and doesn't represent the recommendations of any particular manufacturer. Use it as a general reference.

### Radial Tire Load (pounds) vs. Inflation (psi) Charts

| Tire Size | 25 psi | 30 psi | 35 psi | 40 psi | 45 psi | 50 psi |
|---|---|---|---|---|---|---|
| 30/9.50-15LT | 1,240 | 1,410 | 1,570 | 1,715 | 1,855 | 1,990 |
| 33/9.50-15LT | 1,565 | 1,780 | 1,980 | 2,170 | 2,345 | 2,510 |
| 31/10.50-15LT | 1,400 | 1,595 | 1,775 | 1,945 | 2,100 | 2,250 |
| 32/11.50-15LT | 1,575 | 1,795 | 1,995 | 2,185 | 2,360 | 2,530 |
| 33/12.50-15LT | 1,765 | 2,000 | 2,225 | | | |
| 35/12.50-15LT | 2,015 | 2,295 | 2,555 | | | |

## Suggested Trail Tire Pressures

*Courtesy Oasis Off-Road Manufacturing*

John Williams at Oasis created the chart below, which outlines some heavy-duty four-wheeling pressures based on GVW and tire size. These suggestions are subject to three general rules that John has also supplied.

1. Increase pressure approximately 3 psi for each 10 miles per hour over 20 miles per hour, until normal highway pressures are reached. For example: A 3,000-pound vehicle with 31x10.50R15 tires traveling at up to 40 miles per hour should have about 15 psi in them (9+3+3=15).

2. Decrease pressure by approximately one-half for extremely soft snow. The exception to this is a 33x9.50R15 tire, which usually benefits from an increase in pressure.

3. Decrease pressure approximately 1 psi for every 2 inches tire diameter is increased beyond this chart, assuming a corresponding increase in width of the tire.

| Tire Size | GVW | | | | | | |
| | 2000 | 3000 | 4000 | 5000 | 6000 | 7000 | 8000 |
|---|---|---|---|---|---|---|---|
| 215/75R15 | 11 | 13 | 15 | N/R | N/R | N/R | N/R |
| 235/75R15 | 10 | 12 | 14 | 16 | N/R | N/R | N/R |
| 29x8.50R15 | 10.5 | 12.5 | 14.5 | 15.5 | N/R | N/R | N/R |
| 30x9.50R15 | 9 | 10 | 12 | 14 | 16 | N/R | N/R |
| 31x10.50R15 | 8 | 9 | 10 | 12 | 14 | 15 | N/R |
| 32x11.50R15 | 7.5 | 8.5 | 9.5 | 11 | 13 | 15 | 18 |
| 33x9.50R15 | 9 | 10 | 12 | 14 | 16 | N/R | N/R |
| 33x12.50R15 | 7 | 8 | 9 | 10 | 12 | 14 | 16 |
| 35x12.50R15 | 6 | 7 | 8 | 9 | 10 | 12 | 14 |
| 36x14.50R15 | 5 | 6 | 7 | 8 | 9 | 10 | 12 |
| 38x15.50R15 | 4 | 5 | 6 | 7 | 8 | 9 | 10 |
| 225/75R16 | 11 | 13 | 15 | N/R | N/R | N/R | N/R |
| 245/75R16 | 10 | 12 | 14 | 16 | N/R | N/R | N/R |
| 265/75R16 | 9 | 10 | 12 | 14 | 16 | N/R | N/R |
| 285/75R16 | 8 | 9 | 10 | 12 | 14 | 16 | N/R |

# Chapter 3

# SUSPENSION & STEERING

## Long Legs

If you look at the first military jeep of 1940 and compare the suspension to this 1995, you will find only a few concept changes. It didn't change all that much, because it worked! The best part is that it's highly adaptable. The intro of the TJ coil spring suspension marked the transition to a new Jeep utility era.

The suspension is a vital part of making your Jeep perform, both on and off the trail. The suspension fits in with both parts of our traction and clearance equation for Jeep performance. A tire off the ground delivers no traction, so a suspension that keeps the tires on the ground aids in traction. A raised suspension can also provide more clearance.

If you improve on the suspension's ability to deliver traction and clearance, you will have certainly improved your trail performance. As discussed in Chapter 1, you may have to trade some on-road performance and drivability toward this goal. Be sure you are willing to do so before making the change.

The other factor to consider is legality. Every year more laws are enacted by various states to define or limit suspension modifications. In some cases, it's a "let's-do-something-even-if-it's-wrong" opportunity for politicians looking for publicity. In other cases, it's a legitimate response to totally unsafe modification practices that cost lives. Most states have suspension modification laws on the books, and it's your job to determine what they are.

Before we get into the nuts and bolts, let's define a couple of terms that are often mixed up. *Articulation* describes how well the suspension conforms to the ground. If one tire is stuffed into the wheelwell and the

*Left:* The 1 3/4-inch-wide spring was used through 1975. It's adequate, though the springs were usually short. Note that this spring has a military wrap, meaning that the second leaf wraps around the eye of the main leaf. It stemmed from a World War II military requirement that ensured the GI-spec rig could keep going with a broken main leaf. It's still a good idea, though improved steel has made it less necessary.

other is hanging down, or drooped, the suspension is articulated. *Travel* is the total up and down movement of the suspension with the axle in a level plane.

## Suspension Modification Goals

The common goals for Jeep suspension mods are increased articulation, better ride quality, more load capacity, or a lift to carry larger tires. These are all achievable via modifications, and if done correctly and in moderation, the negative effects on street drivability and safety can be minimal.

On the other hand, you may be inspired by some long-legged, high-tech Jeep buildup in a magazine and want to emulate the 35 inches of articulation you saw. Well, cool is cool and to be admired, but cool is not always practical. For the most part, these rigs are not driven daily, and those that are have very tolerant or daring drivers. These drivers have also spent copious amount of time and bucks getting their rigs built.

## Jeep Leaf Spring Suspension

The perennial Jeep suspension is pure simplicity. Take four underslung leaf springs (a.k.a. spring under, the spring being mounted under the axle) and

four tubular shocks, and there you have it. Jeep traditionally mounted a set of shackles at the leading end of the front springs. This basic setup remained in the Utility models until the last YJ Wrangler of 1996. The XJ Cherokees continue to use a leaf spring in the rear. The reason leaf springs have lasted so long is that they work!

The leaf spring goes way back in history. There are three basic styles, full elliptic, semielliptic (or half-elliptic), and quarter-elliptic. Semielliptic is the form that finally found favor, but recently some hard-core types have been experimenting with quarter- elliptics or three-quarter-elliptics on trail-only machines.

### Understanding Leaf Spring Rate

Leaf springs are generally constant rate, meaning they will require the same effort to deflect, or flex, all through their travel. Spring rate is expressed in pounds per inch, or pounds/inch. This is the amount of weight it takes to move the spring 1 inch. To move the spring 2 inches, it takes twice the weight, and 3 inches takes 3 times the weight, etc. Obviously, the higher the rate, the more the load capacity and the harsher the unloaded ride. The rates are chosen to balance these two elements.

Dual-rate leaf springs are also used. By design, the first inch or so of travel is a softer rate, but at some point in the spring travel, the rate increases. The spring rate of a dual-rate spring might be expressed as 155–230 pounds/inch, for example. Often this is done by combining a relatively soft spring with a stiffer overload leaf.

In day-to-day use, friction affects a spring's performance. Since the leaves have to rub and slide along each other, if they get rusted or gummed up, their movement and effectiveness will be impaired. Most of the movement (and therefore restriction) is at the ends of the leaves.

The manner in which the spring is clamped can also affect the spring's ride and flex. Clamps are necessary to keep the leaves parallel to each other. Commonly, these clamps are riveted to the leaves and crimped around the spring. If the spring is clamped too tightly, movement, especially downward movement, is

Longer springs are more flexible than short ones. These National springs are 10 inches longer than the stock front springs, and this Jeep flexes like no tomorrow. Notice also that shackles are reversed.

restricted. The better springs use a bolt clip that leaves the spring plenty of room to move. Better spring makers that still use clamps leave a little clearance above the top leaf when the crimps are made.

Some other tricks for supple, long-lasting springs are to taper the ends of the springs and/or diamond-cut them. Also, the best springs use Teflon leaf pads to lessen the friction between the leaves as they move against each other.

### Wide vs. Narrow Springs

You will see wide and narrow springs on Jeeps. A narrow spring needs more leaves for the same rate as a wide spring. Some folks claim that a narrow spring has better lateral twist than a wide one. This is true in theory but the thickness of the spring pack and the loss of clearance seem to offset any small gains. Lateral flex is more an issue with spring length than anything and since the old narrow springs were short in comparison with newer setups, that point is moot unless you plan some narrow custom springs.

Some Jeepers have successfully transplanted narrow rear springs to the front of early CJs. Since these springs are 7 inches longer, the result was much increased articulation but it also involved reversing the front shackles (read on) and a lot of fabrication.

### Long vs. Short Springs

The length of a spring is dictated by the chassis layout. Still, a longer spring can flex better, deliver a

better ride, and offer better lateral twist. This is why many Jeepers are installing longer springs in any practical way. Just a few more inches in length can produce a marked improvement in articulation and ride quality. Many Jeepers have gotten quite innovative in the quest for longer springs.

The common method for the front involves reversing shackles, and extending the chassis out the front for the front perches, and sometimes mounting the axle off center on the springs. Some Jeepers have mounted longer springs, especially the rear outboard of the chassis, as was done with the stock 1957–65 Jeep Forward Control trucks.

As good as it sounds, swapping longer springs is not a casual modification. Your "shade-tree" engineering skills need to be top-notch and your fabrication skills even better.

### Leaf Count

You'll see Jeep springs range from 12 leaves in an old Universal CJ application to a single leaf rear spring that was used in some 1970s-era J-20s. In theory, you can have equal spring rates with few or many leaves. The advantage of fewer leaves is that friction problems between leaves are minimized. The overall thickness of the spring pack is usually less, as well. On the downside, the thicker material tends to sag and fatigue faster.

More and thinner leaves tend to produce a very flexible spring, as evidenced by National Spring's success with such types. The major downside is that the

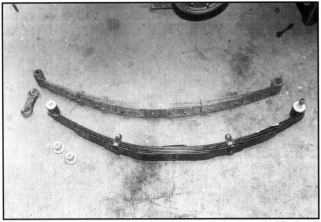

Notice the difference in camber between the 2-inch lift OME spring, bottom, and the original spring. Note also some of the other quality features of the OME, including bolt clips, Teflon pads between the leaves, and a flat spot at the axle pad area. A pinion angle shim is also attached.

Fiberglass springs may be the future of leaf springs. This custom 'glass spring is from Flex-A-Form and weighs a mere 7 pounds (compared to about 55 pounds for the OE steel spring). Being a mono-leaf, it isn't subject to friction. At about 200 lb/in., this spring feels softer. It exhibits properties more like a coil spring. *Courtesy Flex-A-Form*

spring pack is thick. If you are using a spring-under-axle configuration, this reduces your clearance somewhat. Also, this type of spring offers more trouble with friction when age, rust, and mud unite to bind the leaves.

### Camber

Not to be confused with steering camber, this term refers to the amount of arch in the spring. When you get right down to it, the flatter the spring, the better it works. It can move an equal distance up or down. As the camber increases, spring flexibility decreases. A heavily arched spring needs more rate in order to hold its arch. Heavily arched springs usually need their uptravel sharply restricted because if their arch is reversed too much, the springs may break. In a case like this, lift is traded for articulation. Springs with many thin leaves seem to be more tolerant of being reverse arched.

### Composite Springs

Composite springs are built of fiberglass and/or carbon fiber. They have been used in race cars for at least 15 years and are used in some sports cars and at least one non-Jeep SUV. Though they have not trickled down heavily into the 4x4 aftermarket yet, they are the future of leaf springs.

The first big advantage of the composite spring is weight savings. A Jeep CJ spring made by Flex-A-Form, the leading maker of fiberglass springs, weighs only 7 pounds. A standard four-leaf CJ-7 front spring weighs

something like 55 pounds. If you install a set of fiberglass springs on a Jeep, it'll end up about 175 pounds lighter.

A fiberglass spring will also outlast a steel spring several times over. Flex-A-Form tested a bunch of steel springs on a stress testing machine and most of them make it to about 50,000 cycles. A fiberglass spring on the same machine makes it into the millions of cycles. A set of 'glass springs tested at an independent facility showed only a 3 percent loss of spring rate after 200,000 cycles. They also have a better memory (hold their arch) than steel springs.

For an off-pavement vehicle, the only major disadvantage to a fiberglass spring is its lack of resistance to damage. Repeated impacts with rocks and other trail hazards can break the glass fibers and weaken the spring. The answer would be spring guards. Another disadvantage is cost. The price of a custom-built fiberglass spring is a touch under $200 a copy, though if you consider the long-term wear advantage, it becomes more reasonable. If and when mass production starts, the price will go way down.

### Innovative Steel Springs

Going beyond fiberglass springs, there is some innovation in steel springs. Among those that qualify as different would be the Old Man Emu springs. Each leaf is built on its own die and with its own camber. Each leaf is built with a little more camber than the previous leaf so that the point of contact with the leaf above is always at the ends. The springs are made flat at

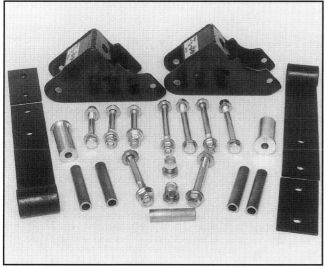

The M.O.R.E. shackle reverse kit for Wranglers features a buggy spring for the rear shackle that enhances articulation droop. This nicely done kit is a bolt-on, but it doesn't hurt to have a torch for removing some of the old parts. *Courtesy M.O.R.E.*

the area where they attach to the axle to minimize any effects from clamping the spring to the axle (this is also being done by other spring manufacturers). Greaseable Teflon pads are placed at the point of contact to minimize friction. The Emu springs are offered with only a modest 2-inch lift, but ride quality is superb.

Another unique design to watch for in the near future is one that is seeing some popularity in Australian and European markets. These are parabolic springs, and what makes them unique is the fact that the leaves are separated by 3-millimeter spacers and formed so that they only make contact at the very end of the leaf. Since there is no contact, except at the ends, friction is almost eliminated. The leaves are also tapered at the ends. Parabolics need about half the number of leaves to get the job done, so they are considerably lighter. At present, I know of no Jeep applications, but stay tuned!

### Shackle Position

This discussion refers to the shackle position of the front springs, which is at the front of the chassis on all stock Jeeps. A leaf spring has one solid mount. Because the arched spring effectively gets longer as it compresses or shorter as it droops, a pivot is needed at the other end. That pivot is called a spring shackle, and there is much debate among Jeepers as to whether the front of the spring is the best position for it.

As far as I can find out, this position is as much historic engineering tradition as anything else. It does tend to allow the vehicle to sit a bit lower and a low silhouette was important to the Army, for whom the first Jeeps were built. Around the world, most other 4x4 builders since then chose the trailing position of the spring for the pivot point.

The M.O.R.E. shackle reversal kit for CJs is similar to the YJ version, but it does not have the buggy spring feature. This one requires some welding for the chassis shackle bushing sleeve but is otherwise a very straightforward installation.

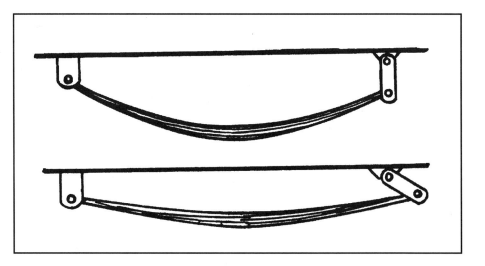

Note the motion of the shackle as the spring flattens out and the eye-to-eye distance grows. Positioned properly, the shackle tilts back slightly at rest (weight on vehicle). The spring end of the shackle should not tilt forward. As the suspension compresses, the shackle leans farther back, and you want the spring to get flat before the end of the spring or the shackle touches the chassis. The bump stop position will limit travel, as will a longer shackle.

One of the newer trends for CJs and YJs is to perform a shackle reversal. The advantages are improved ride quality, less stress on the chassis and spring, plus improved tracking. The reason the ride and tracking improve is that with the OE setup, when the Jeep encounters bumps at speed, the axle is moved up, but also back. It can freely move up, but much of that rearward shock is transmitted to the solid spring pivot. A lot of Jeeps end up with bent and broken springs, broken spring mounts, and cracked chassis when used hard. This is why the later Wranglers used a spring with a huge rubber eye at the back of the spring to help absorb some of that shock. The reversed shackle simply transforms that shock into a little extra shackle movement.

On the downside, besides the extra cost, the tire size on shackle-reversed CJs and YJs is generally limited to about 33 inches. In the reversed setup, the tire moves backward instead of forward when the spring is compressed. Large tires can interfere with the fenders on full compression. CJs are worse than Wranglers in this regard.

There is a group of hard-core rock crawlers who claim that the backward movement of the shackle costs some traction and tends to increase wheel hop. Some folks also prefer not to be limited in tire size. There are as many hard-core types who have shackle reversals and do not agree. This is probably one of those "Ford vs. Chevy" type of debates that will continue forever. Neither side is totally wrong nor right. The debate is mostly in the hard-core realm. People in the middle ground, mostly those folks who use their Jeeps as transportation, seem to prefer the benefits. These make up the majority of the shackle reversal kit buyers.

Several kits are available and some fabricators build them on a custom basis. Care must be taken by fabricators as the tiny nuances to the job are not readily visible. One of them would be that the axle must generally be moved forward. Shackle angle is another key element.

### Shackle Angles and Choices

Modern OE shackles are often a pair of fairly thin pieces of stamped steel. They are stronger than you would imagine, due to the ribbing engineered into them. The earliest OE version was a U-shaped piece that relied on bronze bushings and lots of lubrication from grease guns. In stock configuration and use, the OE equipment is adequate. With the extra loads of big tires, lifts, and torquey engines, the originals may not be adequate. Unless you have the oldest style shackle, a change is fairly easy. If you have the oldest style, the original brackets must be cut from the chassis and new ones attached.

Shackle position, or the direction it leans, either forward or back, is a complex choice derived from spring rate and length. Most often the shackle is tilted away from the axle. As the spring flattens, it gets longer and tilts the shackle farther away.

If you re-arch a spring and add more camber, the eye-to-eye distance decreases and the spring is shortened in effect. The shackle will then be more vertical or even tilted in toward the axle. The effects of this can be mild or wild. On the mild side, a rough ride may result because the shackle is resisting the spring. The bottom eye of the shackle is lowest when vertical. Effectively, the shackle is "longer." If it leans either way, the "length" is decreased. If the shackle is tilted in, then the spring has to effectively "jack up" the weight of the Jeep to get longer. That can cause a very rough ride and early spring or shackle failure.

On the wild side, the wrong shackle angle can cause the shackle and the end of the spring to flip forward and up against the chassis in severe droop situations and be stuck there by the weight of the vehicle. All of this is why aftermarket springs with more arch are made longer to compensate. It's also why consideration of shackle position during modifications is vital.

Shackle length as a means to gain lift is discussed elsewhere, but shackle length is important to ride quality. Shorter shackles react faster, especially if they are near the vertical. They also resist side loads better. Most experts agree that increasing shackle length from stock should be kept to a maximum of 2 inches for these reasons.

As to the shackles themselves, lots of choices are available. Some shackles are nothing more than two pieces of plate steel with holes. In some cases, these are connected by a welded or bolted-on brace for added strength. Some Jeepers claim that these types of shackles reduce the amount of flex available. Currie offers a shackle with a built-in bracket for a tow bar. They also offer their "Boomerang" shackle for Wranglers with highly arched springs (longer than stock) that will allow the shackle movement to flatten out the spring.

With the advent of polyurethane bushings (more on these later), notorious for squeaking, a lubeable shackle bushing soon followed. The bolts are drilled and a zerk fitting is installed. The bushings can then be lubed as necessary. With the right equipment and larger than stock bolts, Jeepers have built their own lubeable setups by drilling the bolts themselves.

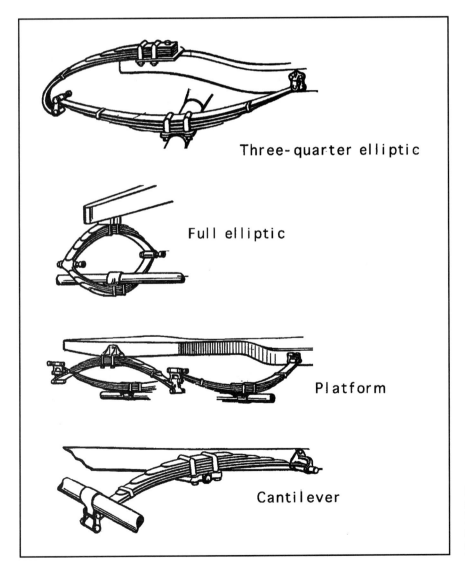

Three-quarter elliptic

Full elliptic

Platform

Cantilever

So you thought quarter- or three-quarter elliptic springs were new stuff. Here are some illustrations from a 1912 shop manual to prove otherwise. Give you any ideas?

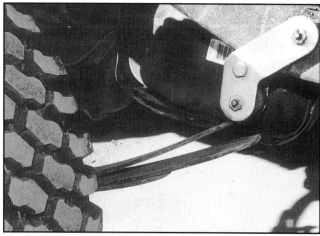

The Boomerang shackle from Currie allows for longer or more heavily arched springs to be used without putting the shackle in a bad position. This Jeep is drooped far enough to plant the center bolt of the shackle against the chassis. Too short a spring, perhaps?

*Right:* A poor setup. At rest, these shackles are tilted forward. As the spring flattens out, it has to lift the weight of the vehicle to push the shackle back. The result is a harsh ride and, depending on the weight involved, this placement could be tough on the spring.

A closeup of M.O.R.E.'s Wrangler shackle reversal kit. The short spring on top makes this setup a three-quarter elliptic. Note that a bolted shackle is used and that the bushings are greaseable.

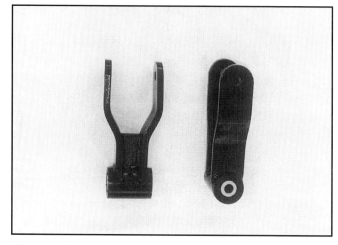

The XJ 1 1/2-inch lift shackle from TeraFlex is designed to match a front coil spacer lift of the same dimension. In order to get a 1 1/2-inch lift, the shackle must be 3 inches longer than stock.

Speaking of bolts, as logic would dictate, larger is stronger. Many shackle kits incorporate larger bolts. Poly bushing can be made a little thinner than rubber, so a larger sleeve and bolt can be used. In some cases, the mounting hardware is altered to accept the larger bolt.

One fabrication trick is to mount shackles on both ends of the rear springs and locate the axle via a pair of arms. Compression and droop are both enhanced, because both shackles allow the spring to freely arch either way. In essence, the shackle movement is divided between the two. The increase in droop is impressive.

Greaseable polyurethane bushings are all the rage. Why? Because they eliminate the raucous creaking that comes from dirt or cold weather. Some Jeepers claim they notice better articulation from freshly greased shackles.

## Leaf Spring Tricks

In the old days, leaf springs were packed in grease and then wrapped with sheet metal or even canvas. This eliminated most of the friction. The problem was that the grease attracted dirt and the job had to be redone periodically. In a 4x4, this would be an ongoing nasty job.

These days, the hot tip is to take the leaf springs apart, clean the leaf faces, paint them (some folks even wax the leaves), and insert Teflon pads between the leaves. These can be a cut-to-fit full-length piece of Teflon, a fitted liner that is ribbed on the sides and designed to fit certain width springs, or a small pad for the high friction area at the end of the leaf. The springs can also be treated by High Performance Coatings to a baked-on coating they call SO2. This mixture of PTFE (Teflon) and graphite makes the leaves very slick but the cost is fairly high.

Some manufacturers, such as Skyjacker, Superlift, National Spring, and OME, offer antifriction protection on their production springs in the form of pads at the end of the leaf. These can be installed on any spring but holes need to be punched in the spring to hold them. This is usually done before the leaf is tempered.

Spring over lifts are somewhat controversial because they can induce spring wrap in some cases. With well-designed springs and/or a traction bar of some sort, the 3 to 4 inches of lift is gained with few problems. As you can see here, the spring remains nearly flat. A flatter spring gives a better ride and better articulation.

Another leaf spring tuning trick involves loosening the crimped-type spring clamps. Some Jeepers open the clamps all the way, cut them off shorter, drill a pair of holes, and insert a spacer and bolt. Voila, instant bolt clip. In some cases, loosening a clamp can result in a noticeable increase in droop.

## Selecting Springs

To make the ideal selection, you will need to weigh your vehicle three ways. Before you do that, decide about your load capacity. If your Jeep is a truck and you use it as such, obviously you need to consider cargo capacity and rate your springs accordingly. If you have an SUV or utility-type rig, you need to consider your "loaded-for-bear" weights, which would include passengers, winch, camping gear, and all the other stuff you normally carry.

If you normally travel very light, so be it, but if you order springs for this condition and then make a change to carry a bunch of heavy gear, the light-rated springs you bought will sag. For best spring results, make an honest and accurate evaluation of use and load.

First, get the weight of the whole vehicle and then get the weight over the front and rear axle separately. Skyjacker uses some nifty formulas to help customers get the correct rates and they are included on page 56. These can be useful with any spring selection situation.

Going beyond rate, you will need to consider other changes you might have made, such as a spring over. A spring that was designed for underslung operation may not be the best choice for a spring over. Speak to the

spring manufacturer for their perspective on using the springs for this purpose. It might not be safe to rely on a local parts store for the best information on such things. Often a custom spring is the answer, because it can be built for this, or any other, specific situation. The more you can tell the spring builder about your needs, the better the result.

### Spring and Chassis Bushings

Early car and truck springs used greaseable bronze bushings for the spring pivot points. By the 1950s, rubber, or more specifically neoprene, was beginning to be used. Neoprene bushings gave a much smoother ride but the bushings had a fairly short life. Rubber technology has improved to the point where the working life of the OE rubber bushings on a street-driven or mildly off-roaded Jeep is essentially equal to the life of the vehicle. Not so for machines that are worked hard.

The latest bushing trend is polyurethane compounds. These bushings have a longer life than rubber in tough situations, but generally are not as soft. The big debate these days is whether to use rubber or poly bushings. If flex is more important than durability, then rubber is currently still the way to go. Manufacturers of poly bushings are closing the softness gap, whereas neoprene manufacturers are working on tensile strength. The softness of bushing compounds is checked with a durometer and rated according to a scale (see page 58 for details). Bushings are also tested for tensile strength, which is a measure of toughness and the ability to carry a load. Typical rubber spring bushings have a 25A–50A durometer rating and a tensile strength between 500 and 1,500 psi. A current Daystar poly bushing that is considered soft has a 1,500-psi tensile strength but a 73A durometer rating. Many poly bushings are in the 85A–95A durometer range with correspondingly higher psi ratings. New technology is improving the material all the time, as evidenced by Daystar's Durothane compound, which has a 73A durometer with a 3,500–4,000-psi rating. They are working on a 60A–65A durometer material at the same psi.

How poly bushings are formed is of vital importance, especially from the durability standpoint. During the mixing process, the material will naturally try to absorb water. If much moisture is allowed in the material, it will tend to make pockets, or bubbles. A dry atmosphere is vital and the better manufacturers mix in a complete vacuum. Poly bushings with a porous look are usually of poor quality and when cut open can yield large voids that weaken the material.

### Leaf Spring Lifts

Lift is needed to fit larger tires, and there are many ways to achieve it. In some cases, lift can also enhance articulation. The first and most common method is via increased camber in the springs. If this is done in moderation, say up to 2 1/2 inches, very few negative side effects are noted. A lift of this dimension does not usually need the bump stop lowered to restrict uptravel, so a gain in articulation is usually achieved. As you get to and exceed 4 inches of lift this way, the bump stop must be lowered to save the spring.

Lift blocks are the cheap lift alternative on rear axles that are spring over. Never, ever use them up front! Even in the rear, this is not a recommended procedure. Once you use a setup like this, you are kissing roadability good-bye. The axle wrap would be horrendous and the strain on those U-bolts massive. Use a better alternative.

## Spring Over

The other common method of lift is via a "spring over" conversion. In all leaf spring Jeeps, except the rear of J-Series trucks and Wagoneers, the spring is mounted under the axle. If you put the axle under the spring, you automatically gain a lift equal to the thickness of the axle tube. This entails torching off the spring perch from the bottom of the axle and welding a new one on the top. The steering will usually require some attention in the form of a dropped pitman arm or another practical method (read on).

The advantage of a spring over is that you can use the springs in their ideal, nearly flat position. Other than the ordinary problems associated with any lift, axle wrap under power can create wheel hop. As torque is applied through the axle to the tires, the axle twists. The spring resists according to its stiffness, but will actually go S-shaped. This happens to all springs, regardless of axle position but in a spring over situation, the extra leverage increases the effect.

The result of axle wrap is that the driveshaft and pinion angle changes and if it changes enough, the U-joint binds and breaks. The other negative effect occurs if the tires lose traction. Suddenly released of torque, the springs snap back again and the driveshaft takes the brunt. Spring rate, the length of the spring, gear ratios, and engine torque all contribute to this tendency.

Several cures exist for axle wrap, whether it comes from a spring over or not. These include stiffer springs and torque rods of all types (a.k.a. traction bars). Some spring manufacturers, most notably Rancho, include a half leaf on the leading end of some of their springs that goes from the eye to just past the U-bolts. Often this is just enough to prevent wrap. Several companies build torque rods but be sure they will not restrict articulation. Some do.

One of the simplest antiwrap solutions is offered by Rubicon Express. Since a spring over requires a new perch on top of the axle, RE developed a perch that features a much longer base for the spring. This has the effect of an extra leaf, and can reduce or eliminate wrap.

## Lift Blocks and Add-a-Leaf

Lift blocks are used primarily on the rear of trucks and Wagoneers that use a factory spring over setup. It's an inexpensive method of getting lift. As the name implies, it's a steel or aluminum block that's inserted between the spring and the axle perch. Longer U-bolts are used with it. Their only advantage is that they are cheap, and they will lift you up.

The disadvantages are numerous. First, they can multiply axle wrap, though with stiff truck springs and mild lifts (say up to 2 1/2 inches), they are bearable. Also, you will be forever retorquing them, as they tend to work loose more often. Nobody recommends lift blocks over 4 inches and never, ever install blocks on the front of anything. If you use blocks, use one single block rather than several. A stack will eventually come apart.

Add-a-leaf products are offered by most aftermarket suspension manufacturers. This is another very inexpensive method of lift and generally preferred over blocks, though the amount of lift available is less. With some small variations, they all involve adding a single, heavily arched leaf to your existing leaf pack. It can raise the suspension 1 to 1 1/2 inches with a corresponding increase in spring rate. An add-a-leaf can also be used to bolster sagging springs. Usually, it's a pretty hefty leaf, but the versions with a longer, thinner leaf provide a better ride than the short, very thick ones.

## Longer Shackles

A longer shackle is one way to gain lift, but it's not the best way. Longer shackles are most useful to "fine-tune" the height of one end of the Jeep to the other during suspension modification. Remember that a longer shackle only lowers one end of the spring. That means your lift will be only half of the extra length of the shackle. It will also change your *pinion angle*. In the

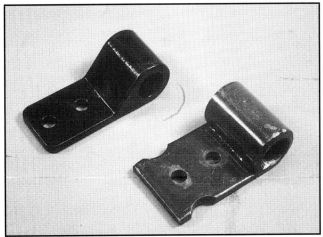

Spring hangers are an often overlooked piece of hardware that can fail in hard use. On the right is a stock type of unit. They usually break between the eye and the first bolt hole. The much stronger piece on the left is a Slickrock Enterprises 4340 hanger.

front, longer shackles on a reversed Jeep would lower the pinion. In standard shackle configuration, the pinion is raised.

Longer shackles could mean having to reweld the spring perches on the axle in a new position to get the correct pinion angle. Too long a shackle could allow the shackle to flip itself against the chassis, perhaps to stay there until you get out with a bar and pry it back.

Longer shackles on the front end of Jeeps with shackles in the stock location could lead to some embarrassing moments. Think of those springs and shackles hanging out there waiting to catch a rock ledge. It happens all the time and sometimes the result is a bent spring.

### Selecting a Lift Kit

The more lift you buy the more money you spend. Don't buy lift for looks—buy it for need, and buy no more than you need. The drivability and safety trade-offs increase with more lift. Giving away your safety for looks is not smart!

Regarding cost, it isn't that 4-inch lift springs cost that much more than 2 1/2-inch springs, it's that you have to make so many other changes to make the 4-inch springs work. If you have limited funds, get a better quality kit with less lift rather than buying a cheap "nose-bleed special" high-lift model that could give you trouble.

How much lift is best? Many Jeepers running CJs and YJs find 2 1/2–3-inch kits to be a good upper limit compromise. They retain a reasonably low center of gravity. The mild lift springs don't usually need the bump stops lowered, so you gain up- and down-travel. Ride quality is good, and owners report that you can fit 32x11.50, 33x9.50, or even 33x12.50 tires.

Most experts recommend a maximum of 4 inches of lift in a bolt-on kit for the short wheelbase rigs. You'll see four-wheelers with higher lifts, but they've either had some serious reengineering done or they're risking their lives. There is little need for more lift with a trail Jeep, unless it's a mud bogger. Usually, raw lift is traded for articulation.

In general, trucks, longer wheelbase, or wider rigs are more tolerant of a bit more lift. Four to six inches is not outrageous for a large truck. Six inches seems to be the generally agreed-upon practical limit for trucks, but the same basic rules apply as with the utilities. Good engineering can get the job done more safely.

### Leaf Spring Lift Complications

Depending on the amount of lift you opt for, complications may emerge beyond those already discussed. One such complication involves the brake lines. More lift or articulation may stretch the brake lines like rubber bands. A kit should include a method of extending the brake lines, if needed. Most commonly, a lowering bracket is included. Sometimes longer brake lines are needed.

Brake lines can be custom fabricated at hydraulic shops or ordered via Stainless Steel Brakes, TSM, or Superlift (and others, see the brake section). In some cases, a longer factory type of line can be found to fit. Not all stainless steel brake cables are DOT legal. Also, in some rare cases, emergency brake cables will end up too short.

One of the complications of lifted rigs or increased articulation is brake lines that are too short. In this case, the brake line is stretched like a rubber band from a sway bar disconnect alone. The cure is longer brake lines, which are available from several sources.

An accident waiting to happen. These U-bolts just cry, "Hit me, hit me." The correct setup is to cut the U-bolts off flush with the nut after the nuts are torqued. This prevents the U-bolts from sustaining massive damage and gives you an inch more clearance under the axle.

If your Jeep uses remote axle breathers, these may also need extending. Since these most often use rubber hose, it's not a big deal to make them longer. Some additional complications are discussed in the steering section further along.

### Other Suspension Hardware

Under this heading come items like spring plates, U-bolts, and shackles. These are items that are not on the "glamour" list for Jeep builders but are worthy of attention nonetheless. Upgrades in these areas can add a good deal of beef to any buildup, and they don't cost a whole lot.

U-bolts and spring plates provide another good area for upgrades. The first is to install larger U-bolts and nuts. With the typical underslung Jeep setup, the U-bolts, plates, and nuts are carrying the entire weight of the vehicle. Even with a spring over, where the weight is carried by the spring pad, the extra force from engine torque is enough reason to upgrade. Even if all you do is add some weight or increase severity of use, a U-bolt upgrade is a good idea. Almost all suspension kits come with new U-bolts.

The upgrade is fairly easy. All you need to do is drill larger holes in the spring plate. Use self-locking nuts on the new U-bolts and make sure the U-bolts are of the correct size for your axle tube. The best U-bolts are made of carbon steel, such as 1341 or 1541, and have the threads rolled rather than cut. Cut threads are easily spotted because the threaded area has been reduced in diameter. U-bolts should not protrude much beyond the nuts. If they do, cut them off just past the nuts. You can also double nut them to protect the threads if they are not hanging too low.

Many Jeep spring plates are notoriously flimsy. Often, the U-bolts get tightened to the point where the stock plate distorts. Sometimes a tough trail or impact with a rock is enough to bend them. Lots of alternatives exist, from simple replacements made from thicker plate, to those that protect the nuts.

Protecting the ends of your U-bolts can save a lot of hassle down the road. The ends of the U-bolts and the nuts are just hanging down there to get hammered and to hang you up. Once the ends are bent or scarred, removing them can lead to busted knuckles and some language you might not want the kids to hear. Several manufacturers make spring plates that have a skid plate to cover the nuts. Be aware that very cheap versions of this design may not leave room for a socket on the nuts. If you want ultimate beef from a traditional design, JKS builds a solid steel plate an inch thick with countersunk holes for the nuts. These plates literally *are* bulletproof.

The Four X Doctor makes a U-bolt reversal kit that moves the plate on top of the axle on Dana 30s, 44s, and AMC 20 axles on Jeeps with underslung axles. These eliminate all the stuff under the axle and gain more than an inch of clearance.

Currie builds clamp-on leaf spring mounts for the rear axles (tube diameter 2.75, 3.00, and 3.25 inches) that replace the spring perches on the axle, the U-bolts, and the spring plate. They allow for infinite pinion angle adjustments and the bracket only protrudes a quarter-inch below the spring.

Another overlooked suspension item, and one that tends to bite back at the wrong time, is spring hangers. These are the brackets that are welded or riveted onto the chassis from which the spring mounts or pivots. Most problems occur on the pivot bracket and while they more frequently appear on the front springs, they can also show up in the rear. In some cases, damage is transferred to the chassis.

Fortunately, the aftermarket has stepped in with some stronger replacements. The cast 4130 steel pieces from Slickrock Enterprises are probably the best known and most popular of these. They are bolted on with

Grade 5 or Grade 8 hardware and usually with self-locking nuts. This is a vital mod for any hard-worked Jeep, regardless of the state of modification. Do it before your chassis gets damaged.

## Jeep Coil Spring Suspensions

Other than some prototypes in the 1950s and the short-lived optional front torsion bar suspension for 1963–66 Wagoneers and Gladiators, the first nonleaf Jeep suspension came in 1984 on the downsized XJ Cherokee. These rigs combined a front coil spring suspension with long, supple leaf springs in back. When the Grand Cherokee debuted in 1993, it came with four coils. So did the updated TJ Wrangler that emerged for 1997.

Coil spring suspensions have many advantages and a few disadvantages. On the good side, all spring friction is eliminated, so "effective" spring rate and ride quality remain constant. Also, the axle is well secured by locating arms, so axle wrap is eliminated. In the case of the Jeeps, the front and rear suspensions are five-link, the axles being located by five arms. Long travel is the prime benefit. In some cases, there may be a reduction in weight. Also, because the axle is "tied down" better, handling is more carlike.

On the downside, coil spring suspension is more expensive and complicated to modify. Many who have switched over from a modified leaf sprung rig to a modified coiler have reported that coils often tend to be a little too soft and the rigs lean and bounce more than desired. This makes the choice of spring rates and shocks very important.

### Coil Springs

Coil springs are rated the same way as leaf springs, by the number of pounds it takes to move the spring 1 inch. Like leaf types, they also come in dual-rate designs. Dual-rate coils can be identified by the first couple of coils being closer together than the rest. Important coil measurements to know are free length, wire size, and number of coils.

The free length is important because if you know your three important vehicle weights (front half, rear half and total; see page 56), the spring rate and length, you can figure the approximate spring length and ride height when loaded. Wire size and number of coils will indicate rate. If the coils are widely separated and climb rapidly, the spring is said to have more ramp or pitch. Coil springs droop well, but the maximum uptravel may be controlled by coil bind, or the point at which the coils stack up into a pile. A long spring with lots of coils will bind faster than one with few coils, but the spring with fewer coils and more pitch may sag faster.

Coil springs are only loosely attached to the vehicle via a small clip at the bottom coil. The weight of the vehicle holds the spring in place. In modified rigs, the suspension can drop farther than the spring and it may pull away from the top spring seat by a little or a lot. In factory applications, the shock will limit downtravel and prevent this from occurring.

Unlike leaf springs, coil springs can retain a similar rate to stock, even when lifted, without any problem. A touch of extra rate is often built in by the kit maker, which may be up to 10 percent per inch of lift. This is

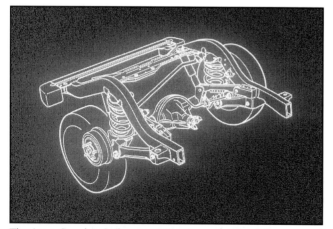

The Jeep Quadra Coil rear suspension consists of four control arms, a transverse track rods and two coil springs. The front is very similar. Coil spring setups have many advantages, not the least of which are a great ride, good articulation, and more carlike street manners. They are, however, more difficult to modify. *Courtesy Chrysler Corporation*

The cheapest and easiest coil spring lifts are via coil spring spacers. This Tera part offers a 1 1/4-inch lift using spacers. When combined with correspondingly longer shocks, ride and articulation are at stock levels. Spacers may also be used to fine-tune spring lifts.

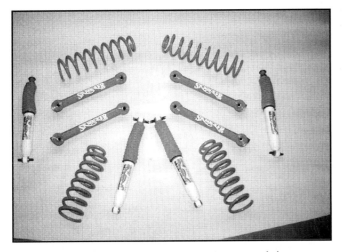

A spring lift is the next step up from spacers, and the parts list gets longer. To correct caster and pinion angle, longer arms are required. This Skyjacker kit is a moderate lift, middle-priced Grand Cherokee application. It's a very simple kit to which many options can be added. *Courtesy Skyjacker*

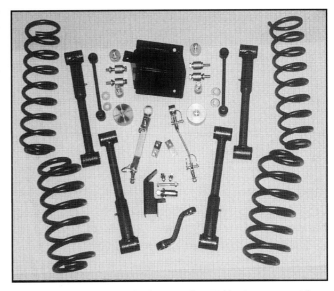

Top dollar setups include this Teraflex TJ kit. It comes with new coils, pivoting lower arms, sway bar disconnects, track bar lifting bracket, and a dropped pitman arm, among other goodies. This ain't a cheap kit, but it's well thought out and has few complications. *Courtesy Tera Manufacturing*

done to compensate for the added leverage of the higher center of gravity, and it helps resist sway. The correct shock choices are more important with a coil spring rig.

### Coil Spring Lifts

Lifting coil spring Jeeps is a bit more complicated than with a leaf spring rig. The simplest and cheapest way to lift a coil spring vehicle is to install a spacer at the top of the coil and a correspondingly longer shock, or a shock extension. These lifts are usually limited to 1–1 1/2 inches but can be found up to 2–3 inches. If combined with a body lift, a spacer lift can offer the room for a moderate jump in tire size. Sometimes spacers are used to augment a spring lift. These spacers are commonly metal, but some companies offer spacers made of hard polyurethane. Both styles are adequate. In moderation, a spacer lift has few complications.

The next step up are longer coils, and the lift values are from 1 to 5 1/2 inches, depending on application and company. These kits will require longer shocks and usually new control arms to correct caster. As with leaf springs, the more you lift, the more it costs. Complete coil spring lift kits above 3 inches of lift can cost as much as 50 percent more than an equivalent leaf spring lift kit.

Any amount of lift has a corresponding change of caster and pinion angle. Front axle caster (explained more in the steering section) is the backward tilt of the steering axis of the front wheels. Caster equates to good

directional stability and tracking down the highway. Pinion angle (explained more in the driveshaft section and also in Chapter 4) is the tilt up or down of the diff pinion.

Lifts move the steering axis more toward the vertical, and directional stability may be lost. "Wanderitis" is the result. This is my word for a condition where the vehicle lacks directional stability and requires constant steering corrections. Small lifts, from 1 to 2 inches, make little difference but after that, correction is often necessary. Changes in pinion angle may cause a similar effect.

The peculiar problem with Jeep coilers is that, unlike a leaf sprung rig, more caster isn't as much of a cure-all for wanderitis. The stock rigs are set at 7 to 8 degrees caster. The OEM arms have adjustable pivots, so that this can be dialed in by an alignment shop. According to Rubicon Express, rigs that are lifted about 3 inches and up track better with less caster, somewhere around 5 to 6 degrees. Several methods exist for correcting caster and pinion angle after a lift, the most common being modified control arms. In some cases, such as the Off-Road General Store and some Rubicon Express kits, a modified arm is used that puts caster and pinion angle back in the "green" zones (whatever they may be for the particular Jeep) and then the values can be fine-tuned with the OEM adjusters. Rubicon Express and Terra Flex use adjustable arms that can be fine-tuned to gain the correct caster and pinion values. Offset cam bolts for the rear, available from Jeep dealers, will help fine-tune rear pinion angle.

One of the limitations to increased articulation in a coiler is the rigid control arms. The amount of twist available is limited to the flex in the bushings. Many of the lift kit manufacturers are therefore offering pivoting arms. These arms are threaded in the center and will pivot during articulation. This feature will also allow the length to be adjusted for caster and pinion angle correction. Bushings are fitted at the ends as normal and, interestingly, these are usually rubber rather than polyurethane. The polyurethane bushings were found to transmit too much harshness, especially in the plush Grand Cherokees.

A variation of the above concept uses Heim joints at one or both ends of the control arm to allow articulation. Heim joints have the needed flex for this but tend to be noisy and transfer lots of vibration, even the versions that are insulated with Teflon. In some instances, a Heim joint is fitted at one end and a big rubber bushing at the other.

As this book was being completed, Currie had just announced its new "Johnny Joints," which have the flexibility of Heim joints but insulate better against noise and vibration. They also have a wider angle of movement. Already, they have been incorporated into arms for coil spring Jeeps.

### Coil Spring Lift Complications

Many of the complications for a lift with coil springs are the same as for leaf springs. These include the need for longer brake lines, or lowering brackets, steering geometry problems, and axle vent problems. Add to them the need to relocate the Panhard or track rod. It's designed to be parallel to the axle. If it's angled, it can cause a form of bump steer (see the steering section).

There are some drivability glitches unique to lifted coil spring rigs. These include a wobble or vibration that sets in at certain speeds or on some road surfaces. The wobble is more prevalent with more lift. It is caused by the changes in caster and the leverage of the control arms being altered by the lift. Very careful tuning can eliminate it in mild to moderate lifts but with tall lifts, it can only be lessened to a point.

The other trademark oddity of lifted or long travel coilers is a "jacking" action by the arms from engine torque. This may lift one end or one side of the vehicle when power is applied against an obstacle or in a turn.

It's usually harmless, only making a tricky trail situation feel more tricky. It isn't harmless if it occurs on the street during turns.

Also noticeable in coilers with lots of articulation is that when the axle moves down, the front wheels will be pulled toward the back of the wheelwell. As they drop, the arms are effectively getting shorter. The reverse happens when it moves up. A similar situation occurs to the rear wheels, in which they move forward as they move down.

Grand Cherokees with large tires and long suspension travel are particularly troubled by wheel position in the rear, because they have small wheelwells. Even with a healthy lift, fenderwell trimming is usually necessary to fit tires larger than 31 or perhaps 32 inches tall.

With radical axle articulation (one wheel up and the other down), the axle may be pulled forward on one side and back on the other. This can input a bit of steering the driver hadn't intended. It feels the oddest when it comes from the rear axle. It's easily dealt with at slow speeds by driving technique but it could be disastrous if encountered going fast, though that is an unlikely possibility.

Most experts recommend that coilers with lots of droop be fitted with lockers at both ends. Why? Imagine a deep crack into which a wheel drops as you cross it diagonally. Because the control arm may be hanging nearly straight down, instead of automatically climbing the other side, the forward motion will try to pull the wheel down and farther back. If the wheel has power applied, of course, it will climb itself out.

Lift kit manufacturers have been constantly work-

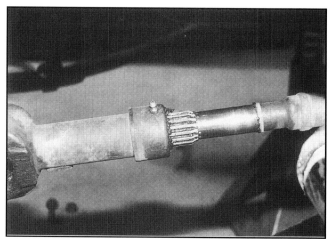

Lifts and other suspension mods can result in driveshaft slip yokes that may pull apart on the trail. This front shaft is about a half inch from doing just that.

ing on these problems and new cures are found every day. With the coil sprung Jeeps being relatively new to the trail scene, it takes a while for the technology to catch up.

## Driveshafts and Pinion Angles

Lift changes driveshaft and pinion angles both front and rear. Changing the operating angles of the driveshaft universal joints can have many negative effects, the mildest of which is vibration and a shorter life. You'll get more detail on universal joints in Chapter 4. Our goal here is to talk about the complications that suspension lift imparts and the cures for them.

To start with, the two universal joints, or U-joints, on each driveshaft should operate at the same angle and at the same speed. That means the pinion end of the differential and the transfer case output must be parallel on two planes. If they are not, then one universal is operating at a slightly higher or lower speed than the other and vibration is the result. The greater the difference, the greater the vibration of the driveshaft. Three degrees or less is usually regarded as "in the ballpark."

The other necessity is that both yokes are in line with each other, or phased. If they are operating more than about 1 degree apart, vibration can result. On driveshafts with slip yokes, it's possible to install the two halves a spline or two off.

The U-joint vibration problem is complicated on full-time four-wheel-drive systems. With a part-time system, you really only worry about rear driveshaft vibration. The front shaft can be a little off parallel because it's operated at a low speed. Not so with the full-time setup, which suffers vibration times two.

Pinion angle can be corrected by tapered shims on leaf sprung Jeeps or a modified radius arm (or caster adjusters in mild cases) on coil sprung rigs. Tapered shims come in a variety of types and are fitted between the spring perch and the spring. The other common method of aligning U-joint angles is by lowering the transfer case. This isn't the ideal setup, due to the loss of clearance and the fact that if you lower one end of the T-case, you raise the other. It works, however, and is better than vibration and wasted U-joints. It may not apply to rigs with the full-time four-wheel-drive problem. Lowering the entire engine and trans assembly would work but isn't practical. Many lift kits come with transfer case lowering kits.

Up front, pinion angle and caster are inexorably linked. If you change one, then you will change the other (see the steering section). The only way to change this relationship is by cutting and rewelding the axle tubes.

Bear in mind that your pinion angle changes with suspension movement or by the torque effect of the axle. The rear pinion will climb under a torque load and the front will drop. If this occurs at low driveshaft speeds, it isn't much of a problem, because the U-joint

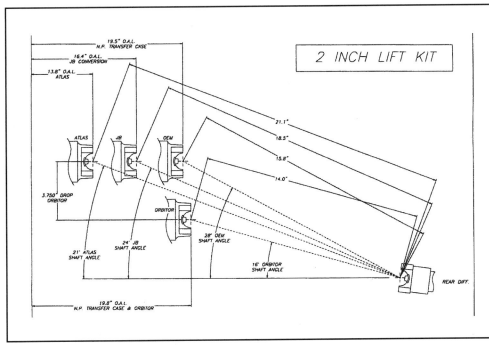

This chart shows the driveshaft angles of a Wrangler with a variety of tailshaft positions when utilizing Orbitor and Atlas T-cases. It's a great illustration of how driveshaft angle is affected by output position. *Courtesy Advance Adapters*

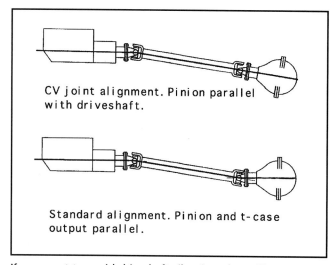

CV joint alignment. Pinion parallel with driveshaft.

Standard alignment. Pinion and t-case output parallel.

If you want to avoid driveshaft vibration after a lift, measure your pinion angle and adjust your axle according to this illustration.

can deal with the extra angularity going slow. If you happen to be spinning the wheels or are in a high gear with the drivetrain turning at a higher speed, it's a different deal, and U-joint failure is possible. Some builders will opt to set the pinion angle a degree lower in the rear and a degree higher in the front to help compensate.

As discussed in Chapter 4, the maximum angularity for most U-joints is about 30 degrees. This is a short-term maximum number. Continuous angularity is rated at 15 degrees for most universals, though service life will be cut by 75 percent at this angle.

Reaching the maximum angularity of U-joints starts to be an issue on short-wheelbase Jeeps at 2 1/2 to 3 inches of lift, give or take, with longer rigs having more leeway. A short driveshaft makes the angle steeper. In addition to the other methods discussed, one cure is a driveshaft-constant velocity (CV) joint. More accurately called a double Cardan, the CV takes two standard U-joints and couples them with a housing that has a centering device. If you have a 20 degree angle, the CV essentially splits this between the two joints, giving them 10 degrees each, well within their operating range.

The requirement for using this setup is that, unlike the single Cardan setups, the diff pinion must be parallel with the driveshaft rather than parallel with the transfer case output. If you have an operating angle of near 15 degrees, you probably should consider a CV joint. If you want long U-joint life, start thinking about installing one when your angle is 8 degrees. A Spicer

1310 series CV has a maximum operating angle of 30 degrees and the stronger 1330 will bind at 25 degrees.

### Tailshaft Kits

As mentioned above, on short-wheelbase rigs, driveshaft and U-joint angles become a problem. Even a longer rig with lots of lift can encounter angularity problems. A longer driveshaft will lessen this angle in all cases. Most later Jeeps use the NP 207, 231, or 241 chain drive transfer case and a slip yoke is used on the rear output. This adds a great deal of length to the case and on Wranglers, it makes for a tiny driveshaft.

Several companies make tailshaft kits that eliminate the slip yoke in favor of a standard yoke. This can add 4 to 4 1/2 inches to the length of the driveshaft and lessen the angle significantly. You could also combine a tailshaft kit with a CV joint. Installing the tailshaft kits entails partially dismantling the transfer case, and this is done most easily with the T-case on a bench. More on tailshaft kits appears in Chapter 5.

### Custom Driveshafts

There are many reasons for a new, custom-made driveshaft. A change of drivetrain components is a common one, as is a suspension lift kit. In any case, the best advice is to do some figuring beforehand to determine what driveline problems may crop up. Forewarned is forearmed.

Before you get a lift kit, you might uncouple the driveshafts from the diffs front and rear and measure how far they drop below the pinion. If you deduct a couple of inches from that distance for safety, you get the approximate amount of lift you can install without major driveline mods. If you lift beyond that, you can figure on spending some extra bucks on driveshaft mods. The lift value you obtain may contradict some lift kit manufacturer's recommendations.

Measuring your Jeep for custom shafts starts with getting all your suspension kit stuff installed and with the vehicle on its wheels. It wouldn't hurt to bounce it a couple of times to settle the suspension. You will

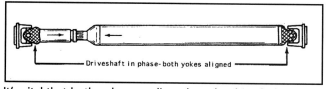

Driveshaft in phase-both yokes aligned

It's vital that both yokes are aligned on the driveshaft. If not, vibration will ensue. In a two-piece shaft like this, the two sections can be accidentally assembled a spline off. In a one-piece shaft, the driveshaft builder would be at fault.

need the transfer case and pinion yokes installed. If you've done engine or running gear swaps, make sure they are in the final position. If you move things around later, your measurements will be invalid. The driveshaft builder will build what you order and will not make refunds if you order wrong. Measure twice, order once.

The measurement you are looking for is the center of the T-case output U-joint cup to the center of the pinion U-joint cup. If you don't have a helper, you can use a clamp or vice grips to clip the free end of the tape to the yoke. The clip end of the tape can induce errors used like this, but if you start at the 1 inch mark and adjust your measurements at the other end (simply add an inch), you'll come out OK.

Many times, you will want to get your old shaft modified. If the yokes are in good shape, they can be cut from the old tube and reused with the new tube. Consider the age and mileage of your rig and that new parts might be cheap insurance.

The driveshaft builder may need to know a few other things. He will need to know if you have a particularly flexible suspension. Longer slip yokes can be installed that will compensate for a large amount of movement. He will need to know which U-joints you want to use and whether you want a CV joint at the t-case end.

## Sway Bar and Track Bar Disconnects

As good street manners and drivability became more important to the 4x4 buying public, various suspension improvements began to be fitted to Jeeps. The first of these was an antisway bar. This torsion bar connects the axle to the body and is designed to minimize body roll, or lean. Body roll is more than just an uncomfortable tilt, it is also a transfer of weight that can affect tire grip, handling, and safety.

When the Wrangler grew out of the ashes of the bad publicity given to the CJ in the mid-1980s, it featured a lower, wider stance and sway bars front and rear. It also contained another safety item known as a track bar or Panhard bar. These arms locate the axles laterally and, combined with the other stuff, make the Wrangler very carlike on the street. The problem is that they affect trail performance adversely. Some Jeepers are out there running round with sway bars and track bars removed needlessly in the name of trail performance. There are now methods of having the best of both worlds.

JKS is famous for having originated the sway bar disconnect, and several other companies have followed suit. With the pull of a pin, you can unhook the sway bar from the axle and gain an instant 26 percent increase in articulation on a Wrangler. CJs and other rigs are similar. When you get back to the pavement, a few minutes will have you hooked back up and ready for road handling. The sway bar disconnects work with the coilers as well as the leaf sprung rigs.

Disconnecting the track bar on Wranglers has a similar effect. It will increase articulation approximately 30 percent, but handling on the street heads straight to the commode. JKS and M.O.R.E. (Mountain Off-Road Enterprises) each developed a track bar disconnect that allows the track bar to be used on the street and then released for the trail. In addition, M.O.R.E. has a track bar that has a Heim joint rather than bushings, and this setup allows much great articulation than the stock setup.

The sway bar disconnects are available for use with stock or lifted suspensions on CJs, YJ and TJ Wranglers, XJs, and ZJs. Nothing is currently available for SJs. Track bar disconnects are made to fit Wranglers. Both devices are valuable additions to the Jeeper's arsenal, whether the rig is a mild or a gonzo buildup.

### Body Lifts

A body lift is a fairly easy and very cheap way of getting clearance for bigger tires or extra articulation. This can only done to Jeeps with a separate chassis and body and not the unibody rigs, such as the Cherokee and Grand Cherokee. It involves lifting the body farther away from the chassis by means of spacers. It's particularly useful for "fine tuning" after a lift or a shackle

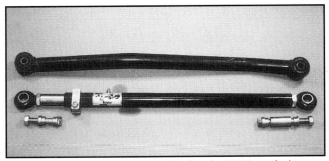

The track bar is largely responsible for the YJ Wrangler's street manners, but it's also true that with the bars disconnected you get an articulation increase of 25 percent. The answer is a track bar that can be released for the trail. M.O.R.E.'s Slip-Loc track bar features Heim joints at both ends but more importantly, it's easily released by means of a 9/16-inch wrench or socket for an instant gain in articulation.

Here's the obvious difference in tire clearance on a Wrangler, with and without the addition of a M.O.R.E. 1-inch body lift—standard height left, and 1-inch body lift right. The lift just about eliminated some heavy tire/fender contact with this Wrangler, which mounts 33x12.50s Dunlops with a 2-inch OME lift and a M.O.R.E. shackle reversal.

reversal. For example, combining the M.O.R.E. shackle reversal kit and the super supple Old Man Emu springs (about 2 inches of lift) with a 1-inch body lift and 33x12.50s is an outstanding combo on a CJ or Wrangler. The bigger meats would not fit otherwise.

The experts don't always agree as to how much body lift is too much. One to 2 inches is certainly safe. Three inches in not uncommon and occasionally OK'd by the pros. After that it's gray area. The longer the bolts, the more leverage on them and during chassis flex, the bolts or the body mount may break. Some states have restrictions on body lift heights, so check before you start.

The most common type of body lifts are simply aluminum pucks that you fit above the original neoprene body mount. These are pretty bulletproof. The least expensive mounts are made of GRP (Glass Reinforced Plastic). The most recent additions are made of Delrin, a synthetic material similar to polyurethane. These will give rather than break but offer some flexibility.

A body lift is simple to perform but not always easy. Rust can take its toll on the body hardware and you may find yourself dealing with broken and seized bolts, not to mention body mounts that tear out of sheet metal. A torch becomes a vital tool in these situations. The various kit manufacturers usually supply the new hardware and these are most often Grade 5 bolts. Grade 8 and harder bolts lack the "give" needed for a constantly flexing body.

Body lift complications include interference with the steering column and shifters, fuel filler neck, and fan to fan shroud. The more lift, the more the problems occur. One inch of lift usually has a minimum of bad side effects.

## Shock Absorbers

Shocks are often called the most misunderstood suspension part. They either become the focus of a "more is better" fixation, or they are completely ignored. All

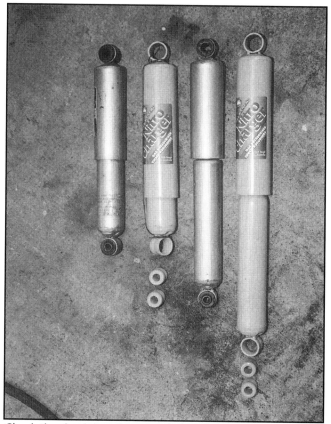

Check the shock lengths extended and compressed. Comparing stock rear Wrangler shocks to a set of OME shocks showed the OMEs were longer than stock extended, but the same length closed. In theory, this means you could install these longer shocks into a stock height rig with a 3-inch gain in droop.

The shock is often the limiting factor to downtravel, modified or stock. You can see how much by running the Jeep up an RTI ramp with the shock disconnected. In this case, at least 1 1/2 inches was gained. You can install a shock that's longer by this amount, as long as the shock doesn't bottom befo re the axle contacts the bumpstop when the axle is all the way up.

vehicles are equipped with one at each corner. The more is better credo dictates that if one is good, two should be better. If two is good, how about four per wheel? Some drivers, such as Baja racers, make expensive modifications to their shocks. On the other side, some Jeepers buy the cheapest shocks they can find and wish they didn't have to buy any. What's best for you probably lies between these extremes.

### Shock Anatomy

Shock absorbers are more accurately described as suspension dampers or spring dampers. The suspension has a frequency, or a rate at which it will respond to bumps. It's usually between one and two cycles per second, with soft springs being at the slow end and stiff springs at the faster end. The soft springs are slower to "snap back" than the stiffer ones. Left undampened, they can bounce and oscillate like a plucked bowstring.

The shocks are designed to dampen the movements of the suspension so that it will return as quickly as possible to the rest position but without bouncing back and creating a jolt. Shocks are most necessary at higher speeds for vehicle control, but even at slow speeds on the trail they help reduce sway and unwanted weight transfer.

There have been several types of dampers over the years, from those that relied on friction, to hydraulic lever types, and finally tube hydraulic types. The tubular shock has been adopted as the industry standard for many good reasons, but you might be interested to know that the earliest of the prototype jeeps used lever shocks.

The common shock is nothing more than a sealed tube that is filled with hydraulic fluid. One end is solid. The other has a hole and seal, through which a movable rod extends. On the inside end of the rod is a piston. The piston has small holes or valves that allow the piston to move up and down the tube. The size of these valves controls how fast the piston can move. With no valves, the piston would move very little because fluid does not compress. This is your basic monotube shock that goes back 70 years.

The monotube shock is vulnerable to damage. One dent will render it useless. Some better monotubes will have a sleeve and some deadspace to protect the hydraulic cylinder, but the single wall units cool better. This leads to the discussion of a more modern shock variant, the twin tube design. Instead of being in the piston, the valves are in the bottom of the cylinder and the outer layer around the hydraulic cylinder becomes the oil reservoir. The twin tube designs run cool.

One of the problems with ordinary hydraulic shocks is that heat and rapid movement can cause the oil to aerate and foam. That's partly because there is a certain amount of air space in the top of the housing so the fluid has room to expand or contract and partly because the heat also makes the oil foam. Once foaming starts, the shock quits doing its job.

It was discovered that if the shock housing is pressurized with an inert gas, the foaming is nearly eliminated. This discovery led to the gas-charged shock. After the oil is installed, the void is filled with 40–150 psi of nitrogen, and then the unit is sealed. Racing shocks may use up to 400 psi to further resist foaming. Unlike standard shocks, gas-charged shocks can be mounted upside down if necessary. The gas charged idea works with both twin-tube and monotube designs. Gas shocks tend to be stiffer than ordinary shocks, depending on how much gas pressure is used.

Variations of the gas shock include the cellular gas and cellular foam designs. The cellular gas shock has a bag often filled with freon at a very low pressure (say 10–15 psi), and this bag expands and contracts to keep the hydraulic oil slightly pressurized. Cellular foam does the same thing, except the bag uses foam, with or without the gas. Neither of these types protects as much against cavitation as a gas shock, but they are softer for low speed work. Some expensive racing shocks, such as Fox Shox, use an external reservoir for cooling and pressurization.

There are also air shocks and coil over shocks. The coil over is a fairly standard shock with a small coil spring around it. It can provide some extra load capacity and perhaps a little lift, at the cost of ride quality. The air shock does the same thing, though via air pressure. The air shock is designed primarily as a load leveling device. The coil over and the air shock put a lot of stress on shock mounts, decrease ride and suspension travel, and do not work well on most four-wheelers.

Among the commonly touted shock specs are piston and piston rod size. In this case, bigger is better, with the larger piston running cooler and dampening better. A variety of seal materials are used, from simple neoprene to Teflon to more exotic materials like Nitrile. The durability of the seal is vital to shock life.

A larger shaft is stronger, though the material it is made from will play a part. They range from cast or sintered iron, to induction hardened steel, to silicon bronze. The best shafts are made from forged steel and machined to a micro finish. The shaft is usually chrome plated, and the quality of this work will help determine how long the shock will last. A poor chrome job will peel and eat the shaft seal. Once the shock loses oil and pressure, it's history.

Some shocks have eyes on both ends or just one end. Either way, the quality of the welding will dictate how long that eye stays attached in tough situations. On cheap shocks, they are attached by a couple of spot welds. Better shocks are continuous or double welded for more strength.

One would suppose that a shock will dampen the same amount in the up or down movements. Many do, and they are called 50:50 shocks. In fact, they can be tuned to nearly any percentage, depending on what is needed. Many leaf spring shocks are 40:60 or 30:70, meaning that they are softer on the upstroke than on the down. Leaf springs, especially stiff ones, tend to snap back quickly. On compression, their inherent friction tends to dampen upward movement a bit. A set of

springs that has been worked over to have less friction might need differently valved shocks than an ordinary spring.

Coils are the opposite. Without the inherent friction, they tend to need more dampening control on compression and less on rebound. A coil spring shock might have a 60:40 or 70:30 bias. A shock valved for the typical leaf spring is a very poor choice for coils.

In the past few years, adjustable shocks have entered the market. Some, like Warn's Black Diamond brand, adjust to road conditions automatically with valves that are sensitive to the velocity of the piston movement. Other shocks are position sensitive and have an area of travel that is very soft in the middle of travel, but that increases in stiffness the farther the piston moves up or down. Edelbrock's new Performer shocks are said to be sensitive enough to be able to tell the difference between body lean and a bump, and adjust accordingly. Some shocks, such as Rancho's RS9000 line, are manually adjustable. The firmness can be controlled by a five-position knob on the body, or even via a remote control setup in the cab. The firmness adjustment doesn't change the shock bias that is preset by the factory.

### Shock Boots

To boot or not to boot, that's the question! The lurid, multicolored shock boots are a common sight on the trail. What are they for? According to the manufacturers, they protect the shaft from dirt and corrosion damage. If the shaft gets corroded or pitted above the shock body, or even excessively dirty, it can cause shaft seal failure when the bad part gets compressed into the shock.

Some Jeepers claim that the boots will hold dirt and moisture, and cause worse problems. This seems somewhat unlikely, because the boots have large drains. Still, the manufacturers may void the shock warranty if the boot is not used. That's enough reason for me to keep my boots on!

### Multiple Shocks

You see dual shocks a lot. Are they really necessary? For some, perhaps. The whole idea of multiple shocks is to share the load. Since shocks turn dampening movement into heat, and heat tends to create foam, two shocks sharing the same load would run half as hot as a single shock. With today's better shocks, the need for dual setups is much less than it was. A single good shock of today can do the work of two of yesterday. A

Do you really need dual shocks? If you like to go fast, perhaps, because the two shocks will share the load and, more importantly, the heat. If you do install duals, a setup like this works well. The shock hoop is braced to its brother across the engine compartment. You can get shock hoop kits from a variety of manufacturers.

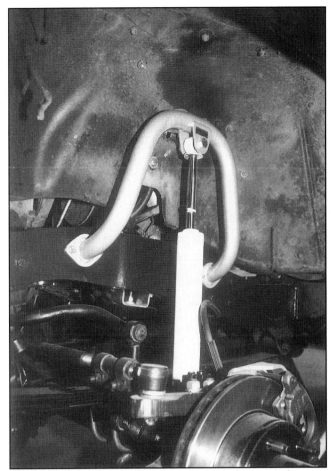

This is a rockcrawler's shock setup. A single long travel Rancho RS-9000 cellular foam shock on a hoop gives this CJ plenty of flex and control at low to moderate speeds. Note that this Jeeper prefers to run shocks without boots. This M.O.R.E. shock hoop kit could easily carry two shocks.

slow-moving rock crawler simply has no need for dual shocks. Still, there are fast movers out there that can cook even the best shocks of today and can use the double dampening.

Shocks must be valved for dual operation. Either they are both softened to provide the dampening of a single shock, or one is tuned to provide dampening upward and the other set to dampen downward. Two standard shocks will most likely make the ride much stiffer.

Dual shock positioning can provide options beyond just dampening movement. To dampen the axle, the shocks are best placed over the axle, perpendicular to it. Some shocks are cantilevered, or angled, forward or back. While this position doesn't dampen quite as well, it can provide some resistance to axle wrap. Especially in the rear, one shock tilted forward and another tilted

back can offer good dampening with some spring wrap control also.

Aftermarket dual shock kits are offered by several manufacturers. The usual setup is for the shocks to be mounted via a hoop kit and used side by side. Often, the two hoops are braced to each other by a bar that crosses over the top of the engine.

### Long Travel

In nearly all stock suspensions, the shock length determines the limit of suspension travel. Ditto for many lift kits. One way to increase articulation is to install a longer shock. Doing so is much more involved than just bolting on the longer item. The shock mounts will need to be relocated as well.

The first step is to disconnect or remove your existing shocks and see how much more travel or articula-

Dropped pitman arms are necessary to avoid bumpsteer during a lift. Always buy a purpose-built unit rather than bending your own. Improper heating and quenching can make the metal brittle, and the piece may break.

tion you can get. Simply disconnect the shocks and jack the vehicle up by the chassis until the wheels are off the ground. Bear in mind that your brake lines may be too short as well and you may have to temporarily disconnect them. If the lower shock mounts are significantly lower than the extended shocks, then you have some long travel potential.

Since you cannot usually just bolt on a longer shock, first measure the distance between the shock mounts with the suspension extended all the way. Then compress the suspension all the way against the bump stop and measure again. Ideally you want a shock that has an extended length about a half inch longer than your extended dimension and one that has a compressed dimension, about 1/2 to 3/4 inch shorter than the distance between the shock mounts with the suspension on the bump stops. The extra travel downward adds a margin of shock and shock mount safety. The collapsed distance is even more important, since the bump stop has some give. If you accidentally bottom the suspension hard, you will still have some shock travel left. Bottoming the shock can damage it and even break off shock mounts.

The shock manufacturers will list the extended and collapsed length of their shocks. If you are lucky, you will find one that fits your dimensions. Most likely, you will have to relocate a shock mount to get the longer shock installed. There are various methods for relocating shock mounts, including kits, fabrication, and a few bolt-on tricks.

A couple of OE parts-shock mount combos work well on CJs. Older CJs used a welded bracket on the chassis for an upper mount and the spring plate carried the lower mount. From about 1982 on, the lower mount was welded onto the axle and the upper mount was a long, bolted-on chassis bracket. An almost identical setup was used on SJ Big Jeeps from day one. If you combine the newer upper bracket (Jeep PN-5364229, 5364228) with the old spring plate-mounted lower shock mount (Jeep PN-5359011, 5359012), you can get a seriously long shock installed with bolt-on parts.

If you have a Wagoneer or J-Series pickup, it's possible to do the same thing by leaving the upper mount alone but adding a new spring plate with a shock mount. Some rear CJ spring plates would work in this case, as long as they are for the later 2 1/2-inch wide springs. With the difference in weight and load capacity, it would be better to buy some beefier units from a source like JKS.

### Choosing Shocks

If you are buying a suspension kit, the shocks are usually included. Does this mean they are the best ones for your situation? Not always, but usually. The lift kit builder will select the shocks that work best with the kit. They may offer a shock upgrade, and this is often a good idea.

The question of dual shocks is one that is answered by how you drive. If you are a fast mover or like to get frequent flier miles, you can probably use dual shocks. If you are a standard-duty Jeeper or a rock crawler, a single high-quality shock at each corner will do you just fine. Save your bucks for something else.

As to the type of shock, the need can be divided by slow movers, fast movers, and rigs that are mostly stock and run on the street. Slow movers are the hard-core or rock crawler types that usually trailer. They stay away from low or high pressure gas shocks, because they can cost some suspension flexibility. A good compromise can be had with shocks that use cellular gas or foam. Another good compromise is adjustable shocks, like Rancho RS 9000s. They offer the flexibility to dial-in the dampening for street or trail. That's why these are one of the most popular shocks on the market.

Fast movers are Jeepers who primarily run desert trails or milder trails where you can get up some speed for more than just a short stretch. For these folks, low

Three things to talk about here. First, the tie rod end has been replaced by a Heim joint and moved to the top of the steering knuckle. A narrowed Chevy truck tie rod is used and is about 100 percent stronger than stock. Installation is simple: drill a 5/8-inch hole and install a 5/8-inch bolt.

pressure gas shocks are a better choice to deal with the heat and foaming that come from taking a bumpy road at speed. If you are a real fast mover, high pressure gas or even remote reservoir shocks may be your ticket to cool shocks. A frequent flier will need the best and strongest shocks money can buy.

If your Jeep is to remain fairly stock or spend most of its time on the highway, then some of the trick, self-adjusting units like the Edelbrocks are a good choice. Low pressure gas is always a good choice for stock or mildly built rigs.

Situations that may change your shock needs include the mounting of larger tires, a change of spring rate, a major change in vehicle weight, or a change in driving condition. In any of these cases, you may have to reevaluate your shock needs.

## Steering

The need to steer is obvious. Hard use can take a toll on the stock steering system. This includes the impact of rocks or logs. Modifications, such as a lift, will change the geometry and leverage of the system. In the case of older Jeeps, the steering equipment is troublesome on the stock rigs. Large tires will double the stress on tie rods, drag links, etc. Big tires can also overload the OEM power steering system. As with everything else, one modification begets another!

Pre-1972 Jeep CJs, 1957–65 FCs, and 1946–65 Willys Station Wagons had a steering system that is not regarded as suitable for a trail rig. The Jeeps from 1941

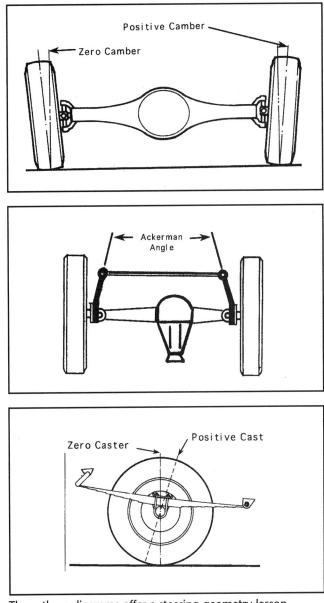

These three diagrams offer a steering geometry lesson.

up used two tie rods attached to a slightly off-center bellcrank that was connected by yet another rod from the steering box mounted well back in the chassis, near the firewall. It's a very complicated setup and prone to bumpsteer (suspension movement steers the wheels slightly), especially when lifted. Power steering was not available. Very often, the steering on these early rigs will be converted to the later style CJ setup that uses two rods.

Gladiators used a bellcrank setup similar to the CJ until 1969, after which the system was improved and became similar to the system found on 1972 and later CJs. Commandos used a setup similar to the later CJs their entire 1967–73 run. YJ Wranglers use a variation of the late CJ setup, with the drag link attached to the far right end of the tie rod instead of the knuckle. XJs are nearly identical to YJs, and this setup seems to be adequate with appropriate mods for lifts. TJs have reverted to a slightly more complicated "Y" setup, which Jeep calls the Haltenberger system, in which the drag link runs from the pitman arm to the right knuckle. A tie rod from the left knuckle attaches to the drag link about a foot from the right end. The Grand Cherokee is similar. This setup appears to have few problems and adapts well to modifications.

### Common Steering Problems

The two most common steering problems associated with all modified Jeeps are durability of the tie rod and drag link, and bump steer. This durability is tested by the addition of large tires or power steering (to a vehicle that didn't come with it), or tough trail conditions. Any one of these is enough to bend a factory tie rod, and these scenarios are often combined.

Several cures exist. On the homemade front, some Jeepers have reinforced the tie rod and drag link with angle iron and the like. They will also fabricate new tie rods from a large variety of materials. As with any home fabrication, how well this works depends on the fabricator's skill and knowledge.

On the store-bought front, several companies offer heavy-duty tie rods. These start with units that are designed to replace the OE setup. First on the list are units made of larger, stronger material adapted to fit Jeeps. Some are adaptations of truck tie rods. Some of these units are narrowed versions of GM truck tie rods and drag link and are plenty strong. They are more robust than the stock Jeep pieces but still of carbon steel. They vary in price but are usually under a hundred bucks.

Next up are replacement tie rods made of 4130 chrome-moly tubing that use the OE tie rod ends. These vary in outer diameter from 7/8 inch to 1 inch, with wall thickness from .188 inch to .250 inch. These are extremely robust pieces. The one disadvantage to 4130 is that if it does get bent, it will usually break when you try to bend it back. Ordinary carbon steel is softer and can be bent back. This is seldom an issue but crops up more often than you would imagine in light of 4130's superior strength.

Bump steer is the condition caused by suspension movement tending to steer the vehicle. This occurs when the drag link is at an angle. When the axle moves up, the rod effectively gets longer and in most cases makes the Jeep steer to the right. Ideally, the drag link should be as level as possible, but lifts make the drag link reach down.

The easy cure to bump steer is often a dropped pitman arm, although the extra leverage makes steering box damage more likely. Do not bend your pitman by any means that uses heat. Heat crystallizes the metal and makes it brittle. Better to spend a few bucks on a made-from-scratch part and stay alive.

### Steering Linkage Mods

Major lifts may require a complete redo of the steering linkage. In the factory steering setup, the tie rod is mounted below the arms and is somewhat vulnerable to damage. Many Jeepers are mounting their tie rods above the arms for clearance. This has the added advantage of lessening drag link angles and minimizing bump steer. Some machine shops can redrill the tapered holes in the steering knuckles to accomplish this.

JKS, for one, takes a slightly different tack and offers kits that do this via a standard bolt and a Heim jointed 4130 tie rod and drag link. A standard 5/8 drill bit is all that's needed. Tri-County Gear takes a completely different approach by offering a kit that incorporates modified GM steering knuckles with the arms relocated on top of the knuckles. This allows the entire steering linkage to be above the spring, even in a spring over situation. The stock pitman arm can then be used.

### Steering Dampers

A steering damper is nothing more than a shock absorber for the steering system. It dampens the effect of tire vibration and feedback from road surface irregularities. These problems are inherent in all vehicles with large tires, 4x4s included. The effects are multiplied when you add even larger tires and lifts, so a steering damper upgrade is a vital ingredient to most buildups.

Like shocks, steering dampers come in a variety of configurations, which include gas charged, twin tube hydraulic, and cellular gas. All the same problems shocks can have apply to steering dampers.

Even with stock rigs in certain driving conditions (fast moving), the stock damper may be inadequate. Tire size is the other controlling factor on whether you need to upgrade your steering damper. Just as with shocks, a larger piston exerts more control, so the upgrade will be larger in diameter.

A damper will not control bump steer. As discussed, this is an issue of steering geometry. Nor will it control the vibrations that come from worn-out steering components.

Most newer vehicles are already fitted with a damper. In these cases, all you need to do is add the

This kit from Tri-County Gear uses adapted GM knuckles on Dana 44s. The steering knuckles are moved to the top and the tie rod mounts on top. This allows the tie rod to be mounted above the spring in a spring over and minimizes drag link angles. It only works for Dana 44 axles.

beefier unit. In older Jeeps not so equipped, the after-market supplies brackets to mount the damper. The key is to have the damper centered in its travel so that it does not restrict steering movement. The unit should be mounted as high out of harm's way as possible, but that may not protect it forever. Steering dampers are often front line casualties in hard-core 4x4 circles. The damper is best mounted to the drag link.

Occasionally you will see two or more dampers used. For most Jeeps, one is plenty. The dual setups come into play with really huge tires. If one good damper doesn't stop the vibration in your CJ with 33-inch tires, you probably have other problems. If you have a Gladiator truck with 44s, then twin dampers may be necessary

### Caster, Camber, and Toe-In

These are the angles of the steering system that commonly are altered to give you an "alignment." In a solid axle 4x4, with the exception of some coil spring rigs, only toe-in is adjustable. The remaining angles are built-in and nonadjustable, except by big rocks applied to the axle at great force.

Caster is the forward or backward tilt of the steering pivot points on the axle measured in degrees. Positive caster means the top of the pivot point is tilted toward the back of the vehicle. Negative caster tilts the top of the pivot to the front. Positive caster makes the vehicle more directionally stable, i.e., it travels in a straight line better. Negative caster makes the vehicle steer easier, but has the opposite effect on directional stability, without other changes being made. All Jeeps run positive caster, from 3 to 8.5 degrees, depending on year and model. Caster is adjustable on coil spring Jeeps via eccentrics on the radius arms.

Camber is the inward or outward tilt of the tops of the wheels. Positive camber tilts them out from the center of the vehicle and negative camber tilts them inward. Camber also relates to directional stability, with slight positive camber the most stable. Preferred settings for Jeeps run from 0 degrees to 1.5 degrees positive.

Related to camber is steering axis inclination. This is an engineered angle that usually places the upper pivot farther inboard than the lower. This aids in directional stability, load transfer, and ride quality. It's nonadjustable.

A close relative to camber is camber roll. If you turn the wheels of your Jeep hard to one side, you can see the inside wheel tilt in and the outside wheel tilt out.

When the wheels are turned, the steering axis inclination and camber combine to increase camber. This aids in cornering.

Toe-in or toe-out is the difference in the distance between the front edge of the tires versus the rear. If the front of the tires are closer than the back, the vehicle is toed-in. If the reverse is true, it is toed-out. If the dimensions are equal, there is zero toe. Toe-in causes the vehicle to have better directional stability. Most Jeeps are toed-in a tiny amount (measured in 32nds of an inch), with some rigs running zero toe.

Toe-out on turns, more elegantly known as the Ackerman angle, is another engineered-in value that allows the inner wheel to steer a greater amount than the outer wheel. To avoid scrubbing, the inner wheel has to turn in a smaller circle. The Ackerman angle is achieved by angling the steering arms on the knuckles inward. This value is actually fairly easy to compute; simply draw an imaginary line from the steering pivot point to the center of the rear axle. Yes, this means that the Ackerman angle is sensitive to wheelbase and that axles or steering knuckles meant for longer rigs may not be ideal in shorter rigs and vice versa.

Caster and camber angles are engineered into the vehicle for stock applications. The problems start when the rig is modified. The driveshaft section of this chapter talks about caster and pinion angle and how lift affects them. The expensive problems come when you have to separate caster and pinion angle. This may occur at lifts over 4 inches.

Pinion angle and caster are locked together. The only way to change their relationship is to rotate the axle tubes in relation to the diff housing. The tubes must be removed to do this and a shop that specializes in such things is the only place to get it done. This work is expensive and tricky.

Once caster is readjusted, then pinion angle can be set by welding the spring perches in a new place. Ordering a new custom axle allows you to get these values dialed in according to your needs, but there are still lots of measurements to take and choices to make. Before you tear everything down, tell the axle builder what you are doing, and he will ask the appropriate questions.

Camber is affected only by a bent axle housing or tubes. Shims are available that fit between the knuckle and the spindle that can correct very minor errors. In some cases, the tubes can be slightly bent to correct inaccuracies. There is no particular advantage to changing the camber on your Jeep from stock specs.

Toe is adjustable. In general, you will use the stock settings. Going down the road will naturally try to pull the tires apart. Larger tires multiply this tendency. Some Jeepers advocate dialing in a little extra toe-in as a way to reduce wander with big tires. As to how much extra toe-in, experimentation seems to be the key. Too much toe will cause abnormal tire wear. A good starting point might be to go to the maximum toe-in listed in the spec range for your rig and increase it, if needed, by minute amounts, monitoring tire wear closely.

### Power Steering

If you have power steering, you have probably ignored it in the buildup process. If you don't have it, you want it. In the first case, help is available to beef up your power steering for better trail performance and longevity. In the latter case, there are conversions for CJs to get the steering out of the "power by Armstrong" category.

Power steering first became available in CJs as an option in 1972. It used the venerable and popular Saginaw box and pump with a very light 20:1 ratio and took 4 1/8 turns to go lock to lock. FCs and Willys trucks never had it. Gladiators to about 1965 had a Thompson system available that used a hydraulic cylinder on the steering linkage and a valve block on the column, similar to Fords of the same era—junk by today's standards. Later SJs (from 1965) used the Saginaw box. Early models used a single ratio box with a 17.8:1 ratio. From 1974, they used a variable ratio box with 20:1 at the center, gradually changing to 16.4:1 on either side. By 1979, this ratio had changed to 17:1/13:1 and later a single-rate 19:1 box was used. Lots of odd changes were made in the SJs but the boxes are mostly interchangeable.

C-101 models did not get power steering until it was introduced as an option for V-6 models in 1970. It used a Saginaw box with a 17.5:1 ratio. XJ and Grand Cherokees all have had standard power steering with most packages and ratios about 14:1. Wranglers used the Saginaw box with a 16:1/13:1 variable ratio.

### Power Steering Coolers

Power steering uses an oil that is nearly identical to automatic transmission fluid, less the friction modifiers, and is subject to the same frailties as the ATF in your transmission (see Figure 6-1, Trans Fluid Temp Chart in the trans chapter). If you ever wondered how hot the power steering can get, look at page 59. Overheated power steering oil can cause a loss of power assist in critical periods and early failure of the parts. Big tires and a hard trail can raise the temps even more.

At about 212 degrees, the oil in the power steering system starts to foam. The first symptoms of this will be a growling noise, which is an indication that the pump is cavitating, followed by intermittent loss of fluid pressure and power assist. Continual high temps will also degrade the internal seals and the hoses.

The answer is a power steering cooler, and this is considered a necessity in many rock crawling circles. The cooler mounts on the low pressure (return) line between the steering box and pump reservoir. Currie offers an extruded cooler kit, but nearly any type of cooler can be used, including small trans coolers and engine oil coolers. If you rig something up yourself, make sure to use power steering–rated, high temp hose.

Power steering coolers have been used from the factory on certain Ford, GM, and Chrysler applications. If you want to do some wrecking yard scouting, look at old police cars and medium-duty trucks. Mopar offers a power steering cooler for certain truck towing packages, and this can be bought in kit form from Chrysler/Dodge dealers under Part No. 52038977. It will fit on later Wranglers with ease and earlier or custom setups with minor fabrication.

The cooler is most needed at slow speeds, so placing the cooler in the fan's airflow can reduce temps more than mounting it just anywhere. Even a spot on a fenderwell that gets some airflow from the fan is better than a dead area. Finding a good spot may be problematic under a tightly packed hood. As with any cooler, placing it in a safe location that is not vulnerable to trail damage is the No. 1 consideration.

Even if you don't mount a cooler, at least change your power steering oil once in a while if you four-wheel hard. Just one hard trip can turn the fluid dark. Just as the fluid does in an automatic transmission, the power steering oil deteriorates and can degrade the performance of the system, even before premature wear occurs.

### Power Steering Conversions

Over the years, many of the more mechanically inclined Jeepers have fabricated the means to install power steering on their Jeeps. Conversion kits have been available from Advance Adapters since the 1970s to give older CJs power steering. These kits may have partial application to Willys trucks and FCs as well, but check with the company before ordering. The common thread is that a Saginaw power steering box is used.

These great units appeared in 1964 and remained almost unchanged until the late 1970s, when a couple of variations appeared. The easiest setup would be to use a Saginaw box and Pitman arm from a Jeep application. Advance Adapters recommends the use of 1987 and later YJ Wrangler boxes and also suggests using the matching Saginaw pump. Mounting the pump where it was originally mounted is easy on engines from GM, Ford, or AMC. If you are converting an engine that did not have this option, the fabrication requirements will go up a few notches.

While the original steering columns are intended to be modified to work with the power steering conversions, Advance Adapters recommends that if you plan to upgrade, use the columns from 1972 to 1979 CJs. Some Jeepers have fitted a variety of other columns from various cars and trucks, some that include a tilt feature.

### More Power for Your Power Steering

More than one Jeeper has found that his original power steering system cannot overcome his locking front differential or fat tires on the trail. Another problem is a power steering setup that is oversensitive and lacking road feel, making the vehicles harder to control in certain street situations. AGR Inc. has done some serious research and come up with several upgrades.

The Superbox 1 has a 17:1 ratio and 3 1/2 turns lock to lock. It also features a larger 3.35-inch piston (stock is 3.1-inch) to increase the amount of push available for big tires and tough trail situations. The improvements in drivability are noteworthy.

The Super Box 2 is similar but has a variable ratio for a more sporty feel. The ratio varies 17:1 near the center position to 13:1 on either side. This makes the box more responsive the more you crank the wheel.

To get the maximum from the new boxes, AGR uses larger Saginaw pumps with more capacity to pump oil. The OE pump flows 2 to 2.6 gallons per minute at 800–1,300 psi. The Super Pump offers 5 gallons per minute and 1,500 psi.

The AGR boxes can be used on almost all Jeeps, but bear in mind that the Saginaw boxes converted to metric attachments in 1980. They changed from flared fittings to O-rings on the hose ends. They also changed input shaft sizes for various years and models, so if you are swapping, you need to know what input is currently on your box. The two common sizes are 3/4 inch and 13/16 inch. It isn't difficult to change the input size on your column if that is necessary.

## FACTORY JEEP SPRING SPECS

| Model | Years | Type F/R | Leaves F/R(opt) | Rate F/R(opt) | Spring L x W, F/R |
|---|---|---|---|---|---|
| CJ-2A, 3A, 3B | 1945–64 | L/L | 10/9(11) | 260/190(225) | 36.25x1.75/42x1.75 |
| CJ-5 | 1955–65 | L/L | 7(10)/9(11) | 240(260)/200(225) | 39.63x1.75/46x1.75 |
| CJ-6 | 1955–65 | L/L | 7(10)/9 | 240(260)/270 | 39.63x1.75/46x1.75 |
| CJ-5, 4-cyl. | 1966–71 | L/L | 5(12)/9(12) | 188(236)/200(410) | 39.63x1.75/46x1.75 |
| CJ-5, V-6 | 1966–71 | L/L | 10(12)/5(12) | 176(236)/230(410) | 39.63x1.75/46x1.75 |
| CJ-6, 4-cyl. | 1966–71 | L/L | 5(12)/9(12) | 188(236)/270(410) | 39.63x1.75/46x1.75 |
| CJ-6, V-6 | 1966–71 | L/L | 10(12)/5(12) | 176(236)/230(410) | 39.63x1.75/46x1.75 |
| CJ-5 | 1972–75 | L/L | 7(10)/5(10) | 190(270)/230(270) | 39.75x1.75/46x1.75 |
| CJ-6 | 1972–75 | L/L | 9(10)/5(10) | 210(270)/230(270) | 39.75x1.75/46x1.75 |
| CJ-5 | 1976–83 | L/L | 4(7)/4(7) | 170(230)/185(250) | 39.75x2.00/46x2.50 |
| CJ-7 | 1976–86 | L/L | 4(7)/4(7) | 170(230)/185(250) | 39.75x2.00/46x2.50 |
| CJ-8(1) | 1981–85 | L/L | 4(7)/4(7) | 170(230)/185(250) | 39.75x2.00/46x2.50 |
| YJ | 1987–90 | L/L | 4/5(6) | 128(203)/170(237) | 39.75x2.00/46x2.50 |
| YJ | 1991–95 | L/L | 4/5 | 113/170 | 45x2.00/45.60x2.50 |
| TJ | 1997–98 | C/C | —/— | 120/160 | — |
| PU | 1946–65 | L/L | 9/11 | 303/370(410) | 36.25x1.75/50x2.00 |
| SW | 1949–65 | L/L | 10/8 | 260/150 | 36.25x1.75/50x1.75 |
| FC-150 | 1957–65 | L/L | 7/9 | 270/280 | 39.63x1.75/52x1.50 |
| FC-170 | 1957–65 | L/L | 6/6 | 260/280 | 46x2.5/52x2.50 |
| FC-170DRW | 1959–65 | L/L | 7/9 | 287/672 | 46x2.5/52x2.50 |
| SJ PU, 1/2 ton (2) | 1963–75 | L/L | 6/8(10) | 216(270)/295(400) | 44x2/52x2.50 |
| SJ PU, 3/4 ton (2) | 1963–75 | L/L | 6/10(9) | 270/400(502) | 44x2/52x2.50 |
| SJ PU, J10 (2) (3) | 1976–75 | L/L | 5/5 | 195(260)/165(340) | 44x2/52x2.50 |
| SJ PU, J20 (2) (3) | 1976–75 | L/L | 2/3(6) | 260(330)/340(510) | 44x2/52x2.50 |
| SJ Wag. | 1963–75 | L/L | 7(5)/4(6) | 160(228)/215(230) | 44x2.5/52x2.50 |
| SJ Wag. (4) | 1975–91 | L/L | 5(6)/5 | 215(260)/160(265) | 47x2.5/52x2.50 |
| XJ Cher. | 1984– | C/L | —/3 | 120/160 | —/51.63x2.50 |
| MJ PU (5) | 1986–92 | C/L | —/5 | 140/230 | —/57x2.50 |
| ZJ | 1993–98 | C/C | —/— | 200/160 | — |
| C-101 | 1967–71 | L/L | 5(6)/1(6) | 160(183)/188(266) | 46x1.75/56x2.50 |
| C-101 | 1972–73 | L/L | 5(6)/3(6) | 158(205)/200(266) | 46x2.0/56x2.50 |

(1) Full Length hardtops had five leaf rear springs.
(2) Many other spring rates listed. Common shown.
(3) SWB shown. LWB 285 standard on rear.
(4) Many other spring rates listed in this era.
(5) Optional spring rates available.

## Calculating Spring Rate
*Formulas Courtesy Skyjacker*

These formulas work for leaf and coil springs. They can help you approximate ride height and your spring rate needs.

1. First, you will need to determine the weight on the front and rear axles. This can be done at a truck stop or any convenient truck scale. If your ultimate goal is to find a spring rate and ride height for a predetermined vehicle setup and load, weigh it in that configuration. If your goal is to determine a load capacity, you will need to weigh the vehicle once empty and once with the load.

*Let's assume a front weight of 2,400 pounds, rear weight of 1,800 pounds.*

2. From the front and rear weights, deduct the weight of the axles, wheels, and tires, since they are not supported by the springs. Here are some educated guesses as to weights for axles, wheels, and tires (front/rear): Dana 30/35 (front/rear)- 250/200 pounds, Dana 44- 300/250 pounds,

Dana 60- 375/300. After subtracting the unsupported weight, divide by two to determine the weight carried per spring.

*Using the Dana 30/35 setup, this yields:*

*Front 2,400 - 250 pounds = 2,150 ÷ 2 = 1,075 pounds per spring*
*Rear 1,800 - 200 pounds = 1,600 ÷ 2 = 800 pounds per spring*

   3. Find the rate of the spring in pounds per inch.

*Assume new spring rates front 230 pounds/inch, rear 175 pounds/inch*

   4. Divide the load per spring (pounds) by the rate per spring (pounds/inch) to get the deflection in inches.

*Front: 1075 pounds ÷ 230 pounds/inch = 4.67 inches of deflection*
*Rear: 800 pounds ÷ 175 pounds/inch = 4.57 inches of deflection*

   5. Now for some practical application. With coils, if you have the free length of the spring, you can calculate loaded ride height difference easily. By determining what the loaded height of the spring will be with the per spring load, you can figure mounted spring-seat-to-spring-seat height. With leaf springs, you need free arch measurements and then you can deduct the loss of arch according to the spring rate and per spring load.

*Sample Solution for Coil Spring:*

*Front free length: 18 inches - 4.67 inches = 13.3 inches mounted height*
*Rear free length: 18.5 inches - 4.57 inches = 13.9 inches mounted height*

*If your original mounted heights were 11 and 12.1 inches, then you would gain 2.3 inches up front and 1.8 inches in back.*

*Sample Solution for Leaf Spring:*

*Front spring free arch: 7.6 inches - 4.67 inches = 2.93 inches free arch mounted at weight*
*Rear spring free arch: 7.25 inches - 4.57 inches = 2.68 inches free arch at weight*

*If your original free arch numbers were 0.9 inch front and 0.8 inch rear, then you would gain 2.03 inches of lift in front and 1.88 inches in back.*

## Spring Dictionary

*Arch:* See camber.

*Bolt Clips:* A device used to keep the spring leaves lined up atop one another. This is the preferred method of doing this because it does not restrict the movement as the "cinch"-type clamps may.

*Camber:* The built-in curve, or arch, in the spring. Also a steering term indicating the inward or outward tilt of the front tires toward the center of the vehicle.

*Droop:* The downward movement of the suspension.

*Deflection:* Movement or compression of the spring.

*Eye:* The loop in the end of the spring into which a bushing is installed and to which the spring is mounted.

*Eye-to-Eye:* The measurement of a leaf spring from the center of one eye to the center of the other. Usually taken unloaded.

*Free Arch:* The distance between the top of the inside of a leaf spring to an imaginary line drawn between the center of the two eyes. The spring is unloaded.

*Free Length:* The unloaded length of a coil spring.

*Main Leaf:* The first or primary leaf. Often this is the only leaf with an eye, though the second leaf may also have one that wraps around the outside of the main leaf.

*Military Wrap:* This is where the second leaf loops loosely around the main eye. As the name implies, this was originally mandated by the Army so that the vehicle was operable with a broken main leaf.

*Pin Offset:* The anchor pin is not always centered on a spring. Pin offset is the distance the pin is off center.

*Pitch:* Also called ramp, pitch refers to how tightly that spring has been wound. Coils close together have less pitch than coils that are farther apart.

*Rate:* The amount of weight it takes to deflect the spring, expressed in pounds per inch. It takes 200 pounds to deflect a 200 pound/inch spring 1 inch, 400 pounds for 2 inches, and so on.

*Scrag:* A.k.a. "presetting." A method of setting the position "memory," or the permanent arch of a spring. After assembly, the spring is placed in a press and deflected a predetermined amount. This is usually past the normal deflection the spring will encounter in use.

*Shotpeening:* Steel shot is sprayed at high pressure on the surfaces of the leaves to compress the surface of the steel and surface harden it.

*Taper:* Some manufacturers taper the ends of each leaf. This allows for a softer rate spring, as compared to a dimensionally similar untapered leaf, and reduced friction.

*Wire Size:* The diameter of the metal bar that is wound and tempered to make a coil spring.

**Load Bearing Qualities of Neoprene
vs. Polyurethane Bushings**

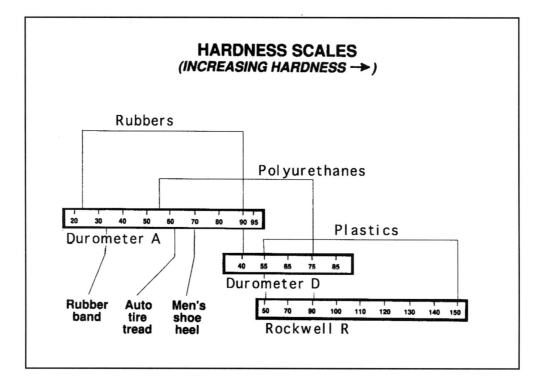

## Ramp Travel Index

The ramp is a useful testing tool. Not only does it give an objective means to measure suspension flexibility, but it also offers a "freeze-frame" method to note some of the dynamics of suspension movement. It can't duplicate all the dynamics that occur on the trail, but it does offer the means to compare and rate suspension improvements against the stock setup. It can also provide fun competition at Jeep meets.

Ramps generally come set at 20 degrees. The 20 degree ramp is most commonly used for all stock and most modified rigs. Some of the long-legged, big dogs can max out a 20 degree ramp easily, so a steeper ramp is used.

The idea is to get as far up the ramp as possible until one of the wheels lift off the ground. The farther you go up without lifting a wheel, the better your score. This is not a banzai charge, but a gentle climb until a wheel, usually the rear, lifts. At that point, the distance the vehicle has traveled up the ramp is measured and divided by the wheelbase, then multiplied by 1,000 to get the ramp travel index

or RTI. A vehicle with a 93.25-inch wheelbase goes 42 inches up the ramp—42 divided by 93.25 = .4504 x 1,000—for a 450 RTI.

Everybody tests a little differently and so you may see varying numbers for the same rig from different sources. Here's a fairly common test standard that I use.

1. I measure the *actual* wheelbase every time. I have found that *true* and *advertised* wheelbases are often different. Also, some modifications change the wheelbase length. A quarter-inch can change the index by a full point.

2. When going up the ramp, I go a little past the point where the rear tire lifts and then slowly back down until the tire *just* touches the ground.

3. I use the centerline of the front hub as a measuring point and take this measurement perpendicular to the ramp surface. A large carpenter's square on the ramp makes an ideal tool for this.

A 20 degree ramp is useful as a tool to check for chassis and tire interference under full articulation, as well as driveshaft problems. This Wrangler is registering an honest 850 RTI. The tools you need for an RTI test: a ramp, a tape, a carpenter's square, pen, paper, and calculator.

## Sample of Power Steering Temps

| Condition | Steering Temp (degrees) | Ambient Temp (degrees) |
|---|---|---|
| freeway, high speed | oil–134<br>pump–139<br>box–102 | 90 |
| city, stop and go | oil–130<br>pump–150<br>box–118 | 92 |
| trail, easy | oil–153<br>pump–168<br>box–172 | 95 |
| trail, hard | oil–193<br>pump–227<br>box–215 | 95 |

Note: Oil temp taken at reservoir (reservoir separate from pump). Pump temp is the exterior temperature of the pump housing. Box temp is the exterior temperature of the steering box housing.

*Chapter 4*

# AXLES, GEARING & DRIVESHAFTS

## Power to the Ground

Next to the tires and the suspension, the axles of your Jeep take the most abuse. The factory usually (but not always!) builds in enough strength for a stock vehicle to tackle moderately severe conditions. Some axles will hold up under extremely rough conditions without modifications and others will not. If you add in the complication of big tires, weight, lots of engine torque, and a heavy foot, you'll need to make some mods or a swap. This chapter will walk you through options to beef up or replace your axles and driveshafts according to need.

### Jeep Axles

Most of the axles that appeared on Jeeps from day one until today came from Spicer, or Dana-Spicer, as it's now called (Dana for short). For a few years in the AMC era (1976–86), a Corporate AMC axle was used on CJs and some SJs. All of these units have a great reputation for durability when used within the limits of their designs. Before you start reciting trail lore about broken parts, remember that the vehicle manufacturers got just what they ordered and your ideas of four-wheeling may far exceed those of a factory engineer.

### *Front Axles*

Jeep front axles fall into two general categories, open and closed knuckle. The early closed knuckle designs, the Dana 25, Dana 27, the earliest Dana 30s, and the first Dana 44Fs (used in the old Big Jeeps; "F" is for front) are all very similar in design. The axle steering knuckles are in a sealed and enclosed housing. The wheel pivot is accomplished via kingpins and bearings.

In the early days, assorted axle joints were used besides the standard Cardan U-joint, including exotica like Tracta-Joints, Bendix joints, and Rzeppa joints

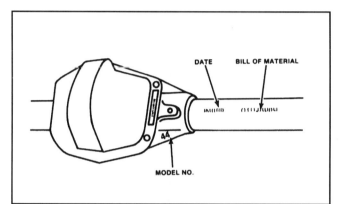

This illustration will help you identify the particular Dana axle in your Jeep, or any vehicle for that matter. The model number and date are self-explanatory (the date does not always appear), but you will need the Spicer catalog to decipher the bill of materials. The B.O.M. lists all the specs and parts numbers for the particular axle, and this is valuable information for swappers. *Courtesy Dana Spicer*

(pronounced "Cheppa"). These pieces are just about impossible to replace and are very weak by today's standards. If you are using them in near stock situations, they can survive. If you subject them to big tires, lots of torque, and hard work, they're goners. Some of the last closed knuckle front axles of the late 1960s, the Dana 27, Dana 44, and the few military Dana 60s, have some potential for beef but hard parts are getting tough to find.

Open knuckle axles appeared industrywide starting about 1970 and have taken over. Their chief advantages, besides ease of manufacturing, are lighter weight, better steering angles (about 7 degrees more angularity for a tighter turning radius), serviceability, and an edge in overall durability. They use pressed-in ball joints for steering.

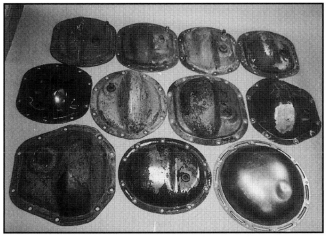

One of the best ways to I.D. an axle visually is via the cover. From the top, left to right, the early World War II era Dana 25 cast cover with vent, the later World War II stamped Dana 25 cover with vent, the early CJ Dana 25 stamped cover with vent, the late Dana 25, 27, and early Dana 30 stamped cover, late Dana 30 stamped cover with rubber fill plug, the Dana 41 cover, the Dana 53 cover, the Dana 44 cover, the Dana 60 cover, the Dana 35 cover, and the AMC-20 cover.

Jeep front axles are full floating units that are normally equipped with locking hubs (except the very early models). One variation appeared in the downsized Cherokee models when they debuted in 1984, and that was the high-pinion, or reverse cut, Dana 30. They also have been used in the Wrangler YJ models since their introduction in 1987. The pinion is designed to operate above the pinion centerline rather than below it as with most diffs. This axle is also equipped with a center disconnect device instead of locking hubs. A Dana 44 version of this was used on the very last Grand Wagoneers. (More on disconnects later.)

One of the weakest parts of any front axle in general is the axle universal joints. They can be upgraded to larger sizes in a few cases (namely some Dana 44s and Dana 30s) by replacing the axle shaft assemblies with those of the larger size (see Figure 4-2). Beyond this, buying name brand pieces, like genuine Spicer, ensures a beefy unit.

Most experts agree that sealed, nongreaseable U-joints are stronger than the variety fitted with zerks. When the cross section of the U-joint is drilled, it weakens somewhat. Spicer claims this decline in strength is 5 percent or less. This strength issue comes into play because in many cases, the U-joint sizes available for front axles are on the small side with no easy cure.

They are also generally operated at more extreme angles than driveshaft U-joints, which makes beef an even bigger issue, but also makes it more difficult to grease if it is equipped with a fitting. More information on U-joints appears in the driveshaft section U-joint.

### Rear Axles

Jeep rear axles can be divided into two general categories, semifloating and full floating. In a semifloating axle, the axle shaft not only bears the weight of the vehicle but also applies the driving torque. With a full-floating axle, the weight of the vehicle is carried by a set of tapered wheel bearings and a stub axle that's very similar to the front wheel bearing arrangement. The axle shaft has only to supply the driving torque.

There are two subclasses, offset and centered differentials. Most Jeeps, from day one to about 1971, used the Model 18 transfer case. This unit had a rear output that was offset to the right side. When the similar Model 20 t-case was introduced in 1972, it used a centered rear output, and so the differentials were centered in the housings. There is only a marginal difference in strength between a centered and offset axle.

Going back to semi vs. full-floating axles, each type has its own advantages. The main four-wheeling advantage to a full-floater is that if the axle breaks, the wheel and hub remain as before. When a semifloater breaks, the vehicle usually is not safe to drive because the hub and wheel may fall off. While a full-floating axle can be built in any level of weight capacity and

The long axle disconnect for Dana 30 and some SJ Dana 44s was used from 1984 to 1996 and takes the place of locking hubs. The sleeve, controlled by a vacuum servo, couples the two axles together. It works well, except in very high HP applications or when there are other complications, such as an automatic locker.

The difference in strength between the 297-X Spicer joint and the 260-X is approximately 30 percent, according to Spicer sources. Prior to 1995, all Dana 30s used the smaller universal. Some mid-1970s Dana 44s used the smaller universal joint also.

For a Wrangler, the 1995 half-axle (above) carried the bigger 297-X U-joints and can be swapped into earlier rigs either used or new. On the side with the disconnect, you need only replace the outer axle.

hub design, they are generally reserved for the HD rigs that have 8- or 10-bolt lug patterns and use special wheels. Only one light-duty full-floater was built for Jeeps, the World War II era 23-2, but it was not particularly strong by today's standards. While swapping in the big beefy full-floater axles adds a great margin of strength, it can be massive overkill and a severe weight penalty in a rig that doesn't need the carrying capacity.

Via lots of fabrication, it's always been possible to convert that standard Jeep axle to a light-duty full-floater. It was not particularly easy for the home wrencher until just recently, when Warn Industries introduced full-floating conversions for Dana 44 axles, as well as the AMC 20. For some time now, Summers Brothers has offered a full-float conversion for the AMC 20 but Dana axles had pretty much been left out till Warn came along. Anyway, all the kits offer the advantages of a full-floater in a standard Jeep axle size and wheel bolt pattern.

Despite the advantages, you may not need a full-floater. When you consider that some of the aftermarket semifloating shafts are virtually indestructible in certain applications, the added expense of a full-floater may be unnecessary.

Semifloating Jeep axles can be divided into three categories, tapered, flanged, and C-clip. Tapered axles were the norm in the old days and were in regular use on Jeeps to about 1970. They featured a tapered shaft that was slotted on the end for a woodruff key, and were threaded on the end. A wheel flange, complete with tapered receptacle, was attached via the very tight

(hopefully!) nut. The weak link is the key, which can shear, and the nut, which can work loose. These older axles usually were either 10 or 19 spline, adding another weak link into the equation.

The AMC Model 20 axle (a transplant from the AMC car line) was used in 1976–86 CJs and some 1970s-era big Jeeps. While it has a fairly bulletproof differential, the antiquated tapered axles are a definite weak link, even though they used splines instead of a keyway. Fortunately, Summers Brothers and others have come to the rescue by building one-piece flanged axle replacements for the Model 20. Similar help is available for the old tapered axle 44s.

Flanged axles are forged so that the shaft and flange are one piece. This eliminates many of the weak links. As with the tapered axles, the shafts are held in by a bearing that is pressed onto the shaft and the bearing is held by a retainer and preloaded via shims under the retainer. If the shaft breaks, the retainer may hold the flange on for a short way at low speeds, but it's nothing you'd want to hang your life on. The flanged axles are also built with 30 splines, making them considerably stronger than the old 19-spline version.

Finally, the Dana 35 C-clip type of axles use a roller bearing, and the axle floats free but is held in place by a C-clip inside the differential. It's actually a pretty good way of retaining an axle—until it breaks. A pin between the two shafts prevents the axles from pushing in and losing the clips, but if the axle breaks, the remainder of the axle—the flange, brake drum, and wheel—are free to part company with the Jeep. Yeeha!

Some owners may opt to eliminate the Dana 30 disconnect. In this case a one-piece axle from a nondisconnect XJ (Quadra-Trac models), as shown here, is a direct replacement. The problem is that you need a method of unlocking the wheels from the axle. Warn will soon debut a new Wrangler Dana 30 locking hub kit that eliminates the sealed bearings and the peculiar hub.

On the left is a World War II era 23-2 full floater (brand-new at Mile-Hi Jeep in Denver) and an early semifloat Dana 44 next. The 23-2 is not a particularly strong setup. The only advantage is that the wheel won't fall off if the axle breaks.

This is an AMC-20 flanged axle. It differs from the Dana 44 in that the Dana unit relies only on a single large keyway. The AMC is a bit stronger with splines and a small keyway. If the nut is kept tight, both styles are reasonably reliable. If not, failure is imminent. The slightest wear on axle, flange, or keyway warrants replacement. Summers, Dutchman, Currie, and Moser all offer one-piece replacement axle shafts.

Warn's full floater kit for Dana 44s and AMC 20s uses internally splined hubs and a 30-spline 4340 alloy axle shaft. A kit for Dana 35 is in the offing, and look for other applications in the future. Warn can supply custom splined axle shafts for oddball spline combinations. *Courtesy Warn*

The only C-clip axles in the Jeep inventory are the Model 35 in Wranglers and XJs from about 1992 up, and the Dana 35s and aluminum cased 44s in Grand Cherokees. Before then, they used a standard bearing and retainer similar to the Dana 44.

Beyond the Warn full-floater conversion that's in the works for the Dana 35 (it may be available as you read this), there is no 100 percent foolproof way to keep a C-clip axle in place when the axle breaks. There are C-clip eliminator kits that add a measure of immediate safety, but the sure way is to either have a spare rear axle shaft and be ready to swap it out on the trail, or buy an axle shaft that you cannot break.

### Ring and Pinions

We got into choosing gear ratios in Chapter 2, but now we get more into the mechanics of gearing choices. Let's start with ways of determining gear ratios. If you have an unidentified axle, whether it's in the vehicle or not, there are three ways of determining

Ring and pinions vary in strength according to size. Here's a sample of Jeep types. From left to right, top to bottom, Dana 60, Dana 44, Dana 35, Dana 30 reverse cut (note the direction of the teeth), Dana 27, and Dana 25.

This is the minimum parts kit for a ring and pinion replacement: RandP, new ring gear bolts, new pinion nut and crush sleeve (if so equipped), pinion bearings and seal, and a set of shims. Add to this a set of carrier bearing if the mileage is high, and a diff cover gasket.

gear ratio. The first is a tag that may or may not be attached to the housing via a bolt. The second method works only with open differentials. You hold one wheel while turning the other exactly two turns and counting the number of times the pinion passes a mark you make on the housing. If it makes 4 full revolutions plus about 1/10 of a revolution, you have a 4.10 ratio. Simple.

The last method involves a little exploratory surgery. You must remove the cover or third member and count the number of teeth on the ring gear, and then divide by the number of teeth on the pinion gear. If you count 41 ring gear teeth and 9 pinion teeth, 41/9 = 4.55.

Since tire size and gearing are so closely interrelated, we discussed choosing the best ratio in some depth in Chapter 2. Once you've decided on what ratio you want, there are a few other considerations. The first is that in changing from a high (numerically low, such as 3.07, 3.31) ratio to a low (numerically high, such as 4.10, 4.56) ratio, you actually sacrifice some gear strength because the ratio of ring gear teeth to pinion gear teeth changes. For example, a Dana 44 with a 3.54 gear ratio has 46 ring gear teeth and 13 pinion teeth. A 4.89:1 ratio has 44 ring gear teeth and 9 pinion teeth. By necessity, the lower ratio pinion is smaller, the tooth contact area is reduced and a margin of strength is lost.

How much this actually matters depends greatly on the inherent strength of the R&P design itself (e.g., a Dana 44 with an 8 1/2-inch ring gear vs. a Dana 60 with a 9 3/4-inch ring gear), the quality of the materials,

the torque output of the engine, weight of the vehicle, and how it's driven. If you determine that you need 5.38 gears and are running a Dana 30, it may prove better to upgrade to a Dana 44 with 5.38 ratio instead so that you retain a margin of strength. The other alternative is to gear for trail work via changes in transfer case gearing (see chapter 5) and maintain a higher axle ratio.

Bear in mind also that carriers and cases are not always compatible with all gear ratio combos. You can see on the top chart on page 79 that you may have to change carriers with the gears. If you are installing a locker that replaces the carrier anyway, you can kill two birds by ordering one to fit the new gears that you have chosen.

### Splines and Things

The diameter of the axle shaft and the number of splines at the driving ends are vital to strength. More splines equals more driving surface with which to transmit torque and a larger material diameter. The fewer the number of splines, the smaller the diameter of the axle at the bottom of the splines. This area is called the "minor spline diameter." Since we know that smaller is weaker, the smallest part of the axle is the place where the axle is going to break. On the typical 10-spline axle, the diameter at the bottom of the spline is 1/8 inch smaller than the outside. Spline depth can be varied somewhat by the pitch of the splines and thus affect the minor spline diameter of the shaft, but the variances in strength are minimal. In general, for every spline you add, axle shaft strength increases by

These are all Dana axle shafts from assorted years. There is more than a 200 percent increase in strength between the 10-spline axle on the right and the 30-spline on the left. The 19-spline unit, about in the middle, has a raised section at the spline. No doubt, this is to keep the minor spline diameters the same as shaft size.

approximately 11 percent (see page 79). Of course, you can only put so many splines on a given diameter of axle.

An axle shaft upgrade can bring a great deal of extra strength into any axle, but you must have the correct matching pieces. Using an old tapered axle Dana 44 as an example, you could install a set of flanged axles with 30 splines instead of 19 by also replacing the differential side gears or installing a locker with 30 splines. This boosts axle strength by more than 100 percent! Summers Brothers makes a 19-spline flanged axle replacement that is stronger than stock by a comfortable margin due to the flanged design and quality of materials alone.

While custom axle shafts can be built for nearly any application, it may be less expensive to swap in a complete used axle assembly, even if some minor mods are needed such as relocating spring perches. The moral here is to choose the largest diameter and highest spline count possible if you are making an axle shaft swap. The need for this sort of beef increases with tire diameter, torque input, and tough driving situations.

### Axle Shafts

Axle material is a vital element in the strength equation. Since the factory axle shafts were made by Spicer, they are high quality pieces, generally built of 1040 carbon steel that is heat-treated for surface hardness. Beware of cheap, no-name replacement axles, as they often range from pot-metal quality to coat hanger material. The science of building an axle shaft involved

finding the balance between hardness and flexibility. If it's too hard, the metal will be brittle and break under load instead of flexing. Too soft, and it bends and tears.

You will see terms like 1340, 1540, 4340, and others bandied about by axle manufacturers. These refer to the composition of the steel in the axle and are issued by a regulating authority, such as the SAE (Society of Automotive Engineers). Each combination has a particular benefit in a particular application. The first two numbers refer to the steel group (Figure 4-9 "Steel Groups"), the second pair to the amount of carbon present in 10ths of a percent; 1040 grade carbon steel contains .40 percent carbon. Steel is nothing more than iron and carbon, which makes the iron harder.

The ideal axle will combine hardness and flexibility. Axles must twist and absorb shock, but the surface must also be hard enough to resist wear. Axles generally come in two types, through-hardened, meaning that the metal is of uniform hardness throughout, or surface hardened, meaning that the material is hard on the outside and gets softer toward the center.

The Rockwell system is used to measure the hardness of metals. For example, 60 Rockwell, a commonly seen number, is hard enough to be used as a bearing surface but an axle through-hardened to this spec would shatter like glass when dropped and would have very little flex. Through-hardened axles will also propagate cracks more easily.

Greg Moser of Moser Engineering has made over 30,000 custom axles and has some interesting comments. "I can make my axles out of any material I choose," he said, "but I prefer to use a high manganese content, H-rated steel. My secret then is in the induction hardening process, and the result is an axle that is 55–60 Rockwell to a depth of about .450 inch and gradually softening to about 40 Rockwell in the center. This leaves the axle better able to flex, gives it high strength and resistance to cracks, but most importantly, it resists fatigue."

Flex and fatigue are two important elements. Axles made of harder materials do not flex as much and they fatigue faster. Remember also, a longer axle will flex more than a shorter one, no matter what the material (a 24-inch shaft will twist more than three times that of a 12-inch shaft). Moser tested some equal length 35-spline, 4340 axles against similar units made of his preferred induction hardened 1340H alloy. The 4340 axles yielded (broke!) at 12,000 lb-ft after having twisted 27 degrees. The 1340H axles yielded at 13,300 lb-ft and 32 degrees of twist.

His cycle-fatigue test was even more telling. Each type was cycled to 80 percent of its yield point until it fatigued and broke. The 4340 lasted an impressive 400,000 cycles. The 1340H lasted over 1,000,000 cycles before it gave up.

How do you know whether your axle shafts are up to the job? Moser uses a method that could be useful with any axle if you have test data on what it takes to break. Since gearing multiplies torque, what your engine puts out will be multiplied by the time it reaches the rear end. Lower gearing multiplies it even more and that's why 4x4s are more susceptible to broken parts than a race car. A drag car with a potent V-8 does not equal the torque generated at the axles of many low-geared six-cylinder 4x4s.

An engine developing 200 lb-ft of torque in front of a drivetrain that has a 4.5:1 first gear, a 2.6:1 low range, and 4.10 axle gears will generate 9,594 lb-ft of torque (200 x 4.5 x 2.6 x 4.10 = 9,594). Moser takes 80 percent of that figure (multiply by .80) to reach a realistic figure. While in theory, the two axles share the torque load, he prefers to see each axle able to handle the max figure. Moser also points out that it isn't often that you will reach the combination of terrain and torque to max out an axle. The engine must be at peak torque, usually a higher rpm than you would use crawling in first gear, to get anywhere close to an axle's limits, but it's nice to have a reserve.

## Hubs

In the earliest days of the four-wheeling sport, the front axle churned along, even in two-wheel drive, to wear itself out at mundane on-road chores. In about 1950, Arthur Warn began the Warn dynasty and invented his first set of freewheeling hubs. This simple device saved wear and tear on the axle, increased fuel mileage, and allowed the tiny Jeep four-banger to put a little more energy into propelling the Jeep. Everybody knows that on the street, a set of freewheeling hubs can add 1 to 3 miles per gallon. On the other hand, freewheeling hubs aren't strictly necessary for the mostly trailered trail Jeep, but when was the last time you saw one without them?

From the first Dana 25 axles through 1980, the CJ wheel bearing hubs were a six-bolt affair, with six bolts holding the locking hub or drive flange in place and transmitting torque from the axle to the hub. Ditto for pickups, station wagons to 1965, Gladiator trucks and Wagoneers to 1973. From 1981 to 1986, CJs reverted to a five-bolt design that is one bolt short of acceptable. These five-bolt jobs soon became notorious, as much for the pot-metal locking hubs that came with them, as anything else. Conversely, the Jeep trucks and Grand Wagoneers from 1974 used an internally splined hub identical to the GM style, and this is a nearly bulletproof setup.

Locking hubs have been a part of the Jeep scene for a long time. While Art Warn pioneered the idea, Cutlass hubs, like these early 1960s pieces, are among the earliest. These "classics" could be useful for a stock rig, but it's doubtful they would be of much use in a built rig. They'd make a nice paperweight or wall ornament. Parts are impossible.

The main strength criterion for hubs is an all-steel body. No sintered steel or aluminum. It doesn't hurt if they are waterproof. No joke, some cheap hubs will freely allow water into the hub. If you are looking for ultimate strength, stay away from automatic locking hubs. *Courtesy Superwinch*

Here is a selection of the common Jeep front bearing hubs. The internally splined hub on the left, from an SJ, is the boss of this group, with no studs to break or work loose. You can adapt this style onto CJs. Next best is the six-bolt hub in the lower middle. Upper middle is the notorious 1981–86 five-bolt hub. The Wrangler style on the right uses a sealed bearing and is actually a fairly strong and trouble-free setup. The main disadvantage is the small wheel bolt pattern.

With the advent of the downsized Cherokee in 1984, the front axle was equipped with sealed wheel bearings and a center disconnect device in place of hubs. When the Wrangler YJ was introduced in 1987, the same design was adopted for the utilities. Though mistrusted, this setup is actually pretty reliable and sturdy with moderate torque loads.

The disconnect uses a two-piece axle on the long (passenger) side and a sliding coupling actuated by a vacuum servo that connects the two axle sections when the transfer case is shifted into four-wheel drive. With an open diff, the effect of uncoupling the shafts is the same as a pair of unlocked hubs, with a lot less mechanical complexity. The sealed splined stub axle and sealed bearing of the Dana 30 disconnect axle is waterproof, unlike the standard open knuckle. The disconnect is a good setup and Dynatrac will even build you a Dana 44 version of it for your YJ.

The ideal, if you don't already have them, is to switch to a set of internally splined hubs like those that appeared on the big Jeeps. This is even a good upgrade for rigs with the 6-bolt hubs. While you can source these pieces from the Dana 44s on big Jeeps, Warn introduced a much stronger aftermarket kit in 1997 that beats them all and uses the standard Jeep 5 on 5 1/2-bolt pattern. An easier alternative for 5-bolt hubs, though not as beefy, is to use the earlier 1977–80 disc brake 6-bolt hubs (a bolt-on job). Short of that, a swap to a set of premium hubs and a set of new studs tightly installed will still add a good margin of beef compared to stock.

One of the perennial problems with all of the externally splined hubs is the bolts working loose or shearing off. Driving torque and vibration tends to work them loose. The first no-no is to use lock washers on the bolts or nuts. They can break and leave the fastener loose. Always use bend-over type locking tabs on bolts. The best idea is to install hardened studs that are Loctited into the hub. Nuts are then installed, torqued to spec, and secured using lock tabs and Loctite. Self-locking nuts can also be used, if hub design permits.

Torquing drive flange or hub bolts (front or rear) is vital, since they transmit torque. The reason for bolt torque specs is to stretch the fastener slightly, which actually makes it stronger. Too tight and stretched too much, it becomes brittle and breaks easily; not tight enough, and it works loose or shears. Get a torque wrench and check these items regularly in hard use!

Choosing a locking hub is fairly simple, as there are only three types: manual, automatic, and (only occasionally seen on late models) solid drive flanges. Manual hubs are just that, you have to get out and lock or unlock them by hand. Automatic hubs save you the trip out by locking automatically when the t-case is shifted into four-wheel drive, but before you get too excited, you should know that some of them will automatically unlock on a steep downhill. Warn, for one, offers on some of its premium auto hubs the option to manually lock them 100 percent to avoid this potentially dangerous situation.

Another option that some folks use is to revert to the old-style drive flanges—nothing more than a heavy flange that bolts to the hub. It's splined in the center to accept the stub axle. For a trail Jeep, this is a cheap, simple, and bulletproof solution, but these flanges can be difficult to find for some hubs.

Other hub selection tips include choosing steel bodied locking hubs over aluminum and buying the top-of-the-line in a particular brand. As a final word, auto locking hubs are generally more fragile than their manual counterparts.

### Complete Axle Assembly Swaps

In many cases, a complete axle swap is the best and cheapest way to build drivetrain beef. A used axle is often less expensive than filling an older housing with upgraded parts. In some cases, there are stronger axle assemblies that are direct bolt-ons, but the correct units may be difficult to find. Most often, the bigger axle was simply not offered, such as a Dana 44 on the front of a CJ or YJ. In these cases, the most dimensionally similar axle from another application (Jeep or not) is modified as necessary to fit. This usually entails narrowing and relocating spring perches.

There has been enough demand for these services that a number of companies now offer upgraded axles that will fit a variety of Jeep applications. You simply call and ask for the axle you want, give them the application, and a bolt-on unit arrives. In some cases, you must provide precise measurements. The product can be purchased in many levels, from a fairly standard replacement to a unit with custom dimensions and

Warn offers a front hub conversion that features internally splined hubs. These are not recycled Wagoneer hubs but new, thicker, better pieces that are designed to work with your old spindles. This is the ultimate front hub setup at the time of this book. *Courtesy Warn*

upgrades like thicker axle tubes, nodular housings, and a wide variety of trick innards.

The big question is, do you need a swap? It depends on a great number of factors, beginning with what's there right now. If you are talking about a big increase in tire size or engine torque, the older axles (Dana 23, 25, 27, 41, etc.) are almost certainly going to need replacing. After that it becomes a formula involving tire size vs. engine torque. Your driving style (lead-foot?) and the type of trails (or type of work) to which you plan to subject the Jeep are also a major factor. The type of transmission used is another big deciding factor. Automatic-equipped vehicles are much gentler on axles than a rig with a manual transmission. Finally, the load-bearing capacity of the axle comes into play if you drive a truck.

Putting all these factors together becomes the final equation. You can go the "unlimited bucks" route or use the charts on page 79 and 80 to get closer to the bone. The chart will give you a baseline to determine whether you need to swap or not. Aftermarket builders often add many enhancements to their axles, so consider the chart's recommendations as applying to baseline or standard spec units.

Besides the strength issue, there are a couple of other elements in the axle choice equation. A beefier axle is both heavier and dimensionally larger (though often the differences are marginal). That means you will end up hauling a few extra pounds around as well as decreasing the ground clearance under the axle. An average semifloater Dana 60 weighs about 40 pounds more than a similar Dana 44 and the bigger unit decreases ground clearance by at least 3/4 of an inch. The moral here is not to trade weight or clearance for braggin' rights alone. If you need the beef, go for it. If not, stick with the smaller unit.

### Aftermarket Axle Choices

The aftermarket consists mainly of variations of three very capable and popular axle choices, the Dana 44, the Dana 60, and the Ford 9-inch. Owners of some bigger rigs also opt for the Dana 70 full-floater, but this monster axle is usually reserved for the heaviest haulers, and we won't deal with it here.

The Dana 44 is most often swapped in as a replacement front axle in CJs, YJs, XJs and TJs when the stock Model 30 is deemed too weak. It can handle a great deal of power and large tires. Its biggest weakness is the U-joints, which are no bigger than many Dana 30s. Dana 44s were used in so many stock applications from

Probably the most common front axle swap is the Dana 44, and for good reasons. The Dana 44 is at least 100 percent stronger, stock for stock, than the Dana 30. This option was not offered by the factory but it's a fairly easy fit. In some cases, such as the narrow track Wagoneer 44, only minor changes are necessary to fit them. In other cases the wider units must be narrowed. Either way, the 44 is an easy and cost-effective front swap for Jeeps needing more beef.

A to Z that they are available by the truckload, and a great deal of expertise is available to build them for every application, stock or custom.

The Dana 60 is usually considered the Schwartzenegger of the Jeep world. They can be built in a variety of nearly bulletproof ways with axle spline counts up to 44 (though a 35-spline axle is usually sufficient). The 60 can be used front or rear. Up front, they mount huge, virtually indestructible axle shafts and U-joints. The older, closed knuckle Dana 60s use smaller U-joints and are considerably weaker than the later open knuckle pieces.

Semifloat Dana 60s are the ultimate beef for the rear of CJs and Wranglers. With a 9 1/2- inch ring gear and 35 spline, 1 1/2-inch axle shafts, they are up to serious horsepower and abuse. This happens to be a high-pinion 60.

The Ford 9-inch is a popular replacement for CJs and YJs. Currie Enterprises is best known for introducing these drop-out carrier axles to the Jeep world about 15 years ago. The axle design itself dates back to the 1950s and has been a perennial favorite ever since. With a 9-inch ring gear, it is just a bit beefier than a Dana 44 in stock form. If you add some of the goodies Currie is famous for, such as nodular iron carriers, beefed-up housings, larger bearings, and 35-spline axles, you're into Dana 60 territory.

The only downside to these units is that prior to 1998, they had a low pinion, about 1 1/2 inches lower than a standard-cut Dana axle. Early in 1998, Currie introduced a high-pinion version that can replace all the low units. With the pinion more than 3 inches higher than before, pinion and driveshaft angles can be easily optimized. Transfer case lowering devices can be removed and in some cases, the engine and trans/t-case can be moved up and tucked between the frame rails.

If you have an idea to build and install a 9-inch of your own, bear in mind that many stock Ford units have small 28-spline axle shafts, relatively weak housings, and small axle bearings. Shop for units from later Ford pickups that use 31 spline axles, large bearings, and the "triangulated" housings.

Some of the typical mods to a custom Dana axle include the replacement of the stock axle tubes to prevent bending and breakage. The OE tubes are generally 1018 or 1026 cold drawn steel that has a welded seam. The first stage is to replace the tubes with better materials. Dynatrac, for example, uses 4130 DOM (drawn over mandrill) seamless aircraft steel tubes that increase strength 40–70 percent. Sometimes the tubing is replaced with thicker walled tubing, but since there is a weight penalty, this isn't always necessary or desirable. In the case of offset differentials, the short tube is often left in stock configuration because it's more resistant to bending and only the more vulnerable long side is beefed.

### High-Pinion Differentials

In high-lift, short-wheelbase applications, driveshaft angles are the perennial problem. There are some axle solutions to these problems as well as those outlined in Chapter 3, and they come in the form of high-pinion, or reverse-cut diffs.

A high-pinion Dana diff places the differential pinion above the centerline of the ring gear, unlike the standard diff, which places the pinion below it. The

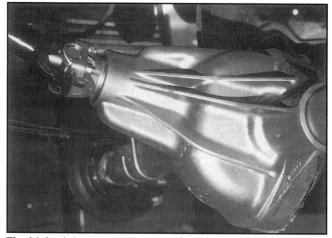

The high-pinion or reverse-cut axles are very useful because they reduce driveshaft angles. The reverse cut axles were designed for front applications and are at their strongest there. Used in rear axle applications, they lose about 30 percent in ring gear strength because they are turning in reverse. This high-pinion 60 is still at least 50 percent stronger than a Dana 44. A reverse cut 44 is deemed too weak for the rear of most Jeeps.

pinion is 2.25 inches higher than a standard Dana diff and about 3.5 inches higher than a low-pinion Ford 9-inch. No, you can't make a high-pinion diff by just turning a standard diff upside down. If you did this, it would soon burn up due to lack of lubrication. The high-pinion housing is specially built to provide the necessary lubrication for the pinion bearings.

The "reverse-cut" term refers to the direction of the

The Ford 9-inch is a popular alternative to Dana axles. They have a 9-inch ring gear (duh!) in a drop-out carrier. In stock Ford applications they used 28- or 31-spline axles, but Currie builds them with special 35-spline shafts. They can be used front or rear. The only disadvantage has been the low-pinion position. Currie now builds a high-pinion version of the 9-inch, and claims it's as strong as a Dana 60. Brave words, but no one who knows Currie doubts it.

spiral cut on the ring gear teeth, which is the reverse of a standard diff. This makes the unit stronger when operating in a front-drive situation. High-pinion diffs can be used in the rear, but in this position, they are about 30 percent weaker, because they are essentially running in reverse of their ideal rotation (a similar problem that the standard diff faces working up front). Incidentally, since the XJ, YJ, and TJ front Dana 30 is a reverse cut, high-pinion unit, it makes a good swap for an older unit in applications where a brute axle is not needed.

High-pinion Dana 44s and Dana 60s are available for front drive applications. Dynatrac is perhaps best known for building high-pinion Dana diffs. Their high-pinion 60 can be used in rear drive application also, though the 30 percent loss of strength must be factored in. Dynatrac doesn't recommend the high-pinion Dana 44 for the rear due to this inherent loss of strength, but the reverse cut 60 is a popular solution and generally rated as somewhere between a "built" 44 and a stock 60 in strength.

## Locker Basics

A locker is one of the most critical choices you will make, both in terms of off-pavement performance and drivability on the highway. Lockers will deliver "true" four-wheel drive and get you through the most amazing situations, but some types may have adverse handling effects on the street. The symptoms include tires chirping plus clicking, clanking, and banging from the

drivetrain when turning. You can also get a tail end "wiggle" on application or release of throttle in turns. On slippery roads, the units can lock and cause partial or complete loss of control. When used in the front axle, a locker makes steering difficult or impossible when in four-wheel drive.

While "locker" is a generic term that encompasses the entire breed, there should actually be two classifications, locker and limited slip. For the most part, you can put locker choices into three categories: limited slips (not truly lockers but often categorized with them), automatic lockers, and on-demand lockers. Which unit is best for you depends on the projected use of your Jeep and your budget.

### Open Differential

This is the standard setup for most Jeeps. Simply put, the open diff supplies equal traction on hard surfaces going straight but allows the inside tire to slow down when the vehicle turns. In low traction situations, torque will flow down the path of least resistance. With one tire on pavement and one tire in goo, the torque will go to the one in the goo. In low traction situations, a 4x4 without traction-aiding devices in the diffs is, in essence, a two-wheel drive—one wheel spinning in front and one in the rear.

### Limited Slip

Limited slips became commonly available for light-duty 4x4s in the mid-1950s in the form of the Spicer Powr-Loc. The limited slip operates more or less like an

In the ever-lasting quest for stronger axles, here's a prototype axle from Summers. Using Dana 60 reverse-cut gears, the custom housing is being tested in full and semifloat designs. No word yet as to a production date, but by the time this book is in print you'll know. Remember you saw it here first! *Courtesy Summers Brothers*

King of the automatic lockers is the Detroit Locker, a.k.a. the No-Spin. Built by Trac-Tech, this is probably the universal locker among Jeepers. It's positive, hard to kill, but lacking in manners. The newer versions are a bit more civilized but in a light Jeep, expect some drivability issues. *Courtesy Trac-Tech*

The EZ Locker from Trac-Tech is easy to install. Simply remove the spider and side gears and replace it with this unit. This is an automatic locker that is fairly positive. It's only failing is that it relies on the OE carrier for strength. *Courtesy Trac-Tech*

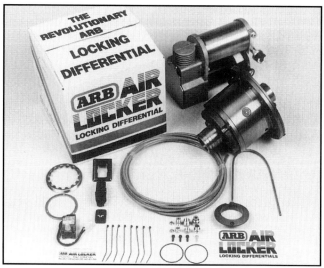

The ARB Air Locker is the king of the on-demand lockers. Using compressed air, the locker engages with the push of a button. The compressor is handy for tire inflation. The carrier is replaced with a unit that is often stronger than the OE piece. Note that the compressor pictured here has been replaced with an improved type. *Courtesy ARB*

open diff in everyday use but in low-traction situations, some torque may be applied to the wheel with the most traction.

Limited slips can be "loose" or "tight," referring to the difference in wheel speed allowed between the two wheels. Loose limited slips can be easily overcome in trail situations where there is a great difference in traction between the tires, such as when a tire lifts. A tight unit will operate better in this regard, but may exhibit some adverse characteristics on the street. Limited slips commonly operate via clutch packs or gears that are calibrated to deliver equal traction until a certain amount of "breakaway torque" is reached and then they release. A limited slip is ideal for the occasional, moderate-duty Jeeper on a budget who wants to add some trail traction without a drivability penalty on the highway. They are generally the least expensive traction aiding device. They can be fitted front or rear in part-time four-wheel-drive rigs, but take care installing a tight limited slip up front, as you may encounter steering problems in four-wheel drive. (Full-time rigs are another kettle of fish —watch out!)

### Automatic Lockers

The earliest automatic locker I have found was the M&S locker that appeared in the 1913 Jeffery Quad and was also used in a few other early 4x4s. A locking differential is defined as one that will achieve a true 50-50 division of torque between the two wheels. Automatic lockers do this in a variety of ways, some more

smoothly than others. All will deliver a 100 percent torque split when slippage is sensed. Under light loads and equal traction, they will mimic an open diff but may exhibit some handling quirks on the street—some more than others. Watch out in slippery weather. They can be very cranky in the rear of full-time systems, though by all reports it depends on your willingness to endure.

Using an automatic locker in front axle applications is often done but drivers of such rigs must sometimes unlock a hub or disengage the front axle in order to make a tight turn. Automatic lockers are generally not much more expensive than a limited slip (in some cases they are less expensive) and are preferred by the harder core crowd that is willing to sacrifice some on-road user-friendliness.

### On-Demand Lockers

On-demand lockers achieve 100 percent lockup by various means but the commonality is that they are all controlled by the driver. They can be operated hydraulically, by a cable, via air or vacuum, or even electrically. The beauty is that until they are actuated, they operate as a normal open diff. No side effects, but 100 percent traction when you need it. This makes them ideal for full-time four-wheel-drive rigs or in front-axle applications. They are the most expensive and the most complicated type of locker. An on-demand locker works well with front or rear axles and is safe with full-time systems. Because they are manually operated, pilot error becomes an issue but, then again, many pilots feel they can "out-think" an automatic locker.

### Locker Choices

A variety of lockers are available. Each has advantages and disadvantages. We'll go though the commonly available units and discuss the merits. In addition to the units mentioned below, the aftermarket will soon debut an electrically actuated on-demand locker. Both Power Trax and Trac-Tech have been working on such an idea.

### Powr-Loc

The granddaddy of limited slips. The Spicer Powr-Loc was available in Jeeps from 1956 through 1970. The Powr-Loc can be identified by a two-piece case and four-pinion differential. It uses clutches that are calibrated to achieve the correct breakaway torque. The Powr-Loc can be "loaded" to increase breakaway torque by adding extra clutches to the pack. It's still available to fit both types of Dana 30s and Dana 44s with either 19 or 30 splines. There used to be a version for Dana 27s. The unit replaces the existing carrier. It's OK for front axles on part-time rigs and for the rear of full-time units.

### Trac-Loc

The Spicer Trac-Loc has a one-piece case and only two pinions (spiders). It became optional in Jeeps in 1971, replacing the Powr-Loc, and is still optional in the rear of various Jeep models. It's generally considered less robust than the Powr-Loc but the application covers both Dana 30s and 19- and 30-spline Dana 44s. Versions are available for both 28- and 31-spline Ford 9-inch diffs. It can be used up front if desired on part-time four-wheel drives and in the rear of full-time rigs.

### True-Trac

The True-Trac from Trac-Tech (say that fast three times!) is a torque-sensing, gear type limited slip differential that is very smooth. Unlike limited slips that use clutch packs, the case is full of gears that allow smooth breakaway operation but only a small wheel speed difference. Applications are for Dana 30s, Dana 35 (retainer and C-clip), 30-spline Dana 44, Dana 70, and Ford 9-inch. With the True-Trac, there is an element of driver control. A touch of brake at the right moment will cause the True-Trac to more fully engage, such as

in a lifted wheel situation. OK for the front or rear of both full- or part-time four-wheel-drive Jeeps (some adverse symptoms in full-time rigs).

### Lock-Right

The Lock-Right comes from Power Trax and is a simple, inexpensive, and easy-to-install automatic locker. It can be a little coarse in its street manners, especially with lightweight rigs, but it more than makes up for this in trail performance. The unit replaces the spider and side gears in the stock carrier, which makes it the easiest type to install, but limits overall strength to that of the stock carrier. The Lock-Right uses splined pieces with center facing teeth on each axle. The stock spider cross shaft is fed through an oval hole in the center of the two-piece center unit. Torque forces the pin to push the center pieces apart and engage the teeth, thus locking the two axles together. Coasting through a turn, most of the torque is released and the teeth are allowed to ratchet. Lock-Rights are available for all Dana 30s, both Dana 35s, 19- and 30-spline Dana 44s, 30 and 35-spline Dana 60, AMC 20, and Ford 9-inch. They are used by some in front axle applications but may be too tight for many. Not recommended for the front of full-time rigs and by some reports marginal (but livable) in the rear of the full-timers.

### E-Z Locker

From Trac-Tech, this unit is very similar to the Lock-Right, which it predates, in operation, installation, and cost. The same pluses and minuses apply. Application guide is similar to the Lock-Right.

### Detroit Locker

From Trac-Tech, this nearly indestructible automatic locker is also known as the No-Spin. It's been around since the 1960s and has a reputation for being efficient and tough. Early units were pretty notorious for their atrocious highway manners but were still widely used because of their brute strength. The newer SofLocker versions are a kinder and gentler adaptation of the original on the highway but with the same beef and lockup characteristics in the dirt. The Detroit Locker replaces the original carrier and fits the late Dana 30, Dana 35, 30-spline Dana 44, Dana 60, Dana 70, and AMC 20. Although it's often used in front diffs, it's not generally recommended for this. OK for the rear of full-time four-wheel-drive rigs, with a few adverse symptoms.

## ARB Air Locker

The ARB Air Locker is an Australian import. An on-demand locker that is actuated by compressed air, it's either fully locked or open, as with a standard diff. The differential unit replaces the original carrier and in most cases it is stronger. The only serious downside is that this is a fairly expensive bit of kit. With the need for an air compressor and air lines running *into* the diff housing, it's also complex. Once installed, it's ideal for use in front or rear diffs in full or part-time situations.

### LOCKER CHART

| Locker | Trail Traction | Street Manners | Installation | Durability | Cost |
|---|---|---|---|---|---|
| Powr-Loc | fair | good | moderate | good | moderate |
| Trac-Loc | fair | good | moderate | fair-good | moderate |
| True-Trac | good | good | moderate | good | mod-high |
| Lock-Right | excellent | fair-good | easy | good | low |
| E-Z Locker | excellent | fair-good | easy | good | low |
| Detroit | excellent | fair-good | moderate | excellent | mod-high |
| ARB | excellent | excellent | difficult | good | high |

## Driveshafts: The Torque Connection

It's easy to overlook the lowly driveshaft in the buildup process. Beyond the length and angle issue issues connected with suspension lifts discussed in Chapter 3, the strength issue needs a few words, starting with the U-joints.

As mentioned in Chapter 3, 15 degrees is the crawling-on-the ground maximum continuous operating angularity for U-joints. Fifteen degrees doesn't seem like much until you consider that most experts consider 8 degrees as the workable compromise between angle and U-joint wear. Even a mild lift will put most short wheelbase Jeeps past 8 degrees.

More angularity equals less U-joint life. For example, Spicer rates their U-joints for 5,000 hours at a 3 degree angle. At 12 degrees, that life is cut to 25 percent, or 1,250 hours. If you don't mind changing U-joints once a year, this is OK. Operating the high angle driveshafts at lower speed, e.g., low-range trail work, will also stretch U-joint life a bit. You can go past 15 degrees for brief periods at low speeds as your suspension moves. Also, if you reduce the torque load when the U-joint is at a severe angle, life increases. That might mean going gently on the throttle when the U-joints are flexed. This definitely applies to the front axle U-joints, as well as the back.

Three sizes of driveshaft U-joints are commonly used on Jeeps: 1310, 1330, and 1350. These refer to the basic dimensions, as shown on page 80. Virtually all the Jeeps, except some of the big Jeeps in the Gladiator era, use 1310 series U-joints. Considering stock gearing, tires, and engine torque, these are adequate. Once you get through beefing your Jeep, it may be short of what's needed. You can get an idea by using the formula on page 80 and checking how your current or projected setup rates, and then comparing it to the torque ratings on page 80.

U-joint selection deserves a few words. Just as with everything else, there are parts and then there are *parts!* There appears to be a large quality gap when it comes to U-joints. While some very good brands are out there, most pros recognize Spicer as being at or near the top of the heap. After all, Spicer perfected the Cardan joint for automotive applications near the turn of the century.

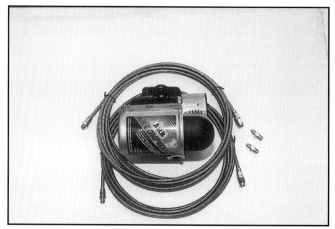

One of the few weak links to the ARB setup is that the plastic air lines are vulnerable to damage. JB Conversions has come to the rescue with a braided steel reinforced line that can eliminate many problems. Shown is the improved ARB compressor. *Courtesy JB Conversions*

The 1/4-inch bolts and straps (right) used on later Jeeps are notoriously weak. Fortunately, the U-bolt type is an easy replacement. You can even buy yoke upgrades to fit larger size U-joints. If you have the strap type and use it in hard service, inspect them often. Use a torque wrench when you replace them and use Loctite.

There are other good name brands but stay away from cheap, no-name parts.

The next question is whether to buy greaseable or nongreaseable U-joints. There is a difference in strength between the two, with the nongreaseable holding the aces by a slim margin. Spicer says the difference is only about 5 percent. The tradeoff is that regularly greasing a U-joint not only provides lubrication, but purges the joint of contaminants like water and dirt. On the other hand, the nongreaseable joint has better seals and will not allow water to enter as easily. Seals on the greaseable type are designed to allow grease to be pumped out in the process of service. A commonsense approach is to stick with the greaseable type, unless you are running your joints on the ragged edge of their strength ratings, and grease them often. Always install the greaseable joint with the zerk hole positioned so that it's in compression when torque is applied. If you opt for a nongreaseable joint, be sure to pack it well with the best grease you can buy before you install it. One constant with U-joints is that they are inadequately lubricated by the manufacturer. U-joints run at severe angles will tend to wear out their grease faster than units run at lesser angles. That means the grease in your nonlubeable joint might fail before the U-joint.

Speaking of grease, use only a grease rated EP ( for extreme pressure). Many U-joints fail because some leftover "covered wagon" grease was used. Chassis grease for wheel bearings, ball joints, and tie-rod ends is not adequate. EP-2 grease is rated by the NLGI

(National Lubricating Grease Institute) to have an operating temperature range of minus 10 to 325 degrees Fahrenheit. Spicer recommends a lubricating interval of 5,000 miles or three months on 4x4s used 10 percent on the trail. Cut that in half, at least, if you 'wheel a lot, and apply a squirt or two after major encounters with water.

### Upgrading Yokes

Upgrading universal joints is possible on most Jeeps, but you can only do so if the correct pinion and transfer case yokes are available. Figure 4-8 rounds up the available yokes for assorted axle/t-case combos found on Jeeps.

In some cases, a downgraded yoke might be necessary. Let's say you are switching to a Dana 60 rear axle on a CJ. Your current 1310 U-joints are adequate but the 60 you selected was fitted with a 1-ton 1350 yoke, so you would look for a 1310 yoke for a Dana 60 to match your existing U-joints. Of course, your driveshaft would probably need shortening in this situation also.

The strongest method for holding the U-joint in the yoke is the U-bolt setup. The strap kits are the simplest method but the Jeep version uses very small quarter-inch bolts. Also, the inside of the straps can gradually wear and cease to effectively clamp the U-joint cup. Tightening the strap bolts will not affect how tightly the cup is clamped. Eventually, they will come unglued. Though you may occasionally see a strap type yoke drilled to accept a U-bolt, it isn't recommended because it will weaken the yoke, and the U-bolt doesn't usually fit well enough to do a good clamping job.

Fortunately, most Jeeps come with the U-bolt type, though a few cautions are in order. The first is to make sure they are evenly tightened and checked regularly. A U-bolt may stretch or distort a little, but it can be tightened to compensate. A U-bolt is properly tight when the two nuts have been evenly tightened to the point where the lock washer goes flat and then about 1/8 turn more. Too tight, and it can distort the cap and kill the joint. Blue Loctite is also required on the nuts or even with the bolts on a strap type setup.

### Driveshafts

There is a definite science to selecting the diameter of a driveshaft. The rear is the most important (on part-time rigs) because they do all the work. The front shaft usually is operated only at low speeds, though a full-time rig might need some special attention.

If you have a driveshaft vibration problem or a severe angle, the double-Cardan, or CV joint, is a possible answer. The CV is at least as strong as the U-joints used in it, but these bad boys will fail spectacularly when bound up. This one is used on a Model 18 T-case in an older CJ, but take note that the differential pinion is not properly aligned. The axle needs to be tilted up parallel with the driveshaft.

The ideal diameter depends on length, with shorter shafts being smaller. A 3-inch shaft is fine for up to 48-inch driveshafts and 3 1/2 inches is good for 49- to 60-inch shafts. Driveshafts longer than 60 inches need a carrier and a two-piece setup. This is only applicable to pickups.

Wall thickness is ideal at 14 gauge (.083-inch wall thickness) but 16 gauge (.065-inch wall thickness) is often seen and is acceptable on moderately stressed rigs. A .120 wall is used for short 2-inch diameter shafts (usually the front) and this is the practical thickness limit. Thicker in this situation is not always better because it increases rotating mass. It's nice to have a piece that will resist a touch on a rock, but overkill isn't necessary.

Another important and often ignored part of the driveshaft is the slip yoke. The splines wear (faster if you don't grease 'em) to the point where there will be noticeable runout. You can feel it by grabbing the shaft near the joint and pulling it side to side. There should only be about .007 inch runout or less on a rear shaft. You can probably get away with a bit more on a front shaft. More runout equals more vibration. Also make sure that there is at least 2 1/2 inches of spline engagement at the stretched-out point. There should also be a bit of travel left when the axle is in its full upward position.

The slip yoke moves less than you might think, because most axle movement is side-to-side articula-

tion. Special slip yokes with lots of travel are available for rigs with especially flexible suspension systems. A boot over the slip yoke will protect it from water and dirt and help it to last a long while.

### Driveshaft Clearance

As you modify your Jeep's suspension and drive-train, it's a good idea to check the flex points of the driveshafts for clearance. At extreme angles, the yokes may touch and when they do, something breaks. Stock rigs do not usually have the legs to cause this, but a Jeep with a very flexible suspension is likely to max out the driveshaft angles. This is something you want to check before finding out the hard way, when you're 50 miles from nowhere.

To check for clearance, max the suspension travel out, up, down, and articulated, and check for at least 1/16 inch of space between all the points of the yokes and U-joints. The simplest and safest method to test articulation is to use or build an articulation ramp (see chapter 3) and slowly run the vehicle up, checking at various points until you max out travel.

To test up and down clearance, simply jack the chassis up until the wheels are off the ground and the suspension is drooping all the way. Be sure to always support the vehicle with stands. It's doubtful that you will have to check with the suspension in the up position because most Jeeps have lots more droop than compression, and any clearancing you do on droop will more than cover compression.

If you find minor clearance problems, you can often grind little corners off the yokes for clearance. Take care with the grinder, as taking off too much material can weaken the yoke. Major problems can be solved by restricting suspension travel, or installing a CV joint if none was fitted before. Some of the driveshaft angle tricks found in Chapter 3 may also help.

## CV Joints

The double Cardan, or CV joint, was invented by A. W. Herrington in 1929 for a front axle design. We now see it used mainly on driveshafts. It can operate at a more severe angle than can a single Cardan joint, though there are some restrictions to its use. CV joints are most often seen on front driveshafts but CJs and Wranglers frequently need them on the rear to counter excessive driveline angles. If you have an operating angle of over 15 degrees, you need a CV joint. A Spicer 1310 series CV has a maximum operating angle of 30 degrees and the 1330 will bind at 25

degrees. As you can see, a CV may solve a lot of driveshaft angle problems.

The CV takes two standard U-joints and couples them together into a housing with a centering device. If you have a 20 degree angle, the CV essentially splits this between the two joints giving them 10 degrees each, well within their operating range. The requirement is that, unlike the phased single Cardan setups, the diff pinion must be parallel with the driveshaft rather than parallel with the t-case output.

Opinions vary as to the strength of the CV assembly itself. Though there is the extra complication of the assembly, you can generally count on them to be as strong as the U-joints they contain. If, however, you manage to bind them up, they fail rather spectacularly.

There are two types of CV joints, the Spicer and the Saginaw. The Spicer 1310 or 1330 unit is commonly seen on Jeeps but you may run into a Saginaw. The Spicer has the better reputation because the trunnions are held in with snap rings. The Saginaw's trunnions are held in with plastic plugs from the factory but the pieces are machined to accept snap rings when you rebuild them.

**Maximum Recommended Tire Sizes for Jeep Axles***
*For highway and moderate off-pavement use, stock engine. Equipment in good condition is presumed.

| Axle | Tire Size (inches) |
|------|--------------------|
| Spicer 23-2 | 31 |
| Spicer 25 | 31 |
| Spicer 27 | 31 |
| Dana 30 | 32 |
| Dana 30 (1) | 33 |
| Dana 35 | 32 |
| Spicer 41-2 | 32 |
| Spicer 44 (2) | 32 |
| Dana 44 (3) | 35 |
| Spicer 53 | 33 |
| Spicer 60 (4) | 33 |
| Dana 60 (5) | 38–44 |
| Spicer 70 | 44 |
| AMC Corp. 20 (6) | 32–35 |

(1) Used in 1987–97 Wrangler
(2) Tapered axle type
(3) Flanged axles
(4) Early tapered, 19-spline axles
(5) Depends on full or semifloat design
(6) Stock tapered axles—aftermarket flanged axles

## JEEP FACTORY AXLE ROUNDUP

| Model | Years | Application | Ring Gear | Axles | Use |
|---|---|---|---|---|---|
| AMC 20 rear | 1976–86 | CJ, SJ | 8 7/8 in | 29/1.25in/SF | 3 |
| 23-2 rear | 1941–46 | CJ, GPW, MB | 7 3/4 in | 10/1.00in/FF | 2 |
| 25 front | 1941–65 | CJ, FC, PU, SW | 7 3/4 in | 10/1.13in/FF | 2 |
| 27 front | 1966–71 | CJ, SJ(G), VJ | 7 1/8 in | 10/1.13in/FF | 2 |
| 30 front | 1972–86 | CJ, VJ | 7 1/8 in | 27/1.13in/FF | 3 |
| 30 rear | 1967–68 | VJ | 7 1/8 in | 27/1.13in/SF | 2 |
| 35 rear | 1987–97 | TJ, YJ, XJ | 7 9/16 in | 27/1.13in/SF | 3 |
| 41-1 rear | 1946–50 | CJ | 7 3/4 in | 10/1.00in/SF | 2 |
| 44-2 rear | 1950–70 | CJ, FC, PU, SJ(G) | 8 1/2 in | 19/1.25in/SF | 2 |
| 44 rear | 1970–97 | CJ, FC, SJ(G), SJ, TJ, ZJ | 8 1/2 in | 30/1.31in/SF | 3 |
| 44F front | 1957–70 | FC, SJ | 8 1/2 in | 19/1.25in/FF | 2 |
| 44 front | 1971–86 | SJ | 8 1/2 in | 30/1.31in/FF | 3 |
| 53 rear | 1957–65 | FC, PU, SJ(G) | 9 1/4 in | 19/1.19in/SF | 3 |
| 60 front | 1967–69 | 715 | 9 3/4 in | 10/1.50in/FF | 3–4 |
| 60 rear SF | 1969–87 | SJ | 9 3/4 in | 35/1.50in/SF | 4–5 |
| 60 rear FF | 1969–87 | SJ | 9 3/4in | 30/1.31in/FF | 4–5 |
| 70 rear DRW | 1959–65 | FC | 10 9/16 in | 23/1.50in/FF | 4 |
| 70 rear GI | 1967–69 | 715 | 10 9/16 in | 10/1.50in/FF | 4 |

*Use Guidelines:*
1. Stock use—light duty
2. Stock use—medium duty
3. Stock use—medium duty, modified- heavy duty
4. Modified—heavy duty
5. Modified—unlimited duty

SF = semifloating, FF = full floating

## FRONT AXLE UNIVERSAL JOINT GUIDE

| Axle | Application | Factory U-Joint | Upgrade |
|---|---|---|---|
| Spicer 25 | CJ, FC, SW, PU | Bendix, Rzeppa, Tracta | 5-74X (4) |
| Spicer 25 | CJ, FC, SW, PU | 5-74X | None |
| Spicer 27 | CJ, SJ(G), C-101 | 5-74X | None |
| Dana 30 | CJ, SJ, C-101 | 5-260X (1) | None |
| Dana 30 | YJ, XJ | 5-260X (2) | 5-297X |
| Spicer 44F | SJ(G), FC | 5-74X | None |
| Dana 44 | SJ | 5-297X (3) | None ( 2) |
| Dana 60 | 715 | 5-74X | None |

(1) Some were closed axle and used 5-74X U-joint.
(2) Disconnect axle. In 1995, 5-297X U-joint adopted. These larger U-joints can be installed with 1995 axle shaft for a 30 percent increase in strength.
(3) Some had the smaller 260X. These can be upgraded to the 297X by changing axle assemblies. Approximately 20 percent stronger.
(4) Requires a conversion kit.

## AVAILABLE FACTORY RATIOS, CARRIER SIZE VS. GEAR RATIO CHART

| Axle | Low Ratio Case | High Ratio Case |
|------|----------------|-----------------|
| 25 | — | 4.27, 4.88. 5.38 |
| 27 | 3.31, 3.54, 3.73 | 4.27, 4.88, 5.38 |
| 30 (std) | 3.07, 3.54 | 3.73, 4.10, 4.27, 4.88 |
| 30 (rev) | 2.73, 3.31, 3.54 | 3.73, 4.10, 4.56 |
| 35 | 2.73, 3.07, 3.54 | 3.73, 4.10 |
| 44 | 2.73, 3.31, 3.73 | 3.92. 4.10, 4.27, 4.89, 5.89 |
| 53 | — | 4.27, 4.88, 5.38 |
| 60 | 3.73, 4.10 | 4.88 |
| 70 | 3.73, 4.10 | 4.27, 4.88, 5.89 |
| AMC-20 | 2.73, 3.07, 3.31, 3.54, 3.73, 4.10 | — |

## SPLINE STRENGTH GRAPH

Approximate. Choose your old spline count on the top line, then work your way down to the level of the new spline count on the column at left to find the approximate increase in strength. Some swaps may not be practical.

| | 35 | 31 | 30 | 28 | 19 | 10 | Old Spline Count |
|------|------|------|------|------|------|------|------|
| 10 | | | | | | | |
| 19 | | | | | | +99% | |
| 28 | | | | | +99% | +198% | |
| 30 | | | | +22% | +121% | +220% | |
| 31 | | | +11% | +33% | +131% | +231% | |
| 35 | | +44% | +55% | +77% | +176% | +275% | |
| **New spline count** | | | | Increase in strength | | | |

### Axle Assembly Swappers Guide

Find the original axle type in Part 1 and note factor. From engine torque column in Part 2, find the range into which your engine fits and note the factor. Finally, look at Part 3 and note the tire size range you intend to run. Add the three factors together and compare the score to the various axles listed in Part 4. If your total score exceeds those listed, then you probably need to upgrade. If your number comes to the edge of an upgrade and you plan on some hard 'wheeling, the best bet is to bump up. If the number just crosses the line and you have an automatic trans or plan light-duty work, you are probably OK.

**Part 1**

| Orig. Axle | Factor |
|------------|--------|
| Dana 23-2, 25, 27 (front or rear) | 9 |
| Dana 30 (early, front or rear) | 8 |
| Dana 41 | 7 |
| Dana 30 (late) Dana 35, Dana 44 (early, front or rear) | 6 |
| Dana 53, 44 (late), AMC 20 | 5 |
| Dana 60 (front or rear) | 4 |
| Dana 70 | 3 |

**Part 2**

| Eng. Torque (lb-ft) | Factor |
|---|---|
| 100–150 | 2 |
| 151–200 | 3 |
| 201–250 | 4 |
| 251–300 | 5 |
| 301–350 | 6 |
| 351–400 | 7 |
| 401–450 | 8 |
| 451–500 | 9 |

**Part 3**

| Tire Diameter (in.) | Factor |
|---|---|
| 27–31 | 2 |
| 31–33 | 4 |
| 33–36 | 6 |
| 36–40 | 8 |
| 40–44 | 10 |

**Part 4**
**Replacement Axles**

| Total is more than: | Then you should upgrade to: |
|---|---|
| *Front Axles* | |
| 14 | Dana 30 (high-pinion) |
| 16 | Dana 44 |
| 20 | Ford 9-inch (Currie 31 spline) or Dana 44 (high-pinion) |
| 22 | Dana 60 |
| 24 | Dana 60 (high-pinion) |
| *Rear Axles* | |
| 20 | Dana 44 (flanged axle) or AMC 20 w/flanged axles |
| 22 | Ford 9-inch (31 spline) or Dana 60 (high-pinion) |
| 24 | Dana 60 |

## Universal Joint Dimensions and Torque Ratings

| Series | Cap to Cap | Cap Diameter | Max Torque Rating |
|---|---|---|---|
| 1310 | 3 7/32 in. | 1 1/16 in. | 1,600 lb-ft |
| 1330 | 3 5/8 in. | 1 1/16 in. | 1,850 lb-ft |
| 1350 | 3 5/8 in. | 1 3/16 in. | 2,260 lb-ft |

## Calculating Driveshaft and Low Gear Torque

Use these formulas to calculate the maximum torque generated by your Jeep in low gear and to determine the approximate amount of torque delivered to your U-joints. If you add the axle ratio to this equation, you can calculate the torque on the axle shafts.

Low Gear Torque = Engine Torque (net) x 1st gear x
low range x .85

Example: A Wrangler with a 4.0L six, 3.93 1st gear, and 2.72 low range, would have:

220 x 3.93 x 2.72 x .85 = 2351.7 lb-ft low gear torque.

## Jeep T-Case and Differential Yoke Availability

| U-Joint Series | T-Cases | Axles |
|---|---|---|
| 1310 | Dana 18 | Dana 25/27 |
| | NP-231 | Dana 30 |
| | NP-241 | Dana 35 |
| | NP-208 | Dana 44 |
| | Dana 300 | Dana 60 |
| | Dana 20 | Dana 70 |
| | Quadra Tr. | |
| 1330 (s. cup) | NP-231 | Dana 30 |
| | NP-241 | Dana 35 |
| | NP-208 | Dana 44 |
| | Dana 300 | Dana 60 |
| | Dana 20 | Dana 70 |
| 1330 (l. cup) | Dana 18 | Dana 25/27 |
| | NP-231 | Dana 30 |
| | NP-241 | Dana 35 |
| | NP-208 | Dana 44 |
| | Dana 300 | Dana 60 |
| | Dana 20 | Dana 70 |
| 1350 | Dana 18 | Dana 25/27 |
| | NP-231 | Dana 30 |
| | NP-241 | Dana 35 |
| | NP-208 | Dana 44 |
| | Dana 300 | Dana 60 |
| | Dana 20 | Dana 70 |

## Common Steel Groups

### 10XX, 11XX, 12XX, 15XX

The carbon steel group. Most standard OEM axles are 1040 grade. OEM axles are generally heat treated to 40 Rockwell in the center with the outer layer at 55-60 Rockwell to a depth of about .180 inch. These grades all carry from 1.00–1.65 percent manganese.

### 13XX

The manganese steel group, which contains 1.45–2.05 percent manganese. If it contains 1.6–2.05 percent of manganese, it can be called an alloy steel. This grade is used by aftermarket axle builders because the high manganese content allows for more flexibility during the heat treating process.

### "H" Rated

These steels contain a measure of silicon but otherwise match the composition of a standard type, such as 1340. Silicon comes from quartz and sand, and when mixed into steel it adds a measure of hardness. 1340H, for example, has .15–.30 percent silicon.

### 43XX, 47XX

The nickel-chromium-molybdenum group. An alloy containing .65–.95 percent chromium, .2–.3 percent molybdenum, and 1.55–2.0 percent nickel. Chromium increases hardness and the elastic limits (when the material is quenched), as well as increasing corrosion resistance. Molybdenum and nickel also increase hardness.

## Available Aftermarket Gear Ratios
Nonfactory ratios are highlighted.

| Axle | Available Ratios |
| --- | --- |
| 25 | 4.27, 4.88, 5.38 |
| 27 | 3.31, 3.54, 3.73, **4.10**, 4.27, 4.88, 5.38 |
| 30(std) | 3.07, 3.31, 3.54, 4.10, 4.27, **4.56**, 4.88 |
| 30(rev) | 2.73, 3.07, 3.31, 3.54, 3.73, 4.10, **4.56** |
| 35 | 2.35, 2.73, 3.07, **3.31**, 3.73, 4.10, **4.56** |
| 44 | 2.73, **2.87**, **3.00**, 3.07, **3.23**, 3.31, 3.54, **3.92**, 4.10, 4.27, 4.56, **4.78**, 4.89, **5.38**, **5.89** |
| 53 | — |
| 60 | **3.33**, **3.54**, 3.73, 4.10, **4.56**, 4.88, **5.13**, **5.38**, **5.86**, **6.17**, **7.17** |
| 70 | — |
| AMC 20 | 2.73, 3.07, 3.54, 3.73, 4.10, **4.56** |

*Chapter 5*

# TRANSFER CASE, OVERDRIVE & SPLITTERS

## Torque Splitting

There are three main versions of the Dana 18 T-case that a re sorted by intermediate shaft size. Starting from the right is the 3/4-inch shaft from the World War II era, also seen in a very few early CJs. In the middle is the much better 1 1/8-inch shaft used from 1946 to 1953 (for sure, and seen occasionally later). Finally, the best and most common 1 1/4-inch shaft that lasted to the end of the Model 18 in 1971.

The Dana 300 T-case replaced the Dana 20 in CJs starting in 1980 and lasted until the demise of the CJ in 1986. It had all the strength characteristics of its ancestors, the Dana 18 and Dana 20, but a much better 2.6:1 low range. The low gearing and cast-iron beef has made it a popular Jeep transfer case.

The transfer case is the heart of any four-wheel drive. Development of a practical way to split the power between front and rear axles was a crucial development in 4x4 history. The transfer case does more than provide a torque split. Most of them also provide an overall gear ratio drop, a *low range.*

As we have discussed in Chapter 2 and Chapter 4, gearing is one of the most important aspects to performance on the trail and on the street. Finding a compromise that works in both venues is the age-old four-wheeler's dilemma. The transfer case low range allows the gearing needed for slow speed trail work, and high range offers standard gearing for the highway.

Potentially, combinations of axle and transfer case gearing are infinite, but we have been limited to what the manufacturer gave us. Recently, the trend from the aftermarket has been to supply transfer cases (or conversion kits) with an extra-low low range. Now it's possible to retain more highway-friendly high-range axle gearing and yet have those stump-pulling low gears for the trail. You can also choose to combine the lower transfer case gears with low axle ratios to get some outrageously low gearing.

### T-case Basics

Transfer cases can be divided into several categories, part-time, full-time, cast iron, aluminum, gear drive, and chain drive. A part-time 'case is one that supplies power only to the rear wheels until shifted into four-wheel drive. A full-time unit is one that supplies power to the front and rear at all times but uses a center differential to allow slippage for turns. Usually, that center diff can be locked, either manually or automatically, to provide a true 50/50 torque split. Some of the latest high tech 'cases are torque sensing, meaning that they will provide the most torque to the axle with the most traction. These setups are nifty for light-duty stuff, snowy roads and such, but are overwhelmed in really tough terrain.

The early transfer cases were cast iron and, overall, are much stronger than the later aluminum units, but at twice the weight. Aluminum T-cases have closed the strength gap, however, so don't automatically dismiss them. Virtually all the current Jeep transfer cases are aluminum, with the last all-iron units phased out in 1986. Most experts agree that the aluminum NP-231 is tough enough for even hard-core Wranglers.

The transition from iron to aluminum also seemed to mark the transition from gear to chain drive innards. Gear drive cases tend to be noisier than chain drive but stronger. They also tend to have a longer life. A set of T-case gears will usually outlast the Jeep, but a hard-worked chain drive unit will often need a chain replacement at 60–80,000 miles. Chain drive 'cases also require religious oil changes to last. Chains usually last longer on part-time 'cases because the chain doesn't come into play until the vehicle is shifted into four-wheel drive. The chain is operational all the time in full-time cases.

Chain units use planetary sets instead of gears and because the dynamics of gear ratios can be built more compactly, it's easier to get lower ratios. While it's unusual to find a gear drive 'case with a ratio much under 2.0:1 (the 2.46:1 Dana 18 and 2.6:1 Dana 300 are exceptions), chain drive 'cases are at 2.57:1 or lower.

### Crawl Ratio

One of the terms you may hear bandied about, especially by rock crawlers, is "crawl ratio." This refers to the overall gearing, or final drive ratio, of the vehicle in first gear, low range. To determine crawl ratio, multiply the ratio of first gear times the transfer case low range times the axle ratio. If your first gear is 4:1, your transfer case is 2.72:1, your axle ratio is 4.10 (4.0 x 2.72 x 4.10 = 44.6), and your crawl ratio is 44.6:1.

A low crawl ratio is very important to a rock crawling Jeep or any other situation where low speed control is needed. The ability to idle over rough terrain at 1/4 mile per hour in total control doesn't usually come with stock gearing, especially with manual transmissions. A low crawl ratio is also an asset on descents, where using engine braking is preferred over using the footbrakes. The availability of low gearing doesn't hurt at high altitudes, when the rarefied air has sapped half your engine power. A deep crawl ratio is less important to a desert Jeep, a mudder, or one that is used primarily in easy situations.

The "ideal" crawl ratio is a debatable topic and one that is subject to a great deal of personal preference. There are some rigs down to 350:1. They can idle in gear and the movement is barely perceptible. Even without going to these extremes, it's possible to go so low that first gear is essentially useless 99 percent of the time. Also, the needs of a manual trans and an automatic are quite different (see chapter 6 for more details).

The crawl ratio needed depends on the type of terrain encountered and how much low-end torque your engine develops. A big, torquey engine can get by with a higher ratio than can a four-cylinder. The key is to be low enough that the engine can essentially idle over obstacles at a very low speed without constantly stalling or forcing the driver to slip the clutch.

After quizzing a number of 'wheelers, I'll go out on a limb and give some crawl ratio ranges. For general purpose wheeling with a manual transmission, a range of 40–60:1 will offer good all-around performance. For automatics in the same situations, 35–50:1 works well. For die-hard rock crawlers with stick shifts, 60–100:1 and beyond can be beneficial. For automatics in the same situations, 45–60:1 works well.

### Factory Transfer Cases

The factory T-cases are pretty good units for the most part. Some may debate the handiness of certain ones, such as the short-lived Dana 21 single-speed case that appeared in the 1960s-era Gladiators and Wagoneers with auto boxes. A few of the oddball big Jeep 'cases of the 1970s and 1980s are also questionable.

If you have an option to swap, there may be some benefits to going for another type of T-case. Generally, you are restricted to a few choices unless you plan to swap in a transmission at the same time. Companies like Advance Adapters and Novak build special adapters that widen your range of choices by a big margin, even to 'cases outside of the normal Jeep realm. Here are a few words on each of the factory transfer cases.

Only in the last couple of years have the gear drive transfer cases received some attention. Currently, the Jeep Dana 18 and 20 and the Dana 300 have had gearsets built. Tera-Low's 4:1 kit for the Dana 300, shown here, drops the ratio from an already decent 2.6:1 to 4:1. This kit is reputed to be very quiet. *Courtesy Tera Manufacturing*

## Dana 18

Developed in 1940 by Spicer, this is the original Jeep T-case, and versions of it were manufactured until 1971. While they were designed for modest power, this cast-iron unit can take a fair bit of torque, especially the later versions. Because they are compact and have a decent 2.46:1 low range, they are still popular in buildups. They use an offset rear output position, so a rear differential with a right offset must be used.

The Model 18s can be divided into three general categories, small-shaft (3/4-inch diameter, used in World War II Jeeps with a 1.97:1 low range), medium-shaft (1 1/8-inch diameter, used from 1946 to 1953 and sometimes found later), and big-shaft (1 1/4-inch diameter, used in most 1953–71 Jeeps). The "shaft" refers to the intermediate gear shaft. The big shaft units are preferred because of the increased bearing surfaces. It's possible to remachine a small or medium case to accept a larger shaft, though the World War II era cases are weak in other areas and are best avoided for perfor-

mance applications. Input shafts have either 6 or 10 splines.

## Dana 20

Another great Spicer cast-iron 'case that first appeared in 1963 big Jeeps with manual trans only. In 1972, they replaced the Model 18 in CJs and C-101 and lasted there until 1979. They use a centered rear output and had a marginal 2.03:1 low range. The Model 20 was a variant of the Model 18, so it's possible to use the low range gearing from the older Ford Bronco Dana 20 to get a 2.46:1 low range (the parts are hard to get). With a fair bit of machining, it's also possible to stuff Model 18 gears into the 20. This is another strong unit for its size and it uses a 1 1/4-inch intermediate gear shaft. Input shafts have either 6 or 10 splines.

## Dana 21

A single speed iron unit that's not worth many words. It was used behind automatics in half-ton Gladiators and Wagoneers from 1963 to 1969. It was reliable and strong but useless for anything but mild off-roading.

## NP-200

A divorced cast-iron 'case (meaning not mated to the main trans and connected via a short driveshaft) that was used in the M-715 military Gladiators that were built from 1967 to 1969. It's a relative of the heralded NP-205. It had a very marginal 1.91:1 low range. A good, bulletproof unit but not worth much space because of its oddball nature and limited application.

## Dana 300

This is another variant in the Model 18 and 20 family that was used from 1980 to 1986 CJs. It featured a great 2.67:1 low range and had a centered rear output. It has proven every bit as durable as the other cast-iron units in this family. The Dana 300 is the most popular gear drive T-case for CJs and many are swapped into earlier and later model CJs and even the occasional YJ.

## BW-1339

The original Quadra-Trac. This Borg-Warner transfer case was introduced into the big Jeeps for the 1973 model year and lasted through the 1979 model year. It found its way into the CJ-7 line from 1976 to 1979 as an option. It was an aluminum cased, chain drive, full-time four-wheel-drive transfer case that was the first American incarnation of this configuration. It was

The BW-1339 "Quadra-Trac" full-time unit has been much maligned over the years but actually was a decent gearbox. This unit has the optional 2.57:1 reduction unit (optional on Big Jeeps, standard on CJ-7). It was also fitted with a limited slip center differential that was manually lockable.

always coupled behind a Turbo 400 automatic, and came with or without a low range in big Jeeps—CJs all had the low range. It had an offset (to the right, like the Dana 18) rear output. When so equipped, it had a neat 2.57:1 low range. The center differential featured a limited slip coupling that could be manually locked for a true 50/50 split. This transfer case has been much maligned over the years but in fact, it was an advanced design and is fairly strong. It did cost some fuel economy. Because it has a clutch pack type of limited slip unit as a center diff, it requires a special oil.

## NP-219

Built by New Process gear, the NP-219 was the second incarnation of the Quadra-Trac used in big Jeeps from 1980–1982. It was an all-aluminum full-time 'case that was very similar to the NP-208 part-time t-case introduced the same year. It was nothing special and is fairly rare. It's a toughie to repair due to lack of parts.

## NP-208

Another New Process box for big Jeeps, introduced in 1980 and called "Command-Trac." It was aluminum cased and chain driven but a part-time setup. Unlike the more common GM variant, it had the T-case output on the left. It also had a fixed yoke rear output, unlike the sliding yoke GMs. It features a nice 2.61:1 low range and was seen behind automatics as well as manuals. It lasted to the end of the big Jeeps as a part-

time option and was often behind six-cylinders. It's a durable unit and one of the better chain drive 'cases.

## NP-229

This New Process case was introduced as an option in the big Jeeps in 1983 as the "Selec-Trac" and had some unique features. It was essentially a full-time case with a center diff that could be locked, but it also had a two-wheel-drive mode. It used an aluminum case with a chain and had a 2.61:1 low range. This unit, which lasted through 1986, has a reputation for being cranky, and is tough to repair for lack of parts.

## NP-228

Very similar to the NP-229, it was minus the two-wheel drive—four-wheel-drive Selec-Trac feature. This full-time case used a 2.61:1 low range and was optional from 1985 to 1991 in big Jeeps. Nothing special.

## NP-207

A lightweight, light-duty New Process chain drive, part-time case that was introduced in 1984 with the midsized Cherokee/Comanche XJ models. It was also used for 1987 in Wrangler model YJ. Essentially, it was an early version of the NP-231 that replaced it for 1988 in XJs and YJs. It had a nice 2.72:1 low range.

## NP-231

Introduced in 1988, this part-time transfer case became the mainstay for the XJ and YJ models and continues in those models to this day as the NV-231 (NV for New Venture Gear, essentially a new corporate

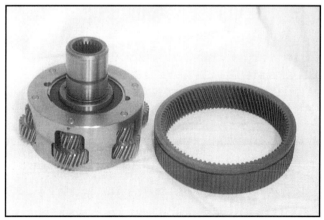

The heart of the NP-231 4:1 low-range conversion from 4 to 1 Manufacturing is this six-gear planetary. Six-gear planetary sets are considerably stronger than the OE three-gear units, but the drop in ratio costs some strength. *Courtesy 4 to 1 Manufacturing*

identity for New Process Gear). It was also used in six-cylinder ZJ models through 1995. Chain driven with a 2.72:1 low range, it's reliable even with more than stock horsepower applied.

## NP-242

Later known as the NV-242. This is a full-time case that was introduced in 1987 for the XJ models as Selec-Trac, and used for a couple of years in the last Grand Cherokee SJ models. The front output was on the left, so it used a front axle so equipped. It's also used on the Grand Cherokee ZJ models as the baseline T-case for six cylinders. It features a lockable center differential and a 2.72:1 low range. Not much use on a dedicated off-highway rig but nice on the highway.

## NV-249

This slick New Venture Gear unit is offered in top-of-the-line Grand Cherokees as the Quadra-Trac. It's a chain drive, full-time T-case with a 2.72:1 low range but uses a viscous coupling to shuttle torque to the front or rear as needed. It's mainly seen behind V-8s. It's pretty user friendly, needing little driver input. In 1996, a lockable center diff was introduced for more challenging terrain, but this is really a Sport-Ute unit that's not suited for hard-core folks.

### *Extra Low Transfer Case Gearing*

Most of these aftermarket improvements come in the form of kits, with one complete T-case available. The kits offer low ranges from 3.5 to 4.87:1, depending on type. The chart in Figure 5-3 shows the crawl ratios available with assorted Jeeps combined with the optional aftermarket transfer case ratios. It's easy to see the benefits of relatively mild axle gearing and deep transfer gears.

A T-case gearing swap could save the expense of axle gearing changes, depending on whether your current axle ratio is suitable for big tires on the street. Still, there are also some potential disadvantages to consider. For one, you are stuck with that very deep low range. With mild gears, it works out fine. When combined with low axle gears, these extra deep T-case ratios can be too low and essentially useless 95 percent of the time. You know best what will work for you.

Also, some of the very lowest gearsets can be noisy. It's not grind-themselves-into-dust noisy, but a harmless, potentially annoying noisy. Considering the benefits, it seems a small price to pay. Here are the various choices by transfer case types.

## NP-231, 241, or 242

The first to debut a kit for these gearboxes was 4 to 1 Manufacturing. The company currently builds two kits for the Jeep, NP-231 (also NP-241 and 242) that offer a 4:1 low range and a 3.5:1 low range. Six gear planetaries are used. A remachined rear case half is also supplied on an exchange basis and the conversion can be done in about 3–4 hours. The 4:1 kit is reputed to be a little noisy in low range but the 3.5:1 kit is very quiet.

Tera-Low, from Mepco Jeep Parts, offers a 4.0:1 low-range kit that is similar in scope but slightly different in execution. It features a new five-gear planetary set and a brand-new rear case half, so you can keep your old stuff for just-in-case.

## Dana 300

Tera-Low 4.0:1 gearsets, mentioned above, are available here as well. This combines deep gearing with an extremely stout cast-iron unit. The gears are high quality items, and the unit is said to be very quiet after the conversion.

## Dana 18

This recently introduced kit from O'Briens 4-Wheel West features a choice of 4.10 or 4.86 low-range gears for the old model 18. The manufacturer claims that these gearsets are stronger and quieter than the originals.

## Dana 20

Hicks 4x4 Specialists makes a kit to drop the Jeep Dana 20 from 2:1 low to a more respectable 2.46:1. The gears are specially made for the purpose. Rumor has it that Tera-Low may have a Dana 20 kit in the offing for late 1998, but details are sketchy.

## Atlas

From Advance Adapters, most famous for providing adapter kits to stuff anything into nearly anything else, comes the Atlas II transfer case. This is an all-new gear-drive case that was designed by Advance Adapters. Though the housing is aluminum, it's heat-treated and quite stout. The Dana 300 and NP-205 provided inspiration for the design. The Atlas II is available with either 3.8 or 4.3:1 low-range gearing. This unit is reputed to be almost "indestructible" (my word, not Advance Adapters') and is the top dollar answer to low gearing needs, combined with a big margin of beef. The Atlas can be configured to replace all the standard Jeep transfers and many other swaps. It's 2 1/2 inches

In the spare-no-expense category, the Atlas II rules supreme. This box was designed from the ground up for beef and utility. This is actually one of the first 3.5:1 prototypes, but the new units offer 3.8 or 4.3:1 ratios in an aluminum case. *Courtesy Advance Adapters*

shorter than the NP-231 with a short tailshaft conversion and 2 inches longer than a Dana 300. At $1,795 (as of this early 1998 writing), it ain't cheap, but it's a lot of beef for the buck.

### NP-231 Tailshaft Conversion

One of the downsides to the New Process chain drive transfer cases in Jeeps is that they are relatively long and have a highly placed, sliding yoke on the rear output. From the OEM perspective, this is fine; it's cheap to build and works well within stock parameters. When it comes to modifications like lifting the vehicle, however, the driveshaft angle becomes a big problem.

The aftermarket has come to the rescue with a number of tailshaft conversions that shorten the NP-231 approximately 4 inches and replace the sliding yoke with a bolted-on yoke. The rear driveshaft must then be lengthened and equipped with a slip yoke. You may also need a CV joint.

The kits from Currie, M.I.T., or JB Conversions are similar in that they come with a replacement rear output shaft, new tailshaft housings, rear output yoke, larger rear output bearings, and installation hardware as needed. They differ in that the Currie and M.I.T. kits use a remachined NP-231 shaft, whereas JB Conversions uses a stronger all-new shaft. In all cases, the net result is a stronger unit. The two kits that use modified 231 shafts retain the strength of the OE shaft, while the JB shaft is about 40 percent stronger than stock. All the kits are good and serviceable but the prices, of course, reflect the differences in the kits.

Advance Adapters recently announced its Orbiter, which is a unique method of lowering the rear output. It's a new housing that bolts to the back of the original case and uses gears to drop the output to lessen driveline angles 50 percent. It does not require T-case disassembly, but does require a new driveshaft.

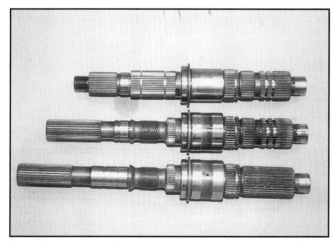

The differences in NP-231 tailshaft lengths are illustrated here. On the bottom is the newest TJ version. In the middle is the standard NP231J version from YJs and others. On top is JB Conversions' heavy-duty shaft. Notice the difference in length as well as diameter.

The typical short tailshaft kit for the NP-231 consists of a short or shortened shaft, rear housing, bearings, and a fixed yoke. Typically, the kits on the market will reduce T-case length by 4-plus inches. Shown is the newest version of JB Conversions' heavy-duty kit. *Courtesy JB Conversions*

## Other T-case and Related Goodies

There are various other t-case–related goodies to consider, including the Currie Twin-Stick shifter for the Dana 300. This item evolved in response to folks running automatic lockers up front. It allows the front axle to be uncoupled from the T-case while in low range. This is easier than climbing out and unlocking a hub in order to make a tight turn or shifting out of four-wheel drive and low range at the same time. It does add another lever to the floor.

The full-time four-wheel drive in a Quadra-Trac can be disabled with a kit from MileMarker. It eliminates the center diff (and the need for the special oil). It will then also require the use of a set of locking hubs up front, also available from MileMarker, Warn Super-winch, or others.

JB Conversions offers a 2-Lo kit for NP-231s that allows you to use two-wheel drive low range. This is useful for Jeepers running automatic lockers up front. The side benefit is that you will have a "true" neutral. Though the current setup prior to about 1996 has a neutral position, it only disconnects the trans from the T-case. It does not uncouple the front and rear outputs. The 2-Lo also provides this feature. This makes the vehicle more easily flat towed.

## T-Case Swapping and Beefing

"Beefing" is a little misleading in the sense that there is little you can do to most T-cases, especially the gear drive units, to beef them up. Most often, a weaker

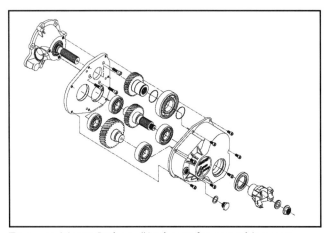

To quote Monty Python, "And now for something completely different!" The Atlas Orbiter is a gear drive unit that bolts on the end of the NP-231 T-case. No disassembly is required. It drops the output 3.7 inches and decreases driveshaft angle by 12 degrees. Transfer case length increases by just over 3/16 of an inch. The unit is very new to the market but looks beefy enough to pass the Jeep owner's durability test.

unit is swapped for a stronger one. There is direct interchangeability between some T-cases, such as a Model 20 with a '69 and a later "big hole" Model 18, but with rear output in a different spot, the rear axle will also need changing. Lots of other pitfalls exist and most often, the swap is done in conjunction with an engine or transmission swap.

Another direct swap possibility is to replace an NP-231 T-case with an NP-241. The late Dodge Ram units with a left front output are suitable. The GM units have the wrong bolt pattern. The 241s interchange with few clearance problems at the skid plate but they will need a tailshaft kit installed because they are longer. This swap has been done to XJ Cherokees with the 231s or to replace later full-time 242 or 249 'cases in Grand Cherokees. Also, the NP231D, a unit used in new Dodge half-tons, can be swapped in with the installation of a tailshaft kit.

As far as strengthening goes, maintenance is a good beginning step. Regular oil changes will keep most T-cases going just about forever. Keep it factory strong longer! Synthetic 90-weight is a good choice for many hard-used gear drive 'cases, because it lessens friction and resists heat better than regular oil. Chain drive boxes can also benefit from synthetics. Fluid changes on chain drive cases should be more frequent due to the heat generated and the light oil used. Careful assembly during a rebuild and quality parts will ensure good performance. In the case of the older small and medium intermediate shaft Dana 18s, a switch to the big 1 1/4-inch shaft can bring some added durability.

The NP-231 has a plethora of modifications available that will turn this already tough T-case into a trail superman. There are three basic versions of the NP-231: the NP 231J is used in Jeeps, the NP231C is used in GM S-series trucks, and the NP231D is used in newer half-ton Dodge Rams.

The NP231J has a three-gear planetary set that can be swapped for a six-gear set from an NP-241. The three-gear piece is rated for 600 lb-ft of torque while the six-gear unit is rated to 1,400 lb-ft. In some cases, you may have to swap in a new input gear as there are early and late planetary sets.

A stronger chain is also available. The 231D model is different in that it uses a 1 1/4-inch chain in place of the 1-inch chain of the 231C and J models. If you buy the chain and sprockets, it swaps right in. The stronger JB Conversions tailshaft kit has already been discussed.

The Warn overdrive for the Dana 18 dates back to the 1960s. A vintage unit is shown here with an optional adapter to allow the use of a power take-off as well as an overdrive. This extremely rare piece was designed to run PTO winches. The modern version of the Warn overdrive is built by Advance Adapters. It's essentially the same unit as before and features a planetary gear with a .75 step up, a fourth or fifth gear if you will.

## Overdrive

Only one overdrive is available for Jeeps as a bolt-on and it fits only the Model 18 'case. The Advance Adapters Saturn unit is one that was invented and marketed by Warn in the 1960s and went out of production in the 1980s. Advance bought the tooling and patents in 1990 and reintroduced it.

The Saturn plugs into the PTO (power take-off) hole of the Dana 18 and provides a 25 percent (.75) over-

drive. The unit uses a planetary set that is operated by a lever. The unit can be used to split gears (a shift to third OD might pull a hill while fourth won't) or as a "fifth" gear for highway cruising. When they took over the product, AA also became a welcome source of repair parts for the old units.

The Saturn is easy to install and durable to 300 lb-ft.

## Splitters

A splitter is essentially a device that fits between the trans and T-case or between the bellhousing and the transmission. It can provide overdrive gearing or underdrive gearing. The units presented here differ in gearing method but all will increase the length of the trans/T-case assembly, decrease the length of the rear driveshaft, and increase the length of the front shaft. This may not be an option in short wheelbase Jeeps that already have driveshaft problems. A splitter could be ideal for a Jeep pickup, Wagoneer, CJ-6, Scrambler, or Jeepster.

The Gear Vendors unit bolts on the back of certain transfer cases and provides a 22 percent overdrive. Since it fits on the rear output, it operates in two-wheel drive only. It's a fairly long piece, so it's suitable only for pickups and other long rigs.

US Gear builds a two-speed unit that fits between the transmission and transfer in just a few applications,

This two-speed splitter fits between the trans and the T-case. Built by 4 to 1, it is optional with planetary sets in 2.72, 3.5, or 4:1. The advantage is that you can operate in standard ratios or extra low, as needed according to terrain. The only disadvantage, beyond the extra torque load on the T-case, is that the unit is 6 3/8 inches long. This requires some play in the wheelbase length. The CJ-7 and YJ are probably the shortest Jeeps that can use one. A 5-inch unit may be available by the time you read this. *Courtesy 4 to 1 Manufacturing*

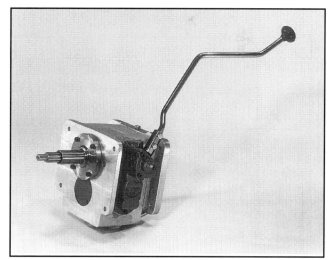

The Ranger two-speed torque splitter was designed and built by Warner Gear in the 1960s. Advance Adapters purchased the design in 1975. It fits between the bellhousing and transmission of certain manual transmission rigs. It's beefy and able to handle 420 lb-ft of engine torque. It can be ordered in a 27 percent (.73) overdrive or 17 percent underdrive (1.17:1). The high range is 1:1. Obviously, with a 7-inch unit length, you need the driveshaft length to play with for this piece. *Courtesy Advance Adapters*

and comes as either a 20 percent overdrive or a 2.25:1 underdrive. Again, it's suitable only for longer rigs.

The Ranger II units come from Advance Adapters and bolt between the bellhousing and the trans. The application is only for a small number of four-speed manuals using Ford, GM, or Dodge bellhousing patterns. The unit can be purchased as a 27 percent overdrive or a 17 percent underdrive. The Ranger is intended more as an aid to towing than a serious off-highway tool, but can be used as such if you have the driveshaft length (4.8–5.2 inches) to spare. It will handle 420 lb-ft of torque.

4 to 1 Manufacturing builds a splitter that provides a 2.72:1 underdrive (essentially, it's the planetary set from an NP-241 in a special case) to which you split or combine gears. Optionally, you can have it fitted with 3.5:1 or 4.0:1 gearsets. With the 2.72:1 unit, if you leave the transfer case in high and shift the splitter into low, you end up with a 2.72 ratio. If you kick in the T-case low (say it's a Dana 20 with a 2.03:1 low range), your ratio becomes 5.52:1. In some ways, this is better than an extra-low low range because your gearing can reflect what is required by conditions. The downside is that the unit increases the length of the gearbox by 6 3/8 inches, making it suitable for trucks and long wheelbase rigs only. Ask about a shorter unit about 5 inches long, which is expected soon.

## FACTORY JEEP TRANSFER CASE ROUNDUP

| Model | Low Range | Type/Output | Drive | Years | Application |
|---|---|---|---|---|---|
| Dana 18 | 2.46:1 | gear/offset | part | 1941–71 | CJ, FC, PU, SW, C101 |
| Dana 20 | 2.03 | gear/center | part | 1963–79 | CJ, SJ, C101 |
| Dana 21 | 1.00 | gear/center | part | 1963–69 | SJ(1) |
| Dana 200 | 1.91 | gear/center/ divorced | part | 1967–69 | M-715 |
| Dana 300 | 2.60 | gear/center | part | 1980–86 | CJ |
| BW-1339 | 2.57 | chain/center | full | 1973–79 | SJ(2) |
| NP-219 | 2.60 | chain/center | full | 1980–82 | SJ |
| NP-208 | 2.61 | chain/center | part | 1980–91 | SJ(3) |
| NP-229 | 2.61 | chain/center | part/full | 1983–86 | SJ(4) |
| NP-228 | 2.61 | chain/center | full | 1985–91 | SJ |
| NP-207 | 2.72 | chain/center | part | 1984–87 | YJ, XJ |
| NP-231 | 2.72 | chain/center | part | 1988–97 | TJ, YJ, XJ, |
| NP-242 | 2.72 | chain/center/full | part/ | 1987–97 | XJ, ZJ |
| NP-249 | 2.72 | chain/center | full | 1996–97 | ZJ |

1. A single speed case used with automatics.
2. The original Quadra-Trac full-time case.
3. The optional part-time case.
4. Selec-Trac, a unit that features both full- and part-time modes.

### Transfer Case/Trans Adapter Availability Chart
Covers Popular Manuals and Automatics. Mfrs. offer many more possibilities.

| T-Case to Trans | Manufacturers |
|---|---|
| Dana 300 to Ford T-18 | Advance Adapters and Novak |
| Dana 18 and 20 to Ford T-18 NP-231 to Ford T-18 | Advance Adapters |
| Dana 300 to Ford T-19 | Advance Adapters and Novak |
| Dana 18 and 20 to Ford T-19 NP-231 to Ford T-19 | Advance Adapters |
| Dana 300 to Ford NP-435 | Advance Adapters and Novak |
| Dana 18 and 20 to Ford NP-435 NP-231 to Ford NP-435 | Advance Adapters and Novak |

Twin stick T-case kits are available for certain applications that allow a shift from four-wheel drive to two-wheel drive while in low range. This is useful to Jeepers who have an automatic locker fitted up front. In some cases, the locker will engage during maneuvers on the trail and tuning gets difficult. Disengaging the front axle allows for tight turning without having to get out and unlock a hub. This kit is from Mepco. *Courtesy Mepco*

This is a typical T-case adapter. This Advance Adapter kit mates a TH-400 to a Dana 300 T-case. The kits available usually reflect the good combinations. If you have an idea for a swap and can't find an appropriate kit in the Novak or Advance Adapters catalog, it's probably either a bad match or really obscure, like a Studebaker 289 to a LaSalle four-speed to a Dana 300. *Courtesy Advance Adapters*

| T-Case to Trans | Manufacturers |
|---|---|
| Dana 300 to GM NP-435 | Advance Adapters and Novak |
| Dana 18 and 20 to GM NP-435 | |
| NP-231 to GM NP-435 | Advance Adapters |
| Dana 300 to Dodge NP-435 | Advance Adapters and Novak |
| Dana 18 and 20 to Dodge NP-435 | |
| NP-231 to Dodge NP-435 | Advance Adapters |
| Dana 300 to SM-420 | Advance Adapters and Novak |
| Dana 18 and 20 to SM-420 | |
| NP-231 to SM-435 | Advance Adapters |
| Dana 300 to SM-465 | Advance Adapters and Novak |
| Dana 18 and 20 to SM-465 | |
| NP-231 to SM-465 | Advance Adapters |
| Dana 300 to WC T-5 | Advance Adapters |
| NP-231 to WC T-5 | |

| T-Case to Trans | Manufacturers |
|---|---|
| Dana 300 to NV-4500 | Advance Adapters, Novak , and JB Conversions |
| Dana 18 and 20 to NV-4500 | Advance Adapters |
| NP-231 to NV-4500 | Advance Adapters, and JB Conversions |
| Dana 300 to TH-350 | Advance Adapters, and Novak |
| Dana 18 and 20 to TH-350 | |
| NP-231 to TH-350 | Advance Adapters |
| Dana 300 to TH-400 | Advance Adapters, and Novak |
| Dana 18 and 20 to TH-400 | factory parts, Advance Adapters, and Novak |
| NP 231 to TH-400 | Advance Adapters |
| Dana 300 to TH-700R4 | Advance Adapters |
| Dana 18 and 20 to TH-700R4 | |
| NP-231 to TH-700R4 | |
| Dana 300 to 727 Torqueflite | factory parts |
| Dana 18 and 20 to 727 Torqueflite | Advance Adapters |
| Dana 300 to Ford C4 | Advance Adapters |
| Dana 19 and 20 to Ford C4 | |
| NP-231 to Ford C4 | |
| Dana 18 and 20 to Ford C6 | Advance Adapters |
| NP-231 to Ford C4 | Advance Adapters |
| NP-231 to Ford AOD | |

## SELECT LOW-RANGE CRAWL RATIO COMBINATIONS

**4.0:1 first gear**

| Axle | | | | | T-Case Ratio | | | | |
|------|------|------|------|------|------|------|------|------|------|
| Ratio | 2.00 | 2.46 | 2.60 | 2.72 | 3.00 | 3.50 | 3.80 | 4.00 | 4.50 |
| 3.07 | 25.6 | 30.2 | 31.9 | 33.4 | 36.8 | 43.0 | 46.7 | 49.1 | 55.2 |
| 3.55 | 28.4 | 34.9 | 36.9 | 38.6 | 42.6 | 49.7 | 53.2 | 56.8 | 63.9 |
| 3.73 | 29.8 | 36.7 | 38.8 | 40.6 | 44.8 | 52.2 | 56.7 | 59.7 | 67.1 |
| 4.10 | 32.8 | 40.3 | 42.6 | 44.6 | 49.2 | 57.4 | 62.3 | 65.6 | 73.8 |
| 4.56 | 36.4 | 44.8 | 47.4 | 49.6 | 54.7 | 63.8 | 69.3 | 73.0 | 82.1 |
| 5.38 | 43.0 | 52.9 | 55.9 | 58.5 | 64.6 | 75.3 | 81.8 | 86.1 | 96.8 |

If you have a Quadra-Trac (BW 1339) and want to eliminate the full-time four-wheel-drive feature, Mile-Marker has been building a kit for many years. The kit includes new chain and gears and, optionally, new locking hubs (the OE axles were not fitted with hubs). The new chain is a good idea because, being an offset rear output, the chain is in action all the time. *Courtesy Mile-Marker*

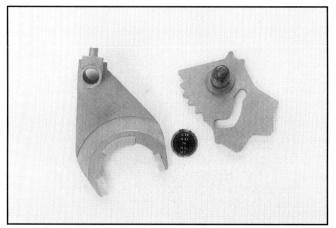

Drivers of Wranglers like their automatic front lockers as much as anyone. A means to disconnect the front axle in low range was a hot item when JB Conversions debuted a 2-Lo kit last year. Up to 1996, the NP-231 did not have a "true neutral" position, meaning that the front and rear outputs were still connected in neutral. This made flat towing a problem. The 2-Lo kit includes parts for this upgrade. *Courtesy JB Conversions*

# TRANSMISSION
## Multiplying Torque

Transmission swaps rate somewhere between axle and engine swaps in popularity with Jeepers. Often an engine and tranny swap go hand in hand. Lack of strength or reliability is one issue, gearing is another. Either way, you have many options.

What does the transmission do? It's a torque multiplier, of course, but it does more. Unlike an electric motor that makes full torque as soon as power is turned on, your Jeep's internal combustion engine must be running at some speed to do it. In order to get your engine turning at a speed sufficient to generate the necessary torque for moving the vehicle, we must have a device that gears the engine down to a ratio that allows it to run at a higher rpm than the output of the gearing device. Since we typically need a wide range of speed options, from three to five speeds (even six in some of the latest vehicles) are provided.

Transmission types are divided into two very distinct categories, automatics and manuals. Though they perform the same job, they do it in completely different ways. These differences used to be the source of heated debates among Jeepers but most of the furor has died down to "drive what you like." Still, there are advantages and disadvantages to each transmission type. We'll cover them separately so you can go to the section that applies to your vehicle.

### The Automatic Transmission

The automatic transmission uses a fluid coupling, called a torque convertor, and hydraulic pressure to provide the connection between the engine and the transfer case. Most automatics have three mechanical speeds, many have four, some of the latest have five, and a very few have six. Automatics have all but taken over the trail scene. While many dedicated stick-shifters will curl their lips into a sneer at the thought, the automatic is superior to the manual in many ways out in the boonies.

With an autobox, you can get away with somewhat

taller gearing because, in effect, the torque converter is a variable-ratio first gear. The mechanical first gear ratios of most automatics, 2.4–3:1, don't sound impressive until you multiply by the torque converter ratio, typically 2.0–2.5:1, to get the effect of a lower gear. Remember, however, that the "ratio" changes with engine speed. You might have a 2.5:1 converter ratio at 850 rpm but by 1,000 rpm, it's down to about 1.5:1 and by 1,500, the converter is locked up at nearly 1:1.

One advantage to autoboxes is that they can be almost infinitely tuned. They can be made to shift harder, softer, faster, or to shift manually. The torque converter ratio can be altered. The mechanical gearing can be changed. In short, you can have it how you want it.

There are some tradeoffs and caveats with autoboxes. For one, you are trading the flexibility of that

Reworked automatics can be had from a variety of sources and built to a plethora of specs. This B&M TH-350 is equipped with performance friction plates, an adjustable modulator, improved bushings, a recalibrated valve body, and a bevy of other improvements that make this unit a massive improvement over the original design. For a hard-worked trail machine, a tranny like this could be a durability asset. *Courtesy B&M*

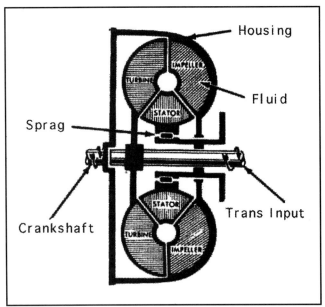

The torque converter laid bare. This is your basic converter. More modern units also feature a lockup device that couples the turbine to the housing and eliminates slipping. The sprag may be the weakest link in a hard-worked torque converter.

variable-ratio first gear for heat. Especially with tall gears, that automatic can get roasting hot on the trail very quickly. That means every automatic-equipped trail Jeep ought to have a temp gauge hooked up and monitored at all times. You may have to buy an auxiliary cooler to maintain safe temps. Deep oil pans and shift kits can also reduce automatic transmission temperatures.

Another automatic tradeoff is decreased engine braking on descents when compared to a manual trans. That variable-ratio converter only works in one direction, with engine power applied. The converter slips some on downhills, so you'll have to use the footbrakes more than with a manual. Lower axle or T-case gears help.

Because of the fluid coupling of the torque converter, automatics are much gentler on the drivetrain than manuals. Often, depending on your driving style and engine torque, you can get by with slightly lighter-duty drivetrain components. For example, a CJ-7 with a 300-horsepower 350 Chev and a manual transmission will definitely need a Dana 44 front axle. The same rig with an automatic could probably survive with the stock Dana 30.

### Torque Converter Tech

The torque converter is both a fluid coupling and a torque multiplier. Unlike a standard manual trans clutch, there is no direct connection between the engine crankshaft and the trans input shaft. So how does this wondrous device work?

The torque converter has three main components. The impeller is a set of turbine blades that is directly connected to the engine via the main housing of the unit. In a mirror position directly opposite the impeller, but not connected to it, is the turbine. The turbine is connected to the input of the gearbox via a shaft. Between is the stator, which is another turbine-like device. The whole convertor is filled with automatic transmission fluid, which is basically a 10-weight hydraulic-type oil, that is pumped through the converter by a pump at the front of the transmission housing.

Driven by the engine, the impeller spins and its curved blades scoop oil from the center of the housing. Directed by the impeller blades, centrifugal force throws the fluid with great force into the turbine, whose blades are curved in the opposite direction of the impeller's. Faced with massive amounts of fluid at high speed, the turbine has no choice but to move and power is transmitted.

By itself, these two turbines are inefficient, because the fluid coming off the turbine blades is traveling against impeller rotation and tends to disrupt flow. The stator in the middle is the key element. At low speeds, the stator changes the direction of the returning fluid from the turbine and gives it a smooth path back to the impeller. Because of the way the stator vanes are angled, fluid pressure from the turbine tries to turn the stator in the opposite direction, but a one-way clutch (called a sprag) locks it into place.

As the turbine speed increases, centrifugal force begins to throw the fluid in the turbine back into the fluid coming from the impeller. A pressure spot is created at the outermost part of the convertor, where the turbine and impeller meet. As this pressure increases, a hydraulic lock occurs and the turbine begins to match impeller speed. The sprag clutch releases and the stator begins to rotate with them. By about 2,000 rpm (or wherever stall speed is designed to occur), the speeds of these components have matched and the convertor is 96 percent locked up.

Without a lockup device, lockup efficiency peaks at about 96 percent because torque convertors are not a perfect coupling. There is always some slippage, and 4 percent is considered good. This 4 percent, along with the extra power required to turn the automatic (20 to

Keeping your tranny cool starts with a gauge kit. The sending unit goes into the return line from the cooler. This return oil is used to cool and lubricate hard working parts. Monitor your tranny temp under a variety of conditions and preferably at the maximum ambient temp you may encounter. Then you can start shopping for an appropriate cooler. *Courtesy B&M*

40 horsepower vs. about 11 horsepower to turn the average manual trans), are the reasons that performance and economy are slightly less with an automatic than a manual. The extra power is wasted due to fluid pumping losses and slippage.

In late model transmissions, the slipping problem at cruising speeds is eliminated by installing a lockup device in the torque convertor. This device completely locks the converter at road speeds, providing a true 1:1 coupling and greatly adding to highway fuel economy. Since slippage also results in heat, the lockup convertor also reduces trans temps.

### Stall Speed

Stall speed is one of those definitions that is difficult to pin down because it has so many caveats. In general, the stall speed refers to the amount of slippage built into the converter. The more specific definition is the maximum rpm the engine will attain with the trans in gear, the brakes on hard, and the engine floored. This may be a difficult situation to attain because some V-8s are powerful enough to overcome the brakes.

Another term in this category is "flash" stall speed, which is the rpm attained by the engine from a full throttle start from a dead stop. Of the two, the first definition is the one used by OE and aftermarket builders to define their product's performance. The second one may be more useful to compare old and new convertors in the same applications.

The problem with pinning down stall speed is that it's infinitely variable according to engine torque, vehicle weight, and gearing (which includes the effect of tire height). Say a stock Jeep with a 258-cid, 215-lb-ft engine, 4.10 gears, and 33-inch tires has a 1,500-rpm stall speed. Then the owner swaps in a 401 V-8 with 325 lb-ft. The same converter might produce a 2,000-rpm stall speed.

### Selecting a Converter

Choosing a converter is done on two levels, via performance and via durability. The durability question really only comes into play with high power rigs. A stock type converter is plenty strong for most Jeepers, but if you think your monster engine will break a stock unit, there are superbeefy race converters out there to fit your needs.

Many Jeepers' first impulse is to choose a "loose" converter with a higher stall speed. Often this may be necessary for an engine that has a torque band that starts at a higher rpm. The pros of this choice are increased torque multiplication and the effect of a lower gear at low speeds. The cons are decreased downhill engine braking and more heat. If you choose a converter with a high enough stall speed, you can create what is called the "Dynaflow" effect. This effect is really nothing more than continuous slippage at cruising speed. If you choose a converter with a 3,000-rpm stall speed and your vehicle cruises at 2,500 rpm at 60 miles per hour, the converter will be continuously slipping at that speed, generating lots of heat and wasting fuel.

On the other side of the coin, some Jeepers choose a "tight" converter with a low stall speed. This reduces the gearing and torque multiplication effects, which are the cons to this scenario. On the bright side, smart builders will counter their tight converters with lower trans gears, or axle gears to compensate. These mods create better low rpm throttle response, much less heat, and better downhill braking.

Converter stall speed is controlled by the internal design but in general, the diameter of the converter can be used as the indicator of stall speed. If the 11-inch converter in your Torqueflite is too tight for your V-8 power, you could install an OE type 10-inch converter from a less powerful engine to gain some stall speed. The reverse is also true. Bear in mind that installing a converter designed for a 150-horsepower engine into a 300-horsepower engine may result in durability problems. But in many cases, the same internal pieces covered a wide range of power outputs.

### Sprags

One of the weak links of a hard-worked converter is the sprag. As mentioned earlier, it's a device to prevent the stator from turning in a reverse direction. When a converter fails, this is typically the piece that goes. A broken sprag is usually an issue with high power/torque applications. A stocker or mildly modified rig is unlikely to have trouble, but the rigors of a hard-core rock crawler might overcome a stock sprag. Race converters will usually have an improved sprag installed, while street/trail performance converters may use the OE style. This is something you can talk over with the converter builder.

### Transmission Temp Control

Some transmissions run hotter than others. Taller gears, more weight, and higher stall speeds can create more heat. So does towing and four-wheeling. Have a look at the trans temp chart in Figure 6-1. Three hundred degrees is not uncommon for a four-wheeling Jeep on a hot day. At this temp, your fluid gets fried in a short time. To avoid heat problems, Step One is to install a temp gauge. If you do nothing else with your automatic, do this. At least, when you get into a critical temp zone, you can stop and let it cool down before it cooks.

Opinions differ on the best place to install the trans temp gauge sender. B&M recommends installing it on the *return* line from the cooler to the trans. This is logical since the returned oil is used for cooling and lubricating the planetary gears and clutch packs. Hot, cooked oil doesn't lubricate well. On the other hand, some Jeepers think it's more useful to monitor the actual temp of the fluid by installing the sensor on the transmission out line. A compromise is to install sensors in both lines, with a switch so you can monitor both temperatures.

Ideally your temps will run at 175 degrees, on a hot day or a cold day. In reality, if it runs over 160 on the cold days and less than 220 on hard-working hot days, you're doing well. Keep in mind ambient temps when testing; given the same type of work, a cool day will show lower temps than a hot one. If the temps are under 220 degrees under the hardest conditions and hottest days, don't sweat the extra cooler. If you see 250 degrees your trans needs help.

Before you run off to buy a cooler, bear in mind that other modifications may affect trans temp. If you plan some mods ahead, such as a change of torque converter, tire diameter, or gears, best wait until all your

A high-performance clutch for your modified stick shift Jeep could be the difference between supplying that stump-pulling torque to the wheels or using it to fry your OE clutch. This Centerforce diaphragm clutch features counterweights on the diaphragm fingers to increase clutch pressure with rpms. This feature may not help you as much on a slow speed trail as would increased clamping pressure or a higher coefficient of friction on the disc. Finding the right clutch for a modified Jeep could turn into a fine balancing act. *Courtesy Centerforce*

other mods are done so you can gauge cooling needs against your final conditions. A swap from 3.08 gears to 4.10s, for example, could drop your working temp down 40 degrees. Overcooling the automatic is also possible.

### The OE Transmission Cooler

There are several ways to cool an automatic. The first is already built in—the radiator cooler. Don't knock it! This cooler sits in the "cool" radiator tank and can knock up to 40 degrees off the trans fluid temp. It also warms the fluid on cold days to prevent your trans from collecting moisture in cold weather. Increasing your engine cooling system (a larger radiator) will enhance the tranny cooler as well. Your radiator shop can often install a larger cooler in the radiator.

Though not actually a cooling method, a change of oil in a hard-worked trans can keep it going longer. If your Jeep regularly sees high temps, at least change the fluid before it breaks down and eats your automatic (use the trans temp chart as a guide). Also, synthetic transmission fluids are capable of withstanding higher temperatures before breaking down. Ditto for high-performance fluids like B&M's Trick Shift. These items are also nice enhancements to any other steps you take.

### Deep Pans

One of the simplest cooling solutions is a deep pan. Built by a number of manufacturers out of stamped steel or cast aluminum, these pans hold a few extra quarts of vital fluid. There are also trans pans with cooling fins or cooling tubes. Finned or tubed pans are reputed to knock 20-50 degrees off trans temps, if they get airflow. (Airflow on a rocky trail at two miles per hour, right!)

Honestly, the above ideas are best used to supplement a more ideal solution, such as an external cooler.

### External Transmission Coolers

External coolers come in a couple of designs, fin and tube, and stacked units. The stacked coolers are more efficient and more compact than the fin and tube style, but much more expensive. Remember that how well any air-to-air cooler does depends on the size of the cooler, the heat differential between the oil and the air, and the amount of airflow. Unfortunately, there is no easy formula for a tranny cooler choice. Most manufacturers rate them according to GVW ratings (since they are sold mostly for towing and RV applications), and this doesn't give the Jeeper much to go on.

On average, a large, efficient cooler will knock 50–100 degrees off the oil temp, if there is sufficient airflow. To maximize cooler effectiveness, make sure it has airflow. So much the better if the cooler is placed in front of the radiator and the engine cooling fan helps with this at low speeds (bear in mind any potential engine cooling problems first). Some folks have installed coolers with auxiliary fans that are thermostatically controlled to start as needed.

### Automatic Gearing Changes

A gearing change can enhance the performance of your automatic transmission. Automatics have only recently been available with lower ratio gearings, both from the factory and aftermarket. These gears, usually first and second, fit many existing Jeep automatics (see page 102). You can either drop your overall first gear ratio (mechanical plus converter) or go to a tighter converter and balance this loss with a drop in mechanical ratio.

A-1 Transmission offers low ratio first and second gear sets to fit many popular automatics, including the Chrysler Torqueflites and GM TH-400s used in some Jeeps. The current Jeep Wrangler three-speed auto already has a 2.74:1 first, as did many of the 999 and 904 boxes of CJs in years gone by. Nothing is available for the current line of Aisin-Warner automatics.

We've only talked about lower gears so far, how about overdrive units? Many of the late-model factory Jeep automatics use four-speed autos, the fourth being an overdrive gear. These Aisin-Warner gearboxes offer the best of both worlds and have proven plenty tough in hard work situations, even with enhanced engine power outputs.

Other units can be swapped in, such as the GM 700R4 (later versions are called 4L60 or 4L60E) and the Ford AOD (not common). These automatics are longer than the 'box they replace, so you need to have adequate wheelbase. They can be adapted to the stock Jeep engines, but they are generally seen with engine swaps. For more information on overdrive options, see chapter 5.

## The Manual Transmissions

The manual gearbox has a direct connection to the engine, via the clutch, so the ratios are lower than with an automatic. They offer more precise control than an automatic but they require much more skill from the driver. Choosing gear ratios (trans, T-case and axles) is much more important with the manual because there is no variable ratio torque converter to take up the gear ratio slack.

In the old days, three-speed manuals were the norm. They used relatively tall first gears (in the 3.0:1 range). These were fine for mild situations but four-wheelers (moderate and hard-core alike) soon learned that a minimum of 4:1 is needed for most trails. A torquey engine can get by with a 3.0:1 manual, but the problem is that you can't go slowly enough in some situations so you have to slip the clutch or stall a lot.

The first improvement discovered by Jeepers was the truck four-speed. These usually had a low "granny" gear, from 6 to 7:1. Second gear was usually about equal to the OE three-speed's first. The Warner T-98, the GM SM-420, and the New Process NP-420 and 435 became popular Jeep swaps and remain so today.

Still, things have changed. For one, many newer Jeeps come with four- and five-speeds with adequate ratios. The Wrangler YJ and TJ AX-15 five-speed is not only durable but it has a near 4:1 first gear and an overdrive fifth to boot. There was also the T-5 and Peugeot BA-10 five-speeds, but these had marginal reliability records.

Going further back, the 1970s and 1980s CJs had optional Warner T-18s with 4.03 or 6.32:1 first gears. Going even further back, the T-98, with a 6.40 first, appeared in a wide range of Jeeps back to 1955. The Tremec T-176 was another decent four-speed of the late CJ era.

As to popular modern HD four-speed swaps, in addition to the old stand-bys listed above, the SM-465 (an updated SM-420) can be added to the list, but the trend lately has been toward the New Venture NV-4500 five-speeds. These combine the truck beef of the old New Process four-speeds with an overdrive fifth.

Two versions of the NV-4500 have been available since their 1992 debut. From 1992 to 1994, GM offered a version with a 6.32:1 first. Dodge has also offered the NV-4500 since 1992, but its had a taller 5.61:1 ratio, which GM now also uses. The lower-geared box is preferred but is expensive and very hard to find.

As you would guess, the NV-4500 is longer than most of the trannys it replaces, so this makes them most suitable for longer Jeeps, such as the CJ-7, YJ, TJ, and, of course, trucks. A commonly noted disadvantage with the NV-4500 is its wide gear spacing. This isn't usually a problem with very torquey engines, but can result in a lot of shifting with less powerful ones. Adapters are made by Advance Adapters, Novak, JB Conversions, and others to fit these beefy boxes to a variety of engine/transfer case combinations.

### Manual Trans Mods

There isn't much in the way of hop-up stuff for manual gearboxes. One enhancement is to switch to synthetic gear lube, or at least more frequent oil changes. The synthetic oil will resist high temps and help your manual to shift smoothly in hot or cold conditions.

In some cases, it's possible to swap gearsets to obtain different ratios. The T-18 is one such candidate. You can upgrade synchronizers and shafts also, but this gets highly technical and often it's cheaper to find the better tranny and swap it in.

## Clutches

The connection between the engine and the manual trans is often forgotten in the buildup process. Any significant modification that affects the drivetrain should be accompanied by a new look at the clutch components to make sure they are up to the task. Those mods would include an increase in engine torque, change of gearing, change of wheels and tires, or a significant increase in weight.

In some cases, there will be enough reserve in the OE style clutch assembly to absorb the extra loads. All that may be necessary is a change to higher quality parts to give you back a reserve. Other times, an upgrade is necessary and this could occur on many

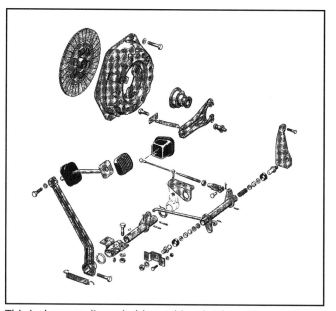

This is the complicated old stand-by clutch mechanism for most Jeep products to 1972. The pedal comes up through the floor, and chassis flex can bind the pedal or the linkage. Chassis flex or weak engine and trans mounts can actually allow parts of this assembly to fall off. *Courtesy Jeep, from the 1972 parts book.*

levels. OE Jeep clutch information can be found on page 103.

The clutch uses three principles to achieve a torque connection: friction, lining area, and pressure plate spring pressure (or the pressure at which the clutch plate is gripped between the pressure plate and flywheel). How much of each is dependent on the design of the clutch itself, and there are unlimited combinations. Obviously an 11-inch clutch disc has more lining and friction area than a 10-inch disc, but if the smaller piece has a pressure plate that exerts more clamping pressure, they may be equal in torque capacity.

### Clutch Discs

Just as with brakes, the lining material on the disc plays an important part in clutch performance. In fact, the materials are very similar (see chapter 9 for more on lining materials). Different linings have different friction coefficients and different resistance to heat. Performance clutch manufacturers are going more and more to composite materials, due to their increased resistance to wear and heat resistance.

The clutch disc consists of five elements: the splined hub that slides along the tranny input shaft, the drive plate, the back plate, the lining, and the springs. The disc actually pivots a little around the hub.

This movement is dampened by small coil springs in the center of the disc that smooth the engagement. More springs means a smoother engagement.

### Pressure Plates

The pressure plate is the most complicated part of the clutch assembly. Not only does it have to securely clamp the disc, but it has to smoothly release. Jeep pressure plates come in two common styles, the diaphragm style and the lever type. There are some subcategories within each type but the details are not helpful.

The diaphragm clutch is the new guy on the block and has all but taken over, due to its light weight, ease of manufacture, and compact dimensions. A piece of spring steel with fingers cut in provides the clamping force, which is very even. In its basic form, the diaphragm clutch does not use centrifugal force to apply extra pressure at high rpms. Performance diaphragm clutches from Centerforce, however, have flyweights added to the fingers to deliver additional clamping force at high revs. The old lever type clutch applies pressure through coil springs (between 3 and 12 depending on which Jeep) between the cover of the unit and the cast-iron pressure plate The effect is heightened by a built-in centrifugal assist device that applies more clamping force at higher rpms. Most older Jeeps have this type of pressure plate. These clutches are large, heavy, and don't dissipate heat well. They also tend to apply a somewhat uneven pressure.

### Clutch Selection Basics

The first bit of advice you will hear from anyone in the performance area is to always use new pieces as opposed to rebuilt. Rebuilt stuff can be OK, but apparently the quality is spotty, and sometimes a piece that should have been trashed ends up being rebuilt.

The second bit of advice is to reevaluate the clutch system every time the engine torque or the weight of the Jeep is increased, or the gearing is changed (which includes adding taller tires). Oddly enough, a change to taller gears can induce clutch chatter in some cases.

If you're thinking about an engine swap, a clutch upgrade is a no-brainer. The old clutch may look similar and even bolt up to the new engine, but it may still may be inadequate. One easy solution is to use a clutch that came with the bigger engine. In addition, the aftermarket offers upgraded assemblies. Centerforce's Gold line offers a bolt-on 30 percent increase in capacity with no tradeoffs beyond a higher cost. Other

manufacturers offer similar upgrades and you can go up from there.

Another reason to look for a stronger clutch is heavy-duty use. Remember that tough terrain where you had to slip the clutch so much that you were smelling roasted clutch for days afterward? A clutch with a better lining can withstand the heat better.

Since clamping pressure is part of the game, you may consider stronger springs in the pressure plate. This may work, but bear in mind that it will increase clutch pedal effort, may overstress the clutch release mechanism, and can make the clutch grabby and hard to control.

A racing clutch is an option, but may not be a good one for a 4x4. Most racing clutches rely on rpm and centrifugal force to apply extra clamping pressure. Both of these are in short supply on a rocky trail at 1,200 rpm. If you fit into the as-slow-as-possible crowd, look for a clutch that has more static pressure or a higher friction coefficient. Finally, if you have an odd combination, the clutch manufacturer can help you make the choices for your particular application.

### The Clutch Release Mechanism

To 1972, the Jeep CJs, the Willys Pickups, FCs, and Station Wagons used a mechanical bellcrank- the floor. This setup is cranky but livable in light-duty situations. For more difficult situations, chassis and body flex can

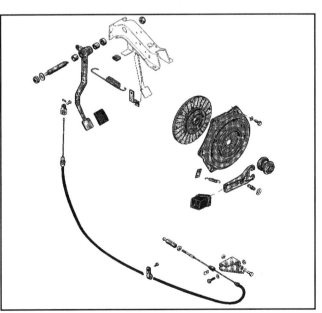

Next to hydraulic clutches, a cable setup is the most adaptable type of clutch linkage. This setup was used for 1972–73 Jeepsters and a similar setup was fitted to a few other Jeeps. *Courtesy Jeep, from the 1972 parts book.*

cause it to fall apart, bind, break, and release the clutch all by itself.

The 1972 CJs used hanging pedals and a cable, which was much better, but 1973–79 rigs kept hanging pedals but went back to a bellcrank-style linkage. In 1980, when the new four-cylinder CJ debuted, it used a hydraulic setup with a slave cylinder outside the bellhousing. The sixes kept the bellcrank setup right to the end. A cable-operated oddball appeared in 1986 2.5-liter fours, mixed in with the hydraulics.

Jeepsters from 1967 to 71 used hanging pedals and cables that eliminated some of the problems, but they still had a trans-to-frame bracket that could cause trouble. The 1972–73 Commando models used a cable that was similar to the CJ.

Big Jeeps used hanging pedals from their debut in 1963 and used a rod-style mechanical linkage well into 1971 for V-8s, when they went to a cable setup. Oddly, the 230 OHC sixes had a hydraulic setup. Like the other rigs in the Jeep stable, the big Jeeps went back to a rod and bellcrank setup in 1973, for reasons that are not clear.

The YJs and XJs use a hydraulic setup with the slave cylinder and throwout bearing as a single assembly mounted inside the bellhousing. This assembly is plastic and somewhat prone to trouble. Some owners have upgraded to an all-metal unit built by Advance Adapters.

## Upgrading Clutch Linkage

Whether to upgrade the clutch release mechanism is often an issue with the rigs using the awful mechanical setups. The usual choice is to go hydraulic, swapping in hydraulic pieces from the 1980–86 four-cylinder rigs. This is almost a bolt-on, with some minor adaptation necessary. Often this is accompanied by a swap to the 1973 and later hanging pedal assemblies.

Another linkage problem is increased clutch pedal effort, due to a stronger pressure plate installed with an engine swap or an upgrade. This is an issue of simple leverage. If you have retained the old bellcrank linkage, Advance Adapters has a chain-operated clutch control kit that offers better leverage. Some owner/fabricators modify the linkages by welding on longer arms to the bellcrank assembly to gain some additional leverage over the stiffer clutch.

When dealing with hydraulic clutches, the same hydraulic principles apply that you will read about in the brake chapter. A smaller bore, longer stroke clutch master, or a larger bore slave cylinder will decrease pedal effort.

Engine swaps from a kit often include the necessary clutch pieces but sometimes the gear will come from the donor engine. Overall, a hydraulic setup is the most easily fitted.

A tranny cooler in this locale will benefit from airflow both from road speed and fan. This fin and tube unit covers nearly half the radiator. If this Jeep had an engine cooling problem from an engine swap, this tranny cooler could be the answer. Fin and tube type coolers generally need to be larger than stacked coolers to do the same job. If a cooler this big were actually needed (doubtful), then a stacked cooler only half this size could do the same job, thus uncovering more radiator area for engine cooling.

### TRANSMISSION FLUID TEMP CHART

| Constant Temperature (degrees) | Approximate Life of Trans. Fluid (miles) |
|---|---|
| 175 | 100,000 |
| 195 | 50,000 |
| 212 | 25,000 |
| 235 | 12,000 |
| 255 | 6,250 |
| 275 | 3,000 |
| 295 | 1,500 |
| 315 | 750 |
| 335 | 325 |
| 355 | 160 |

## FACTORY JEEP TRANSMISSION SPECS, 1946–1998

**Part 1. Jeep Manual Transmissions**

| Type | Speeds | Shift | 1st | 2nd | 3rd | 4th | 5th | Rev. | Years | Note |
|------|--------|-------|-----|-----|-----|-----|-----|------|-------|------|
| T90 | 3 | col/flr | 2.79 | 1.55 | 1.00 | — | — | 3.79 | 1945–72 | 1 |
| T98 | 4 | flr | 6.40 | 3.09 | 1.69 | 1.00 | — | 7.82 | 1955–70 | 2 |
| T14 | 3 | flr | 3.10 | 2.61 | 1.00 | — | — | 3.10 | 1967–71 | 3 |
| T89 | 3 | flr/col | 3.17 | 1.92 | 1.00 | — | — | 4.12 | 1963–68 | 4 |
| T15 | 3 | flr | 2.97 | 1.55 | 1.00 | — | — | N/A | 1970–79 | 5 |
| T86cc | 3 | flr | 3.39 | 1.85 | 1.00 | — | — | 4.53 | 1967–71 | 6 |
| T86aa | 3 | flr | 2.88 | 1.68 | 1.00 | — | — | N/A | 1967–71 | 7 |
| T150 | 3 | flr | 2.99 | 1.75 | 1.00 | — | — | 3.17 | 1976–79 | 8 |
| T18 | 4 | flr | 4.03 | 2.42 | 1.69 | 1.00 | — | 4.73 | 1971–85 | 9 |
| T18a | 4 | flr | 6.32 | 3.09 | 1.69 | 1.00 | — | 7.44 | 1976–79 | 10 |
| T176 | 4 | flr | 3.82 | 2.29 | 1.46 | 1.00 | — | 3.52 | 1980–87 | 11 |
| SR-4 | 4 | flr | 4.07 | 2.39 | 1.49 | 1.00 | — | 3.95 | 1980–81 | 12 |
| T-4 | 4 | flr | 4.03 | 2.37 | 1.50 | 1.00 | — | N/A | 1982–86 | 13 |
| T-5 | 5 | flr | 4.03 | 2.37 | 1.50 | 1.00 | 0.76 | 3.76 | 1982–86 | 14 |
| BA10 | 5 | flr | 4.03 | 2.33 | 1.45 | 1.00 | 0.79 | N/A | 1987–89 | 15 |
| AX-4 | 4 | flr | 3.93 | 2.33 | 1.45 | 1.00 | — | 4.74 | 1987–90 | 16 |
| AX-5 | 5 | flr | 3.93 | 2.33 | 1.45 | 1.00 | 0.85 | 4.74 | 1987–94 | 17 |
| AX-15 | 5 | flr | 3.93 | 2.33 | 1.45 | 1.00 | 0.79 | 4.22 | 1989–97 | 18 |

1. By Warner Gear. Had many variations. Has a six-bolt top cover and "T90" cast into side of case. 1945 and 1946 CJs used a column shift variation (side shift on case), as well as the Tuxedo Park CJ. Used in CJ four-cylinder to about 1972. Used in six-cylinder Wagoneer 1963–69 and four-cylinder FC-150 to 1965. Good 'box within the limits of its design. Sometimes handles V-8s but not recommended.

2. By Warner Gear. A grandfather of the T18 series. Optional in most CJs from 1955 (except V-6) to about 1970. Optional in Gladiator trucks to 1969 as well as the Forward Control trucks (optional in FC-150, standard FC-170) to 1965. "T98" cast into housing. Some minor variations according to year. Very strong gearbox but unsynchronized. OK for V-8s.

3. By Warner Gear. A heavier-duty three-speed for V-6 powered CJs from 1967 to 71 and 232/258 inline sixes through 1975. Jeepster Commandos used them from 1967 to 1971. Casting number of "T14A" or "1302" on housing. Moderately strong and reliable but OK only for sixes.

4. By Warner Gear. A heavy-duty three-speed used in Gladiator trucks from 1963 to 68. Housing has a cast "T89." Not common. OK by all accounts. Up to V-8 power.

5. By Warner Gear. A very-heavy-duty three-speed that was used behind V-8–powered CJs and 1972–73 Commandos. Used in some 1970–79 Wagoneers, J-Series trucks, and Cherokees with both 258s and V-8s as large as 360 cid. Casting number of "T15" or "1307" on case. Very strong and reliable. Up to V-8 power.

6. By Warner Gear. "CC" models were floor shift and used for four-cylinder Commandos to 1971. They are also found in 1966–69 V-6–powered CJs. Very similar to the T90. Weak and unreliable.

7. By Warner Gear. "AA" models were also floor shift and were seen with some V-6–powered Commandos to 1971. Very similar to the T90. Weak and unreliable.

8. By Tremac. Used behind V-8 and six-cylinder engines in CJs 1976–79. Has cast "2603983" or "2603347" on case. Moderately good gearbox.

9. By Warner Gear. A close ratio trans similar to the T98 but with better oiling. Optional in six-cylinder. CJs through 1979. Optional in J-Series trucks 1969–85 and certain Wagoneers 1970–79. Casting number is "T18" or "1301." Great gearbox, limited only by its 4:1 first gear. Up to V-8–power.

10. By Warner Gear. Again, a derivative of the T98. A wide ratio trans with a creeper first gear optional in six-cylinder CJ 1976–79 and optional in J-20 truck 1980–83. Casting number is generally "T18A." One of the best you can get. Definitely up to V-8 power.

11. By Tremac. Manufactured in Mexico. Almost identical to a similar era Ford four-speed. Has aluminum case and was used with six-cylinder and V-8 1980–86. Casting number "2604203." A moderately good box. Up to V-8 power.

12. By Borg Warner (formerly Warner Gear). A very-light-duty trans used behind the 150-cid four-cylinder CJ in 1981 and 1982. Has casting numbers of "13-32" on aluminum case. Very weak and best swapped out.

13. By Borg Warner. Similar to the SR-4. Used in CJ and 1984–86 Cherokees and Comanche pickups. Casting number "13-51" on aluminum case. Very weak and best swapped out.

14. By Borg Warner. Identical to the T-4 but with a fifth gear added. Used in 1982–86 CJs, 1984–86 Cherokees and a very few J-10 trucks 1980–84 and some of these had 0.86 fifth-gear ratios. Weak but improvable. The "World Class" T-5 a possible swap.

15. By Peugeot. Similar to AX-5 but much less reliable. Used for six-cylinder Wranglers from 1987–89 and in Cherokees and Comanche pickup for the same period. The worst Jeep gearbox ever offered by all accounts.

16. By Aisin-Warner. Used in four- and six-cylinder Cherokees and Comanche pickups from 1987–90. An OK box. Not up to V-8 power.

17. By Aisin-Warner. Used in four and some six-cylinder Wranglers 1987–88 and was used in four-cylinder Wranglers until about 1994. Also used in Cherokees and Comanche pickups for the same period. Another OK box not recommended for V-8s.

18. By Aisin-Warner. Used in six-cylinder Wranglers, Comanche pickup and Cherokees from 1989–97 and includes the new TJ. In TJ, it is used in four- and six-cylinder applications. Reputedly a great thing. Marginal with a V-8, but possible, according to some.

## PART 2. JEEP AUTOMATIC TRANSMISSIONS

| Model | Speeds | 1st | 2nd | 3rd | 4th | Rev. | Years | Notes |
|---|---|---|---|---|---|---|---|---|
| AS-8F | 3 | 2.40 | 1.46 | 1.00 | — | 2.0 | 1963–69 | 1 |
| TH-400 | 3 | 2.45 | 1.45 | 1.00 | — | 2.08 | 1965–79 | 2 |
| 727 | 3 | 2.45 | 1.45 | 1.00 | — | 2.00 | 1980–91 | 3 |
| 999 | 3 | 2.75 | 1.55 | 1.00 | — | 2.20 | 1982 | 4 |
| 904 | 3 | 2.74 | 1.55 | 1.00 | — | 2.20 | 1984–86 | 5 |
| AW30-40 | 4 | 2.80 | 1.53 | 1.00 | 0.71 | 2.39 | 1987–97 | 6 |

1. A Borg-Warner unit that was used in Wagoneers and Gladiator pickups and offered only with the Dana 21, single-speed transfer case. Reliable but uninspiring. It was offered with both the 230 six and the V-8.
2. A nearly bulletproof GM design that was mounted behind V-6 engines in the Jeepster Commando from 1967 to 73, and in Wagoneers and J-series pickups from 1970 to 79.
3. This beefy Chrysler three-speed Torqueflite carried the Wagoneer from 1980 to its end in 1991. J-Series pickups were similarly equipped. Some six-cylinder SJ applications used the smaller 999 tranny.
4. A lighter-duty Torqueflite with a lower first and second gear and a large bellhousing and torque converter. Used in CJs from 1980 to 1986 and in some six-cylinder Wagoneers and J-Series trucks from 1982 to 1984.
5. A very-light-duty Torqueflite used in XJ Cherokees and MJ Comanche behind four-and six-cylinder engines from 1984 to 1986. A variant, the 909, which features a lockup torque converter, has also been used in XJs and in YJ Wranglers and, with electronic controls, in the new TJ.
6. The Aisin-Warner transmission is a four-speed automatic with an overdrive fourth. Similar in concept to the GM TH-700R4. It uses a lockup torque converter and has been in service in Cherokees since 1987 and is also used in the Grand Cherokees.

## Gearing Change Options for Assorted Automatics

| Trans | 1st Gear stock/mod | 2nd Gear stock/mod |
|---|---|---|
| Ford C4 | 2.45/2.71 | 1.46/1.55 |
| Mopar 727 | 2.45/2.77 | 1.45/1.55 |
| TH-350 | 2.52/2.75 | 1.52/1.57 |
| TH-400 | 2.48/2.75/3.00 | 1.48/1.57 |

## OE JEEP CLUTCH SPECS

| Years | Application | Disc, Std(Opt) | PP Type/# Spgs | Release Type |
|---|---|---|---|---|
| 1941–68 | MB, CJ w/ L-4, F-4 | 8.5 in. | L/3(6) | B |
| 1968–71 | CJ w/F-4 | 9.25 in. | L/9 | B |
| 1972 | CJ w/232, 258, 304 | 10.5 in. | L/12 | C |
| 1973–82 | CJ w/232, 258, 304 | 10.5 in. | L/12 | B |
| 1967–71 | C-101 w/F-4 | 9.25 in. | L/9 | C |
| 1967–71 | C-101 w/225 V-6 | 10.4 in. | D(L) | C |
| 1972–73 | C-101 w/232, 258, 304 | 10.5 in. | L/12 | C |
| 1946–65 | SW, PU w/L-4 or F-4 | 8.5 in. | L/3 (6) | B |
| 1954–65 | SW, PU w/226 | 10 in. | L/12 | B |
| 1957–65 | FC-150 w/F-4 | 8.5 in. (9.25) | L/6 (9) | B |
| 1957–65 | FC-170 w/226 | 10 in. (10.5) | L/12 (12) | B |
| 1963–65 | SJ w/230 OHC | 10.5 in. | L/12 | H |
| 1965–68 | SJ w/327 V-8 | 10.4 in. | L/12 | B |
| 1968–71 | SJ w/350 V-8 | 11 in. | L/12 | B |
| 1971–72 | SJ w/304, 360 V-8 | 11 in. | L/12 | C |
| 1973–87 | SJ w/258, 360 | 10.5 in. (11) | L/12 | B |
| 1984–85 | XJ w/2.5L | 9.59 in. | D | C |
| 1986–90 | XJ w/2.5L | 9.13 in. | D | H(C) |
| 1991–95 | XJ w/2.5L | 8.88 in. | D | H |
| 1984–86 | XJ w/2.8L V-6 | 9.13 in. | D | C |
| 1987–95 | XJ w/4.0L | 10.5 in. | D | H |
| 1993–95 | ZJ w/4.0L | 10.5 in. | D | H |
| 1987–95 | YJ w/258, 4.0L | 10.5 in. | D | H |

B = bellcrank, C = cable, H = hydraulic, L = lever, D = diaphragm, ( ) = optional or preferred upgrade

## JEEP TRANSMISSION RATINGS

| Model | Rating | Comments |
|---|---|---|
| Aisin-Warner AX-15 | Good | |
| Aisin-Warner AW-4 (four-speed auto) | Good | As a stock automatic for many late model Jeeps, this trans is a very good one. It has few problems and holds up well with stock power outputs. |
| Borg Warner World Class T-5 | Very good | A good swap if a very low first gear is not needed. Standard T-5 not as good. |
| GM TH-350 | Good | A good swap for Chevy-powered short Jeeps. It's compact, common, stout and beefable. Note the "K" on the bellhousing, which indicates a 4x4 unit. The four-wheel drive trans had a stronger housing and a short tailshaft. |
| GM TH-400 | Good | One of the strongest automatics of all time. It was fitted to a large number of Jeeps. |
| NP-435 | Good | Reasonably popular Jeep swap; more difficult to swap than a Warner T-18. Used with Ford and Dodge engines, this is the tranny of choice with a Ford or Dodge engine swap. |
| NV-4500 four-speed | Very good | All the stump-pulling guts of the old four-speed truck boxes with the benefit of an overdrive fifth. An outstanding swap if you have the driveshaft length to play with. |
| Peugeot BA10 | Poor | |
| Tremec T-176 | Good | Able to handle V-8 power, but without the deep first of some other truck trannies. It isn't a popular swap. |
| Warner T-18 | Good | The most popular manual four-speed swap. Offered by Jeep for several years, the Ford truck units are popular for swapping, especially with compound-low first gear. |

*Chapter 7*

# WINCHES & RECOVERY GEAR

## Inertially Challenged

Do you really need a winch? How about a snatch strap or a Hi-Lift jack? The answers to these questions lie in the type of Jeeping you do. If your Jeeping consists of more than a once-a-year foray down a dirt road, then yes. Choose a commonsense array of recovery equipment for those moments when you are inertially challenged.

The first remedy for getting stuck, of course, is not to get stuck in the first place. Some folks, often those in the harder-core groups, argue that money is better spent building a more capable Jeep than in buying a lot of expensive recovery gear. There is some logic to this, but these folks are forgetting the No. 1 cause of being stuck—pilot error. Human error can overcome the best equipped Jeep. We all have days we would rather forget.

### Towing Points

There is a bare minimum of recovery equipment for any Jeep that ventures forth into the outback. First on that list is solid towing points front and rear. Solid means hooks, rings, or brackets that are solidly mounted to the chassis or via a strong, chassis-mounted bumper. The No. 1 cause of recovery accidents is failure of the towing points.

Towing points are also a trail etiquette item. When you are inertially challenged on the trail and another Jeeper offers assistance, it's expected that you will have solid, convenient places for him to hook you up. Poor towing points often results in jury rigs, damage, and accident.

These hookup devices should be designed for recovery use and rated for approximately 1.5 times the GVW of your rig. Tow hooks, etc., are available via many

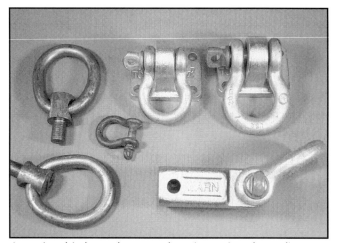

A receiver hitch can be a good towing point, depending on the plug-in used and the receiver. Do not use a tow ball, as they can break off and go ballistic. Here are a variety of attachments. The two rings at the left are military surplus pieces made of 4340 steel and rated for about 10 tons. At the top are two RandP 3-ton brackets, one fitted with a 5/8-inch shackle and the other a 3/4-inch shackle. At the bottom is a cast Warn receiver hitch attachment for a 3/4-inch shackle. The small shackle is a 1/2-inch piece that is rated only for about 3,000 pounds.

parts supply places, but often a marine chandlery or rigger will carry useful items. Some of the stock pieces that appeared over the years are adequate, especially the military items. Your receiver-type trailer hitch may serve but do not exceed its rated capacity.

### *Hand Tools*
#### Shovels

Another must-have is a shovel. There are many uses for a shovel in the Jeeping world, from recovery to camping. A folding GI shovel is the minimum and is adequate in some Jeeping venues. If you are in a place where mud running is common, you'll soon upgrade to a larger shovel out of necessity. Unless, of course, you enjoy groveling on your knees getting up close and personal with your problem. A short-handled shovel increases the workload, as anyone knows who has scooped up a shovelful of the kinda mud that will suck your boots off.

There's more to shovels than grabbing the first one you see at the hardware. The folding GI shovel is convenient, easy to pack, and useful for close-in work, such as making a flat spot for a jack. Because it folds and locks, it can be used as both a shovel and a pick. Many Jeepers carry them along with a larger shovel.

Next up are the short, D-handled shovels. These are very sturdy, and while they take you a little farther away from your work, they still involve some stooping. They're small enough to make stowage fairly easy, but not quite long enough to reach under the middle of a Jeep.

Finally, the long-handled shovel is the best for frequent use because it has leverage and reach. Unfortunately, it's a bear to stow, but people who run mud will often find a way. Get one with a beefy handle, as the extra leverage makes them easy to break in hard use. Shovels come with square or round points. The round point pierces the ground better but the square point cuts roots better.

## Axes and Saws

People who regularly travel wooded areas usually have an axe and or saw along. Treefalls and hanging limbs make these items a necessity for the woods Jeep. Often a small hatchet or small saw is sufficient. Some folks carry full size items, or even a chainsaw. Choose your weapon according to need, but don't overload. A hatchet is often more useful as a single tool than a saw.

## Picks

Some folks carry picks. They can be useful in rare circumstances but they will most often be just added weight. Think about bringing one on particularly remote or extended trips.

## Max Multipurpose Tool

If you carry all the stuff listed above, you'll use up a fair bit of space. A good compromise is the Max Multipurpose tool. Designed for remote firefighters, it's a tool that has interchangeable heads that include an axe, shovel, rake, pick, and adze. It doesn't work as well

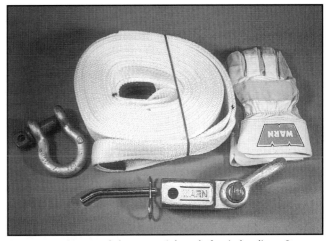

A towstrap is one of the essential tools for 'wheeling. Straps can be purchased in a variety of sizes and types, but Warn offers this recovery kit complete with a 30,000-pound strap, two shackles, a receiver attachment, and a pair of nifty work gloves.

in each of its guises as the single purpose tool would, but you can have them all at your fingertips and it's easy to stow.

## Straps

A tow or snatch strap is another must-have that also falls into the trail etiquette area. Straps are quick and convenient to use and should be carried by any trail bound rig. Most of the time these straps are nylon straps or ropes.

Some Jeepers still rely on chains or cables for recovery but these can be cumbersome and dangerous. There is zero give in chain and very little in cable. That means every shock and jerk is transmitted to the towing points and this transfers a very high shock load that can cause damage. A nylon strap or rope absorbs shock loads and is more gentle to towing points. Many Jeepers will not hook up to a chain to tow you out.

Straps come in different thicknesses, widths, and weight ratings. There are so-called "snatch" or recovery straps and tow straps. Though similar in design and construction to tow straps, recovery straps are longer and will therefore stretch more. Most tow straps are 10–20 feet long, while snatch straps come in 25–30-foot lengths. The general rule of thumb for recovery straps is to pick one with a rating three to four times your Jeep's GVW. Weight rating, length, and width commonly represent the strap's capacity, with 30-foot, 2-inch straps capable of pulling 15,000–20,000 pounds, 3-inch straps around 20,000 pounds, 4-inch straps around 40,000 pounds, and 6-inch straps about 60,000 pounds.

Straps are not without danger, either. Like a rubber band, the strap will stretch and absorb kinetic energy. That energy can be used to multiply the force used for recovery. It also multiplies the danger if a towing point comes loose. It's akin to shooting a paper clip with a rubber band, except that a 3 pound hunk of metal hurtling at 100 miles per hour is lethal. When using tow straps try to keep yourself and others out of harm's way.

Rope can also be used for recovery but in order to get a rope in the same weight classification as a strap, you'd need to go to a ship chandlery and pick up something about 4 inches in diameter. It's much tougher to stow than a strap that you can roll up. Ropes for towing can be more modest in dimension.

### Jacks

At the very least you should carry an OE-style telescoping jack to change your flat tires. If you changed tire size, make sure the OE jack has enough reach for the job. Also, take a quick assessment of the jack's quality. OE jacks run from OK to junk. The bumper jacks are usually borderline dangerous, especially on a loaded rig. You can upgrade your jack as necessary, perhaps with a telescoping hydraulic unit.

With any jack, you need to have a 1x1-foot piece of wood for a base to prevent your jack from burying itself in soft ground. Marine plywood, at least 3/4 inch thick, is better because it doesn't split.

The so-called sheepherders, or Hi-Lift, jack is a useful upgrade.

Hi-Lift is a brand name but other manufacturers make comparable jacks. The Hi-Lift brand lifts 7,000 pounds and comes in four sizes, 36-inch, 42-inch, 48-inch, and 60-inch. This will lift your rig well free of the goo! The slick part is that they can also be used as a manual 7,000-pound winch that will pull (or push) you 3–4 feet at a time. It ain't as easy as an electric winch but it gets the job done. Storage and weight can be a problem in some rigs but many rack and bumper manufacturers offer built-in storage brackets for them.

## Winches

The recovery tool most four-wheelers choose is a powered winch. Winches have been around almost forever, and there are many types and capacities. The first power winches, still used today, were run by a PTO (Power Take-Off) from the transfer case or transmission.

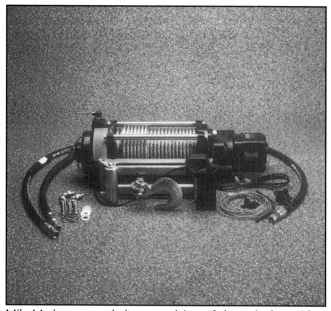

Mile-Marker responded to complaints of slow winches with this two-speed model that is about as fast as a typical electric winch. Since these hydraulic winches hook up to the vehicle's power steering system, Step One during installation is to flush your power steering system and install fresh fluid for maximum performance. *Courtesy Mile-Marker*

A small driveshaft runs the power to the winch. Hydraulic winches date back a ways also but, until the recent intro of the MileMarker unit, they didn't see much use in the recreational 4x4 market. These days, most winches are powered by electricity.

Winches are rated by their single-line capacity in pounds. Occasionally, the stall load is given, meaning the weight at which the winch will no longer pull at all and stalls. Most winches use 5/16-inch wire rope and the heavier-rated units use 3/8-inch wire rope. Common 5/16-inch wire rope has a breaking strength of 9,800 pounds, while 3/8 inch is good for about 14,500 pounds. Various wire rope manufacturers have ratings that are higher and lower than these, with cost related to strength.

### Hand Winches

If you are into recovery by "Armstrong" or simply don't want to shell out the big bucks for a powered winch, a hand winch is an alternative. You'd be surprised at how many people go this route. The advantages are cost, a weight savings over the power winch (both in terms of the winch itself and any extra battery or equipment), and the fact that it will work regardless of whether the vehicle is operable. Disadvantages are the extra effort required, the short cable length, and low capacity of most units. In many cases, having an effective hand winch involves making up some extra sections of wire rope to extend the reach. A come-along extraction is a time-consuming operation, so make sure your trail buddies are into it before you hold up the parade unnecessarily.

### Capstan Winches

These are not just for boats, but it's probably been a lotta years since you've seen one on a Jeep. They are worth a mention because they make a great working accessory. You use ordinary nylon, sisal, or hemp rope with them and control the load with the number of wraps around the capstan and the tension you put on the outcoming rope. They can be used for recovery but are inconvenient in this role. Some capstan winches are electric but most are PTO-powered, many off the front of the engine. Most are rated at or below 2,500 pounds single-line pull, and the ultimate rating depends on the rope used.

### PTO Drum Winches

The Koenig Iron Works, Braden, and Ramsey made some fine PTO winches for Jeeps in years past and they still turn up. A PTO is a rugged, heavy winch that is best suited to hard work rather than recreational recovery. The winches are powered by the engine, via the t-case or trans, and controlled by engine speed or the trans gear selected. One 8,000-pound Koenig PTO winch of years past was powered off the engine crankshaft.

The advantages to a PTO winch is that it is usually built very stoutly and will work all day without complaint. With speed controlled by the gear ratios of the trans, plus engine speed, it is very flexible and can run extremely fast or very slowly (see page 114 for line speed comparisons). Being a worm gear setup, it can last through decades of work.

Disadvantages are that it is difficult for one person to operate or to operate outside the cab. Also, if the engine isn't running, neither is the winch, though one of the old Koenigs had an optional hand crank. PTOs are also very heavy, at least twice the weight of an electric. PTO winches are being manufactured still, but there are no recreational 4x4 applications to speak of. The old winches are difficult to repair due to being out of production for many years.

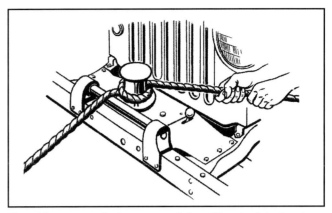

The old capstan winch was a useful working tool, but not hot for recovery because it required two men for safety. As on ships, ordinary rope was used. They offer very fine control, but are seldom seen these days, except on restored classic Jeeps.

### Hydraulic Winches

Hydraulic winches have been popular in industrial circles for many years for their excellent control, high capacity, and adaptability. This popularity trickled down to Jeeps a few years back when MileMarker introduced its line of hydraulic winches. Instead of being powered by a PTO or electric-driven hydraulic pump (they can be if desired), these winches are powered by the vehicle's power steering pump. A priority valve ensures that the steering gets access to hydraulic pressure first.

The advantages of a hydraulic winch are the ability to run all day without strain, very precise control, built-in overload protection, light weight, and reliability. They also stop immediately, unlike many electric winches that will roll on a few inches after the switch is released. Disadvantages are few with hydraulics in general. One might be that some of them will slowly unwind a bit when holding a load.

The MileMarker is the only such winch on the market. When MileMarker introduced its first generation units, the only complaint was the tediously slow line speed. Some regard line speed as important, some don't. Either way, MileMarker responded with a two-speed unit that is essentially as fast as the majority of electric winches.

Perhaps the biggest trouble with the MileMarker has nothing to do with the winch itself but with its use of the vehicle's power steering as a power source. How well the winch works depends on power steering pump pressure and volume. If your Jeep has the prerequisite 1,400–1,600 psi and 4 to 6 gallons per minute capacity, your winch will operate as advertised. If not, it won't. Also, it's possible to overheat your power steering system, but this seems to vary from vehicle to vehicle.

If you acquire this type of winch, be sure your power steering system is in top shape. Get your power steering fluid changed ASAP. Old, broken-down fluid doesn't have the viscosity to produce ideal pump performance, and winch performance will suffer. A tired pump can also contribute to poor performance. The flow rate of the pump, in GPM, is most important but almost impossible to test. Generally, if the pump will pass the OEM pressure tests outlined in the manual, it is likely OK.

### Electric Winches

Electric winches are the mainstay of the recreational 4x4 market. They are light, easy to install, and reasonably priced. Most are not heavy-duty or industrial strength units, even if they have a high load rating. Unless you have some special need, that's OK. Most folks only use their winches a few times a year. As a reference point, our discussions on electric winches will deal with real world winches, 6,000 pounds and up.

The electric winch is designed to run off your 12-volt electrical system, and how much the motor will draw depends on the load. The chart on page 113 rounds up some popular winch specs, and you will be amazed at some of the near 500-amp draws at full load. This kind of draw will kill a battery pretty quick, so it's

fortunate that the overwhelming majority of winch pulls are at a much smaller load. The typical pull is somewhere around 2,500 pounds and at this rating, the average winch will draw 150 to 200 amps.

Electric winch motors range in power from 1.4 to 2.5 horsepower for winches from 6,000 to 12,000 pounds. Two types of motors are used, series wound and permanent magnet. The motor power is chosen according to the designed pull of the winch, so you don't have a choice there. The type of motor is important from a durability standpoint.

Permanent magnet motors are definitely the light-duty choice. While they draw fewer amps than a series wound for the same horsepower, and are somewhat lighter and smaller, they go up in smoke much quicker in hard use. Since you never know how hard you might have to work your winch in a critical recovery, a series wound motor is the better choice. A series wound motor, however, typically requires an upgraded electrical system.

The electric winch has a gear ratio. Just like the Jeep, it's geared according to motor power and load rating. Ratios range from 130:1 to 470:1. Just as with the drivetrain, a tall (numerically low) ratio gives you speed and if you want power with it, you need a bigger motor. The lower (numerically higher) ratios are slower but more powerful.

The drive system of the winch gives you a few choices. Two types are commonly used, worm gear and planetary gear. The venerable and popular Warn 8274 dares to be different and uses a spur gear drive. Each type has advantages.

This is one of the earliest Warn electric winches. Evolved from the Bellevue winches of the 1950s, these spur gear units became the Warn winch mainstay for many years. These early winches were cable operated, and some did not have a power-out feature. Note that the 8274 mounts vertically to an angled plate that attaches to the front frame and bumper.

The newest Warn 8274 model is the only spur gear winch on the market. Recently upgraded and now manufactured with new tooling, this design is favored because of its very fast line speed and large 150-foot cable capacity. A true classic! *Courtesy Warn Industries*

The worm gear setups are much stronger and more reliable but they absorb more power from the motor and generally have a higher amp draw than a planetary unit. They have the advantage of not always needing a brake. Because the worm, or cylindrical, gear is opposite the spur gear (see page 113-114), in theory, the load cannot cause them to free wheel. Worm gear winches are more costly and require oil changes in the gearbox.

Planetary drives are more common because they are lighter, more compact, and draw fewer amps. They allow for a wide variety of gearing choices. They do require the use of a braking mechanism. They tend to be noisier than worm gear winches and are not nearly as strong as a worm gear setup.

Spur gear winches are close to worm gear winches in beef but without the extra drag. They need a sizable brake. The choices in gearing are a little limited compared to a planetary, due to the physical limitations of the design and application.

### Choosing a Winch

As you can see, there are many types of winches and what's best for you depends on your needs. For most of us, with only occasional use in mind, a standard electric, planetary drive, drum winch is more than adequate. For continuous or commercial use, a more industrial-strength unit, such as a hydraulic or PTO winch, is in order.

The size of winch you select is also important. If it's too small, it either won't get the job done or will heave its guts out trying. Winch selection starts with your gross vehicle weight, obtainable from the GVW tag on your door post. Two general rules of thumb for winch selection are: a) take the curb weight of your rig and double it, or b): take the GVW of your rig and add 50 percent.

Most folks underestimate the weight of their rig in its "loaded for bear" state. It's a reality check to load it up as you would for a trip, fill the fuel tank, and get it weighed. If you are like most of us, your eyebrows will crawl to the back of your head in amazement. Look at the info on page 114 as well to get an idea on how terrain affects winch pull.

Keep in mind that winch ratings are taken from the first layer of cable (the bottom-most layer). The winch's rated pull decreases with each layer by approximately 10 percent. Using the drivetrain comparison again, this equates to the effect of tire size on

the overall ratio. Compare your loaded weight with the lowest rating of a particular winch.

How much cable is on the winch is worth considering, even though no matter how much you get, someday you will find yourself 20 feet short! Many winches have 90–100 feet of wire rope. Some carry 150 feet and a few of the old timers carried a bit more.

There are several thoughts to keep in mind with regard to cable length. You need to keep five wraps on the drum, so whatever cable length is listed, deduct about 5 feet. A double line pull—occasionally neces-

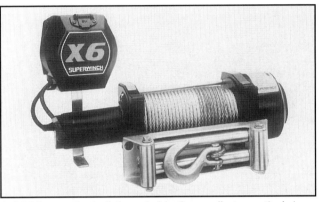

A 6,000-pound winch is probably the smallest practical size for recovery, even for light Jeeps. This Superwinch X6 is a planetary gear model with a 1.6-horsepower motor, but it still draws 400 amps at max load. It isn't much lighter or much less expensive than the Superwinch X9 9,000-pound unit that draws only 35 amps more. *Courtesy Superwinch*

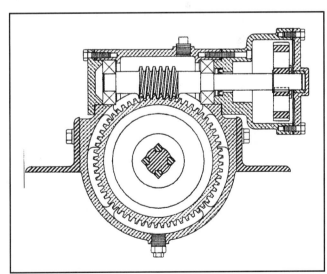

The worm gear winch is powerful and long wearing, but generally slower than an equivalent size planetary style. The worm drive unit is a bit heavier but it does not often require a brake. Because the worm is perpendicular to the spur gear, neither can move unless power is supplied to the worm gear. Note the drain at the bottom. The housing is filled with oil, so regular service ensures long life. *Courtesy Ramsey*

The newer winches often feature integrated solenoid packs. This makes installation a two-wire hookup. The only disadvantage is the possibility that long-term weather exposure will damage connections. In the case of this Superwinch 9,000-pound unit, the controls are under a tight cover, vulnerable only to complete immersion. Note the optional roller fairlead. *Courtesy Superwinch*

*Right:* Permanent magnet motors can be replaced by series wound in some cases. It's also possible to replace a smaller motor for a larger one where the family of winches allows it. In the case of this Warn 6,000-pound winch, a series wound, higher horsepower motor is replacing a permanent magnet type.

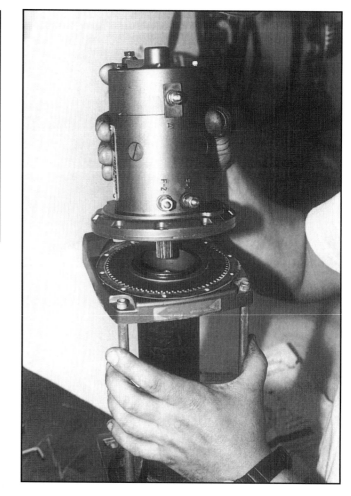

sary—cuts your reach in half. Since more cable out gives you more pull from the winch, you may need to use a double line pull more often, just to get into the "power" ratios for the winch. Also, more cable means more chances for snarled and balled cable on the drum. Lastly, do you travel in an area where "deadmen" (solid winching points) abound, or are they scarce? In scarcer areas, a longer cable is more handy.

The winch motor is controlled by solenoid packs that consist of two sets of solenoids, one for in and the other for out. Sometimes these pieces are integrated into the winch assembly, sometimes they are remotely mounted. The integral solenoid packs are convenient but increase the space needed for the winch and require the winch to be disassembled when solenoid service is needed. You may have special reasons for wanting the solenoids mounted elsewhere, such as under the hood, but the integral setups are usually preferred.

### Choosing a Winch Mounting System

Picking a winch mounting system is a question of

strength, minimal effect on approach angle, and aesthetics (hey, it's gotta look good too). Obviously, the mount you select should be rated for the same capacity as the winch. How much the setup weighs should be a consideration, or you may have to uprate your front springs. Some brands of winches will interchange among mountings, many will not.

Most winch mounts will affect approach angle to some degree. Pick one that minimizes the loss. So called "hidden" winch systems are a pain because you cannot properly rewind the cable without risking injury to your hands. Better to have the winch exposed so you can safely work with it.

Portable, or "receiver hitch," winches are available and can be adapted to the front of a vehicle. They have advantages and disadvantages. The good part is that they can be used front or rear, or left at home when not needed, thereby saving weight. The bad part comes when you are stuck bumper deep and have to dig a big hole to install the winch. They have a major effect on approach and departure angle and can become a dri-

The receiver type mounts can be handy or a hassle, depending on conditions. You can use them front or rear, or leave them at home. They have a large effect on approach or departure angles, as you can see here. They don't tolerate side pulls as well as a solid mount. If you are stuck bumper deep, you may have to dig to install it. Still, some folks find them practical and suitable for their mild or infrequent trail situations.

ving impediment when left installed. They also do not tolerate side pulls very well.

### Winch Accessories

Other than common sense and respect, the most important winch accessory is a set of leather-palmed gloves. It's inevitable that a few of the outer strands of the wire rope will fray, and these will poke out. Sailors who work with wire rope call these little buggers "fishhooks," and yes, they will rend flesh! Cutting

them off with wire cutters as they appear is good maintenance but the gloves will protect your hands in the meantime.

Another important winch accessory is a roller fairlead. Some manufacturers include them with the winch, others supply a hawse-type fairlead as standard and offer the roller unit as an upgrade. It's worth a few extra bucks because it prevents the cable from chafing and allows the limits of cable angles to be stretched a little. Even though a hawse fairlead is made of mild metal, it will still wear a cable. Roller fairleads do hang out there a bit more and in some cases this becomes a clearance problem.

The shackle (clevis, d-ring) is a universal hook-up tool for winches. They come in a multitude of sizes, from jewelry size to those that you'd need a 3/4-ton truck to carry. The common sizes for 4x4s are 5/8-inch and 3/4-inch. These sizes refer to the thickness of the pin. They are rated for a safe working load and should be so

The Pull Pal ground anchor can dig into the ground like this and hold 8,000 pounds. The holding power is subject to the type of ground, but it will hold in snow, sand, mud, gravel, dirt, and even loose rocks. If you are stuck to your axles with no deadman in sight, this is a winching tool that can pay for itself in one use. It folds to about the size of a Hi-Lift jack.

A solid winch mount, like this one from Stage West, has a minimal impact on approach angle, plenty of beef, and a secure place to mount these nifty IPF driving lights. The tow bar points are an optional feature. The only thing missing is a good towing point.

marked, usually in tons. Most 3/4-inch shackles are rated for 13,000 pounds and 5/8-inch for 9,000 pounds.

Another vital necessity is a tree strap. One of the big "never-evers" is using a bare cable around a tree. Often as not it kills the tree—and it can get you a fine. If you wanna keep trails open and trees alive, use the tree strap! It comes in handy for other stuff as well, not the least of which is to provide a towing bridle for an ailing rig.

A pulley, or snatch block, of appropriate capacity will double your winch's pulling power (while cutting the speed in half). It will also offer you many angle options in tricky recovery or winching situations, such as winching around a corner.

A choker chain is useful for logs, rocks, or other surfaces that might chafe a strap. Some folks add a length of appropriately sized chain to the end of their winch cables to prevent cable damage. A choker can also be handy in field repair situations.

What do you do if you have nothing nearby to winch from? A ground anchor can provide the necessary purchase. Several are available (including the old stand-by Danforth boat anchor) but the unit that combines convenience with effectiveness is the Pull Pal. Looking much like an old time horse-drawn plow, it will hold up to 8,000 pounds in dirt, mud, sand, snow, and gravel. One will suffice in most conditions, but if you have an especially heavy rig, you might need two. It folds for easy storage.

Another tricky situation is trying to winch another

There were many brands of Power Take Off winches back in the old days. This 1965 Ramsey PTO winch has probably seen some hard use. The unit drives off the transfer case via a driveshaft. PTO winches are very useful for situations that require long duration winching, but are heavy and unhandy in some trail recovery situations. They are very strong and long wearing, but parts for some can be difficult to obtain. Like this one, many of the old PTOs carried large drums with 150 to 200 feet of 3/8-inch cable.

vehicle that may be heavier than yours. This might just pull you over the edge along with the rig in trouble, with your brakes locked or not. Sometimes you can hook your Jeep to a deadman and sometimes not. One solution in this predicament is a set of wheel anchors, such as those from SureClaw. These folding tools wedge the front wheel and have a plow that digs in, as well as straps to prevent the tire from jumping the anchor. These are pretty specialized pieces. If you don't do frequent rescues, you may not want to devote the weight, space, and bucks to such gear.

If you are into remote controls on the couch, you may be into them for your winch. Wireless remote controls are available for some winches, both from the manufacturer and from outside sources. They have maximum ranges of up to 125 feet.

### Prepping Your Jeep for a Winch

While you can get away with just hooking up your new winch to the Jeep's battery and heading off, there are some pitfalls. The usual bare minimum for a battery is 550 CCA (Cold Cranking Amps) to operate a winch. In reality, there is more to consider. First is that a starting-type battery may not be up to snuff for repeated winching. Not only can repeated discharges be harmful to the battery, but it may not be capable of supplying the amps the winch motor needs for a hard pull.

The cures come on several levels. Replacing your starting battery with a dual-purpose marine-type battery is the easiest first choice. Dual batteries, with one being a deep cycle dedicated to the winch, is a second choice, and a larger alternator is a good step either way. We get into details on batteries, isolators, and mega power alternators in Chapter 11, but remember that many folks have been stopped by dead batteries after a long winch pull. Also, a winch motor will more likely go up in smoke trying to suck amps from a nearly dead battery. Low system voltage is one of the main causes of winch motor failure, along with excessive heat. The winch should not be operated when the system voltage drops below 10.5 volts. On a long pull, it pays to stop periodically to let the winch motor cool and the batteries to build back up.

## COMMON WINCH SPECS, 6000 POUNDS AND UP

| Manufacturer | Model | Capacity (lbs) | Rope Dia-Lgth | Motor Type/ HP | Amp Draw Max | Max Load Speed (FPM) | Drive/Ratio |
|---|---|---|---|---|---|---|---|
| MegaWinch | MW-12000 | 12,000 | 3/8-125 | SW/2.5 | 425 | 1-3 | W/468/133:1 |
| MileMarker | MMW7000 | 7,000 | 5/16-100 | Hyd. | 2 | | 8:1 |
| MileMarker | MMW9000 | 9,000 | 3/8-100 | Hyd. | 2 | | 6:1 |
| MileMarker | MMW10500 | 10,500 | 3/8-100 | Hyd. | 2 | | 6:1 |
| Pierce | PS654 | 9,000 | 5/16-150 | SW/1.5 | 400 | 3 | W/460:1 |
| Pierce | PS-654-M | 12,500 | 5/16-150 | SW/1.5 | 400 | 2 | W/720:1 |
| Ramsey | REP-6000 | 6,000 | 1/4-100 | PM/1.6 | 230 | 6 | P/294:1 |
| Ramsey | REP-8000 | 8,000 | 5/16-95 | PM/1.8 | 280 | 4.5 | P/210:1 |
| Ramsey | REP-9000 | 9,000 | 5/16-95 | SW/1.9 | 400 | 2 | P/138:1 |
| Ramsey | ProPls6000 | 6,000 | 1/4-100 | SW/1.4 | 250 | 2.5 | P/210:1 |
| Ramsey | ProPls8000 | 8,000 | 5/16-95 | SW/1.9 | 350 | 4 | P/210:1 |
| Ramsey | ProPls9000 | 9,000 | 5/16-95 | SW/1.9 | 405 | 4 | P/138:1 |
| Ramsey | RE 8000 | 8,000 | 5/16-150 | SW/1.9 | 345 | 3 | W/360:1 |
| Ramsey | RE 10000 | 10,000 | 3/8-100 | SW/1.9 | 330 | 2.5 | W/470:1 |
| Ramsey | RE 12000 | 12,000 | 3/8-100 | SW/1.9 | 390 | 2 | W/470:1 |
| Superwinch | S6000 | 6,000 | 5/16-100 | PM/1.6 | 400 | 2.5 | P/253:1 |
| Superwinch | S9000 | 9,000 | 5/16-100 | SW/2.0 | 435 | 2 | P/253:1 |
| Superwinch | X6CD | 6,000 | 5/16-100 | PM/1.6 | 400 | 2.5 | P/253:1 |
| Superwinch | X9 | 9,000 | 5/16-100 | SW/2.0 | 435 | 2.0 | P/253:1 |
| Superwinch | Husky 8 | 8,500 | 5/16-100 | SW/2.1 | 405 | 1.5 | W/229:1 |
| Superwinch | Husky 10 | 10,000 | 3/8-90 | SW/2.1 | 450 | 1.5 | W/294:1 |
| Warn | M8000 | 8,000 | 5/16-100 | SW/2.1 | 423 | 3 | P/216:1 |
| Warn | X8000i | 8,000 | 5/16-100 | SW/2.1 | 423 | 3 | P/216:1 |
| Warn | M8274-50 | 8,000 | 5/16-150 | SW/2.5 | 435 | 3 | S/134:1 |
| Warn | XD9000 | 9,000 | 5/16-100 | SW/2.5 | 400 | 5 | P/156:1 |
| Warn | XD9000i | 9,000 | 5/16-125 | SW/2.5 | 400 | 5 | P/156:1 |
| Warn | M10000 | 10,000 | 3/8-125 | SW/2.5 | 475 | 3 | P/199:1 |
| Warn | M12000 | 12,000 | 3/8-125 | SW/2.5 | 400 | 3 | P/261:1 |

Abbreviations: SW = series wound motor, PM = permanent magnet motor, P = planetary drive, W = worm gear drive, S = spur gear drive.
(1) A two-speed unit.

## How Terrain Affects Winch Pull

Terrain has a big effect on line pull. No matter how big your winch, there may come a time when you wish it were bigger. Remember that in extreme situations, a pulley, or snatch block, available from most winch manufacturers, will double your line pull (while cutting line speed in half). Here are some ways to determine the approximate line pull that various terrain situations will impart on your rig. This can be used to help you choose a winch or for general information. Simply add the terrain or slope factor to the loaded weight of your vehicle to make the estimate.

**Ground Condition, Add For**

| | |
|---|---|
| Pavement | 5% |
| Grass | 10% |
| Wet sand or gravel | 15-20% |
| Dry sand | 25-35%+ |
| Light, shallow mud | 35%+ |
| Heavy, deep mud | 50-60%+ |

### Slopes

A slope will have its own factor, to which you will add the aboveground condition factor. Calculating the effect of slope is simply done by approximating the slope in degrees, dividing it by 60, and then multiplying it by the loaded weight of the vehicle. Whatever figure emerges, add this to your loaded weight to determine the approximate pull required. Then add the appropriate percentage of that weight that the ground condition will account for.

$$\frac{\text{Slope (in degrees)}}{60} \times \text{loaded wt (lb.)} + \text{loaded wt (lb.)} = \text{Winch Pull}$$

Winch Pull x Ground Factor (in percent) = Additional Load

Winch Pull + Additional Load = Total Load on Winch

Let's use a Wrangler as an example. It weighs about 4,500 pounds with all the gear we've installed and we've added 300 pounds of gear and supplies, making it 4,800 pounds total. We're trying to winch it up a 50 degree slope consisting of light mud:

$$\frac{50}{60} \times 4,800 = 4,000 \text{ pounds} \quad 4,000 + 4,800 = 8,800$$

8,800 x 35%= 3,080

8,800 + 3,080 =11,880 pounds total winch pull

---

**NO-LOAD LINE SPEED COMPARISON**

| Drive System | Winch | No Load Line Speed |
|---|---|---|
| PTO (from trans) | Koenig 14RT73* | 56 FPM (top gear, 2,000 eng rpm) |
| Electric, Spur Gear | Warn 8274-50 | 52 FPM |
| Hydraulic | MileMarker | 36 FPM (in high gear @ 1,400 psi) |
| | | 6.42 FPM (low gear @ 1,400 psi) |
| Electric, Planetary | Warn XD-9000i | 32 FPM |
| Electric, Worm Gear | Superwinch Husky 8 | 18.3 FPM |

* This winch out of production.
Note: All specs taken on first cable layer. Upper layers are faster.

---

*Chapter 8*

# CHASSIS, BODY & INTERIOR

## Skin and Bones

The chassis is the backbone of any Jeep. Certain models, most notoriously the CJs, are known for chassis problems in tough trail situations. All Jeeps are subject to the ravages of time and climate, and rust can weaken them and make them even more susceptible to the rigors of off-highway travel. Chassis and body repairs are often a part of a Jeep CJ buildup.

There is also the modifications viewpoint. Are there any chassis or body mods that enhance performance or increase durability? The trail puts a whole new set of forces to work that can cause breaks, cracks, and metal fatigue. The modern Jeeper is tackling trails that were science fiction just a few years ago. This is putting even more stress and strain on a chassis, and failures are much more common now than they were just a decade ago, even on rigs that were previously not known for such problems.

### The Jeep Chassis

With the exception of the unibody XJ and ZJ, all Jeeps use a separate chassis/body design. They are all a little different, but we will deal heavily with the CJs since they are most often in harm's way and have most of the problems. Look at Figure 8-1 for chassis specs for assorted Jeeps.

There are basically four chassis designs for the CJ and Wrangler, starting with the early flat-fender CJs. This unit was a ladder-type built of two mild steel C-section rails, with five cross-members (one that unbolted). It also used a "K"-frame at the rear to provide a strong towing point.

The CJ-5 design that followed was very similar. The CJ-5 piece was a little longer and was built to provide an 81-inch wheelbase. The CJ-6 chassis was identical

but had an extra 20 inches added for the 101-inch wheelbase. This general chassis design was used with a few minor changes through 1971.

The pre-1971 chassis can be identified by their U-section front cross-members and K-frames. The K-frames are not always seen, especially nearer the end of the Kaiser era. The pre-1971 chassis were boxed up front to an area just past the rear front spring hanger. Overall, they were pretty weak and will not stand much abuse, by today's standards at least. If you add some performance mods, you will be stressing them even more. You will need to get out the welder and reinforce heavily if you expect such a chassis to survive the rigors of a big engine or extreme use. Often, the chassis will be in a sorry state when you get it, so plan on spending

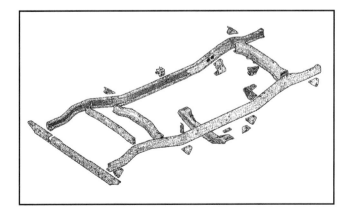

This is the CJ-5 chassis that was used from 1955 to 1971. It was often fitted with a rear "K"-frame for towing or drawbar use. It is very similar to the previous flatfender chassis. Note that the only boxing is at the motor mount area. This is the weakest chassis you will find. For hard-core use, this chassis would need a lot of reinforcement.

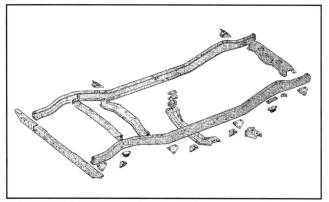

This is the 1972–75 chassis. It's a little stouter and a bit longer (84- vs. 81-inch wheelbase). Notice that the front cross-member has been moved forward to accommodate the longer six-cylinder AMC engines. It's boxed a little more at the front, but it doesn't amount to much extra beef. In many ways, this chassis ends up weaker due to the more powerful line of engines available.

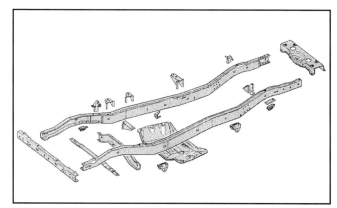

This 1976–77 is among the best CJ chassis. Notice that it's boxed almost all the way. In 1978, they boxed it all the way to the back. The Wrangler chassis is similar, but stronger materials are used, and the construction is improved.

a few bucks. We'll talk more about how and where to reinforce the chassis further along.

Next up are the 1972–75 chassis. It was similar in many ways to the earlier style, but because the engine options were changed, the wheelbase was stretched from 81 to 84 inches. The U-section front cross-member became a stamped piece that was moved right to the front of the chassis. It lacks the rear K-frame to accommodate a rear-mounted fuel tank, and the front

section is boxed from the front cross-member to the rear front spring hanger. This chassis was stronger than the previous design but still not great, especially considering that a high torque V-8 was on the options list.

The 1976–86 chassis took a big jump in beef and were boxed almost to the rear cross-member through 1977. They were a boxed all the way from 1978–on. They also were widened by a few inches in the back, and the wider stance made them a little more stable. The longer wheelbase CJ-7 and CJ-8 models were introduced in this era and shared these design elements. Most experts regard the latest chassis as the best because of the lessons Jeep had learned along the way.

The 1987–on Wrangler chassis is a fully boxed chassis that is not known for breakage problems in any but the most severe and abusive conditions. It's so good that some CJ owners have adapted them to carry the earlier body, though one would wonder at the cost effectiveness of such a change. Why not just drive a Wrangler? The chorus of snarls you just heard was from the round headlight crowd, who would rather spend a year's pay than adopt the square headlight!

### Chassis Failure

The CJ chassis is very flexible. This adds somewhat to axle articulation, and many Jeepers regard it as a big plus. The problem is that metal flexed regularly eventually fatigues and breaks. Jeepers sometimes enhance

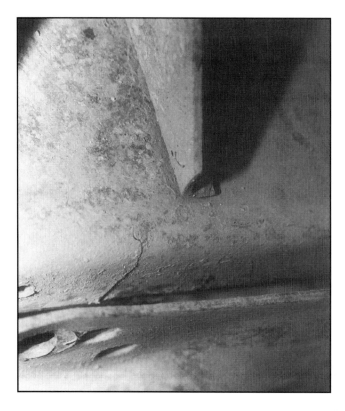

*Left:* Here you see the beginnings of a chassis failure on a 1980 CJ. This crack will continue to propagate until the chassis breaks in two pieces. The crack is located at the middle bolt area of the trans cross-member.

Here's an obvious substandard repair. The chassis is actually broken in two pieces behind the reinforcement. The area near the spring hanger is a common failure point.

With the front of the CJ chassis the most vulnerable to damage, M.O.R.E.'s chassis repair plates provide a method of repair or reinforcement. The chassis behind already has the plate fitted. This plate will not help with a badly rusted chassis.

chassis flex to obtain more articulation but spend more time on chassis repairs.

The CJ chassis has several very common breakage points, the most common being in the area of the rear front spring mount. The crack starts at the bottom near the mount. If left unattended, the crack will propagate all the way to the top of the rail and eventually the two sides will separate.

Another hot spot is at the steering box area of units with power steering. It's also not unusual to find the stamped front cross-member broken on 1972–86 rigs. Some experts have reported the front body mount brackets breaking. When you get right down to it, the chassis can crack anywhere. The moral here is to regularly check your CJ chassis and do it more often if you are a hard-core type. We'll discuss some chassis defense strategies a little later.

On all Jeep utilities, the body plays a big part in the structural integrity of the vehicle and is subject to the same stresses as the chassis. The body mounts are the first places for trouble. Sometimes they will rust away from the body or even tear away while under stress. Also, some of the spot welded seams may also give way. Age and rust will weaken it and since the body and chassis are tied together structurally, a failure on one side can cause a failure on the other.

### Protecting the Chassis

The first and cheapest level of defense is a watchful eye. Repair little problems before they become big ones. Make sure all your body mounts are tight and in

solid condition. Make sure that rust doesn't weaken the chassis or body.

The second level of defense involves some modifications. If your Jeep has power steering, add a steering box brace. Available from a variety of manufacturers, this simple, bolt-on item will help prevent breakage at the steering box area. If you do a power steering conversion on an earlier rig, the same advice applies. Many Jeepers report that a set of strong bumpers will also add a little extra beef to the chassis.

A nice, soft suspension is another item that offers some chassis protection. Ditto a shackle reversal kit. The pros and cons of shackle reversals are discussed in some detail back in Chapter 3, but the benefits to the chassis are not in much doubt. In the stock setup, shock is transmitted to the rear pivot point and eventually results in breakage. With the pivot point up front, the spring and shackle can absorb most of the shock.

If you are stripped down to a bare chassis and have the time, skill and money, you can take a number of

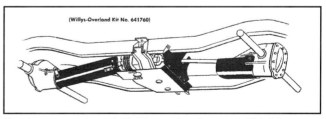

Here's some very cool CJ-2A-era chassis armor. This kit was intended more for Jeeps operating in the farm environment than those on the trail.

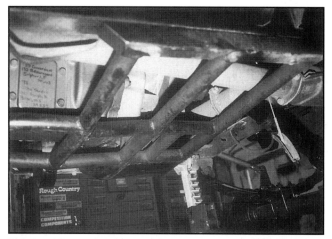

This is an example of a custom trans cross-member that accompanied an NV-4500 tranny conversion. There is no doubt that a setup like this is bombproof and adds a margin of beef to the chassis, as well as supporting and protecting the gearboxes.

useful steps. One of the easiest, and one that you can also do without a complete teardown, is to use Mountain Off-Road Enterprises frame plates. These 4-foot plates weld onto the outside of the vulnerable front horns of the CJ. They come with all the proper-sized holes in the correct spots. They are a reinforcement that can be used on previously repaired chassis as well as a "virgin" chassis, but they do not work well with rusty, deteriorating pieces. If you have the fabrication skill, you could build a similar setup yourself.

Getting well into the fabrication area, some Jeepers have boxed the entire length of their CJ chassis and reinforced it in areas where experience dictates. They may also weld in the cross-members rather than rely on the rivets. This really works but gets mighty expensive, even if you do it yourself. You have to gauge your needs and finances against a major step like this. It becomes a more cost-effective proposition if you need to strip the Jeep down for major work anyway.

Another expensive but easier step is to buy a new chassis. Not an OE replacement (there are still a few New Old Stock (NOS) chassis out there) but one that is scratch built out of superior materials. So far, only one company could be found that's doing this on a big scale and that's Matkins, of Billings, Montana. This company uses square tubing, either 1/8- or 3/16-inch wall, to fabricate a replacement chassis. All cross-members are welded and the body and other hardware just bolts on as with the stock chassis. This is the top-of-the-line chassis at the time of publication.

Extensive reinforcing or a Matkins chassis will eliminate chassis flex and may restrict articulation a bit. It

seems like a small price to pay for the extra beef, but if chassis flex is a part of your battle plan, you will need to be careful about where you beef up the chassis. Consider, however, that extra articulation is easy enough to get from the suspension and you can probably easily make up the loss from a more rigid chassis.

### Unibody

The ZJ and XJ have successfully translated unit body construction to the off-highway environment. They have a very rigid structure that appears to hold up well. You can have major problems if this structure gets damaged, from either an accident or from trail work. In the case of the latter area, it doesn't happen much. When it does, it's usually impact related, as opposed to stress. At the moment, the jury is still out on how well unibodies hold up in the tough trail scene.

### Chassis Armor

The chassis itself doesn't need impact protection, but some of the goodies that live there do. A list would include the fuel tank, transmission/transfer case, axles, engine oil pan, and driveshafts. The CJs and Wranglers come with minimal protection in the center of the vehicle. Some of the other Jeep products have very little protection, but this tends to be because of their intended use.

The big question is: Do you really need chassis armor? It comes down to your rig and how you drive it. Jeep CJs and Wranglers from 1976–on have a built-in skid plate/cross member that does double duty. The trans and T-case are reasonably well protected. This middle area is where most rigs need protection due to the *breakover angle* of the vehicle.

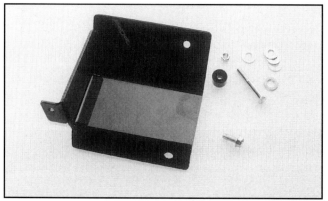

This TJ steering box skid plate from Tera Manufacturing is one of those little details that are often overlooked, until power steering fluid is running onto the ground from a split steering box. *Courtesy Tera Manufacturing*

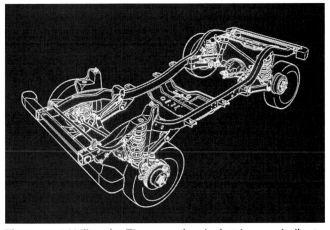

The newest Utility, the TJ, uses a chassis that is very similar to the YJ but features all the brackets needed for the coil springs. So far, this chassis seems to be as indestructible as the YJ.

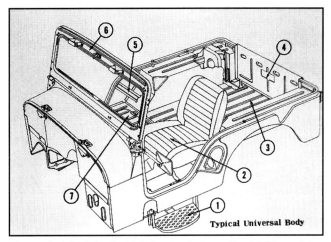

The typical CJ-5 body. This is a body from the 1968 model year, but only a few changes were apparent from 1955 to 1971. Most of the changes happened in front of the firewall. It wasn't until the CJ-7 "door era" that some fairly major changes were made.

Also, certain parts are more vulnerable than others. The older cast-iron transfer cases are usually up to a few moderate hits, but the aluminum 'cases are very vulnerable. Ditto the cast-iron vs. aluminum-case transmissions. With regard to diffs, the cast iron housings and tubes are tough but the sheet-metal covers can be caved in and punched through. Engine oil pans are vulnerable but usually up to some minor love taps from hostile rocks. Driveshafts are vulnerable but it isn't practical to cover them, although I have included an illustration from an old Willys catalog that shows a setup that was available for CJ-2As.

The fuel tank may be one of the most important areas to have skid plates, especially if you have installed a larger capacity unit that hangs down a bit. While punctured fuel tanks seldom ignite, that deadly possibility still exists. Many factory rigs come with a fuel tank "skidplate" but this is usually little more than sheet metal. Buy or build some fuel tank protection if your rig is vulnerable there. Late CJs and Wranglers are hanging out there a bit.

Only a few skid plates are made to order, but a good fabricator can build some very trick ones that make your underside ready to handle landmines. The downside is added weight. If your Jeep's belly doesn't get into harm's way much, careful driving might be the easiest and most cost-effective defense.

## Jeep Bodies

The Jeep CJ body has remained very similar, in design and construction, since the "round hood" CJ-5 was launched in 1954. The so-called "short-nose" bodies

lasted to the intro of the longer wheelbase 1972 models. The extra wheelbase and body length were added up front to accommodate the new line of AMC sixes and V-8s, so the hoods and fenders were a little longer. When the CJ-7 debuted in 1976, the line evolved into hard doors and hardtops but still remained essentially the same. The Wrangler isn't all that much different, even the latest coil-spring TJs.

Jeep CJ bodies are particularly vulnerable to rust. Wranglers are a bit better. Most other Jeep body styles are also fairly vulnerable all the way through the AMC era. When Chrysler took over, rust protection rapidly improved and it's now as good or better than any other manufacturer. Older bodies will also acquire cracks and tears in the course of a hard life.

### Body Defense Strategies

Body defense strategies include regular maintenance like routinely hosing off salt from the underside and out of every nook or cranny that might hold it. Don't let water stand in the interior for long periods. If your rig has carpets and they get wet, pull them out and let them dry. Finally, fix any rust so that it doesn't become a structural problem.

It is widely reported that permanently sealing up the tailgate of a CJ (if so equipped) results in a stronger body. This makes some sense if the job is done with more than just a piece of sheet metal. Some square tubing in the gap will do the trick.

In the course of major rebuilds, some owners have completely stripped the body, repaired any problems,

A typical CJ body failure in a typical area. Eventually this fender will fall off. Other areas to look at are where the front fenders join the firewall and anywhere there are spot welds, including along the floor seams. This Jeep has led a hard life, spending most of its 25 years on rough back roads and snowplowing.

Fiberglass bodies have been popular for a long time. Putting the rust aspect aside for the moment, fiberglass is generally well suited to the twisting and flexing that go with Jeeping. Fiberglass body kits come pretty much as you see this one. You will have to get out the saber saw and cut out the headlights and grill, as well as instrument holes, fuel filler, etc. *Courtesy AJ's Sales and Manufacturing*

and then gone the extra mile and rewelded all the body panels that are spot welded. This does add a bit of extra structural integrity, but whether this step is worth the extra effort is debatable. If you are into no-holds-barred maximum effort for maximum performance and longevity, by all means do it.

A good paint job not only adds rust protection but it makes your Jeep purty. Wanna make on the cover of a magazine? Paint it red, yellow, or a particularly bright shade of green. Avoid dark colors or shades that seem to suck up the light. Remember that with all the body flex, a very brittle type of paint will crack and flake more easily. Any paint can become brittle if improperly applied. Your paint and body person can recommend paints that have some natural flexibility.

Don't overlook spray-on coatings like Rhino Lining, Durabak, or Zolatone. These are very durable coatings that you can apply inside, or if you like the "Flintstone" look, on the outside. Either way, they provide solid protection against rust and damage and they do a fair insulating job as well.

### Replacement Steel Bodies

There may come a time when your Jeep body has reached the limit of practical repair. In these cases, a replacement body, or parts, may be in order. Complete replacements are available, as well as bits and pieces. Most universal types are available brand new. Some repro body parts are available for Wagoneer and Gladiator models as well a limited number of pieces for

Willys trucks and wagons. If you have a Forward Control or a Jeepster, you are out of luck at the time of this writing. As these rigs get more popular, you may begin to see these pieces reproduced.

Most of the bodies are produced overseas, with companies in India and the Philippines (where they *love* Jeeps) being the major manufacturers. In quality,

With the colors built into the body, fiberglass can stay looking good for a long time. The color is put into the smooth gel coat, which is sprayed into the mold first. Fiberglass can also be painted, either right away or down the road. A few special procedures are necessary, but the process is no worse than painting steel. In some ways painting fiberglass is easier because you have no rust to worry about. *Courtesy AJ's Sales and Manufacturing*

### Fiberglass Bodies

Fiberglass bodies for Jeeps have been around for quite some time. Their advantages are light weight, no rust to worry about, and a finish that will last a long while. Glass bodies also will withstand the natural flex of a Jeep chassis much longer than steel bodies. Compared to steel, 'glass has an almost infinite "flex-life." The only generic disadvantage to 'glass is that the wiring needs to be altered. Since the new body does not conduct electricity, ground circuits need to be run to the chassis. This is actually beneficial to the electrical system but involves extra work for the installer.

There are other disadvantages, such as cracking and poor resistance to impact but these are usually attributable to poor construction. As with other products, quality ranges from cheeseball to A-1. The weight advantage is sometimes overrated as well, because the weight of a good fiberglass body may still be within 20 percent of a steel body.

There are three common ways to manufacture fiberglass bodies and parts. They all start with a sprayed-on *gel coat* applied to the inside of a mold. This will become the exterior surface. From that point, the construction methods differ. The best are hand-laid bodies, where the woven fiberglass material is hand-laid in sheets inside the mold. The material is then soaked in resin and the air bubbles are worked out by hand. More layers are laid on diagonally to the previous ones. As you can imagine, this is a very time-consuming (read expensive) process. Vacuum forming is another method that is very good but is not a suitable process for large parts and requires expensive machinery.

Chopped construction, the most common type, uses a special gun, called a chopper, that sprays resin and chopped up fibers like paint. This is the weakest type of construction but the most cost-effective. A hand-laid body can be made very strong with minimal thickness and weight but a chopped body can be built to equal the hand-laid for strength by using extra chopped material and reinforcements that are encapsulated into the material. By necessity, it makes the chopped body heavier and negates some of the weight advantage over a steel body.

Good fiberglass body makers use marine-grade balsa wood, steel, and aluminum to reinforce the body in

these bodies run from very poor to good. The best advice is to carefully inspect a replacement body, before plunking down the cash. Look at fit and finish, as well as the quality of the welding and the thickness of the material. The body should at least match the OE. If you are talking early Jeep, let's be honest and say it was so-so from the factory anyway, so the standard to match is not all that high!

In the opinions of most of the folks consulted, one of the main problems with the cheeseball bodies lies in the quality of the steel. They will rust quickly and some are so bad that you cannot stop them from rusting, even under paint. The welding is another item to look at closely. Some Jeepers have gone over the bodies and rewelded the seams. In rare cases, the fit is so bad that the bodies require alteration to get them bolted up to the chassis. Finally, if you are looking for a 100 percent period accurate replacement for a restoration, you probably won't find it in the replacement body markets, though Archer Brothers comes pretty close with its early CJ bodies.

high stress areas. These areas include the floors, door latch areas, tailgate latch mounts, and corners. Sometimes plywood is used as reinforcement material instead of balsa, but plywood tends to warp over time. Good manufacturers use steel plates in body mount areas. Lesser builders simply reinforce with extra fiberglass. Some do not reinforce at all if they can skate by.

### Off-Highway Body Armor

Body damage is not an inevitability with four-wheeling, but it comes very close. The harder you 'wheel, the more likely it becomes. The hard-core types usually invest in body and chassis armor of some type so that the bumps and grinds of four-wheeling don't leave too many battle scars. The goal is to provide protection without compromising a millimeter of clearance. Sometimes compromises in clearance must be made, but the artful aftermarket and the talented home fabricator can usually minimize the loss.

The most vulnerable areas are the rocker or sill panels and the rear quarter panels. Starting with rockers, the protection can be as simple as a piece of angle iron on the bottom edge of the body, to something supported by the chassis. The latter style is stronger structurally, and this type of setup is called a "rock slider" or "nerf bar." Good rock sliders will support the weight of the vehicle if need be.

A rock slider is a useful bit of kit for any Jeep, but the applications are narrowed to the most popular types (CJ, YJ, XJ, ZJ). Fortunately they are relatively easy to produce, and a good fabricator can build a 'slider for just about any Jeep.

The rear quarter panels can be protected with *applique armor,* to use the old tanker terminology, that bolts on over the panel. Many times, these pieces are

made of aluminum diamond plate to avoid corrosion. Bear in mind that rust can start underneath these plates. A minimum is a good coat of wax on the body before you install the armor. Some Jeepers seal the plates with silicone and others remove the plates peri-

This is your basic nerf bar. Built of tubular steel, it attaches to the chassis and protects the lower body from rock damage. Some of these types are "show" pieces and will bend or dent when actually put to the ol' rock test. Bear in mind also that with this type of setup, you lose clearance in the amount of the bar thickness.

Here's a piece from Stage West that's more accurately called a rock slider. It's made of heavy plate and attaches to the lower body. The marks above are the owner's inspiration to install the 'slider. In this case, clearance is maximized and the angles of the piece promote the vehicle sliding off any rock it encounters. It integrates well with the fender flares.

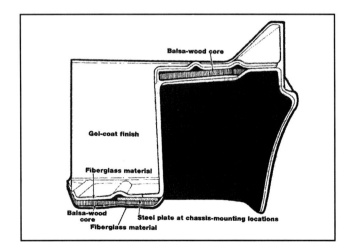

*Left:* Here are some of the features of a quality-built 'glass body, like those from AJ's. Reinforcement comes from marine grade balsa, which is light but holds its shape. Steel plates are installed wherever a body mount is located, or in strategic structural areas. *Courtesy AJ's Sales and Manufacturing*

odically to clean under them and rewax. Similar plates are available for the rocker area, some of aluminum and some of stainless steel.

### Bumpers, Body Hardware, Brush Bars, Etc.

There is so much stuff on the market that fits into this area that I'd need another book to cover it all. The problem is that most of it comes under the heading of cosmetics, and I have no business commenting on what you like to look at. In this case, the main goal is to help you look for quality-built pieces in whatever style strikes your fancy.

At first glance, you can tell garbage from the good stuff by the quality of the welding and the finish. With regard to welding, for the most part, if it looks good, it probably is good, and vice versa. In some cases, spot welds are a sure sign of cut corners. Look also at material thickness. Really tinny stuff is easily damaged on the trail.

The finish is more than cosmetic. You don't want rust settling in anywhere. Obviously, parts painted by spray can are a no-no for a mainline manufacturer. With the ease of getting things powder-coated these days, there is little excuse for a poor finish, no matter how small the company. In fact, the Eastwood Company offers a powder-coating kit that you can buy and use at home. Powder coating is a process

that electrically attracts a colored, powderized material to the piece. The coated part is then heated in an oven at 400 degrees, the powder melts and flows to a durable, even finish. Your oven at home will work, though you'd better ask your spouse first!

Other finish choices include various plating, such as chrome and nickel, or anodizing. If well done, all of these materials hold up for a long time. Stainless-steel

Fenderectomy! Some nice work from a talented and ingenious Canadian yielded a fabricated bolt-on fender for Wranglers that changed the whole character of the vehicle. There was talk that this would go into production, but apparently the people involved have moved on to other things.

The rear quarter panels on most Jeeps are vulnerable. For the venerable CJ, this type of bolt-on "armor" plate is a means to keep the panels nice, or to hide a panel that's not so nice. Only your bodyman knows for sure!

*Right:* Bumpers and tire carriers have come a long way. This unit from Stage West features a built-in receiver, beveled edges for clearance, and a burly swing-away carrier. This Wrangler owner also added a spare wheel bearing hub to mount the tire on. That way, he has a spare part that doesn't take up space inside.

In the old days, if you had padding under your butt, you considered yourself lucky. These days, folks demand more comfort. Recaros certainly provide that, along with side support. The bolstering of these seats will keep you square and secure in the seat at any angle. If there's a downside to seats like these (other than the cost), it's that they are difficult to get in and out of. If you've lost some of the limberness of youth, a few years of going in and out of these will get it back for you!

The interior of a soft top Jeep faces extra problems from the environment. For minimalists, a more common and cost-effective seat transplant comes in the form of units like these Bestops. They are weather resistant but more comfortable than the OE standard seats. Calibrated test-butts agree, however, that the Wrangler Sahara seats have the edge in comfort over the Bestops, while being more vulnerable to weather. Seat covers may be an answer to the comfortable but vulnerable seat problem. Several types are available.

parts and hardware are also popular and good looking. Keep in mind that poor quality stainless steel rusts. Polished aluminum is also attractive. Usually it's treated with a clear coat to prevent oxidation. Eventually, this coating gets rubbed or scratched off and the aluminum may need to be polished.

In some cases, the design of the accessory is a problem. Perhaps not so much in how it looks but in what trouble it causes once it's bolted on. Unfortunately, you may not find this until you've owned it a while. Maybe you will find that you have to remove the whole thing to change a marker light bulb, or the hood hits, or the door won't open all the way, or the piece rattles. Try to look for these drawbacks before you install the item.

Look at the quality of the instructions and whether there is some method of calling for help if assembly gets too tough. How the piece fits is another matter of some importance. There is a lot of fitment leeway needed for a hard-worked trail Jeep that has been tweaked, flexed, and twisted every which way. On the other hand, you shouldn't have to reengineer the vehicle to bolt a simple part on, assuming the part is designed to directly fit your application.

### Interior

Again, this is eye-of-the-beholder stuff. Some things to keep in mind are the material's resistance to rough conditions. Obviously, you don't install velour seats on a machine that runs topless 99 percent of the time. Bestop and Steelhorse, among others, make seats and interior trim that's up to some sunny days, trail dirt, and a little wetness.

On the other hand, "If in doubt, strip it out." That's what one hard-core Jeeper told me once. A trail Jeeper lives a minimalist existence. There is no need for many frills. A semicomfortable seat is really all you do need. This approach does eliminate a lot of expense and trouble. Whether you can live this Spartan existence day-to-day is a matter between you and your iron will.

In the case of SUVs, good compromises are waterproof seat covers, like those from Wet Okole, and footwell liners like those from Fox. Cargo area liners are available also. All these things can help keep your Grand Cherokee grand on the days when you get down and dirty. They are not quite as much fun as taking the hose to the inside of your Jeep, but there are compensations.

### Soft Tops

If you happen to be among the open air crowd, here are a few words on tops. Tops can range from the simple canvas units of the early rigs, to the elaborate vinyl and plastic creations of the newer rigs. Durability and convenience are the Jeeper's two main laments. By nature, ragtops are fairly short lived, with the maximum

Tops can be the source of major annoyance. Not only can taking them down and putting them up be a pain, but they may only last 5–6 years. Get the most out of your top by maintaining it. Also, buy a good one. This trick idea, called the Sunrider, comes from Bestop. Like a sunroof, it makes open air Jeeping a breeze. *Courtesy Bestop*

life in continuous use somewhere around six years. They are also known as a pain in the wazoo to put up and take down. The companies that make strides in these two areas find themselves very busy.

Many CJ, YJ, and TJ Jeeps are ordered with soft tops. The factory tops are of good quality, as are the mounting systems. Aftermarket top manufacturers will usually build tops to replace the OEM top using the original hardware. In very old applications, you may need to upgrade the mounting system to a newer style. The aftermarket seems confident that it can outdo the OEM setups for convenience, so sometimes the upgrades are worth a look. Certainly, if you are converting from a removable hardtop, the aftermarket hardware might be the better choice, though personal preference does enter into the equation.

Vinyl backed by cotton is the material of choice these days, with canvas as the main choice for restorations. Canvas has a certain "look" and it is surprisingly durable, but it is harder to get a good fit and to make the plastic windows seal. Vinyl, on the other hand, can be made in a large variety of colors and styles, it resists significant shrinkage, and window sealing is a breeze. Velcro is often used to achieve sealing in trouble areas.

There used to be a half-dozen top aftermarket manufacturers, but attrition has brought the market down to two big ones, Kayline and Bestop. Both are good companies with good products. They each have trademark features, and the competition between them has

brought out a variety of innovations. You can still find some upholstery shops who will make or repair tops, but they generally have a tough time completing with the "Big Two."

### Storage

Especially if you are driving a little Jeep, the problems of storage can be maddening. You can pile it all in and have it roll around like marbles in a can within ten miles. Theft is also an issue. With a ragtop, a sharp knife is as good as a key if some tasty morsel is left in view.

Some people create their own storage solutions by using military surplus ammo cans, or similar containers, with locks added. Canvas bags or even small wooden crates may be viable solutions. With these, or anything else you can come up with, the main storage requirement is satisfied, but whatever home method you concoct should be secured to the vehicle in some way. As discussed in Chapter 12, loose gear is a potentially lethal hazard.

A variety of storebought solutions are available, starting with the heavy-duty metal boxes from Tuffy. These things are probably bulletproof and it's easier to steal the Jeep than to pry one open. Their

Storage is the perennial problem with Jeeps. Theft comes a close second. You can combine solutions with aftermarket storage boxes. They can range from something you buy at the surplus store, to lockable plastic boxes, to metal units like these from Tuffy. Unless you have the key, it almost takes a cutting torch or explosives to get into these boxes.

If you have a thirsty V-8, that dinky 15-gallon CJ fuel tank won't last long. Many Jeepers will switch to larger tanks, like this 24-gallon unit from Northwest Metal Products. Even though the tank hangs a bit, it's protected by the springs and by a skid plate.

Carrying extra fuel is sometimes a necessity. Everyone has seen the American version of a "blitz" or "Jerry" can. Many people know that the basic design was invented by the Germans for World War II, but not many people have seen the original style. These German-made cans are now commonly called "NATO" cans and are a close representation of the original design. They are a bit stouter than our version and certainly seal better. The bigger one is 20 liters (5.2 gallons) and the smaller size is 5 liters (1.32 gallons). They are available from a variety of surplus outlets.

sole disadvantage is weight. They are built as console boxes, rear fenderwell storage, or, if you are willing to give up the back seat, as cargo storage. Radios or CBs can be mounted in them and Tuffy offers some with built-in speaker positions.

Bestop is also well known for creative storage solutions, but its boxes are made of plastic. This is an advantage in some ways. First, the material can be easily molded to fit in a variety of locations. It's also very light. It locks, though as one can imagine, it isn't as theftproof as steel. There are a variety of other outfits offering storage materials, so it's just a matter of finding the one that suits you best.

### Fuel Tanks

If you have a thirsty V-8, a diminutive 15-gallon tank empties pretty fast. Even if you don't have a thirsty engine, you may want more range to take you farther between fuel stops, or farther out into the boondocks. Factory fuel tank capacities are listed on page 128. Many Jeepers opt for oversized or auxiliary fuel tanks to increase range. They may also choose to carry five-gallon cans to supplement their supply. Not too many years ago, you could easily find a shop to build you a tank or a company that built them. Because of emissions regs and legal issues, the field has narrowed a lot, and choices have become more difficult.

The emissions issues come first. Modern fuel tanks are not vented to the atmosphere. Instead, the fumes are fed to the engine to be burned and the tanks are vented via a charcoal filter canister. Emission regs

require that all replacement fuel tanks, even a second tank, be fitted with the correct emission pieces. That means if there are emissions tests in your area, your new fuel tank needs to have the proper fittings. The companies that sell tanks nationally generally carry *C.A.R.B.* (California Air Resources Board) certification, so this usually makes them legal everywhere. A custom or homebuilt tank may or may not have the right hardware, but if it doesn't have certification of some type, it may not be legal.

There is a durability issue that comes with an aftermarket tank. Modern alcohol-blended or oxygenated fuels are hard on fuel lines and tanks. A plain steel tank can corrode very quickly when used with these types of fuels. Even galvanized tanks are vulnerable. Polyethylene (plastic) tanks are immune to this and aluminized steel tanks are resistant. Good aftermarket tanks are made of one of these two materials. Even the welding rod used must not be vulnerable to rust.

Choosing a fuel tank will involve several levels of thought. One is weight. If your Jeep's payload capacity is 800 pounds with a full 15-gallon tank, then adding another 10 gallons will decrease it by the weight of the fuel. Fuel weighs approximately 7 pounds per gallon, so an extra 10 works out to 70 pounds.

The other issue is clearance. In pickups, a rear tank

or a saddle on the opposite side can be added without a major loss of clearance. With a CJ or YJ, the only direction to expand is down and that may decrease clearance and your departure angle. It may also require a skidplate or a stouter skidplate to avoid damaging the more vulnerable tank.

### Fuel Cans

Carrying extra fuel in cans is another time-honored option. From the time the "Jerry" can was invented by the Germans in World War II, it's been a useful addition to a Jeeper's kit. There are pluses and minuses to their use.

The plusses of a Jerry can include not always having to carry a huge tankful of gas around, at the expense of fuel economy and cargo capacity. On many serious expeditions, fuel is deliberately carried in cans, because they can be unloaded if the vehicle gets stuck or encounters very difficult obstacles. In the case where a larger tank costs clearance, your overall trail performance is better with the extra fuel in cans.

On the downside, cans usually have to be carried outside the vehicle (NEVER carry gas cans inside the passenger compartment). This usually puts them in an area where they may help raise the center of gravity adversely. Also, they may be vulnerable to damage. Another NEVER is driving around town with full cans strapped on the back of your Jeep. It may even be illegal in your area to carry a full gas can on the outside of a vehicle.

There is also a distinct difference in types of cans. Forget plastic containers because they can crack and chafe. Ditto for those tinny little cans. Use these two types for your mower. The most common type of can is the five-gallon Jerry or Blitz can. Blitz is one of the best known manufacturers and these cans can be bought cheaply most everywhere, and racks are common that can handle them. They are cheap and easy to find, but

A popular accessory these days for rock crawlers is "Moab Rollers." Projecting just past the point of contact at the approach or departure angles, they can deflect an impact and allow the projection to "roll" past. This is a custom application only. So far, nobody is offering a ready-made kit.

in this author's experience, they always seem to weep fuel at the cap. They are pretty rugged and I've dropped one off the back of a speeding 4x4 and gone back to find it dented but intact.

The better five-gallon cans are the NATO style. These more closely resemble the original German design. They are harder to find and much more expensive but they have a cap that *does not leak* in my experience. They pour better and the spouts that are commonly available seem to be easier to use. They are as durable as the other cans, but it's harder to find a proper mounting for them, at least in the United States.

If you opt for cans, use a very secure mounting system that is not just attached to sheet metal. Forty pounds of fuel can tear a Jerry can mount off most sheet metal in very short order. The best idea is to use a rack made of tubing and whose weight is carried by a stout bumper or solidly mounted bracket.

## JEEP CHASSIS SPECIFICATIONS

| Model | Overall Length | Frt. W. | Rear W. | Section Modulus* |
|---|---|---|---|---|
| CJ-2A, CJ-3A | 122.97 | 29.25 | 29.25 | 1.493 in. cu. |
| CJ-3B | 122.97 | 29.25 | 29.25 | 1.493 in. cu. |
| CJ-5, pre-1971 | 128.44 | 29.25 | 29.25 | 1.493 in. cu. |
| CJ-6, pre-1971 | 148.44 | 29.25 | 29.25 | 1.493 in. cu. |
| C-101, 1967–71 | 159.00 | 29.25 | 29.25 | 2.247 in. cu. |
| C-104, 1972–73 | 164.88 | 29.25 | - | 1.493 in. cu. |
| Wagoneer | 173.96 | 38.00 | - | 2.050 in. cu. |
| J-2000, 1963–69 | 183.75 | 44.50 | - | 3.500 in. cu. |
| J-3000, 1963–69 | 195.75 | 44.50 | - | 3.500 in. cu. |
| CJ-5, 1972–75 | 131.38 | 29.25 | - | 1.493 in. cu. |
| Pickup, 1947–65 | | | - | 2.581 in. cu. |
| FC-170 | 171.50 | 44.50 | - | 2.581 in. cu |
| J-2000, 1970–87 | 183.75 | 44.50 | - | 3.610 in. cu. |
| J-4000, 1970–87 | 195.75 | 44.50 | - | 8.000 in. cu |

* A measurement of the area, in cubic inches, of the inside of the c-section.

## FACTORY FUEL TANK CAPACITIES

| Model and Year | Main, Std/Opt | Location* |
|---|---|---|
| 1945–61, CJ-2A, 3A, 3B | 10.5 | US |
| 1954–69, CJ-5, CJ-6 | 10.5 | US |
| 1970–81, CJ-5, CJ-6 | 15.5 | R |
| 1982–86, CJ-5, CJ-7 | 15.0/20.0 | R |
| 1981–85, CJ-8 | 15.0 | R |
| 1987–96, YJ | 15.0/20.0 | R |
| 1997–up, TJ | 15.0/19.0 | R |
| 1947–65, PU, SW | 15.0 | R |
| 1957–65, FC-150 | 16.0 | S |
| 1957–65, FC-170 | 22.0 | S |
| 1963–65, Gladiator PU | 20.0 | S |
| 1966–69, Gladiator PU | 18.0 | S |
| 1970–73, Gladiator PU | 20.0 | S |
| 1974–75, J-Series PU | 19.0 | S |
| 1975–78, J-Series PU | 19.0 (20.0 Aux.) | S/R |
| 1979–86, J-Series PU | 18.2 | S |
| 1963–69, Wagoneer | 20.0 | R |
| 1970–80, Wagoneer | 22.0 | R |
| 1981–91, G.Wagoneer | 20.3 | R |
| 1984–90, Cherokee | 13.5/20.2 | R |
| 1991–97, Cherokee | 20.2 | R |
| 1986–92, Comanche PU | 16.0/18.0/23.5 | S |
| 1993–up, G. Cherokee | 23.0 | R |
| 1967, Jeepster | 15.0 (9.5 Aux.)** | R |
| 1968–71 Jeepster | 15.0 | R |
| 1972–73 Jeepster | 16.5 | R |

* Location Glossary: US = underseat, R = rear mounted, S = side or saddle mounted.
** Some conflicting info whether this was available or not. The Jeep Data Book for 1968 does not show this option.

# Chapter 9

# BRAKES

## Whoa Nellie!

Most folks would agree that being able to stop is more important than being able to go. In stock form, modern Jeeps have adequate, if not very good, brakes. And then there are the old-timers. There was a good reason why Roy Rogers' TV sidekick was always going, "Whoa, Nellie," when bringing that tired old CJ-2A to a stop. Beyond the inadequate brakes of yesteryear, the problems for most Jeepers come when the vehicle is modified.

The brakes on Jeeps from any era were designed to match the operational limits of the vehicle. If you exceed any of these limits, by changing major components or the way the vehicle is used, you may find that the Jeep is underbraked. This may manifest itself in accelerated wear on brake components or a decrease in braking performance, or both. Depending on your modifications, the decrease in performance can be alarming or more subtle.

The chart on page 138 rounds up the original equipment in some detail, but basically drum brakes lasted into the early 1970s, when disc brakes took over stopping duties in front. Rear drum brakes have lasted to this day in all but the most expensive Jeep applications, usually due to cost and complexity issues. Making the rear brakes perform dual duties as parking brake and service brake is much easier with drums than discs. Currently, only the high-dollar Grand Cherokees use four-wheel disc brakes.

Brakes of any type share a common concept, to turn energy into heat. The brake will create friction that slows the movement of the vehicle and in doing so turns the energy of that vehicle in motion into the heat of friction.

### Disc vs. Drum

The drum brake is the granddaddy of brake systems and has been around since the beginning of the motor vehicle era. It has changed little in concept over the years. It uses an internal friction surface around the circumference of a drum and expanding shoes on the inside. Via a hydraulic cylinder (in modern times at least, as the first systems were mechanical), the friction lining of the shoes are forced against the friction surface of the drum.

Disc brakes date back almost as far as drum brakes but they didn't find practical application until the 1950s and total acceptance until the early 1970s. Disc brakes use two friction surfaces on either side of a disc, called a rotor. At some point around the circumference, a caliper is fitted that contains two brake pads, one on either side. The hydraulic caliper squeezes the two pads toward each other, clamping the rotor.

Disc brakes are superior to drums for several reasons. For one, they are more resistant to fade because

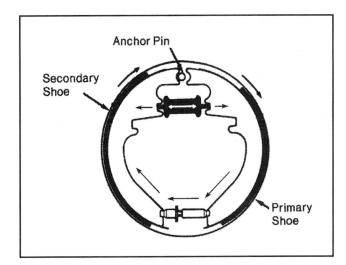

The best drum brakes are self-energizing, meaning that they convert some of the friction into added braking force. This is why many drum brake setups work well without a booster and those that have boosters may be hypersensitive to pedal pressure. If you've ever driven an old Caddy, you know what I mean. Just wave your foot over the brake pedal, and the brakes lock.

they dissipate heat better. Why? Because the swept area (the friction surface for the pad) is directly exposed to the air. Just one side of a disc brake may have as much swept area as a similar-sized drum. A drum brake must first heat the exterior of the drum to dissipate heat and the friction surface can get very much hotter than the cooling surface of the drum, causing fade.

Disc brakes are also more resistant to dirt, mud, and water because they are self-cleaning. The pad, always lightly rubbing against the surface of the rotor, keeps it mostly clear of mud, dirt, or water. Drum brakes can pack with mud and when they get wet, take four times as long to dry out. Water is, after all, a lubricant and lubricants don't combine well with devices that depend on friction. If you need to make a fast stop after a water crossing with drum brakes, you'll find out what, "Whoa, Nellie," is all about!

Drum brakes, however, are not without benefits. The actual braking performance between drums and discs is not large (given a roughly equal playing field). They have more lining area and because the modern designs self-energize (essentially braking force is multiplied, see Figure 9-3), they can generate some serious friction with less pedal effort than can a disc brake. That's why disc brakes almost always use power assist, when many drum brakes do not.

## Why You Need Improvements

The most common reason for an improvement to the brakes is the addition of larger tires. The taller tires increase the torque arm effect, and this decreases the

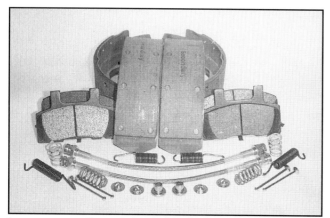

In many cases, the only level of brake improvement needed is an improved set of shoes and pads. This set is from Praise Dyno Brake and features composite linings with a higher friction coefficient than stock linings. This brake set could very well compensate for those bigger tires. *Courtesy Praise Dyno Brake*

leverage the brakes are able to exert on the wheels. Since the brakes have to work harder, they get hotter and wear out faster, and the Jeep may not stop as well.

This could be a serious problem if you combine 33x12.50s with the 9-inch brakes of an old CJ. The effects are less with modern disc brakes or larger drum brakes, but they still exist. Combine the above scenario with the increased speed potential of a modified Jeep, and the vehicle is more at risk. Consider also that most modified rigs have gained a bit of weight, further stressing the brakes.

### *Brake Improvements: Linings*

The beginning level of improvements for any set of brakes is changes in lining material. You might combine this step with any of the others that follow. Until recently, brake linings came in three common types, organic, semimetallic, and metallic, but the new trend is in the composite materials.

### Organic Linings

This type of brake lining material is a compound of organic materials that are bonded together with resins. Until recently, this included asbestos, which is now essentially outlawed due to health risks. It has been replaced by glass fibers and other synthetic materials. Organic linings have improved substantially over the years. Good organic linings provide quiet operation, combined with good wear characteristics. As friction material, they work best at low temperatures, making them most suitable for low speed and unstressed work. The average organic brakes are good to about 500 degrees and then will fade away very quickly and wear faster.

### Semimetallic

Next up the brake food chain are semimetallic linings. The material in these linings contains steel fibers (essentially steel wool), as well as some organic materials and resins. They wear better and resist heat better than pure organics. Some semimetallics will handle up to 1,000-degree temperatures. The semimetallic pad is known to work better at relatively high temperatures and in most cases requires more pedal pressure when cold. These materials tend to be noisy as well. Many newer Jeeps already use semimetallic linings, but they may be unnecessary for an earlier rig unless some factor is increasing the workload of the brakes, such as larger tire diameters or heavier loads. Semimetallics may increase brake drum or rotor wear.

## Metallic Linings

These may consist of sintered metal (powdered metal that is fused together by heat) or steel wool that is compressed and fused with other materials. This material has been used exclusively for racing or aircraft brakes. They can tolerate very high temps but they are of little use to the average Jeeper, because they only really start to work well at temps that would fry the average lining. They also will eat up standard rotors and drums like candy. The only reason I even mention them is that some nonracing folks still ask for them. They usually regret it in everyday use.

## Composite Linings

Composites are the future of brakes that are here now. Composite linings are made from carbon, carbon fibers, Kevlar, and/or polymer compounds, along with a few other goodies. The new materials allow for much longer wear (next year an OEM manufacturer will offer a 100,000-mile brake warranty), much higher resistance to heat, quiet operation, and excellent compatibility with rotors and drums. The range of friction coefficients can be made to any desired level. Praise Dyno Brake of Royse, Texas, was the first to offer a production composite material, back in 1982.

### Hard vs. Soft Linings

These rather dated terms refer to the friction coefficient of the lining material. The actual figures are more useful. The current industry standard uses a two-letter designation, with the first rating being the coefficient of friction of the material in a cold state and the second letter its rating hot. Each letter covers a .10 range. For example, the OE industry standard is an EE lining, which equates to a coefficient of friction of .25–.27 hot or cold. An "F" rating has a .27–.37 coefficient of friction, and a "G" rating, which is about the highest standard commonly seen for street use, has a .37–.47 rating. Some race cars use linings at .80–.90 coefficient of friction, but these are not practical for everyday use. How high a coefficient of friction you can use will depend on how much grip your tires have on the road surface, the weight of the vehicle, the torque arm effect of tire diameter, and how much force your hydraulic systems can generate. If your linings are too "grippy," you may experience early tire lockup. On the other hand, a tall and wide tire swap could use a higher rated pad.

### Riveted vs. Bonded

Brake linings are attached to shoes or pads in two common ways, via rivets or by bonding with a glue. More modern brake builders can mold the brake material to the pads. Riveted linings are just that—they are riveted to the metal shoe or pad. This entails countersinking the rivet into the lining material. One advantage to a riveted shoe is that it transfers heat a little better than a bonded lining. On the downside, countersinking tends to weaken the lining and it can crack. Also, the usable lining stops at the point where it wears down to the rivet heads. The absence of rivets gives bonded shoes more usable lining material. This also translates into more material, since the rivet holes reduce the surface area of the lining somewhat.

### Brake Improvements: Drums

In the old days, brake improvements came in the simple form of larger drum brakes. The popular trick was to swap the 9-inch drums for 10- or 11-inch self-energizing units from Jeep Station Wagons or pickups, or the even better 1960s-era Gladiator pieces. This is still a somewhat popular conversion for vintage Jeeps with a bias toward practicality, but good used parts are hard to find and many new parts are out of production.

Increasing the diameter of the drum increases the leverage of the brakes on the wheel, as well as the swept area and lining area. This knowledge can be useful for front or rear brakes. To maintain the same ratio of leverage, a rule of thumb for drum brakes is to increase the diameter of the drum by the same percentage as you increased the diameter of tire. If you go from a 29-inch tire with a 10-inch drum to a 33-inch tire, you are gaining a 15 percent increase in tire diameter. Ten inches increased by 15 percent is 11.5 inches. By uprating to 11-inch drums, you would be getting into the ballpark. The limiting factor will be how much room is available inside the wheel and the brakes. Whatever brake you choose, you need about 3 inches difference between the diameter of the outside of the drum and the inside of the wheel for cooling.

### Front Disc Brake Conversions

There are gearheads out there who relish the challenge of "making it work"—sourcing parts, trying them out, adapting, playing around with various ideas. These are people who would rather do it all themselves. The results can be a work of art or junk, depending on how well those DIY desires match up to the skill and expertise applied. Think about your brakes and what they do before taking an experimental approach.

We'll start off here by outlining a few of the retrofit bolt-ons that have been used over the years. One front disc brake option for CJs going back to the flatfender era is to use the bits and pieces from the later disc brake CJs. The 1977–80 disc brake option is practically a bolt-on to Dana 25, 27, and 30 axles, though this setup is getting hard to find.

The 1977–80 setup uses a six-bolt, bolted-on caliper bracket that matches the six bolts of the stub axle mount and a 12-inch diameter rotor that is 1.2 inches thick. Though a thinner rotor was used from mid-1978 on (apparently there was a period when they were mixed), the six-hole bracket remained through the 1980 model year. Calipers need to match thick or thin rotors.

In 1981, the calipers were changed to a more compact unit and a two-hole bracket was used that mounted to cast-in ears on the knuckle. This will swap over if you use the Dana 30 knuckle that came with them. This makes it a more complicated swap, but the parts are a little easier to find.

If you have or have installed a Dana 44 open knuckle axle, you can adapt Chevy truck calipers and brackets to the knuckle and use a 1976–86 Ford Bronco rotor and wheel bearings, along with a 1974–76 Bronco or F-150 spindle. The smaller 1972–76 Chevy truck caliper bracket is preferred.

Much of the above would apply to Jeepsters, FCs, Willys Station Wagons and pickups, or even the early Wagoneers, that used a Dana 25 or 27 front axle. Some Dana 30s and old, closed knuckle Dana 44s are more problematic.

On the other hand, companies like Stainless Steel Brake Corp., Foothill 4-Wheel Drive, and others take all the guesswork out by offering front disc brake kits. Everything you need is there. No complications. No guesswork. Application is usually for most of the common varieties of Jeep that use Dana 25, 27, 30, or 44 axles.

### Rear Disc Brake Conversions

Disc brakes in the rear have all the advantages of a front conversion, though one could argue about the bang-for-buck aspect. This option becomes more cost-effective if you absolutely need a brake upgrade and especially if you are doing an axle assembly upgrade.

The aforementioned GM caliper brackets can be used in back with Jeep rotors. In order to have an emergency brake, calipers from Corvette, Cadillac Eldorado, or Lincoln Versailles must be used. These used a

Rear discs are a common mod, especially as an accompaniment to a rear axle swap. This is a set that is commonly found on Ford Explorers and Expeditions. A rear disc kit using these pieces is offered by Ford Motorsports but it doesn't fit Dana axles. In this case, Currie used Ford axle and wheel bearing hardware on a custom Dana 60, so the setup fits well.

mechanical, cable-operated actuator that you can adapt to the Jeeps OE e-brake cables, or if it has a T-case e-brake, you can choose to leave these calipers out and go with the standard type, or install a later type e-brake assembly.

All of the above involves scrounging, fabricating, adapting, and general fooling around. There are probably some dollar savings in doing it this way, if you don't pay yourself for the time. An easier alternative is to buy a bolt-on kit, such as one of those from TSM, Stainless Steel Brake Corporation or Rubicon Express. These kits are available for the front or rear of many drum brake Jeeps, and they supply everything that's needed.

A higher buck alternative that simplifies the emergency brake situation is to use 1995 and newer Ford Explorer rear brakes that have a small, drum type emergency brake in the rotor hub. Installing this setup entails welding a Ford 9-inch style axle end onto the axle tube (a benefit to this is that you can use the big Ford 9-inch axle bearing). Currie Enterprises has been building such setups for a couple of years now with good success. If you are having a Currie axle built, this may be an ideal way to go. The brake kit comes from Ford Motorports and is designed for Mustangs.

### Hydraulics

Changes in the hydraulic system will go hand-in-hand with many other brake system changes you

This is the common Jeep CJ booster bracket. In addition to mounting the booster, it transfers pedal motion to the booster with a bit of a ratio. It actually decreases the ratio a bit. By moving the firewall mounting holes down 1/2 to 3/4 inch and moving the rod from the pedal down on the arm by the same amount, you can increase the pedal ratio. You will also need to shorten the rod on the booster or install an adjustable rod. This bracket is adaptable to many earlier applications, but is getting hard to find.

might make. The hydraulics need to match the friction-producing setup at the wheels. The brake system balances the amount of force applied to the hydraulics, the hydraulic pressure generated, the coefficient of friction from the brake linings, the tire grip, the weight of the vehicle, and torque arm effect of the wheels. If you

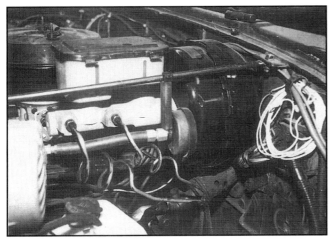

This setup combines an Off-Again dual diaphragm booster with a Corvette disc brake master cylinder. The booster is mounted directly to the firewall in this case, but it could be mounted to the CJ style bracket. The dual diaphragm doubles the power of a given diameter booster. The CJ doesn't have room for a large diameter booster, so the Off-Again setup offers the means to increase power assist in limited space.

change one part of the equation, you may need to change another.

### Hydraulics 101

Without getting into physics overmuch, I'll just state a few commonsense facts for you to consider. First, the hydraulic system converts the forces generated by your leg on the brake pedal into hydraulic pressure by pushing a piston down the bore of a master cylinder. Since brake fluid (or any other liquid) cannot be compressed, the piston increases the pressure in the system. The pressure is converted into force again at the other end of the line, when the caliper pistons or wheel cylinder pistons have no choice but to react. The brake pads or shoes are forced against a rotor or drum to create friction.

The master cylinder creates pressure and displaces a given amount of brake fluid at the same time. How much fluid the master cylinder displaces and how much pressure it generates depends on the stroke and surface area of the piston. The amount of pressure and displacement is carefully calibrated to match the pistons in the calipers or wheel cylinders to generate a predetermined amount of force needed to apply the brakes.

If properly designed, the hydraulic system will multiply the force you apply at the pedal several times. The basic formulas for this are included in Figure 9-2. The more force multiplication you get, the more pressure is applied to the brake linings and the more friction is generated.

The force generated at the caliper piston or wheel cylinder depends on the size of these pistons versus the size of the master cylinder piston. If you had a 2-square-inch master cylinder, a 2-square-inch caliper piston, and applied 50 pounds of force to the master, you'd still have only 50 pounds of force at the caliper. If you increased the caliper piston to a 4-square-inch piston, you'd have 100 pounds generated. An 8-square-inch caliper piston would generate 200 pounds of force, and so on. The same principle works with drum brakes, though they need less pressure because of the servo action discussed earlier.

The problem is that you can only have caliper pistons so big. A 4-square-inch piston is 2.25 inches in diameter and that's pretty big for a caliper piston. In most cases, 200 pounds of force isn't enough for a disc brake caliper. Help for your legs comes in the form of some mechanical leverage from the brake pedal assembly. By changing the pedal ratio as shown on page 138,

On this 'glass bodied flatfender, a dual diaphragm master cylinder is mounted without a booster. You can see the mounting bolts for the pedal assembly behind the cylinder. This rig also uses four-wheel discs, so it must have an outrageous pedal ratio. Note the clutch master on the right.

that 50 pounds at the master cylinder can be turned into more using that mechanical advantage. Typical manual brakes have a pedal ratio of 4 or 5:1 while power systems are often about 3:1, depending on the amount of servo action supplied by the booster. (Read on.)

Using our previous formula with a 5:1 ratio, that 50 pounds from your leg becomes 250 pounds. Our 2-square-inch master cylinder sends that down to our 4-square-inch caliper piston and we get 500 pounds of pressure, and this is in the ballpark of many brake systems.

### Brake Master Cylinder

When it comes down to nuts and bolts, the changes you make at the wheels could result in increased pedal effort or a very touchy pedal that will lock the wheels at the slightest pedal movement. If these modifications are carefully selected, the odds are good that the impact will be minimal and few changes will be needed.

An example of this would be a rear disc conversion on a modern Jeep that already has front discs. Some kits recommend removing the *proportioning valve* (a device that lessens the pressure to the rear brakes) or the *residual pressure valve* (a device that holds a tiny bit of pressure in the drum brakes) because of the differences in disc versus hydraulic brakes. Other kits include a new master cylinder as needed.

Older rigs or pre-1966 units that do not use a dual cylinder are good candidates for a master cylinder swap. In the case of the dual cylinder, this is a good

safety step because it has two separate circuits, front and rear. If one circuit develops a leak, you will still have 50 percent of your brakes.

In the case of the early rigs, many of them used pedals that came up through the floor and had master cylinders mounted on the chassis. In extreme use, chassis flex can cause the body to interfere with brake pedal operation and often this, combined with an inadequate master cylinder, makes them prime candidates for a hanging pedal swap. These units can be removed from later Jeeps, or even non-Jeeps and retrofitted to the earlier rigs.

If you do a brake swap and end up with a hard pedal, there are a few options. If you don't have power brakes, this is an obvious solution (discussed shortly). Several companies, such as Off-Again, offer a power brake swap. If you already have power brakes, a master cylinder swap may be in order.

You can use the formulas on page 138 to determine what size master cylinder you need and match this up to a mounting system or a booster. If you determine you need more volume, you can increase the size of the cylinder and compensate for the lower pressure with a booster, a more powerful booster, or a change in pedal ratio.

In a master cylinder swap, look for one that is set up for rear disc brakes, if these are what you plan to install. Most disc brake masters do not have a residual pressure check valve and if you get one that does, you may have to remove it from the master cylinder or end up with dragging brakes. Corvette master cylinders are popular in Jeeps with four-wheel discs because they are built for discs all around.

### Disc Brake Calipers

A multitude of caliper types are available but only a few are easily retrofitted to the Jeep. There are two basic types of caliper designs, fixed and floating. Fixed calipers use a piston or pistons on either side of the rotor. Hydraulic pressure operates the pistons individually.

A floating caliper uses one piston on the inside of the rotor. The caliper slides on a bracket and when the piston is pushed against the inside pad, the force is transmitted though the caliper housing to the pad on the outside and roughly equal force is applied to both sides of the rotor.

Fixed calipers are generally adjudged to be superior, but more expensive to produce than sliding calipers. The performance differences are not worth noting for most Jeepers and a sliding caliper has much more flex-ibility for adaptation. If, for example, you are swapping in a sliding caliper and the rotor is offset a bit more to one side or the other than it was in the original appli-cation, the sliding caliper has the flexibility to still work. A fixed caliper will need to be positioned exactly.

### Proportioning Valves

Brake bias, or the percentage of braking done by the front and rear, is an important topic. The deceleration of braking tends to transfer most of the vehicle weight to the front. Not only that, most Jeeps are heavier in the front than in the rear. This is especially true of pick-ups. The end result is that the rear brakes will tend to lock up sooner than the front and everyone knows that skidding tires develop less grip. The answer to this problem is the proportioning valve.

A proportioning valve limits the amount of pressure to the rear brakes to help prevent lockup. Most Jeeps (and certainly any with OE disc brakes) have them and they usually work well, even in a case where a mild level of brake modification has been performed. The problems start with the addition of rear discs or front discs in place of drums. The original proportioning valve, if one is fitted, may be doing the exact opposite of what is needed.

Fortunately, adjustable proportioning valves are available and you can then dial in the amount of brake bias required. Since correct brake bias depends on load, you can experiment and adjust the bias as needed, depending on how much gear you are carrying.

### Brake Lines and Hoses

Since the brake system can operate at up to 1,000 psi, it becomes important to have lines and hoses up to the job. The material used is not just your average hardware store household stuff, but is specially made to withstand high pressure, corrosive elements, and fatigue. Do not substitute copper or nonbrake rated tubing unless you have a death wish.

The metal tubing is double-wall material that is tin-plated to resist rust. Even so, it will eventually corrode under the severe conditions of salted roads. Any brake mods should include a thorough inspection of the metal lines.

Many modified Jeeps will include the replacement of all the brake lines. You can buy brake line on rolls and with a tubing bender and a double flaring tool, you can replace all the line and route it wherever you want. The lines must be double flared, as shown in Figure 9-

Many times during the brake modification process, the OE proportioning valve (if one was even fitted) is inadequate. Adjustable proportioning valves, like this Wilwood unit, allow you to dial in the rear braking to suit the vehicle.

5, for strength and to prevent leaks. A single flare leaves the edges prone to cracks. You can also buy prebent, presized, and flared brake lines to fit nearly any Jeep from companies like Classic Tubes.

The flexible brake hoses are made of neoprene with a fabric "net" embedded in them and often have a Teflon liner inside. They are designed to resist "bal-looning" in response to increased pressure but they all will expand to a small degree. This tendency will increase with age. When this occurs, it increases the amount of fluid the master cylinder has to push. Steel braided lines are popular, because the steel mesh pre-vents the lines from ballooning.

Replacing the flexible brake lines is common for many reasons. On lifted rigs or those with more articu-lation than stock, the brake hose must be long enough to reach from chassis to brake in all suspension and steering positions. In some cases, a longer OE style line may be found by a diligent search, but many Jeep builders use premade lines from Earls Performance Products, Skyjacker, or other sources. Some hydraulic shops will also build you custom lines. Keep in mind that not all braided lines are DOT legal.

### Brake Fluid

Most common brake fluid is a glycol-based liquid that has several important properties to include resis-tance to boiling, freezing, and corrosion. It must also have some lubricating properties. Unfortunately, brake fluid is hydroscopic, meaning that it will absorb mois-ture from the air. As the percentage of water increases, so does corrosion but most importantly, the boiling point is lowered. Boiling fluid gets aerated and a spongy pedal is the result.

A DOT 3 fluid has a boiling point of 400 degrees Fahrenheit (contrast that to water at 212 degrees). With just 2 percent (by weight) of water, the boiling point drops about 100 degrees. By the time the water content reaches 6 percent, it has dropped to 285 degrees. The moral here is to regularly change your brake fluid, more often in humid climates than dry ones. Don't use brake fluid that has been left open for long periods or that has been opened and stored for long periods.

Brake fluid is graded by the Department of Transportation. DOT 3, DOT 4, and DOT 5 are the common ratings. DOT 3 is the standard for most vehicles and has a boiling point of 401 degrees. DOT 4 is used in many high-performance car brake systems for its 446 degree boiling point. DOT 5 has a 500 degree boiling point and is used in racing and some high-performance street cars. DOT 3 is adequate for most Jeepers, with DOT 4 for highly stressed Jeep brake systems. DOT 5 is usually overkill and not cost-effective, but knock yourself out if you need the edge.

An alternative to glycol-based fluid is silicone-based fluids. Unlike glycol, silicone does not absorb moisture and it also will not eat paint (regular fluid will, so be careful). Silicone fluid is required to meet DOT 5 specs. It's best installed with the brake system dry, as in an overhaul, because the presence of even some glycol tends to reduce its performance.

### Brake Boosters

Having a brake booster is equivalent to having speed skater Eric Heiden's legs. It multiplies the amount of force applied to the master cylinder. This is often the cure for a hard pedal. Jeeps have had power brakes available since the debut of the Gladiator and Wagoneer in 1963. The CJs first got power brakes in 1976 for the drum brake setup, and later it came as standard for the disc brake setups. The CJ booster is now out of production, and while used ones are available, many Jeepers are adapting other styles to fit.

Two types of booster are commonly available, the single-diaphragm and the dual-diaphragm. Both are operated by engine vacuum. The double-diaphragm booster is more powerful than the single unit. How much assist a booster can generate is dependent on the size of the diaphragm. The large diameter unit will supply more boost but if underhood space is limited, so is booster size. That's where a dual-diaphragm booster is useful. It nearly doubles the power of a small-diaphragm booster and is perfect for limited space applications.

A few Jeepers have adapted the GM style Hydro-boost system. This uses hydraulic pressure from the power steering system to supply boost. This is a complicated conversion but not without merit. Because engine vacuum can be affected by things like altitude and camshaft profiles, you may not always have maximum boost available. The hydroboost supplies 100 percent boost as long as the engine is running. This makes it useful for diesel engines, or high-performance engines with low-engine vacuum.

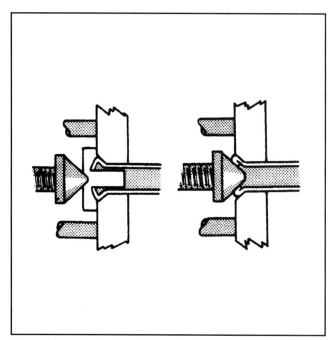

If you do any brake line fabrication, you absolutely must have a double flaring tool. It's a two-step process. First, with a small arbor, the line is accordioned a precise amount. In step two, the accordioned part is folded down and shaped. Single flared lines tend to split, and with lives riding on the brakes, you don't want a hydraulic leak.

### Brake Drums and Rotors

Most rotors and drums are made of gray cast iron. This material provides a good friction surface but is fairly rigid and has a high melting point. Some high-performance pieces may have a higher nickel content to increase hardness. Rotors come in two guises, solid and vented. Solid rotors are thinner and used in less stressful environments, such as light vehicles or in rear brake applications. Vented rotors are thicker and have vanes between the two friction surfaces that provide extra cooling.

The emergency brake is always a problem with rear discs. With many kits, a Lincoln or GM caliper is used that incorporates a parking brake feature. In this Ford-type rear disc kit, a set of miniature drums operate inside the disc hub. Both types work well enough, but not generally as well as the original drum brake setup.

Brake drums are generally built of the same gray cast iron as rotors. Sometimes they are made of composite materials, such as a stamped sheet steel drum with an iron friction surface cast in. Some drums have exterior cooling fins cast in, which also adds some strength. The more metal in the drum, the longer it takes to heat up and better able it is to resist fade on a hard stop. It will, however, hold heat longer.

Beyond the size issues discussed earlier, there is lit-

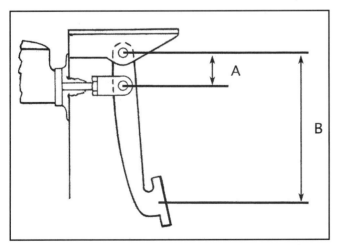

Like so many other things on your Jeep, the pedal assembly has a ratio. The mechanical advantage of the pedal, or lack thereof, will contribute to a hard pedal. By lengthening distance B or shortening distance A, you can increase the leverage and decrease pedal pressure. If distance A is 2 inches and B is 6 inches, you have a 3:1 pedal ratio.

tle to choose in a rotor or drum. Obviously, the quality of the casting can be suspect so the cheapest of the cheap is best avoided. A vented rotor is a definite good choice for the front—perhaps also in the rear, in a highly stressed set of brakes. Ultimately, your choices of rotor and drum are going to be dictated by what will fit.

### Parking Brakes

In the old days, a single-drum-style parking brake was mounted on the transfer case and worked well when not soaked with oil from the inevitable T-case seal leakage. In truth, this brake setup is not a terrible concept, because not only are all four wheels locked (if the Jeep is in four-wheel drive) when the brake is applied, but it has the leverage of the axle ratio working for it. The advent of the Dana 20 finally put an end to the T-case mounted parking brake, and a cable-operated system was adopted that utilized the rear brakes.

Parking brakes or emergency brakes—whatever you call them—can be an important part of four-wheeling. They can be used for more than just keeping the vehicle from rolling away when parked. If your parking brake works well, you can use it to hold the vehicle on a hill while you let out the clutch. Some Jeepers will apply a little parking brake on a descent in low gear and not use the footbrakes. How well these scenarios work depends on which type of actuation system you have.

Just as with the main brakes, the performance of the emergency brakes depends on the force applied. In the case of the e-brake, the mechanical leverage is what gives you that force. Overall, most 4x4 folks prefer the euro-style lever that is mounted between the seats. It has good leverage and if you depress the button, you can operate the brake one handed while using your feet for the clutch and gas. Unfortunately, this setup is only fitted to the very latest Jeeps, but the assembly can be retrofitted if you are clever.

The foot-actuated e-brake is most common and while this works well as a parking or e-brake, it's impossible to use as a hill holder unless you have three feet (and if you did, you'd use the footbrake). The oldest type of Jeep e-brake has the lever coming out of the dash. This one can be used as a hill holder, but you need a strong arm! It's a bit short of leverage.

**JEEP OE BRAKES ROUNDUP**

| Year | Model | Front Type/Diameter | Rear Type/Diameter |
|------|-------|---------------------|--------------------|
| 1945–63 | CJ (1) | drum, 9 x 1.75 in. | drum, 9 x 1.75 in. |
| 1964–71 | CJ | drum, 10 x 2.00 in. | drum, 10 x 2.00 in. |
| 1972–76 | CJ (2) | drum, 11 x 2.00 in. | drum, 11 x 2.00 in. |
| 1977–78 | CJ (8) | disc, 12.00 in. | drum, 11 x 2.00 in. |
| 1978–86 | CJ (3) | disc, 12.00 in. | drum, 10 x 1.75 in. |
| 1987–96 | YJ | disc, 11.02 in. | drum, 9.84 x 1.77 in. |
| 1997–98 | TJ | disc, 11.00 in. | drum, 9.00 x 2.50 in. |
| 1947–65 | PU, SW | drum, 11 x 2.00 in. | drum, 11 x 2.00 in. |
| 1957–65 | FC-150-170 | drum, 11 x 2.00 in. | drum, 11 x 2.00 in. |
| 1959–65 | FC-170 | drum, 12 x 2.00 in. | drum, 13 x 2.50 in. |
| 1963–72 | SJ PU,W (4) | drum, 11 x 2.00 in. | drum, 11 x 2.00 in. |
| 1967–73 | SJ PU,W(5) | drum, 12 x 2.00 in. | drum, 12 x 2.00 in. |
| 1974–91 | SJ PU,W(6) | disc, 12 in. | drum, 11 x 2.00 in. |
| 1974–87 | SJ PU (7) | disc, 12.50 in. | drum, 12 x 2.00 in. |
| 1984– | XJ | disc, 10.98 in. | drum, 10 x 1.75 in. |
| 1993–98 | ZJ | disc, 11.2 in. | disc, 11.2 in. |
| 1967–73 | C101 | drum, 10 x 2 in. | drum, 10 x 2 in. |

(1) Also 1965 except Tuxedo Park.
(2) Standard from 1975 to 86.
(3) Optional from 1975 to 77. Used a six-bolt caliper bracket and 1.1-inch-thick rotor.
(4) Standard on Wagoneer and PU under 7,000-lb GVW.
(5) Over 7,000 GVW, std on all 1973 SJ.
(6) J10 and Wagoneer.
(7) J20. 1980–84 J20 had 12 x 2.5 in rear brakes. 1985–87 J20 had 12.52 x 2.5 in rear.
(8) The mid-1978 and later brakes used a thinner .8890-inch thick rotor. In 1981, a smaller caliper was used that mounted to a knuckle assembly that had two mounting bolts for a two-bolt bracket.

## Useful Hydraulic Formulas

*Calculating System Pressure in PSI*
1. Calculate area of master cylinder piston in square inches.
   a. Formula: Area = 3.14 x Radius squared (radius is 1/2 diameter).
   b. For a 3/4-inch master cylinder, the formula would be:
3. 14 x 0.140 = 0.4396 square inches
2. System Pressure = Force on master cylinder ÷ Area.
   a. 100 pounds ÷ 0.4396 = 227 psi

*Calculating Correct Master Cylinder Displacement*
1. Calculate the displacement of each of the pistons and add them together. We'll use 2.25-inch front caliper pistons and 1.5-inch rear calipers for an example. Remember that calipers don't move much and will have a short stroke. The .020-inch stroke used in the example is an average for a generic caliper. To get piston area, use the formula for finding the area of a piston that you used for calculating master cylinder piston area. The 3.97 and 1.76 numbers used below are the area of a 2.25- and a 1.5-inch caliper piston.
   a. Displacement = Stroke x Area.
   b. 0.020 x 3.97 = 0.0794 x 2 = 0.1588 cubic inches front
   c. 0.020 x 1.76 = 0.0352 x 2 = 0.0704 cubic inches rear
   d. 0.1588 + 0.0704 = 0.2204 cubic inches
   e. Add a safety factor of 100 percent to account for deflection, hose swelling, etc. That would be 0.4408 cubic inches.
2. To find the master cylinder displacement, we will use a stroke of 1.25 inches, since this is a common length. We must then convert the displacement into a master cylinder diameter.
   a. Piston Area Needed = Displacement ÷ Stroke
   b. 0.4408 ÷ 1.25 = 0.352 square inches
   c. 0.352 ÷ 3.14 = 0.112, Ã 0.112 = 0.334 (radius) x 2 = 0.668 inch diameter, or 21/32 inch - make it 11/16 inch.

# ENGINE & ENGINE SWAPS

## Go-Power

You're probably wondering why the engine section is way in the back of the book. That's because, with a few exceptions, the engine is one of the least important factors in the trail performance equation. Did you gasp? I know, I know! More power is part of the American way and it borders on the sacrilegious to dismiss it so quickly, but let's look at it from a logical standpoint for a minute.

Out on the trail, your engine is loafing along at idle to 2,000 rpms, with an occasional spurt up to three grand. The tires, suspension, and drivetrain are doing most of the work. In this case, having 300 horsepower is no better than 150, since horsepower is a product of engine speed. More engine speed equals more power. The real power issue for many is highway performance. On the trail, however, what you are really looking for is torque. Many stock Jeep engines are adequate in this department, some are not.

There are a lot of good reasons for an engine swap or a performance buildup, especially if you already have the more important stuff done like the suspension, tires, and lockers. It may be that your engine is ready for an overhaul and if you gotta buy the parts, why not buy better parts! It may also work out that swapping in a good used V-8 may be close to the price of rebuilding that six cylinder. Some mods, like fuel injection, not only increase power and torque, but make the engine immune to the typical problems of carb flooding due to severe angles on the trail.

A lot of good performance stuff has been left out here due to space considerations. This chapter hits the high spots that seem to bring the most trouble to Jeepers. Other books on the detailed specifics are included in the bibliography.

### Power and Torque

Knowledge is power—in this case horsepower! We'll start by talking about the relationship between horsepower and torque. By definition, horsepower is work times speed, or the rate at which work is done. In general, the more rpms an engine can generate, the more horsepower it will make. Horsepower is almost always measured at a high (relative to the engine's basic design) engine speed. For the average Jeeper, an increase in horsepower is most desirable and useful in the street environment, certain types of competition, or just plain ol' pedal-to-the-metal fun.

Although horsepower is a more universal language, for four-wheeling, torque is often more important. Torque is force times distance. Put a pound of weight on the end of a foot-long bar and you are generating 1 lb-ft of torque. Add another pound and you are generating 2 lb-ft. Lengthen the bar to 2 feet, reduce the weight back to a pound and you are still generating 2 lb-ft. When the engine fires that mixture of fuel and air, the piston is forced down the bore and generates torque via the leverage of the crankshaft and connecting rods. Most stock engines generate max torque at the lower revs, 1,500 to 2,500 rpms, and it's this grunt that gets you up the hill and over the rock.

### Building for Torque

The generally perceived ideal torque curve for a working Jeep would be generous low-end grunt and a strong midrange. We're talking usable torque from idle to about 4,000 rpm, with a very strong punch from idle to 3,000 rpm. This is essentially what a stock engine delivers, but with carefully selected aftermarket parts it can be improved upon. It's very easy, however, to lose low rpm performance by selecting the wrong pieces. The best part about an engine built for torque is that it will generally be very economical at the same time.

Whether your current torque is adequate depends in large part on the weight of the vehicle. If you will glance at page 162, you will see a selection of the torque-to-weight ratios for a variety of factory-equipped Jeeps. GVW is used since few of us operate Jeeps at shipping or curb weight. The chart shows the number of pounds of weight each lb-ft of engine torque has to move. You will notice the ratios get more favorable with the bigger engines or with lighter rigs. If your performance is unacceptable, you are left with losing some vehicle weight or gaining some torque.

You've heard it before: "There's no substitute for cubic inches." It's true. Any engine's torque characteristics can be improved but there comes a "wall" past which a smaller engine cannot climb, no matter how much money is thrown at it. The moral is that if you need the extra torque, your money may be better spent on a larger displacement engine rather than trying to make a small engine perform big engine tasks.

For example, replacing the 232-cid six in your Jeep J-20 with a 401 yields a 65 percent increase in torque, stock engine to stock engine. Since this is almost a bolt-in swap, it could be a very cost-effective mod. It gets more problematic when you want to perform a more diverse swap, such as a Chevy V-8 into a four-cylinder flatfender. The installation costs are much higher due to the necessary drivetrain swaps and fabrication. Odds are good that most of the J-20's drivetrain is up to handling V-8 grunt, while the flatfender's gear is weak.

In some cases, it's possible to increase the displacement of the engine by changing bore or stroke. Boring a 232 six (actually 231.8 cid), .040 inch over increases the displacement to 236.8. Installing a 258-cid crankshaft and con rods, which offers a .040-inch increase in stroke, boosts the displacement to 258 ci. A within-the-limits bore job will offer little torque increase, but an increase in stroke gives the piston more leverage. The 258 beats the 232 by an easy 12 lb-ft. In actuality, few of the Jeep engines are this interchangeable (only the 1972–91 V-8s and the inline sixes) but you get the idea.

An increase in compression ratio generally produces an increase in torque, as well as improvements in high-altitude performance. The increase is usually fairly modest, within the realms of nonrace engines and standard fuel. An increase from an 8.0:1 CR to a 9.0:1 CR produces approximately a 2 percent increase in torque without changing the engine's general torque-at-rpm characteristics. The mileage will increase also, perhaps as much as 4 percent, with a one-ratio jump. This could be good news at the pumps, but the costs of getting the compression up may exceed the ideal bang-for-buck ratio. You may also be forced to run premium fuel.

The two standard methods for increasing compression are via a change of pistons and by decreasing the combustion chamber size in the cylinder head. This can be done by swapping to a head with a known smaller combustion chamber (not always possible) or by milling the head (limited by the safe amount you can remove). If you are in the midst of an engine overhaul, the piston change or head mill might be more cost effective.

### Camshaft, Carburetor, and EFI

Excluding making changes to stroke, changes to the camshaft and the induction system (either a carburetor or a fuel injection system) will have the greatest effect on torque. These are also two items that get messed with more often than not. Let's start with cams.

Many factory cams can equal aftermarket cams in torque up to about 2,500 rpms, but they fall off rapidly

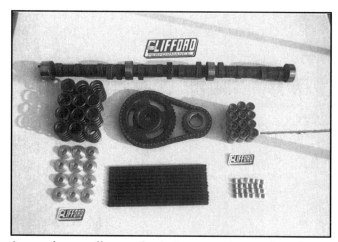

A cam change offers moderate torque and power benefits. This Clifford kit for the 258 six is well thought out and very complete. The cam and lifters are included, of course, but a double roller timing chain ensures accurate long-term cam timing. The new valve springs match the cam profile and rpm range. The alloy pushrods are sized to ensure correct lifter preload. The aluminum valve spring retainers and alloy keepers are gravy, but they do lighten the valvetrain a bit. *Courtesy Clifford*

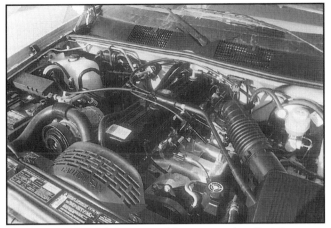

The factory EFI engines are multiport, meaning that they have an injector for each cylinder. This system allows for very precise metering and outstanding power outputs. This injected 4.0-liter six is a sweetheart, and many late model Jeepers are satisfied with it as-is. There are many speed parts for this engine, though not all of them keep emissions legal.

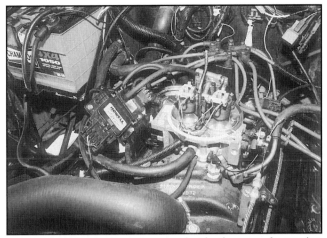

TBI fuel injection systems are popular, both as an aftermarket bolt-on, or as the original system retained on swapped-in engines. This setup happens to be a Howell bolt-on kit. Howell and Holley both base a bolt-on kit on the GM idea, but make it more adaptable to a variety of engines. A TBI doesn't make the engine much more powerful than a good running carbureted engine, but drivability is radically improved.

after that. The right aftermarket camshaft will pull just as hard down low but allow the engine to keep pulling well beyond the stock cam and extend the usable torque range—and increase the horsepower to boot. This is the best combo.

How much benefit there is to a cam upgrade depends on how well the factory profile fits your driving style. Generally speaking, a grind with duration close to a stock cam but with more lift will result in more torque. The nice part is that the extra lift won't cost significant fuel economy or drivability, but there is a practical limit.

The more lift, the less time is available to open the valve, and the more the valve rate increases. This puts heavy loads on the cam and valvegear. The maximum practical lift amount depends on the engine. Look at between .450 and .500 inch as your absolute maximum gross lift unless the cam grinder tells you different.

The amount of time the valve is open, the duration, is even more important to consider. The longer the valve is open, the more air and fuel the engine can take in. This is especially conducive to high rpm power production. Down at low speeds, however, the traditional long duration and overlap, high lift camshaft may cause the engine to idle poorly and lose low-end throttle response. Corruption of the intake flow by exhaust gases, the reduction of engine vacuum, and the resulting carb/EFI metering problems are caused by the overlap period of long duration cams. Wider lobe center angles can negate much of this detrimental effect and,

in essence, you can have the benefits of a longer duration without all the bad side effects.

Duration and compression ratio have an important relationship. A short duration cam combined with a high compression ratio can increase cylinder pressure enough to cause pinging. Conversely, a low compression engine with a long duration cam will be a slug, due to a lower "effective" compression ratio.

The correct approach is to pick the cam according to your compression ratio. The cam manufacturer will often have a compression ratio recommendation for each cam. If your engine has between 8.6 and 9.5 to 1, your cam selection choices will allow you a pretty flexible rpm range. If you have a very low compression engine, 8.0-8.5, you'll need to stick to short duration cams and will probably have to sacrifice some upper end capabilities to keep cylinder pressures up at low speeds. For high altitude operation, a shorter duration cam usually works best.

Cam selection will be greatly influenced by your driving habits, both on the trail and the street. Some Jeepers use their rigs in sand or mud drags, or other types of competition requiring high rpm capability. You know who you are and what you need. The rest of us see 4,500 rpm only rarely, and we're interested in a nice snappy engine with decent economy.

To make the ideal selection, you will also need to determine your cruising rpm and general operating range by monitoring your tach for a period of time

One of the best bolt-ons is the MPI kit for 258 sixes from Mopar Performance. It basically takes the MPI from the 4.0-liter and adapts it to the 258. It's said to add 40 horsepower, and it makes the engine run as smooth as silk. It's a complicated kit, but worth the effort.

while driving "normally" (for you, at least). You may be surprised by what you find. Some folks who clamor after off-idle grunt often find themselves very seldom below 1,500 rpm. At the other end, guys wanting high revs often find themselves revving past 5 grand about twice a year. The more accurate you can be in evaluating your needs, the better results you'll get. It doesn't make sense to build an engine for that once-a-year wild ride on main street.

The power and torque curves for a given cam change according to engine displacement. The rpm range drops slightly as the displacement increases. In engine families that have an interchangeable cam, such as the AMC V-8s (304, 360, 401 cid) that appeared in Jeeps from 1972 to 1991, a cam that's a smooth and docile "torquer" in a 401 might turn the 304 into a gutless wonder at low revs and give it an idle lope like a top fueler. If your engine is at the low end of the displacement range for a particular cam, conservative cam choices usually give better torque results.

Your cam choices may narrow considerably with EFI engines. They are extrasensitive to changes in engine vacuum. Choose a cam that maintains stock or near-stock idle vacuum or be prepared to spend some hefty bucks recalibrating the EFI. The cam manufacturers can recommend a profile that will minimally impact your EFI setup.

Cylinder head mods can have the same effect as a cam change. Increasing airflow through head work allows better breathing and higher horsepower with no loss of good torque characteristics. It's usually very

expensive compared to a cam change and not an "eyeball" measurement type of job. A very cost-effective enhancement to a cam change might be a good three-angle valve job, match-porting the heads to the manifolds and cleaning out the worst of the crud in the ports.

Remember to keep the engine's ability to breathe in mind when selecting a cam. Overcarburetion is a common mistake. If you combine a nice moderate duration cam that generates good idle vacuum with a Godzilla four-barrel big enough to feed a Pratt & Whitney aircraft engine, your puny V-8 will fall flat on its face when the throttle is opened. If you put in more cam than the carb can handle, the engine runs out of airflow just as the cam is going strong.

For 4x4 purposes, the stock carburetion or fuel injection systems on most engines are usually decent in terms of capacity. The common OE four barrels flow about 600 cubic feet per minute. That's enough theoretical airflow to rev a 360 V-8 past 5,500 rpm. The later model EFI systems have a similar capacity, relative to engine displacement and, amazingly, the old two-barrels and one-barrels aren't all that far behind.

This doesn't mean you have to stick with the OE carbs. There may be other reasons for a carb change. Some factory Jeep carbs are notorious for flooding on the slightest angle or for poor reliability. These are reasons enough for a change, but think long and hard before you increase the capacity of the carburetor in a big way if you want to maintain the engine's docile, low-rpm manners. The text on page 163 shows you how to select a replacement carb based on what your engine needs. Bear in mind that you can see dyno tests that demonstrate higher peak torque figures with bigger carbs, but that peak is always at a higher rpm. Pay attention to what the torque figures are in your usable rpm range before you jump on that bandwagon.

The original intake manifold may still serve your engine well. As with camshafts, however, the aftermarket offers intake manifolds that combine improvements in low rpm torque with the ability to produce a sizable horsepower increase in the middle and upper rpm ranges. Again, the best of both worlds. Usually, the aftermarket manifolds are aluminum, and you can also save some weight.

In the high-tech realm of factory fuel injection, there is little to wish for in terms of performance. Late model fuel-injected engines are powerful and have broad power and torque bands. They are economical and immune to stalling due to angles. Complexity and serviceability are issues that concern many home tinkerers, but fortunately the modern systems are very reliable. When they do have trouble, however, you are usually up the proverbial malodorous creek without a paddle.

In recent years, the aftermarket has put a great deal of effort into bolt-on electronic fuel injection systems. They come in two types, the more common being a throttle body type (TBI) designed to bolt up in place of your carburetor. Some OE Jeep engines came with a TBI system, most notably the 1987–90 2.5-liter fours. Many late Chevy V-8s are swapped into Jeeps, complete with the GM TBI system.

The aftermarket TBIs come in two-barrel or four-barrel configuration (with either two or four injectors) and are usually based on the GM system. The fuel is mixed at the throttle plates, as with a carburetor. While they deal handily with the flooding and drivability issues on the trail, they don't produce a great deal more power or torque than does a properly set-up carburetor. They do allow for some serious fine tuning to enhance performance, with or without other mods.

The more expensive aftermarket multiport (MPI) EFI systems (meaning that there is one injector per cylinder that sprays directly into the intake port) offer a measure of extra performance but at a greater cost and with somewhat limited applicability. The late model Jeep engines, namely the 2.5-liter four, 4.0-liter six, and the 5.2- and 5.9-liter V-8s, come equipped with port injection and the power outputs reflect it! Also,

many Chevy Tuned Port Injection (TPI) engines have been swapped into Jeeps of all types.

Chrysler offers a kit to convert the 232/258 AMC style sixes to the same port injection system that's used on the 4.0-liter. Edelbrock and others also offer MPI setups for Chevy and Ford V-8s. On the AMC sixes, eliminating the troublesome and notorious Carter BBD two-barrel is worth a 40 percent increase in power and great drivability at any angle.

When other engine modifications change the calibration requirements of your factory engine, there are aftermarket sources for recalibrated PROMs (Programmable Read-Only Memory—a.k.a. "chip" or "brain"), as well as performance pieces to enhance your fuel-injected engine. These would include enlarged throttle bodies, improved intake manifolds, high-flow injectors and fuel pumps, and adjustable or rising rate fuel pressure regulators.

### The Exhaust System

Some of the biggest gains in power and torque can come from exhaust system mods. Strictly speaking, the exhaust system begins at the exhaust valve and ends at the tailpipe. Installing an efficient exhaust system can mean power or torque increases as much as 10–15 percent, depending on how poorly the original system flowed, and increases in economy at near the same percentage. Exhaust system modifications are among the few you can make where power, torque, and economy increase together.

As with other performance modifications, there are a lot of myths to be challenged. Regarding exhaust

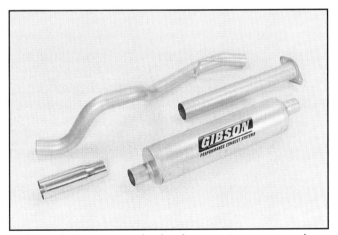

In this emissions age, cat back exhaust systems are popular additions. Eliminating restrictions after the catalytic converter is usually good for a minimum of 5 percent and up to 15 percent improvement in power and torque. It all depends on how well, or poorly, the OE system flowed. This Gibson stainless system is mandrill-bent 2 1/2-inch inch tubing. *Courtesy Gibson Performance Exhausts*

Headers are available for many swapped in combinations, like this CJ-5/Chevy combination. These Advance Adapters units incorporate a built in set of glasspacks. There is a space problem with CJ-5s, so no crossover pipe is installed here. *Courtesy Advance Adapters*

systems, one of the most common says that "engines need back-pressure to operate efficiently." This myth can even be supported by dyno test information that shows a drop in power when a zero-backpressure system is installed on an otherwise stock engine. What needs to be remembered is that the induction system was tuned to the restrictive exhaust system. Add a free-flowing exhaust and the fuel mixture can get lean enough (less fuel-more air) to cause a drop in power.

Often, but not always, a carburetor must be recalibrated to compensate for the leaner mixture and then power and economy will increase beyond stock levels. Many EFI systems will adapt to the lower backpressure and allow a power increase but some will not. If it doesn't have a MAP (Manifold Absolute Pressure) sensor, chances are it won't.

Another of the popular exhaust system myths involves the size of the pipes. Bigger is better, right? Not necessarily. Most experts regard maintaining velocity as the most important consideration, and the pipes must be *correctly* sized to maintain that velocity. A sewer-pipe-sized system on an engine that doesn't need it may actually impede performance—and it will definitely be louder.

The exhaust leaves the engine at a temperature of 1,600 degrees or more. By the time it leaves the tailpipe, it's cooled to 150 degrees, or less. At the hot end, a fairly large pipe is needed to efficiently carry the flow. As the gases cool—and this occurs rapidly—the pipe may be smaller to maintain the velocity.

More times than not, mufflers are the main culprit when you go looking for lost power. Often a muffler change alone can make a significant increase in power. Performance mufflers come in a variety of configurations that boil down to two general types, the straight through type, where the exhaust noise is dampened by perforated tubing and fiberglass or stainless-steel padding, or the "mousetrap" styles, where the exhaust is baffled and redirected with (in the better ones) little loss of velocity. There is ample evidence that both types do the job. In the course of the muffler selection process, remember that one of the primary purposes of the exhaust system is to quiet the controlled explosions of the engine. Unless you yearn for hearing loss, remember there are quiet mufflers that are just as efficient as noisy ones.

Another important aspect to exhaust system selection is the way the pipes are bent. Too many bends in the system tend to slow the flow. The flow problems

with bends are made even worse when a standard pipe bender constricts the area of the bend in the process. Better exhaust system builders use mandrill bending machines that do not decrease the inside diameter of the pipe. This is accomplished by pulling a metal slug though the pipe as the bend is made to maintain the inside diameter.

Another myth concerns dual exhausts. Are they really 100 percent necessary? Not always. The facts are that a single pipe exhaust system is more efficient than dual pipes, up to the point at which the single pipe runs out of flow. In a single pipe, all the exhaust pulses are blended together and this aids in maintaining exhaust velocity. A well-designed 3-inch single pipe can handle a 350-cid Chevy to 5,500 rpm. Not only that, but you only need a single muffler and room for one pipe.

Dual exhaust is sometimes necessary on a V-type engine of large displacement or with V-type engines in a chassis where there is no room for two headpipes to join. In these cases, the major need becomes a crossover pipe so the exhaust pulses can balance. There is usually a small crossover in the OE intake manifold (some aftermarket manifolds don't have them) but this is the bare minimum. Better dual systems run a crossover pipe that connects the two sides together near the front. Dyno tests have shown that this modification alone can make increases in the 5 percent range over a standard dual system. This works because the crossover allows each bank to share the flow capacity of the other. It also tends to make for a quieter system.

Catalytic converters are a fact of life. Fortunately, modern cats of the honeycomb type are only marginally restrictive. The old pellet-filled jobs were terrible. Frontal area at the honeycomb interior of the cat is what you look for in a cat convertor. The larger the frontal area, the better the flow. Remember that a cat needs to be run very hot and near the engine to work efficiently. If it runs too cool, it will quickly deteriorate and plug up, not to mention increase emissions output.

Exhaust manifolds can restrict power no matter how good the rest of the system. Some factory manifolds are better than others but headers are the usual cure and the benefits can be monumental or marginal depending on the quality of the header and the parts being replaced. A good header, properly selected for the application, will add torque, power, and a touch of economy.

There are two styles of headers, four-into-one headers and Tri-Y. Four-into-one headers are the most common and use four equal-length tubes that feed into a single collector. The length and diameter of the tubes are critical. Short tubes tend to enhance high rpm power and long ones low rpm power. Tubes should be approximately 20 percent larger than the diameter of the ports in the cylinder head. Larger than necessary tubes tend to cost low-end torque. Collector sizes (where the four equal-length pipes come together) should vary also according to rpm usage—large collectors (and short tubes) for high rpm power, smaller collectors (and long tubes) for low rpm power. Four-into-one headers are very common for many stock engine or swapped applications.

Tri-Y headers are less common (fewer Jeep applications) and more expensive but they are better for low and midrange torque. With the Tri-Y header, the cylinders are paired according to the firing order of the engine. On the left bank of a V-8, cylinders 1 and 5 are paired and 3 and 7. About 2 feet down (the actual length varies according to the tuning requirements), the pipes are paired again, giving a total of three "Ys," or pairings, per bank. Here's how it works.

Cylinder No. 1 fires, and exhausts and the hot gases flow down the pipe. As it passes the runner from No. 5 cylinder, the flow creates a partial negative pressure in that runner. When No. 5 exhaust valve opens, the exhaust is effectively "sucked" out and the cylinder is cleared of exhaust just that much better. The pulses alternate and "draw" the flow from the opposite pipe. The Tri-Y design tends to enhance low end torque to about 2,500 rpm. As the rpms increase, the effect gradually lessens and by 4,000 rpm, is essentially nullified. At that point, the free flow mufflers and larger pipes are just outgassing large amounts with little finesse.

## Forced Induction

One of the simplest ways to radically increase power and torque outputs is via forced induction. The advent of fuel injection has brought a new age to forced induction and now everyone can avail themselves of the benefits without many of the adverse side effects previously attributed to the modification.

Several well known manufacturers build forced induction systems—Banks, Paxton, Edelbrock, B&M—but for the most part, they are not designed for Jeep applications. Rimmer Engineering is building supercharger kits that are designed specifically for 2.5-liter and 4.0-liter Jeeps. A 5.2 V-8 kit will be finished by late 1998. These kits are C.A.R.B. legal and offer at least a 30 percent boost in power. Torque is also increased, because the boost comes in right off idle.

### Forced Induction Basics

The naturally aspirated engine has to rely on air pressure (14.7 psi at sea level or 1 atmosphere—essentially the weight of the air over the Earth) to fill the cylinder. A good, naturally aspirated street engine will draw in about 80 to 85 percent of the volume displaced by the piston. There isn't enough pressure to fill the cylinder in the few milliseconds of time allotted during the intake stroke and the faster the engine runs, the less air it can take in. Generally restrictive intake systems contribute to the inefficiency, and cams are designed to minimize the losses.

Outside factors also affect how well the engine inhales. Changes in barometric pressure, altitude, and air temperature can all cause an engine to lose or gain power. That's where forced induction comes in; the air is literally pumped into the engine. The benefit, of course, is increased power—but why?

Because the air is pushed in under pressure, forced induction essentially nullifies intake system inefficiencies. More air and fuel are packed into the cylinder, to at least 100 percent of the cylinder's capacity and often from 110 to 150 percent. More air and fuel means a bigger, stronger "explosion" and more power. The only trouble comes when the mechanical design limits of the engine are exceeded. It's kind of like shooting a Magnum round through a barrel not designed for the extra pressure. Something blows!

The best part about a forced induction engine with EFI is that you can more easily retain drivability, emissions, and fuel economy at the same time you enjoy the benefits of a radical power increase. If you compare two engines of a given displacement and design, with similar horsepower-to-displacement ratios, the forced-induction engine will be the more docile of the two by far.

### Turbochargers vs. Superchargers

Forced induction comes in two common forms, turbocharging and supercharging. Both systems use high-capacity air compressors but their drive systems differ. A turbo uses the exhaust of the engine to drive the compressor. This seems fairly efficient on the surface, since a by-product of the combustion process is used to drive the compressor. On the downside, a turbo generally requires higher rpms to develop pressure. The engine will retain its normally aspirated slow speed

Superchargers and modern MPI engines were made for each other. A supercharger is the simplest way to get a big jump in power and torque in a modern engine. The Rimmer Engineering kit gives this 2.5-liter Jeep four a 30 percent boost in power, and is emissions legal. Installation time is about 4 hours. The Eaton blower is geared to provide boost the moment the throttle is opened and is at max boost by 1,500 rpm.

characteristics until pressure is generated by rising engine speed. The application of power builds suddenly as pressure rises and you go from measured acceleration to being pinned in the seat. This is called "turbo lag," and good turbo systems minimize these characteristics but never completely eliminate them.

No matter how you do it, compressing the air generates some heat (especially the centrifugal compressor used with turbos) but because there is heat transfer from the exhaust side to the compressor side, a turbo heats the intake air even more, up to 300 degrees. Since hot air holds less oxygen, some of the benefit of the forced induction is lost. There is also a durability question when the engine is run on this very hot air.

Turbocharged air can be cooled with the addition of another component, called an intercooler, installed between the turbo and the engine intake. This air-to-air cooler (generally, there are other types) drops the intake air temp proportional to the amount of heat generated vs. the ambient air temp. Cooler air drops the pressure a bit and the denser air requires additional fuel to make the ideal mix.

A supercharger is simpler in so many ways and the explanation is shorter. It's mechanically driven by the engine, so in theory, it can be geared to provide pressure (or boost, as it's correctly termed) at any speed. It also generates less heat than a turbo (depending on compressor type), and generally does not need an

intercooler, though it can still be beneficial and is often necessary at boost pressures over 6 psi. It does require a little, or a lot, depending on the type of compressor, of the extra power developed to drive it. Most modern superchargers draw minimal power, usually less than the AC or even the alternator.

## Forced Induction Requirements

How much boost an engine will tolerate depends on the engine design and the compression ratio. The compression ratio is the first direct controller. Since the cylinder is already at some pressure from the blower at the beginning of the compression stroke, it leads to an increase in the "dynamic" compression of the engine. An engine with a 9:1 mechanical compression ratio given a boost pressure of 7.5 psi has a dynamic compression ratio of about 11:1!

In the old days, this meant that you had to seriously reduce the compression ratio of the engine to keep it in one piece. Today's EFI system, especially those with knock sensors (a device that detects detonation) and MAP sensors, lend themselves to supercharging because they can automatically back off timing and increase fuel rate under boost.

Most modern EFI engines with high compression ratios (8.5 to 9.5:1) can handle a 4–6 psi boost fairly easily with their original fuel injection systems untouched. With mods or a drop in compression ratio, higher boost is possible, but the engine will no longer be emissions legal.

## Carburetors and Angles

The perennial problem with carburetors on the trail is loading up and flooding. Bouncing or severe angles allow the floats and needle-seat assemblies to overfill the float chamber and the result is an overrich mixture. The engine falters, blows black smoke, and dies. In older carbs, the fuel spills out of the vent tubes and kills the engine immediately, with fuel soaking the spark plugs and making it hard to restart. This is a design issue. Why hasn't anyone designed a carb especially for trail work?

Some carburetors are better than others at resisting these problems, but there are steps you can take with any carb. The first is to lower the float level a bit. This entails carb disassembly. How much you can or should lower the float level depends on the individual carb. If you can find a carb specialist with experience in dealing with a specific carb in the off-highway environment, great. If not, the best advice is to consult a shop manual. Most carbs have more than one application, so look in the specs and find the *lowest* float level listed for that carb and use it as a baseline. Trial and error will determine if you can go lower.

Second, you can reduce fuel pressure. Often, fuel pressure can overcome the needle and seat to cause flooding. Fuel pressure regulators reduce the pressure, not the volume, so your engine should always have enough fuel available. A 1–4 psi regulator will work well for most trail applications. Simply dial in the lowest pressure that allows enough fuel delivery. Sometimes, you may have to use a trail and a street adjustment.

In some cases, special kits are available to modify the carb fuel inlet to resist angles better. These kits usually spring-load the needle and seat or change the pivot point of the float to better resist angles; the former are available for the AFB style carb and the latter are available for the Holley carbs.

Since the flooding often manifests itself by fuel sloshing out the vent tube(s), a quick solution is to install extensions on these tubes or replace them with longer tubes. The quick and dirty fix can be as simple as a piece of hose clamped to the tube.

In general, dual float carbs or units with a centralized float bowl are best. To name a few brand names, the four-barrel Rochester Quadra-Jet is the hands-down best according to many four-wheelers, due to its centralized and small volume float chamber. Unfortunately, it will fit only GM engines with a spread bore manifold. The Carb Shop, in Rancho Cucamonga, California, is best known for tweaking the Q-Jet.

One of Edelbrock's carbs, formerly known as the Carter AFB, is another good one because it uses a dual float design with twin needles and seats. Edelbrock also builds an off-road needle and seat assembly (No. 1465) to make these carbs even better. The smallest size offered by Edelbrock is a 500-cubic feet per minute model, which is ideal for small displacement V-8s or the larger V-6s.

The Rochester 2G two-barrel carburetors are also good. They appeared mostly on 1955–81 GM cars and trucks as well as the 1966–71 Jeep 225-cid V-6. They are adaptable to a variety of other engines. They come in two varieties, small bore and large bore, and The Carb Shop is an expert on these as well.

The Carter YF, the single-barrel that appeared on early 1970s 232 and 258 sixes, is also a decent off-roader by all reports, unlike its replacement, the two-barrel Carter BBD.

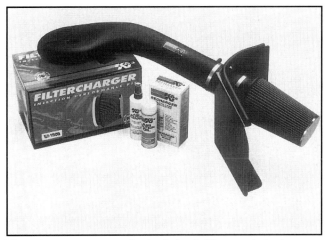

There is some power to be had via air filters and air cleaner tuning. In this case, K&N does the work for you. This 5.2-liter V-8 kit is dyno tested to deliver 23.3 more horsepower and at least 23 lb-ft of torque. *Courtesy K&N Engineering*

## Air Filters and Snorkels

Air filters are an important aspect to Jeeping from two angles. The first is dirt. The 'wheeling environment is a dirty one, and you don't want that dirt getting inside your engine. The other is performance. The restriction, or lack thereof, will dictate how well your engine breathes.

Snorkels, which raise the point from which the engine draws air, are a small part of the U.S. four-wheeling scene but in the outback of Australia, they are regarded as a necessity. Most people think of them in terms of deep fording situations and might be surprised that they have particular benefits in very dusty conditions.

### Air Filter Types

Stock Jeep filters can be divided into two categories, oil bath and paper element. The last oil bath filters went away in the early 1970s for most Jeeps. The oil bath filter works by directing the air over a pool of oil, which attracts dirt. Additional dirt is captured by a steel mesh filter that gets oiled by mist from the oil. The oil bath is cleanable and lasts forever. Keeping the oil at the prescribed levels is vital to filtering efficiency, and the level gradually goes down with use. In general, oil bath filters are not particularly efficient and are also restrictive.

The paper filter has taken over the OEM industry. The early units used wax impregnated paper. The later ones use synthetic materials impregnated with resins and oil. The material consists of irregular passages between the fibers that trap particles on a "go/no-go" basis. While paper filters can be "dusted off," they are designed to be replaced at intervals.

The aftermarket offers two other types of filtering media, oiled cotton gauze and oiled foam. Both are cleanable and both types are relatively free of restriction. The typical cotton gauze filter, produced and made famous by K&N Engineering, consists of layers of pleated surgical cotton fabric sandwiched between wire mesh. Most of the dust is captured at the outside layers and as it soaks up oil, it becomes part of the filtering media.

Foam filters contain irregular passages through the material that trap dirt. The larger particles are captured on the outside, and the smaller chunks work their way into the passages and are trapped on the oily walls.

### Filtering Efficiency

Filtering efficiency is measured by industry standards. The motor industry filtering standard is 95 percent. That means an OE replacement filter must trap at least 95 percent of the particles encountered. The test uses a special dust that has specified amounts of material in certain sizes. Here is a breakdown of the material's particles from a MIRA (Motor Industry Research Association) test:

| | |
|---|---|
| 0-5 microns | 12% |
| 5-10 microns | 12% |
| 10-20 microns | 14% |
| 20-40 microns | 23% |
| 40-80 microns | 30% |
| 80-200 microns | 9% |

Note that a micron is one-thousands of a millimeter, or .0000394 inch. This "coarse" mix is regarded as

one commonly used for street rigs. A Jeep on the trail might see a "fine" mix that has more of the small particles. The industry generally regards anything under 4 microns not to be harmful to the engine, but many people debate this figure.

I scoured various sources for filter tests and came up with a few, but none specific to Jeep filters. Averaging the results, oil bath filters are from 95–98 percent efficient; paper filters run from 96 to 99 percent efficient and are about even with cotton gauze filters, such as those from K&N Engineering. Certain dual stage foam filters, namely those from Amsoil, have tested as well or better. Some tests I found on single stage foam filters ran from 70 to 93 percent. The density of the foam plays a large part in how well or poorly it catches dirt. A foam "sock" over any filter element adds to capacity and efficiency.

With both cotton gauze and foam filters, the special oil supplied is the vital element. A test of an unoiled foam filter yielded 25 percent efficiency and gauze would be little better. That means if you use these types of filters, good oiling is essential to good performance.

### Filter Capacity and Flow

Oil bath filters have a high capacity to carry dirt. Up to the point where the reservoir turns into oily mud, it will trap dirt. They generally do not "plug up" but they can in severe enough conditions. Paper filters have a low tolerance in this area, because of the go/no-go filtering method; the tiny holes gradually get plugged up and restrict the flow of air. Oiled cotton gauze, at least as employed by K&N, has a very high capacity. Most foam elements fit somewhere between paper and gauze according to available tests, though a recently received test from Amsoil on its two-stage filter showed it higher than the other types. Foam uses a maze of passages that, combined with the oil tack barrier, will trap lots of dirt on the outside as well as on the inside.

In airflow tests of equivalent-sized filters, cotton gauze filters come out on top, followed by foam a few steps behind. Paper is far back and oil baths are dead last. What does this mean to you? It means that if your

A homemade adaptation on this 4.0-liter Wrangler moved the air intake up from its creek-sucking position near the radiator, and freed up the breathing to boot. The engine is drawing in warm air, so the breathing gains may be lost by the hot air. The unit is also still vulnerable to splash, though an easily made shield covering the front half could be easily fabricated. Better yet, a closed element filter could be fitted.

paper filter is inadequate, an oiled cotton gauze or foam filter in your stock housing may provide more than enough airflow for your application. That assumes the air cleaner assembly itself is no restriction.

Flow rates decrease as the filter carries more dirt. Eventually, it will affect performance. As available flow decreases, vacuum increases and it can begin to "suck" dirt right through the filter. If you have a filter on the small size, this could cause you problems in severe dust conditions.

### Open vs. Closed Element Filters

You see a lot of open element air filters on the trail. This is a street car performance trick, but there are some disadvantages. The first is that the filter is more exposed to the dirty off-highway environment. Dust, dirt, mud, and water all have easy access to the filter. Mud can clog the filter and the fan can sling back water to soak it. Extremely wet filters essentially cease to flow. In the case of dust, the filter will obviously get dirty faster.

A covered filter resists water and mud and at least some of the dust that blows through the engine compartment. An OE style filter housing with an air horn can be modified by pointing or ducting the intake away from potential sources of water or dirt.

From the performance standpoint, there are two points to consider with an open element. The primary goal of these filters is maximum airflow. A laudable sentiment but consider that a performance filter in a good flowing OE style housing may effectively do just as well. The other concern is engine heat.

An open filter draws its air from the hot engine compartment. Power is lost to warm intake air. It varies considerably from engine to engine, but in one dyno test I personally attended, the difference in power between 88 and 155 degree intake air was 15 horsepower at 3,600 rpm. This means that ducting some cooler air to the intake is beneficial. You certainly do not want to duct the air from the front, where it can be drawn in during a creek crossing.

### Choosing an Air Cleaner

The first thing to remember is that your air filter has adequate flow until it does not. In other words, the restriction may be nil or minimal to 3,000 rpm and then gradually increase. It also may be good right up to 5,000 rpm. As a general statement, the OE air filters are adequate for stock engines at stock engine revs, perhaps with the exception of the oil bath filters.

Flow and rpms are directly related. If you take two engines of the same displacement, one that maxes out at 4,800 and the other at 5,500, the higher revving engine will need a bigger filter. If you use the formulas on pages 163 and 164, you will get a good idea what your engine needs. I flow-tested two air filters for an OE application, one a Fram stock replacement and the other a K&N replacement. The Fram flowed 726 cubic feet per minute, the K&N 1,250 cubic feet per minute. The engine only needed 400 cubic feet per minute to make redline. Either filter would have been fine on paper, but we still got a 5 horsepower increase with the K&N.

In cases of swaps, you can go with a generic open element filter, or find a closed filter that fits. The formulas on page 164 will help you evaluate your current filter element (except an oil bath) but it does not take into account possible restrictions in the housing and the air horn. A trip to the wrecking yard yields many possibilities. The popular Chevy and Ford swaps are particularly easy because the engine manufacturers offered high-performance engines with big single or dual horn filters that breathed well. If you put a 454 air cleaner on a 350, for example, you'll get plenty of air. The only requirement is space.

### Snorkels

Snorkels have two direct benefits to the Jeeper: They raise the air intake above any possible water ingress,

For those of you with nautical aspirations, a snorkel might be the hot idea. There are three advantages, the obvious one being the relocation of the intake away from possible water ingress. The same applies for dust, with less being present at roof level. The cooler outside air could up the ponies by one or two also. So far, only ARB is building snorkel kits for Jeeps, with applications for Wrangler and Cherokee. The Wrangler kit is adaptable to CJs, according to ARB. *Courtesy ARB*

and they raise it out of the source of major dust. The side benefits are cooler air and, in some cases, a ram air effect. Combined with cooler air, this can add a couple of ponies.

The downside is that they may be restrictive. Any time you make a torturous passage for the air, it can cost power. There are only a few systems available for Jeeps. ARB markets a kit for YJ Wranglers and XJs. A kit for TJs is in the works. Because of the similarities in bodies, CJ owners report that the YJ Wrangler kit is easily adaptable to long nose CJ-5, 6, 7, and 8s. With regard to power loss, ARB claims there are no negative effects on power.

The ARB kits represent the only Jeep snorkel kits on the market here, other than some surplus military fording kits for M-38A1 Jeeps. Owners have fabricated their own snorkel systems out of PVC and other materials with good results, as long as pipe sizes match engine capacity. Just to give you a little ammunition for a homebuilt snorkel, a piece of unbent 3-inch pipe can flow over 1,000 cubic feet per minute.

## Engine Waterproofing

The military was particularly adept at developing waterproofing kits. GI Jeeps came equipped with waterproof distributors and plug wires, intake systems with snorkels, and even stacks for the exhaust. These rigs could drive in water deep enough to drown the driver. In a few cases, you could adapt this equipment to your older civvy four-cylinder Jeep, but why? How many people need 6-foot fording capacity?

For practical purposes, you can make your Jeep water resistant but not waterproof. Most Jeepers don't need any more and some don't need even that much. The major areas of vulnerability on the engine are the intake, the ignition, the crankcase breathers, the dipstick, and, if so equipped, the EFI components. The starter and alternator are also vulnerable to a degree.

The general waterproofing philosophy is to make all your vital components safe to the same water level. Otherwise, you are safe only to the lowest point where water ingress will kill the engine. Have a look at the vital systems and make cures for the problem areas.

### Intake System

For those of you with late model Jeeps of all types, bear in mind that the air intake is at the front and vulnerable to water ingress. If you are into water crossings, it would pay to relocate the intake to a less vulnerable position. Any vehicle that has the air intake ducted to

the front is also potentially vulnerable. A major amount of water taken into the engine will result in major damage. Since water does not compress, if enough gets into the cylinder (a cupful is enough), split pistons and bent con rods are the result. Bad news.

Even if your intake is safe from immediate water ingress, an often-missed spot is the preheat hose that goes from the air horn down to the low-mounted exhaust manifold. In some cases, water can be drawn up this tube. Since this preheat is a valuable winter driving and emissions piece, just disconnect it temporarily when deep water is encountered.

If you run an open filter element, at least mount a splash shield to protect the filter from a major deluge. The cotton gauze style seems to hold up best in water. Some informal tests done by K&N at my request showed that all filters, even theirs, stop flowing when soaking wet, but theirs will atomize small to moderate amounts of water without harm. Foam and especially paper filters do not readily do this. Gauze and foam filters dry quickly but paper filters take forever to dry and water may damage certain paper filters permanently.

### Ignition Systems

If the ignition system gets wet, the engine dies. There are some waterproof distributors available from military GM and Dodge applications (the GM CUCV and the Dodge M-880). They were not particularly common or efficient (points type), but they can be had through some surplus outfits and retrofitted if you have a GM or Dodge small-block.

The next step is to have very high quality spark plug wires, in good condition, with nice tight boots, and then spray them with silicone spray. This helps repel moisture. You can also pack the boots and connections with dielectric silicone grease. Do not use silicone sealer, as it can attract and hold moisture. If necessary, Accel makes a self-vulcanizing tape to use on the booted wire ends.

The distributor can be sealed at the base of the cap with silicone as this is a less sensitive area, but the tape may work equally well. Some debate persists as to whether the distributor vent hole (usually at the bottom of the unit) should be left as-is or vented to elsewhere via a hose. Unless your engine is immersed to that point, the hole is usually safe from water splash. A front-mounted distributor is more vulnerable to splash, so a vent hose and good distributor sealing may be more important.

Most electronic ignition control modules can take a

good spraying but not dunking. The connections are usually the vulnerable area. Some Jeepers have mounted their modules inside waterproof boxes. At the least, make sure the wiring connections are sealed.

As a final word on ignitions, a powerful electronic ignition system is more likely to keep your engine running in a wet environment than a weak, points-type system.

### Fuel Injection

Protecting your EFI comes down to three main areas, the control module (ECU), the connections, and the MAP sensor. The other sensors are generally sealed, but take a look to make sure they are not just covered by a snapped-on plastic cover. The ECU can be mounted inside a waterproof box or relocated to a higher area.

The sensor and electrical connections are often water resistant but should be packed inside with dielectric silicone grease and sprayed on the outside with silicone spray. They could also be taped with waterproof tape.

The MAP sensor reads manifold pressure but may also read barometric pressure. To do this, it has a pinhole on the back or bottom. This must stay clear of mud and water and has to remain open to the atmosphere. A splash shield is the minimum protection, and relocation is about the best you can do.

### Dipsticks and Breathers

If your engine was built after 1966, it should have a closed crankcase breather system. Older engines can benefit from retrofitting a PCV (positive crankcase ventilation) system. This eliminates the possibility of the crankcase drawing water. Some Jeepers modify their OE systems by mounting a separate breather filter in place of the air cleaner-mounted piece. This is fine, but like the open air filter, it should be protected from water splash ingress.

Some dipsticks use a rubber seal and will resist water. Other types just have a metal cap. It may be possible to retrofit a seal onto an older dipstick or replace the dipstick with one that seals. Otherwise, a cover is necessary to prevent water from entering. It may not be an issue except on engines with very low dipsticks.

The charcoal canister for your evaporative emissions may suck up water in certain circumstances if it's submerged. Vacuum and purge lines run to the intake system and in just the right circumstances, the vacuum/purge lines might suck up water. Most units are

mounted high and not a problem. If not, the answer is to relocate the unit to a higher spot.

### Starters and Alternators

Both of these components are up to some minor dunking. Clean water doesn't really harm them, unless they are used when full of water, but dirty or sandy water can kill them quickly. The starter is likely to be submerged most often and the quandary is whether to seal it well (in which case if water does get in, it will stay there) or to keep it open so that water will enter and drain just as quickly. There are good arguments on both sides. In the latter case, try to avoid using the starter while submerged or until it has drained.

The outside of the starter is splash resistant but careful sealing of the caps, covers, and joints with silicone sealer will help it stay dry when submerged. The high torque Mean Green starter, mentioned in Chapter 11, is particularly resistant to water. The major area of water ingress for most starters, however, is from the drive area. Water fills the bellhousing and then works its way into the starter from the back side. It's difficult to seal the bellhousing completely, though some 4x4 manufacturers do have sealed bellhousings and have a removable plug at the bottom that can be installed prior to fording.

The alternator is usually high enough not to be a problem and because it has more open holes for cooling, it is nearly impossible to seal. It drains well! Some deep-water Jeepers will remove the cooling fans from alternators to prevent them from blasting water into the unit. The unit does need this fan for cooling in ordinary use.

## Roundup: The Factory Jeep Engines

In order for you to make educated choices, here are the OE Jeep engines for you, with a few words on what makes them perform better and how they interchange with other Jeep engines.

### 1940–1953 L134 "Go Devil" Four-Cylinder L-Heads
Application: MB, GPW, 1945–53 CJ, 1946–50 PU, and
    SW, DJ
Displacement: 134 cubic inches
Common Power Output: 60 hp @ 4,000 rpm
Common Torque Output: 105 lb-ft @ 2,000 rpm
Bore and Stroke: 3.12 x 4.37 inches
Common Compression Ratio: 6.48:1
Performance Potential: very limited
Performance Parts Availability: nil

Comments: Though replaced for 1953 in CJs, this valve-in-block four-cylinder was used into the 1960s in the DJ-3A Dispatcher Jeeps. The 1951–53 Kaiser Henry J automobiles used a 68-horsepower, 109 lb-ft version of the Go Devil. Part of this power increase was due to the increase in compression ratio to 7.0:1 and a slightly larger carb. A Henry J head can be used or the old head can be milled to gain the higher ratio. Also, the Henry J intake manifold allows the use of the Rochester model B carburetor (the smallest, manual choke version that came on late 1950s–early 1960s Chevy 235-cid sixes) for an improvement in breathing. Many years ago, aluminum heads and hot cams were available and these may still be found and used. The L-134 will interchange with the later F-head engines.

### 1950–1968 F134 "Hurricane" Four-Cylinder F-head

Applications: 1953-71 CJ & DJ, 1950–65 PU, and SW, 1967–71 Jeepster
Displacement: 134 cubic inches
Common Power Outputs: 69–74 hp @ 4,000 rpm
Common Torque Output: 115–117 lb-ft @ 2,000 rpm
Bore and Stroke: 3.12 x 4.37 inches
Common Compression Ratio: 6.9:1 or 7.4:1
Performance Potential: very limited
Performance Parts Availability: nil
Comments: A variation of the earlier L-head engine, in which the exhaust valves remain in the block but the intakes are moved into the head. With larger valves, the F-head breathed better, so torque and power outputs were higher. A few performance parts were built but will now be found only in museums. Interchanges with the earlier L-head if hood clearance permits.

### 1980–83 2.5L "Iron Duke" Four-Cylinder

Applications: 1980–83 CJ
Displacement: 150 cubic inches
Common Power Output: 82 hp @ 4,000 rpm
Common Torque Output: 125 lb-ft @ 2,600 rpm
Bore and Stroke: 4.00 x 3.00 inches
Common Compression Ratio: 8.2:1
Performance Potential: fair to good
Performance Parts Availability: fair to good
Comments: This engine was purchased from GM for just three years and is a fairly rare find in Jeeps. The engine itself was used in a variety of GM cars (generally attributed to Pontiac) from about 1979, and it earned a good reputation. OK for light Jeeps, but as

with any four-cylinder, there is a limit to what can be done to make it generate torque. Most of the performance products are for high horsepower applications. No interchange among other Jeep engines, but the engine has a standard Chevy bellhousing bolt pattern. The trans that came with it, however, was weak stuff.

### 1984-1998 2.5L AMC Four-Cylinder

Applications: 1984–88 CJ-7 and XJ, 1987–97 YJ, XJ, TJ
Displacement: 151 cubic inches
Common Power Output: 105–125 hp @ 4,000–5,400 rpm
Common Torque Output: 125–150 lb-ft @ 2,600–3,200 rpm
Bore and Stroke: 3.88 x 3.19 inches
Common Compression Ratio: 9.2:1
Performance Potential: good
Performance Parts Availability: good
Comments: This engine exhibits a great deal of potential, but vehicle weight must be kept to a minimum. The 1984–86 engines used a single-barrel carburetor. In 1987, a TBI version was adopted, and in 1992, a port- injected version became standard. The late fuel-injected versions are the best. Mopar Performance makes a good number of performance parts, and many interchange between the 2.5- and the 4.0-liter six.

### 1957–64 226 "Super Hurricane" Six-Cylinder

Applications: 1954–64, PU and SW, 1957–65 FC-170
Displacement: 226 cubic inches
Common Power Output: 105–117 hp @ 3,600-3,800 rpm
Common Torque Output: 190–193 lb-ft @ 1,400-1,800 rpm
Bore and Stroke: 3.93 x 4.37 inches
Common Compression Ratio: 6.85:1 or 7.3:1
Performance Potential: limited
Performance Parts Availability: nil
Comments: Essentially a Continental engine that was also used in Kaiser and Frazer cars as well as a variety of industrial applications. Very robust. No significant power output changes and few, if any, performance parts were ever built for this engine. Interchanges with the later 230-cid OHC engine.

### 1963–67 230 "Tornado" OHC Six-Cylinder

Applications: 1963–65 PU, SW, 1967–69 M-715
Displacement: 230 cubic inches
Common Power Output: 140 hp @ 4,000 rpm

Common Torque Output: 210 lb-ft @ 1,700 rpm
Bore and Stroke: 3.43 x 4.37 inches
Common Compression Ratio: 8.5:1
Performance Potential: limited
Performance Parts Availability: nil
Comments: An overhead cam engine developed from the Continental 226-cid flathead. A great idea that fell on its face. A relatively powerful six but troublesome; mainly oil leaks and cam problems. The best units were the military engines because they used block-mounted motor mounts, as opposed to the front cover mounts of the civvy engines that caused oil leaks. Interchanges with the 226 flathead with a few mods —but why?

### 1966–71 225 "Dauntless" V-6

Applications: 1966–71 CJ, 1966–71 Jeepster
Displacement: 225 cubic inches
Common Power Output: 160 hp @ 4,200 rpm
Common Torque Output: 235 lb-ft @ 2,400 rpm
Bore and Stroke: 4.75 x 3.40 inches
Common Compression Ratio: 9.0:1
Performance Potential: good
Performance Parts Availability: good
Comments: Purchased from GM (Buick), this engine was similar to the earlier Buick 215 V-8, 300 V-8, and 340 V-8 as well as the later Buick 350 V-8 and 231 V-6. The old 225s were "Odd-fire" as were some of the early Buick 231s. The 225 used a standard BOP (Buick-Olds-Pontiac) bellhousing pattern, so later 231s interchange—including EFI and Turbo versions. The Buick 350 will also bolt up, though other fitting considerations exist. A good engine and a great swap into a flatfender.

### 1966–76 232 "High Torque" Six-Cylinder

Applications: 1966–76 CJ, 1966–70 SJ
Displacement: 232 cubic inches
Common Power Output: 145 hp @ 4,300 rpm
Common Torque Output: 215 lb-ft @ 1,600 rpm
Bore and Stroke: 3.75 x 3.50 inches
Common Compression Ratio: 8.5:1
Performance Potential: good
Performance Parts Availability: good
Comments: An AMC engine first purchased by Kaiser Jeep for Wagoneers and trucks but later used as the baseline engine for CJs. With seven main bearings, it's a durable engine. Essentially a shorter stroke version of the 258 that appeared later. Everything that works for the popular 258 will work on a 232.

### 1971–90 258 "High Torque" Six-Cylinder

Applications: 1971–86 CJ, 1987–90 YJ, 1972–73 Jeepster, 1971–87 SJ, and J-Series PU
Displacement: 258 cubic inches
Common Power Output: 150 hp @ 3,800 rpm
Common Torque Output: 240 lb-ft @ 1,800 rpm
Bore and Stroke: 3.75 x 3.90 inches
Common Compression Ratio: 8.4:1
Performance Potential: good
Performance Parts Availability: good
Comments: A long stroke version of the 232-cid. An excellent seven-main bearing engine, considered to be more than adequate power for CJs. Some leaking problems on later engines with plastic valve covers. Also, the carburetors starting in the late 1970s units are notorious for flooding and drivability problems. Used in big Jeeps as the baseline engine until 1987.

### 1984–86 GM 2.8L V-6

Applications: 1984–86 XJ, MJ
Displacement: 173 cubic inches
Common Power Output: 115 hp @ 4,800 rpm
Common Torque Output: 145 lb-ft @ 2,400 rpm
Bore and Stroke: 3.50 x 2.99 inches
Common Compression Ratio: 8.5:1
Performance Potential: good
Performance Parts Availability: good
Comments: A GM engine generally regarded as having a dubious reputation for reliability. Power output from the carbureted Jeep version was marginal. Used by GM into the 1990s with many improvements, such a TBI injection. The GM truck versions with TBI were rated at 125 horsepower and 150 lb-ft in the same era as the Jeep. Some of the "hot" car versions produced 135 horsepower. Very compact and light.

### 1987-up 4.0L "Power Tech" Six-Cylinder

Applications: 1987-up YJ, XJ, MJ, ZJ
Displacement: 241 cubic inches
Common Power Output: 190 hp @ 4,750 rpm
Common Torque Output: 225 lb-ft @ 4,000 rpm
Bore and Stroke: 3.88 x 3.14 inches
Common Compression Ratio: 8.8:1
Performance Potential: good
Performance Parts Availability: good.
Comments: A great engine! There is a lot of potential in this powerplant but many users find it near perfect in stock configuration. The "Last Hurrah" from AMC, this engine was a development of the

2.5-liter four and strongly influenced by the 258. Port injection makes this engine very tractable and economical. Lots of aftermarket goodies for this engine, including a great selection from Mopar Performance.

### 1964–68 "Vigilante" V-8

Applications: 1964–68 SJ

Displacement: 327 cubic inches

Common Power Output: 250 hp @ 4,700 rpm (2 bbl); 270 hp @ 4,700 rpm (4 bbl)

Common Torque Output: 340 lb-ft @ 2,600 rpm (2 bbl); 360 lb-ft @ 2,600 rpm (4 bbl)

Bore and Stroke: 4.00 x 3.25 inches

Common Compression Ratio: 8.7:1 (2 bbl); 9.7:1 (4 bbl)

Performance Potential: fair

Performance Parts Availability: almost nil

Comments: Originally offered by Nash in 1957 as a 250-cid, the engine was purchased from AMC by Kaiser Jeep for the Gladiator and Wagoneer SJ big Jeeps. Robust and long wearing, it has now become relatively difficult to find parts for this engine. Came in two- or four-barrel form. The four-barrel carb appeared only on the limited production Super Wagoneer (1965–68) but identical engines appeared in early and mid-1960s Ramblers, many of them with four-barrels.

### 1968–71 "Dauntless" V-8

Applications: 1968–mid 1971 SJ

Displacement: 350 cubic inches

Common Power Output: 230 hp @ 4,400 rpm

Common Torque Output: 350 lb-ft @ 2,400 rpm

Bore and Stroke: 3.80 x 3.85 inches

Common Compression Ratio: 9.0:1

Performance Potential: good

Performance Parts Availability: good

Comments: Another engine bought by Kaiser Jeep from Buick. A great powerplant, with many connections to the Buick V-6 engines. Appeared only in big Jeeps for a couple of years in two-barrel form. Used BOP (Buick-Olds-Pontiac) bellhousing pattern and transmission patterns matched. This engine was used by Buick from 1968 until about 1978. There were some Buick hi-po versions with 315-horsepower and 410 lb-ft in the early 1970s, but the common Buick four-barrel engine made 285 horsepower.

### 1972–91 AMC V-8

Applications: 1972–79 CJ (304), 1972–91 SJ

Displacement: 304 cubic inches; 360 cubic inches; 401 cubic inches (1974–78)

Common Power Output: 150 hp @ 4,200 rpm; 175 hp @ 4,400 rpm; 215 hp @ 4,400 rpm

Common Torque Output: 245 lb-ft @ 2,500 rpm; 285 lb-ft @ 2,900 rpm; 320 lb-ft @ 2,800 rpm

Bore and Stroke: 3.75 x 3.44 inches; 4.08 x 3.44 inches; 4.16 x 3.68 inches

Common Compression Ratio: 8.40:1; 8.25:1; 8.35:1

Performance Potential: good

Performance Parts Availability: good

Comments: These engines evolved from the AMC 290 that debuted in 1966. These engines are interchangeable and share a bellhousing pattern with the 232 and 258 sixes. Putting an AMC V-8 into a CJ that had a 232 or 258 is literally a bolt-in. Ditto going from a small displacement to a large displacement. They appeared in identical form in same-year AMC cars, but are also interchangeable with the earlier AMC car 290, 343, and 390 engines. They are highly underestimated and make a great Jeep powerplant.

### 1993–97 Mopar V-8

Applications: 1993–97 ZJ

Displacement: 318 cubic inches

Common Power Output: 220 hp @ 4,400 rpm

Common Torque Output: 300 lb-ft @ 3,200 rpm

Bore and Stroke: 3.91 x 3.31 inches

Common Compression Ratio: 8.9:1

Performance Potential: good

Performance Parts Availability: good

Comments: A port-injected variation of Chrysler's A-block engine that appears only in the Jeep Grand Cherokee and dates back to 1967 and the 273-cid. Much improved since then. The A-block is very similar to the Poly-head 318 that appeared in 1959. Lots of go parts for this mill. The 360 V-8, which is appearing in the 1998 Grand Cherokee, is a potential swap, as well as the 360s that appear in late model Dodge trucks.

## Swapping Basics

In theory, you can drop almost any automotive engine into any Jeep. It all depends on how much time, effort, and money you want to spend. The engine swapping that goes on is usually confined to a few types that fit particularly well or for which there are good adaptation resources.

The weight of the engine deserves some consideration both from the standpoint of added weight on the front suspension and from the standpoint of how that weight will affect handling and traction. The weight issue can be dealt with by the appropriate changes in spring rates but the handling is forever affected, unless you intend hanging railroad iron on back for balance. Engine weight can also be a moot point, since many of the slow turning engines of old outweigh a modern V-8 by a comfortable margin.

Most Jeep CJs are known for marginal chassis strength (the Wrangler is much tougher by all accounts), and the extra torque of an engine swap may cause breakage. Again, appropriate mods made at the time of the swap can forestall problems.

Cooling problems are probably the most common problems, and inadequate frontal area for the radiator is the usual cause. We'll get into cooling problems in depth later on.

### Popular Swaps: The Chevy Small-block V-8

The Chevy small-block is probably the most commonly swapped engine for the Jeep crowd and there are many good reasons. It's available in factory displacements of 265, 267, 283, 302, 305, 307, 327, 350, and 400 cubic inches (not including some oddball truck displacements). They can be stroked and bored to fit in between these figures or beyond them. A huge, and I mean HUGE, aftermarket is devoted to them, and the few bugs they once had have long since been worked out.

The real beauty is that they are virtually interchangeable, share the same basic external dimensions and weight, and many parts may be swapped between them. They are so common and inexpensive that they can be a very cost-effective solution to a lack-of-suds problem. They can be built for torque or to rev to the moon. They are durable and long wearing. Detractors usually find little ammo to use against them and a wall of defenders shoulder to shoulder to argue with. Adapters are built to put them in nearly every type of Jeep, but they are most commonly seen in CJs or Wranglers.

One combined advantage/disadvantage is the rear-mounted distributor. It's protected from water but sits close to the firewall and can be damaged when the frame flexes. The average small-block weighs 550 pounds, which is slightly less than the AMC V-8 and about the same as the Jeep sixes (except the 4.0-liter). The 350 is the most popular. The 267 was a low-pro-

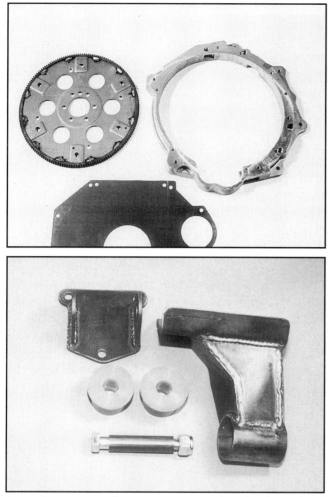

An engine swap can be easy or very tough. A lot depends on how popular the swap happens to be. Popularity will dictate the amount of expertise being applied by the aftermarket. Here are some of the basics you'd need for the most popular Jeep swap, a Chevy small-block. The bellhousing adapter, flex plate, and cover from Advance Adapters mate the Chevy to a Jeep CJ Torqueflite. The M.O.R.E. "Bombproof" motor mounts also are for a Chevy engine in a CJ chassis. *Courtesy Advance Adapters*

The beginning question for an engine swap is, How much engine do I really need? Refer to page 162 for some torque-to-weight ratios. Find the ratio that works for you and emulate it. The next question is, Will the OE drivetrain handle it? Often, this is a moot point because the builder will be swapping in a more desirable combination anyway. The last question is, Will it fit? Dropping a Chevy V-8 into a late CJ or Wrangler makes for a tight but workable fit. With a flatfender, you generally have to reassemble the vehicle around it! While the Sawzall and torch are definite answers to fitment problems, they are not always clean and elegant answers.

**Top Swaps** Here are some of the most successful and interesting swaps I have run across in the past couple of years. Some are common, others are esoteric or blatant overkill.

2.3-liter Ford 4-cylinder in CJ-2A.

231 Buick V-6 in CJ-2A

4.0-liter Jeep MPI six in CJ-8.

340 Dodge V-8 in CJ-5.

401 AMC V-8 in CJ-7.

350 Chevy TBI in Wrangler.

350 Corvette MPI in CJ-7.

351 Ford V-8 in CJ-7.

440 Chrysler in CJ-5.

duction "economy" unit of the 1970s and a bit of a dog. The 302 was a Z-28 hi-po engine and is rare. The 265, and to a lesser extent, the 283, 327, and 307, are a bit antiquated and have oddball accessory mountings. The 400 is the "big-incher," but the block has a few quirks and has been out of production for a long time. One hot torque trick is to use a 400 crank (3.75 inch stroke vs. 3.48 stroke) in a 350 block to get 376 cubic inches. The 400 crank is externally balanced so you need to use a 400 flywheel or flex plate.

## The Ford Small-block

Less common than the Chevy are the Ford small-block swaps. This is another great engine with a following

equally as rabid, but fewer in number than the Bowtie bunch. The Ford mill came in 221, 260, 289, and 302 displacements. The 221 and 260s were real oldies and are not sought after. The 289 is almost in this category. The 302, in continuous production since 1968, is the best of the small displacement bunch.

These engines are generally fitted into the "Windsor" category making the 351-cid 351W a direct relation. The 351W is slightly larger and heavier than a 302, but its displacement offers a 20 percent boost in torque over a similarly equipped 302. It appeared in 1969 and was used in cars into the 1980s, and variants are still used in trucks.

At only 480 to 500 pounds, Ford engines are

156

somewhat lighter and smaller than the Chevy small-block, so they fit a little better in tight engine compartments. They use a front-mounted distributor. Most Ford passenger car engines used a sump located at the front of the engine or had dual sumps. To install a Ford into a Jeep, a rear sump pan must be used from a Bronco or truck. The front-mounted oil filter can interfere with the steering components and must be remotely mounted in some installations. The aftermarket supply is not quite as extensive as for the Bowtie, but still gigantic. Used engines, especially 302s, are very common and reasonably priced.

## The 90 Degree GM V-6

A derivative of the small-block V-8, the V-6s share the V-8's durability and interchangeability but are much smaller and lighter. They share the same bellhousing pattern and general accessory mountings as an equivalent year V-8. Power outputs are similar to the smaller V-8s. The basic design appeared in 1978 as a 200-cid, basically a 267-cid V-8 with two cylinders sliced off. In 1980, the 229 debuted with the same bore and stroke as the 305 V-8. In 1983, the 262-cid (a.k.a. the 4.3-liter) appeared and was essentially a 350, less two jugs. The 262 is the most desirable. The beauty of these V-6s is that they share many internal parts with the V-8s. They came carbureted, with TBI and the late Vortec engines port injected. The Vortec engines are the best choice, with power and torque outputs almost 40 percent over the earlier mills. The V-6s weigh in the neighborhood of 450 pounds and are a full 4 inches shorter than the Chevy V-8. They are often compatible with the stock cooling systems in later CJs and are less known for overheating troubles.

## The Buick V-6

Introduced in 1961, the Buick V-6 has a large and long-standing following among Jeepers. It was actually owned by Jeep from 1965 to 1974, after GM sold the tooling and rights. Buick bought it back for the gas-starved middle 1970s. It originally appeared as a 198-cid unit but soon was punched out to 225-cid. It remained as such through the Jeep years and then when Buick reacquired it in 1975, they immediately bored it out .050 inches (no, you shouldn't bore a 225 .050 inches) and made it a 231.

The engines are all very similar to about 1977. These were "odd-fire" units, meaning that the V-8's firing order was used, less the gaps for the missing cylinders. The only downside was that the engines were inherently a little rougher. For midyear 1977, the engines were redesigned as "even-fire." This entailed a new crankshaft that is reputed to be not quite as strong as the odd-fire part. In 1980, a 252-cid version was offered in assorted Buicks and transverse mounted 3.0- and 3.2-liter variants (not interchangeable with the early units) remain in production today.

The Buick V-6 weighs about 390 pounds and fits particularly well in flatfenders and pre-1972 round-fender CJs. It has adequate power outputs for all but the most adrenaline-charged drivers. Turbocharged versions were used in 1980s-era Buicks. They are economical and durable, and the aftermarket has devoted a fair bit of expertise to adapters and performance products. The engine is noted as particularly easy to keep cool.

## AMC V-8s

Versions of these engines were offered in Jeeps from 1971 to the demise of the Grand Wagoneer in 1991. They are comparable in dimensions and weight (560 pounds and slightly longer) to a Chevy small-block. Power and torque outputs are comparable with the stock carbureted Chevy engines, but the ultimate high rpm performance potential is generally adjudged to be less (though lots of AMC fans will argue stridently). As a stock torquer, it actually may have a better curve than the carbureted Chevy, though not by much.

These engines were built from 1966 to 1991 in 290, 304, 343, 360, 390, and 401-cid displacements, with only the 304, 360, and 401 used in Jeeps. The 304 and 360 are by far the most common. They are all interchangeable, though there are some minor differences by era. The best part is that these V-8s share a bellhousing pattern with the 232 and 258 sixes. Whether you have a six-cylinder CJ or SJ, you can swap a six for a V-8 with bolt-on parts. You can also swap a smaller V-8 for a bigger one.

The aftermarket has so far offered a moderate selection of goodies for the AMC, though it's more than enough to get the job done. It usually costs 40 percent more to rebuild or build up an AMC compared to a Chevy. They are reasonably common and low-priced in used form (mostly from junked Wagoneers) with the 401s being the most sought after.

## Other Swaps

The Ford 2.3L OHC fours, offered from 1974 to date, are reasonably popular swaps for flatfenders. They weigh considerably less than the flathead or F-head

Fitting V-8s into early "shortnose" CJs is often tricky. To save fabrication effort, you can replace the nose and radiator supports with the 1972–79 V-8 style. Then you can install a V-8 type radiator easily. The OE nose is out front and the V-8 piece has been attached to the fenders.

(325 pounds vs. 470 pounds) and have 50 percent more net power and 30 percent more torque. They fit nicely and are reliable.

The GM "Iron Duke" is also seen in light rigs. It's arguably somewhat more reliable than the Ford (it has a timing chain rather than a belt), makes a bit more power and torque, but is heavier and larger.

GM 2.8L 60 degree V-6s are sometimes seen in flatfenders but not often in other Jeeps. Narrow, light, and reasonably powerful, they suffered from a marginal reliability record in their early years.

GM diesels, 6.2 and 6.5L, are sometimes seen in Wagoneers and J-series pickups. With a Chevy bellhousing pattern, they are the approximate size and weight of a GM big-block (396-, 454-cid). They have unbelievable off-idle torque and fuel economy well into the 20s. They have even been seen in CJs. They are not difficult to fit in a big Jeep but you gotta be a diesel nut.

Big-block Chevy engines, 396s and 454s, are sometimes used by the "wild and crazy" CJ crowd. They share the Chevy bellhousing but are a tight fit in a CJ and are overkill (relative to some people!) for power

and torque. They could make a nice swap into a big Jeep, but has anyone seen one?

Chrysler small-blocks are a good choice and are seen occasionally in CJs. They are a bit larger and heavier than a Chevy but are the Bowtie's equal in the performance department. They can be made to fit nicely in a CJ if you use Mopar transmissions or bellhousings.

Chrysler bigblocks, 361, 383, 400, 413, and 440, are sometimes seen in Jeeps, but unless you are talking a big Jeep, they are overkill. At over 650 pounds, they are a monster to fit, but they have been installed in CJs.

The aluminum Buick 215 V-8 used to be a popular swap into flatfenders. Rover has been producing this engine since 1967 and has worked out many of the design faults that plagued GM. At 325 pounds ready to run, these steel-sleeved, all-aluminum V-8s have been offered by Rover in 215 (3.5-liter), 241 (3.9- and 4.0-liter), 251 (4.2-liter), and 275 (4.6-liter) displacements with stock power outputs up to 225 horsepower and torque to 280 lb-ft. Great potential here, but the downside is lack of adapters and the relative expense of used engines.

## Cooling System Tips

The biggest problem an engine swapper faces is usually one of adequate cooling. A bigger engine generates more heat so at the very least, a larger radiator is needed. The problems can go way beyond just a simple radiator replacement, and the further you go outside

Heavy-duty cooling, or heavy-duty cooling problems! This VHP (very high performance) supercharged Chevy V-8 sports a gigantic custom aluminum radiator. It has an equally huge engine oil cooler and trans cooler. The trans is running a very loose torque converter that generates some serious heat. The supercharger will generate extra engine heat, so the oil cooler deals with that issue. Relocating the oil coolers might improve cooling.

of the stock design parameters, the more trouble you will encounter.

One of the first questions you may ask is, How hot is too hot? Well, water boils at 212 degrees. When it boils, it creates steam pockets in the engine and hot spots. This can damage the engine. The water can be prevented from boiling by keeping it under pressure (more pressure equals a higher boiling point) and by adding coolant (a 66 percent coolant mixture is ideal but 50/50 is OK).

Getting down to brass tacks, most modern engines (mid-1970s-up) with high pressure cooling systems (14–17 psi) are perfectly fine running at 200–220 degrees, with short spurts even higher. All the components (gaskets, hoses, radiator, etc.) are designed for the higher temps and pressures. Oddly, one of the main reasons for the higher operating temps is that they aid in emissions reduction and economy.

Older low-pressure systems (4–10 psi) need to run cooler, perhaps 160–180 degrees, with a rare spurt up to 200 degrees. In theory, an older engine could be modified to handle a higher pressure, but the gaskets, hoses and radiator structure must be up to the extra pressure.

The cooling system is basically a heat exchanger. It dumps excess engine heat into the air. It's designed to dump the specific amount (with a little overkill to compensate for climatic or work conditions) that an engine of a specific size and power output generates. There is usually enough extra capacity in the stock cooling system to handle the stock engine with a modest power increase, but when it comes to swapping engines you are usually in need of serious work. A major increase in power amounts to the same thing.

If you have overheating problems with your Jeep after a swap and you've eliminated the engine stuff, they usually fit into two categories: 1) It runs cool while going down the road but gets hot at low speeds (This is usually a problem with the fan setup, the shroud, the fan, or placement of the fan. It could also be a water pump that is running too slow); or 2) It runs cool at low speeds but gets hot at speed. This is often a radiator that's too small or a water pump of insufficient capacity. It could also be an air blockage problem (e.g., stuff in front of the radiator).

### Radiator

Get a bigger engine, get a bigger radiator, right? Very true, but there are physical limitations. One is the available frontal area of the vehicle. The frontal area of the radiator is vital to cooling performance and the bigger the better.

As you know, the radiator consists of fins and tubes. The airflow around and between them is what hauls off the heat. A single row of fins and tubes with a large frontal area is the ideal, although the design of the body limits this space, so a second, third, or fourth row of tubes is necessary to carry off more heat. The problem is that these following rows are not as efficient as that first row that gets the coolest air. Their airflow is reduced and warmed by the row that precedes it. That's why increasing the number of rows doesn't always work as a cure to a hot engine.

So what is the ideal frontal area of the radiator? When swapping, measure the frontal area of the radiator that cooled the engine you are planning to install (length in inches times width in inches equals area in square inches). Note also the number of cores and the general application (was it a light car or a hard-worked truck?). Try to match these dimensions and characteristics in an off-the-shelf radiator to fit your body or give them to the radiator man to custom build you one. Odds are good in a CJ or YJ that you are not going to be able to match the donor car or truck radiator for frontal area. Adding a row of extra cores is one answer but it doesn't always do the job as discussed earlier. If this is the case, you need to substitute other characteristics for frontal area.

Many modern radiator manufacturers built what are called "high-efficiency" radiators. These units are designed to maximize the heat exchange by increasing

You can save 5–15 horsepower by installing electric fans. This pair from Flex-a-Lite pulls 2,000 cubic feet per minute and is designed to fit a Wrangler. Although 2,000 cubic feet per minute is pretty good, it's not quite as much as the stock engine-driven fan at its peak. The engine fan, being variable speed, is really efficient at one specific speed. The electric runs at peak performance all the time, and doesn't run at all when not needed.

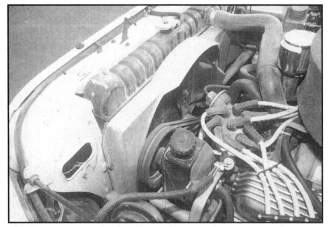

The importance of a fan shroud cannot be overstated. In a swap situation, a good shroud can mean the difference between hot and not. This one was custom made for a CJ-7/401-cid combo. With this engine cranking out a dyno tested 390 horsepower, it needed all the cooling help it could get. The owner fabricated a shroud and, combined with a big engine driven fan, this 401 thumper runs cool as a cucumber.

the number of cooling fins and placing them more strategically. The number of fins is measured by fins per inch (FPI), which is the number of fins along 1 inch of one tube.

Years ago, the FPI was usually 10–14. Nowadays, 18–20 is the norm, and an increase from 10 to 20 FPI can knock 20 degrees off the temp in many cases. If the fins are too tightly packed or if there are too many cores, airflow through the radiator is restricted and cooling is reduced. Most experts regard a 2-inch-thick core as a balance point between rows of cores, fins, and airflow.

Radiator material has traditionally been brass and copper. Some late model cars used plastic and aluminum, which are efficient but not very durable. Custom and racing radiators are often built of aluminum. While brass and copper conducts heat better, aluminum is stronger. This translates into being able to build an aluminum radiator with 1 1/4-inch tubes instead of the standard 3/8- or 1/2-inch tubing of the brass radiator. The bigger tubes carry more water, and a two-tube aluminum radiator from Griffin Racing Radiators can out-cool all three core radiators of the same frontal area and most four-cores.

### Airflow

The best radiator in the world is useless without air. At high speeds, enough airflow is usually generated to carry off heat. At low speeds, the fan or fans take on

that job. Airflow problems are the number one cooling system problem and the answers to this are the ones most often missed.

Once you have a radiator with the proper capacity as discussed above, make sure it has adequate room to breathe. Do you have a winch, horns, lights, oil coolers, grille guards, or anything that is blocking airflow in a big way? If so, remove or relocate the part.

The next item is a fan shroud. This is an absolute must and if you have to have one fabricated, it's worth the expense. In some custom engine swaps, this might be tough order. A good shroud increases the efficiency of a fan by leaps and bounds. Ideally, the fan will project about 1/2 inch into the shroud and have 3/4-inch clearance at the tips. A tighter fit is better, but you have to account for frame flex. A trail Jeep might need 1 inch of tip clearance.

The fan is an important item. Engine-driven fans are usually the best because they pull more air than most electrics. Electrics can be useful as auxiliaries but if you can find an electric fan that fits and pulls more than 2,300 cubic feet per minute, it might be a possible engine fan replacement. The engine-driven fan ideally covers as much of the radiator as possible, even if the shroud extends above or below the radiator by a distance. An inch more of fan diameter can equate to a 15 percent increase in airflow. The engine-driven fans can suck up some power so a thermostatically controlled unit can save horsepower by freewheeling when not needed. Ideally the fan should be not less than 1 and no more than 2 inches away from the radiator. Again, bear in mind frame flex, etc.

Finally, the air must have a way out of the engine compartment. If there isn't room for adequate flow around the engine and under the Jeep, the engine can run hot. This is why you may see louvers cut into the hoods of some rigs. They are designed to allow more hot air to escape.

### Water Pump

Water pumps are not created equal. Just like any pump, there are differences in capacity. When dealing with an OE replacement pump, always opt for the units noted as for "air conditioned" or "heavy-duty cooling" applications. These have a higher flow rate than the standard unit. You can go outside the factory and into the aftermarket pumps, such as those from Edelbrock, Flowcooler, Milodon, and others. These aluminum pumps can double the capacity of a stock pump and are built with aircraft quality components that ensure that

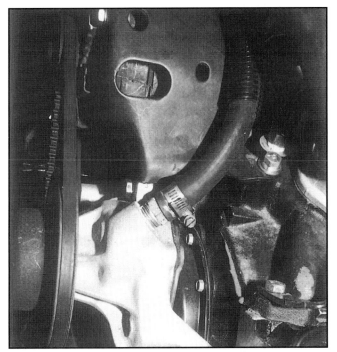

Hi-flow water pumps are available from a variety of manufacturers. Though they can be made of iron, the highest performance units, like this Edelbrock, seem to be cast aluminum. Even if you don't step up to an aluminum unit, at least buy the OE pumps designed for heavy-duty cooling or A/C-equipped models. A smaller water pump pulley can speed up the pump for better flow.

this will be your last water pump. These hi-po pumps may be limited to the popular performance engine applications.

Water flow is also controlled by how fast you spin the pump. Sometimes a change of pulley can be all that's needed to make a big difference. By going to either a larger crankshaft pulley or a smaller water pump pulley, the water pump can be sped up to increase flow. Generally, you want the water pump turning 30–35 percent faster than the crankshaft. If you are a high revver, take care not to overspeed the pump (see the alternator section in Chapter 11 for pulley gearing tips).

Many people think that the thermostat is a throw-away part and a cure for cooling system woes. Not true. It's a temperature control device to help the engine warm up and keep it operating at a designed temp. A lower temperature thermostat will not let more water through, it just opens sooner. There are high-flow t-stats available, such as those from Milodon, if you need them to enhance flow.

Removing the t-stat to increase water flow can be counterproductive in some cases, by rushing the water through the block too quickly and not giving it a chance to pick up heat. The ideal is to keep the water in the block as long as possible, then push it more quickly through the radiator.

### Oil Coolers

In many cases, relieving the radiator from duties such as cooling the automatic transmission may make a difference. An engine oil cooler may also help incrementally. The problem with both of these partial solutions is that, especially in the winter, you may overcool both the engine and tranny oil, which should both be maintained at no less than 160 degrees to cook out moisture buildup.

Obviously an oil-line thermostat could be used or a manual valve to bypass the coolers but unless you have an oil temp problem, these are stopgaps and you are best off finding the true solutions to your cooling system problems.

## Emissions Regulations and You

Talking about engine mods and swaps is fine, but be sure you embark on a little research in your home state and city before you start. In some areas, these actions are strictly controlled via regulations. As rankling as it may be, the law is the law, and when you watch the smog roll by, you should realize that there is at least some justification to the rules. Each state or city is slightly different and research into every nuance of the laws is beyond the scope of this book. There are common threads to many of the regs and we'll cover some of them here.

In general, any emission controls that were installed on the engine or vehicle at the time of manufacture must remain in place and operational. With regard to engine swaps, the regulations usually require that the emission controls match the year of the engine—not the year of the vehicle. Many states also require that the replacement engine be of a similar year or newer. That may preclude putting that 1966 hi-po 289 with solid lifters in your 1986 CJ-7, for example.

High-performance parts are often required to be certified via testing that they do not degrade the emissions performance of the engine. California leads the nation with the strictest exhaust emission regulations and they have a system in place for certifying modified parts. The C.A.R.B. regulates such items, and if the part passes their test (at the cost of the manufacturer), they are issued a waiver and the parts are certified for use.

Many other states have adopted C.A.R.B. certification as the measure of legality.

Finally, in places where smog tests are required, exhaust emissions levels have been adopted for various years and types of vehicles. Some of these regs are quite lenient, while some are Draconian and make it almost impossible for an older vehicle to pass.

Taking the time to research your own area before you begin can save lots of heartache later and potentially some expense. While there are always methods to circumvent such regulations, they can catch up with you at inopportune times.

## Selected Torque-to-Weight Ratios

Ratio of gross vehicle weight (pounds) per pound-foot of torque.

| | |
|---|---|
| 1993 Wrangler 4.0L six: | 19.5:1 |
| 1993 Wrangler 2.5L four: | 30.9:1 |
| 1990 Grand Wagoneer 360 V-8: | 21.3:1 |
| 1982 CJ-7 258 six: | 17.8:1 |
| 1976 Cherokee Chief 401 V-8: | 17.5:1 |
| 1975 Wagoneer 258 six: | 30.9:1 |
| 1974 CJ-5 232 six: | 20.2:1 |
| 1974 CJ-5 258 six: | 19.2:1 |
| 1974 CJ-5 304 V-8: | 15.3:1 |
| 1969 CJ-5 225 V-6: | 15.9:1 |
| 1969 CJ-5 F-134 four: | 32.9:1 |
| 1950 CJ-3A L-134 four: | 33.3:1 |

## Camshaft Dictionary

When you start checking out camshaft catalogs and specifications, you may run into a few new terms that deserve some explanation. Here are some of the heavy hitters.

### Lift

Lift is shown two ways, either cam lift or valve lift, and is measured in thousandth of an inch. One thousandth of an inch is expressed as .001. One hundred thousandth of an inch is expressed .100. The most easily comparable number is cam lift, since this measurement is the actual amount the cam moves the lifter. Valve or "gross" lift, as the term implies, is measured at the valve itself. It's the amount the cam and valve gear actually move the valve.

The important thing to remember here is that cam lift is multiplied by the rocker arm ratio to get valve lift. Rocker arms are offset in such a way that a given lift input on one end is multiplied at the other end. Many times, the actual rocker ratio of the engine is less than the "theoretical" ratio shown by the engine manufacturer and used by the custom cam grinder to calculate the gross lift shown in their information.

### Duration

Next in line is duration. It's most commonly expressed two ways, either at 0.004–0.006-inch tappet lift or at 0.050-inch tappet lift. This means that the duration measurement (the amount of time in crankshaft degrees the valve is off its seat) is not started until the lifter has moved either 0.004, 0.006, or 0 .050 inch from the bottom position. The reason for the 0.050 measurement is that no significant airflow through the valve occurs until it moves well off its seat. The 0.050 measurement is the most accurate indicator of the camshaft's personality for this reason. Sometimes the 0.004–0.006-inch measurement is called "advertised duration."

### Lobe Separation Angle, Centerlines, and Overlap

The lobe separation angle measures the distance, in degrees, between the intake lobe centerline and the exhaust lobe centerline. The lobe centerline is an imaginary line at the nose or "peak lift" point of the lobe. The peak lift period could be 4 or 5 degrees in duration, and the lobe centerline is at the halfway point.

The lobe separation angle is a more modern and technically accurate means of expressing the effects of the overlap period. Overlap is a short period in the cycle when both the intake and exhaust valves are partially open. By spreading the lobes farther apart, overlap is decreased and low rpm power is enhanced to the detriment of hi-rev power. Moving the lobes closer together has the opposite effect of increasing overlap and boosting high rpm power to the detriment of low rpm operation. Lobe design and duration can remain the same while the cam is fine-tuned for the desired rpm range. Wide angles would be between 111 and 118 degrees. Narrow angles are between 105 and 110 degrees.

### Single and Dual Pattern Cams

A single pattern cam has identical lobes on the intake and exhaust. A dual pattern cam has different lobe designs for each. Many engines have problems with flow on the exhaust side, so the exhaust duration and lift are made longer and higher than the intake.

### Symmetrical and Asymmetrical Cams

A symmetrical cam would have the same shape or profile on the opening ramp of the lobe as the closing ramp. This was the industry standard for many years. With computer technology, it's now possible to have different shapes and rates on the opening and closing ramps of the lobe. It might be beneficial for a particular engine to have a steep, fast opening rate but a gentle closing rate to avoid slamming the valve closed.

*Recommended rpm Range*

Depending on the manufacturer, these figures may give the most efficient rpm range (i.e., maximum torque), or the minimum and maximum rpm for a particular camshaft.

Specs may also include the ideal cruising rpm speeds. These figures are important in the cam selection process. If the cam is rated for max torque at 3,000–7,000 rpm, you don't want to put it into a vehicle used at 1,500–3,000 rpm. The cruising rpm figure is a bonus, because you can pick a cam that has max economy at your best cruising speed.

## Figuring Carb Capacity

To find the airflow capacity needed for a given application, you need to know the cubic inch displacement of the engine and the maximum rpm at which you plan to use the engine. Be realistic! If you can't find a carb small enough, chances are a stock type unit will be fine. The ratings are in cubic feet per minute (cfm). The choice of the 0.75 or 0.80 multiplier is given as an option for engine tuning. If you are building a torquer, use 0.75 and input a low max rpm figure. If you are building more of a high revver, use 0.80 and increase the max rpm. If you have a really old, slow-turning engine, like a flathead, use 0.70. A really built engine could use 0.85.

$$CFM = \frac{\text{max rpm x displ in cid} \times 0.80 \ (\text{or } 0.75)}{3,456}$$

Here is a sample using an AMC 360 V-8 intended as a torquer.

$$\frac{4,800 \times 360 \times 0.75}{3,456} = 375 \text{ cfm}$$

## ENGINE SPECIFICATIONS OF POPULAR SWAPS

| Mfr. | Year | CID/cyl. | Power | Torque | CR | B&S | Induction |
|------|------|----------|-------|--------|-----|-----|-----------|
| Buick-C | 1977 | 231/V-6 | 105@3,400 | 185@2,000 | 8.0 | 3.80x3.40 | 2-bbl |
| Buick-C | 1988 Turbo | 231/V-6 | 235@4,400 | 330@2,800 | 8.0 | 3.80x3.40 | MPI |
| Chev-C | 1988 | 262/V-6 | 140@3,800 | 225@2,200 | 9.3 | 4.00x3.48 | TBI |
| Chev -T | 1993 | 262/V-6 | 165@4,000 | 235@2,000 | 9.1 | 4.00x3.48 | MPI |
| Chev-C | 1977 | 305/V-8 | 140@3,800 | 245@2,400 | 8.5 | 3.37x3.48 | 2-bbl |
| Chev-T | 1980 | 305/V-8 | 150@3,800 | 240@2,400 | 8.6 | 3.37x3.48 | 4-bbl |
| Chev-C | 1985 HO | 305/V-8 | 180@4,800 | 235@3,200 | 9.5 | 3.37x3.48 | TBI |
| Chev-C | 1973 | 350/V-8 | 175@4,400 | 270@2,400 | 8.5 | 4.00x3.48 | 4-bbl |
| Chev-C | 1980 | 350/V-8 | 190@4,200 | 280@2,400 | 8.2 | 4.00x3.48 | 4-bbl |
| Chev-C | 1988 | 350/V-8 | 230@4,000 | 300@3,200 | 9.3 | 4.00x3.48 | TPI |
| Chev-T | 1993 | 350/V-8 | 210@4,000 | 300@2,800 | 9.1 | 4.00x3.48 | MPI |
| Chev-C | 1993 'Vette | 350/V-8 | 300@5,000 | 340@3,600 | 10.5 | 4.00x3.48 | TPI |
| Chev-T | 1974 | 400/V-8 | 180@3,800 | 290@2,400 | 8.5 | 4.12x3.75 | 4-bbl |
| Ford-C | 1977 | 144/4 | 92@5,000 | 121@3,000 | 9.0 | 3.78x3.13 | 2-bbl |
| Ford-C | 1977 | 302/V-8 | 137@3,600 | 247@1,800 | 8.0 | 4.00x3.00 | 2-bbl |
| Ford-C | 1986 | 302/V-8 | 150@3,200 | 270@2,000 | 8.9 | 4.00x3.00 | MPI |
| Ford-T | 1991 | 144/4 | 100@4,600 | 133@2,600 | 9.2 | 3.78x3.13 | MPI |
| Ford-T | 1993 | 302/V-8 | 185@3,800 | 270@2,400 | 9.0 | 4.00x3.00 | MPI |
| Ford-C | 1974 | 351/V-8 | 162@4,000 | 275@2,200 | 8.2 | 4.00x3.50 | 2-bbl |
| Ford-T | 1986 | 351/V-8 | 210@4,000 | 305@2,800 | 8.5 | 4.00x3.50 | 4-bbl |
| Ford-T | 1993 | 351/V-8 | 200@4,000 | 300@2,800 | 8.8 | 4.00x3.50 | MPI |

T = Truck, C = Car

## Air Filter Size Formulas

In general, according to K&N Engineering, testing on two-and four-barrel carbs has shown that a short, large diameter filter offers better power than a tall, smaller diameter filter, and suggests that diameter should be as large as practical based on space limitations. There is an ideal ratio of diameter to height for V-8s with two- or four-barrel carbs. K&N thinks the filter height should be between 1/5 and 1/4 of the diameter.

When it comes to single-barrel carbs, the formula is somewhat different. A tall filter may have some power benefit over a short one. The diameter should be at least three times the diameter of the carb throat.

*1. To determine filter area needed for a given application:*

$$\text{Area in sq. in.} = \frac{\text{cid x rpm}}{25,500}$$

For rpm, use your projected maximum or the maximum rated for your engine, usually where peak power is developed.

*2. To determine the effective area of a given filter:*

$$\text{Area in sq. in} = \text{diameter (inches) x 3.14 (pi) x height (inches) - 0.75}$$

*3. To determine if a given filter has enough airflow for your engine:*

$$\text{Approximate airflow} = \text{Area in sq. in x 6.0 cfm/sq. in.}$$
(oiled cotton gauze)*
5.0 cfm/sq. in. (paper)*
4.4 cfm/sq. in. (foam)*

* According to K&N Engineering. These are the rounded best figures for competitors they have tested to date.

*4. To find the ideal height, once diameter has been determined:*

$$\text{Height} = \frac{\text{Area (square inches)} + 0.75}{\text{Diameter (inches) x 3.14}}$$

*Chapter 11*

# ELECTRICAL SYSTEM

## Zap Rap

We are now more than a few steps into the age of electronics—in our vehicles as well as our homes. Fuel injection and electronic ignition dominate our engine compartments, and razzle-dazzle devices of all kinds fill our dashboards. I'll let you decide whether it's all good or not, but we all must bow to the fact that it's here to stay.

This chapter will deal with the electrical aspect of Jeeping and the installation of devices that enhance the performance of your Jeep. In truth, there is very little electrically that has a direct impact on whether you make it up that hill or not, with the possible exception of an electric winch and the oversize batteries and alternators that should go with it. Bare necessity aside, however, the auxiliary lights and all the rest of the electrical stuff we add sure make the job easier in so many ways.

### The Flow of Electricity

If you install something electrical, you must abide by the principles known as Ohm's Laws, named after the German scientist George Ohm. Fortunately, that's fairly easy to do. Before we get deep into *what*, we need to get into a little *how*. I won't turn this into rocket science, but there are some concepts, terms, and formulas you really need to understand in order to work out some of the solutions to your own electrical needs.

The easiest way to understand electrical stuff is to think about it in terms of water. This is a common way to teach the basics. Think of your battery as a reservoir and the wires as small or large pipes. The alternator or generator is a well pump that fills the reservoir. You may have a small or large pump, and how fast the pump works depends partly on how fast the engine

These red-top Optima batteries put out 800 cold cranking amps and are designed primarily for starting uses. These units are hooked up to charge in parallel with no isolator or split-charge unit. The vehicle uses one battery to start and the winch uses the other. An Optima yellow-top deep cycle or the blue marine style would be a better choice for the winch side, or as a single dual-purpose battery. The yellow top puts out 750 cold cranking amps, but is rated for 350 BCI/SAE cycles (drained to 100 percent and recharged). The red top is rated for considerably fewer.

turns it. Think of accessories as faucets of varying sizes, and think of ground wires as drains that go into the earth that will eventually feed the pump.

You go to start the Jeep and your starter motor faucet is a big one. It needs to draw a lot of water through its big pipe, and it draws lots of water from the reservoir. Once the engine starts, it takes a while for the pump to catch up and refill the reservoir.

The engine ignition system only needs a trickle through its tiny pipe, but when you turn on the lights and air conditioner faucets, they are drawing lots of water though medium-sized pipes. So far, the pump seems to be able to keep ahead of the draw and the reservoir is slowly being refilled.

You drive for a while and soon the reservoir is nearly full. When you hit the trail, you turn on three sets of big lights and these faucets take lots of water. The pump can't quite keep up with everything, but the reservoir is only slowly being drained. It can last for a while, though the pump is working very hard. Maybe you need a bigger pump?

A ways down the trail, you get stuck. With the engine idling, the pump slows down and with all those faucets on, the reservoir begins to drain fast. Then, you use the winch and it's as if you pulled the reservoir drain plug. It drains like a broken dam, and no matter how hard it works, the pump cannot keep up with the tidal wave that's going out.

Once you get unstuck, you shut the engine off to wash yourself in a creek. When you come back to start up, only a dribble of water goes to the starter faucet. The reservoir is dry! The pump is smoking hot! You get the idea. As long as you appreciate the amount of draw your engine and all of your Jeep's accessories require to function, you can stay ahead of the game and not run down your reservoir of electrical power.

## The Battery

The battery is the heart of your Jeep's electrical system. There's a lot riding on it. A battery can determine whether you make it into work on that cold winter morning, or whether you make it home from a four-wheeling trip. Whether you need any improvements in this area depends a lot on which extras your vehicle carries and the way you use it. There are also situations in which different types of batteries are needed.

Three basic types of batteries are available, those designed for "normal" use and starting only, those built for deep-cycle use, and combination batteries that are commonly known as "marine" batteries. Each offers the best service in its particular area.

### Starting Batteries

These are designed to supply large amounts of cranking amps to start your rig quickly. They want to be quickly recharged and maintained in a full, or nearly full, state of charge at all times. They will die quickly if used like a deep cycle, i.e., discharged and recharged too many times. They are light, compact, and pack a lot of starting amps.

### Deep-Cycle Batteries

Deep cycles are designed to supply a steady stream of power for a long period. They prefer to be drawn down and recharged regularly. They cannot supply the raw number of amps of a starting battery, but they can supply fewer amps for a much longer period. They usually don't last as long in a starting battery application.

### Marine Batteries

Marine batteries combine the attributes of a deep cycle and a starting battery. They are not great performers in either role (compared to the purpose-built units of either style), but they will happily fulfill a dual role with no loss of efficiency.

Batteries are rated several ways, depending on type.

These Die Hard batteries are among the best representatives of the standard lead acid starting battery. With 900 cold cranking amps, the "Gold" unit would provide a big reserve of power, but the big Group 65 battery might not fit in all battery trays. Always buy the best and biggest battery you can afford. These batteries would not be ideal for use with a lot of winching or with any situation that would draw them down repeatedly. *Courtesy Sears*

Two key ratings for starting and marine batteries are cold cranking amps (CCA) and reserve capacity. CCA is the number of amps the battery can put out for 30 seconds at 0 degrees Fahrenheit before voltage drops below 7.2 volts. Reserve capacity measures the number of minutes the battery can supply a 25-amp load before dropping below 10.5 volts. Obviously, the higher these numbers, the better the performance.

Deep cycles, and some marine batteries, are also rated by an old system called amp-hours (AH). This is the maximum number of amps the battery can supply for 20 hours before the voltage drops below 10.5. A 120-AH battery, for example, can supply six amps for 20 hours.

### Choosing a Battery

The type of battery you choose depends on your needs. How big a battery you should pick depends on some of the same things but may be restricted by physical space. More powerful batteries are usually larger in dimensions. The basic first rule for Jeepers is to fit the most powerful battery that will physically fit in your battery tray and get the highest quality that you can afford. Why?

Things happen on the trail. If the alternator dies, your vehicle will have to run off the battery. The more powerful battery will last longer and may get you to civilization before expiring. Also, in adverse weather conditions, the stronger battery has more juice to get the engine started. There are countless other scenarios where a few extra amps could make a difference. In choosing a starting battery, you want *at least* 1 CCA per cubic inch of displacement, and many people, especially in cold climates, go with much more.

The next complication involves the type of battery. If you don't have a winch, or other big electrical draw item, stick with a starting-type battery. If you have a winch and use it more than a handful of times, it could adversely affect the life of a starting battery. Not only that, a starting battery simply does not have the capacity for an extended winch pull.

In these cases, you have two choices. Install a second battery, a deep cycle complete with isolator (we'll get into this later in the charging system section), or install a marine-type battery that is up to both tasks. While a second battery is the best idea in terms of raw power for the winch, the weight penalty and extra space needed may make it a negative idea. It depends on how much you use the winch. See chapter 7 for more on winches and what they need to survive.

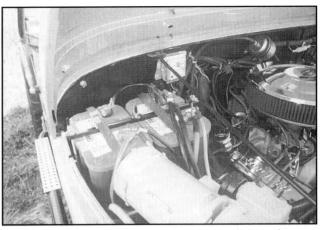

This dual battery setup separates the starting battery from the accessory battery, but allows them to be connected or disconnected via a simple hi-amp knife switch—a simple solution that saves some bucks on isolators or solenoids. It also requires the operator to remember to operate it correctly.

### Dual Batteries

Many Jeepers install dual batteries for a variety of reasons. The extra capacity is usually to drive a winch but there are many other good reasons. Once you decide you need a second battery, the next question becomes how to hook it up.

The easiest approach is to hook them in parallel, which means that the system voltage remains at 12 volts but both batteries combine to produce double the cranking amps. If you have the winch hooked up to this parallel setup, it will draw from both batteries. On the surface, this sounds like a good deal but two problems exist with this setup.

First is that two batteries in parallel will drain each other. If you are planning to use batteries in parallel, you should have two matching batteries. That means brand, size, and even age. Put a tired old battery alongside a new fresh one, and the weak old-timer may start to discharge the newer battery. All batteries self-discharge, and the rate at which they do tends to increase with age. The old battery starts recharging itself from the new one. This process continues until they are both dead.

The second problem is that two batteries in parallel can only be considered one bigger battery. When they're dead, they're dead. Sure, you can winch or crank longer, but eventually they will go dead as a pair just as if they were a single battery.

The next approach is to give the two batteries their separate tasks and use a split charge system to keep them charged. This can be done via mechanical means (solenoids) or via *diodes* (electrical "one-way valves") to separate the two batteries.

Solenoids are cheap and simple but require manual intervention or a voltage-sensitive relay to keep the batteries charged. The simplest setup uses an isolator, which is nothing more than several high-capacity *diodes*. You can wire them up with the alternator output wire going to the center input of the isolator and the outputs get connected to the batteries. The device needs to carry the maximum capacity of the alternator, and units are available into the 250-amp range. You can get them for two, three, and even four batteries.

## The Alternator

You've got a long winch pull ahead of you and you are sucking every amp out of the battery, and the alternator is buzzing at max charge and way too hot to touch. Many Jeepers subject their factory alternators to this sort of abuse regularly and as often as not, the poor thing soon goes up in smoke.

Most newer factory alternators are in the 100-amp range. Some are up in the 120–150-amp range. Older units may be 60 amps or less. If you regularly operate a high draw item like a winch, 100 amps is the crawling-on-the-ground minimum. In a high draw situation, the more amps you can pump into the battery, the longer that battery will hold out. Since a 100-amp unit costs and weighs only marginally more than a 60-amp, you might as well have the bigger one. Same goes for a 120-amp vs. a 100-amp, etc. In addition to amp rating, pay attention to an alternator's duty cycle. This quality is often as significant as maximum amps.

Whatever the stock type alternator's amperage rating, most aren't designed for continuous maximum output. A typical stock duty cycle might be a 60 percent load right after startup that rapidly decreases to a continuous 25 percent, or much less. Put on a continuous 80 percent load and poof! This is especially true of alternators with internal voltage regulators.

The answer comes in the form of heavy-duty, or industrial-type alternators that are designed to be equally happy idling at a 30 percent load or putting out maximum amps until the engine wears out. This gives Jeepers a lot of flexibility when it comes to handling an electrical load.

Selecting an alternator involves finding a unit that will physically fit your mounting brackets and finding one of the right capacity to fit your needs. Starting with capacity, you need to know how alternators are rated. All alternators have their voltage rating and amperage rating stamped on their case somewhere. A typical unit might say 14V 65A, meaning it's rated to produce output voltage at 14 volts and produce a maximum of 65 amps. The amps shown are usually SAE amps and the rating is somewhat misleading.

The SAE rating is the maximum amount of amps the unit can produce in a "cold" state, about 80 degrees Fahrenheit. An alternator remains cold about 5 minutes, or less, under a heavy load. As it warms up, output is reduced because the heat causes resistance in the rotor to increase and output amperage is reduced. Stock-type alternators are more affected by heat than the heavy-duty units. The hot output rating is taken at 200 degrees.

A typical late model stock unit can be rated at 100 SAE (cold) amps. Thoroughly warmed up, the unit might make a maximum of 77 amps, a 23 percent drop. A heavy-duty unit, such as the Premier 170 amp (SAE) rated alternator, produces 146 amps roasting hot, only a 14 percent drop. Their higher output units do even better, with the 220 SAE amp unit, making 200 amps hot, a mere 9 percent drop. These specs are typical of most industrial-type alternators.

There are many other important construction differences between most OEM alternators and the high output jobs. Since heat is a by-product of producing current, an alternator's ability to deal with this is vital to long life and capacity. The first durability factor comes in the form of external voltage regulators—not

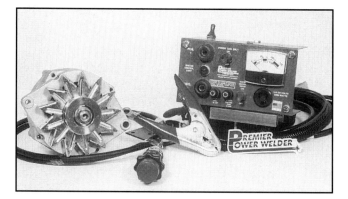

A big industrial alternator is a must for heavy electrical loads. If you have a winch, 100 amps is the minimum size, but bigger is better. This Premier 160 CS alternator is externally regulated, built to industrial specs, and will pump out max amps long after winching work is done. Externally regulated alternators are inconvenient but longer lasting. Alternators reach 200 degrees or hotter, in some cases. Keeping the electronics out of that heat adds to longevity and power output. This unit, along with the underhood welder pictured, fits most early Jeep products. The 170 CS kit fits later Jeeps. *Courtesy Premier Power Welder*

as convenient to wire up but more durable. The mega-alternators use more and higher capacity diodes to convert the alternator's AC current to DC. These diodes are also heat-sinked better than OEM units. Everything in their construction is geared toward durability, including hi-temp bearings.

### Low Speed Alternator Power

If you spend a lot of time idling or at low speeds, it's important to consider the idle output of the alternator. Alternators are built to produce power according to shaft speed. Some are wound to produce as much as 80 percent power at low speeds (about 2,000 rpm alternator speed at 800 rpm engine speed) while most others do about 40–50 percent at that speed. Gearing via pulley sizes is one way to ensure maximum power at idle. A big driven pulley (engine crankshaft) and the smallest available alternator drive pulley ensure a high rotor speed.

The Premier 170CS alternator I mentioned earlier, for example, produces 57 SAE amps at 2,000 shaft rpm. Bump it up an extra grand via pulley changes to 3,000 rpm, and the output jumps to 115 SAE amps. Look at the pulley gearing chart on page 176 for more info, but the handy formula for figuring alternator rpm is to divide crank pulley diameter by alt pulley diameter and then multiply by engine rpm. Take care to calculate your engine redline alternator speed if you have a hi-revving engine. You don't want to be the first person on your block to grenade your alternator. Also, "gearing up" the alternator will draw additional power from the engine. The gearing up idea works for any type of alternator.

### Mounting Mega-Amp Alternators

Mounting a big alternator needs to be given the same consideration that you would when swapping a six for a V-8. In most cases, the new alternator bolts on in place of the original unit, though that isn't necessarily the end of the job. Give some consideration to the quality of the original mounting system. In many cases, you are doubling or tripling the capacity of the alternator. Is the old mount up to the job? A 45-amp alternator at max output draws about 3/4 horsepower. A 220 amp alternator draws about 3 1/2 horsepower.

Even more important is the belt drive. The absolute best setups are the serpentine or v-ribbed belts. They get a very good bite on the pulley and will seldom have slipping problems, regardless of load. Next best are dual v-belt setups and last are single belts. A single v-belt is the most likely to slip in a heavy load situation or to wear out prematurely. In this situation, there are two impor-

tant factors to keep in mind, belt width and belt wrap around the pulley. As a general rule, anything over 120 amps ought to have a serpentine belt or dual belts.

For automotive applications, two common v-belt widths exist, 3/8 inch and 1/2 inch. Half-inch is preferable due to more gripping area, but remember that you can't use a 1/2-inch belt with 3/8-inch pulleys. Belt wrap is the amount of belt that is actually in the sheave of the pulley. The more belt on the pulley, the more capacity it has to drive the accessory. A single half-inch belt wrapped around more than half of the pulley should be adequate for about 120 amps with a tight belt. After that, you get closer to the slippage area.

To find the answer to belt problems, start by looking at other engines in the same family. A trip to the wrecking yard might yield a double pulley or serpentine setup that was optional or appeared later. With no luck there, it's time to find a machinist.

### Underhood Welders

One of the side benefits to the mega-alternators is that they can be used as mini powerhouses. These welders come from companies like Premier Power Welder and Linc-Arc. Imagine having an efficient stick welder, Heli-Arc, or MIG unit wherever you go. These units are real welders, not just emergency equipment. The better underhood welders feature a 115-volt DC power outlet with 20 amps available. Since this outlet

Use the best wire you can find for your Jeep. Better wire has more strands and the insulation is temp rated to a higher spec. This TXL wire from Painless Wiring is one of the better PVC insulated wires and is rated for 275 degrees. The OEM is beginning to use modified polyester wire that has better resistance to oils, solvents, and other damage. *Courtesy Painless Wiring*

supplies DC current, it cannot be used with electronic equipment.

Welding with an underhood unit is easy because it uses high frequency, DC current rather than massive amounts of amps. Most welding units operate at 60 cycles. Underhood welders operate at 6,000–7,000 cycles and can weld at two-thirds the amperage of a conventional welder. With the lower amps, clean welds are easier for novices to make and penetration remains excellent.

## Wires and Cables

To start with, the wiring in your Jeep must be sized properly. The wire size chart in Figure 11-4 gives you the skinny on this, but you may be wondering why. Using the water and water pipe analogy again, trying to put 100 gallons per minute through a pipe designed for 25 gallons could result in a blown-up pipe.

If you put an electrical device on the end of a wire that is too small, two things can happen. One, the wire goes up in smoke. Two, the device does not operate properly, because it cannot get sufficient current. In some cases, operating an electrical device below the required voltage and current is harmful to it.

Another point to consider is that, just like everything else, there is a quality food chain with wire. Better wire has more strands and is more flexible. Given two wires of the same gauge, the one with more strands will have less *voltage drop* and can actually carry a bit more current.

There is also a quality issue in the insulation. The standard run-of-the-mill hardware store wire has a minimum spec of 185 degrees Fahrenheit. Better wire is marked with its temp spec (example 105C, indicating a 221 Fahrenheit rating) or the rating spec under which it is rated, such as UL, MILSPEC, or CSA. Commonly seen wire uses PVC insulation of various compositions and thicknesses to obtain the spec. Going higher up the food chain are wires rated up to nearly 400 degrees, but these are overkill unless you have a very high temp environment. Painless Wiring offers a TXL wire that is rated for 250 degrees Fahrenheit, and this is way over what is generally needed.

### Battery Cables and Connections

When you get to battery cables, you will find 2 and 4 gauge very common. In some cases, these are barely enough to get the juice to the starter in normal conditions, let alone a clutch-out start in a rock crawling scenario. There is another side to this beyond low performance. A starter motor, or any electric motor, dies

Crimp-on terminals are the home mechanic's best friend. Cheap connectors, however, will need to be sealed to avoid corrosion. Better connectors use a coated copper terminal, and the best, like these, have heat shrink built into the insulation to seal the connection. Above are the sealed "weatherpack" terminals favored by GM. These are almost watertight and can be used on a variety electrical devices. *Courtesy Painless Wiring*

quickly if it cannot get a full portion of volts or amps. This is one reason for the bigger-is-better battery discussion above, but if the cables are too small, a battery the size of Texas is of no use.

The simple solution is to install 0 or 00 gauge cable all the way to your starter. It will carry more than enough amps. Also consider that the best battery cable is not battery cable. Many Jeepers use welding cable. Why? It has many more strands than standard battery cable and is very flexible. High quality battery cable, similar to welding cable, is also available from Phoenix Gold or Painless.

The connection at the battery is another weak link. Years ago I was winching a stalled truck up a ramp. I had fixed myself up with dual batteries and a big (for the day) 100-amp alternator. It was a hard pull and all of a sudden the winch quit. It turned out that the lead terminal on the battery had melted. It was a 50-cent piece I had picked up at the local discount auto store.

The major issue in the case above was resistance at the terminal due to a poor connection. Resistance causes heat. Better terminals are made of copper and brass. If you want to go into stellar categories, try Phoenix Gold's gold-plated terminals. They look good enough to hang around your significant other's neck, but they minimize resistance and maximize amperage.

When you are making up your own cables, you may

This Mean Green starter is 6 pounds lighter than the stock Jeep starter, and because of a 2.5-horsepower motor, ball bearings, and a 4.4:1 gear reduction, it delivers three times the cranking torque. Because it's considerably smaller than the OE-style unit, it fits around headers better. According to MG Industries, this starter will deliver 35,000 starts, compared to the OE 4,500. If you do clutch-out starts on the trail, this could be the starter for you. *Courtesy MG Industries*

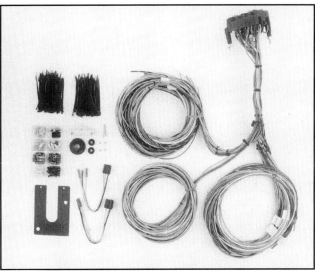

Complete wiring harnesses are available from a variety of sources in OE configuration or updated to a more modern spec. In this shot, we see a Painless kit for a CJ that features better-than-stock fuse protection for the vehicle. You can also buy generic accessory harnesses that connect to a power source and offer protection for all your accessory items without creating a rat's nest of additional wires. *Courtesy Painless Wiring*

be tempted to buy el cheapo terminals. The best are terminals that are molded to the cable, but these are hard to find in the big gauge wire and in the length you may need. In a tie for second are crimped terminals, which take a special tool that auto electrical supply or battery specialists carry, and serrated compression screws. Next are the marine-type terminals that use an eyelet on the cable end. The absolute worst are the cheapest two-bolt, strap type. The GM side terminals are OK but only for moderate amperage.

## Starters

The starter is often ignored in the buildup. It doesn't necessarily need a lot of attention, but there are a number of tricks to keeping them healthy and several upgrades you can make to spin that engine up better. We'll figure that you've already made sure you have enough amps delivered via cable and battery.

One of the most common problems with starters on built-up Jeeps is due to heat. Tight quarters in the engine compartment from a V-8 conversion is one thing, but a header pipe a half inch away is another. A hot starter develops less torque. If you have headers that run close, they can get it so hot that it will not crank the engine over. Two fixes are available here, either insulate the starter with a shield, or use header wrap to keep the heat in the header. Or do both! Nonasbestos header wrap is available from most speed shops, as are starter shields, or you can easily make your own.

Starters are not always "one size fits all." Jeeps used a variety of starters from Autolite, Prestolite, Delco-Remy, Motorcraft and others. These starters were built to spec for Jeep from generic designs used also on other brands. Stage one of a starter buildup would be to check with your local rebuilder and see if an improved unit of the same general type can be made to fit. This is often worth a 25 percent boost in starter torque, and the starters come from truck or hi-po car applications.

The next level is to buy one of the gear reduction, high output starters, such as those available from MG Industries. These units will out-torque and outlast an OE starter several times over. MG Industries earns a little extra coverage here because it covers a very wide spectrum of OE Jeep applications, as well as Chevy V-8 swaps. MG can do custom work for many old-time applications, and has taken strong steps to heatproof and waterproof its starters as much as possible, making them ideal for the trail.

## Accessory Wiring Tips

In many cases, Jeepers will want to wire in just a couple of extras into the existing electrical system. This is fairly easy to do and there are lots of good ways to do it. You don't want your wiring to look like a pack rat's nest! The first problem is finding a power source, and the usual solution is to use the "snap-splice" connec-

Finding a good power source is always a problem. In the case of Wranglers, an accessible spot is at the main feed to the fusebox. Corrosion will not be a problem here as it would at the battery. The No. 4 or No. 8 cable that feeds the fusebox is still capable of being overloaded, so count your amps carefully.

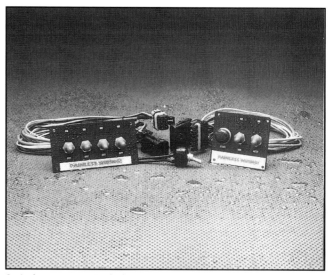

Switches are particularly vulnerable to moisture, but you can buy waterproof units. In this case, Painless Wiring has affixed them to an attractive panel and also equipped them with weatherproof connectors. Packing the connectors with dielectric grease provides even better protection. *Courtesy Painless Wiring*

tors that seem to come with every accessory. These clip onto a wire and provide a quick and dirty power source off an existing wire.

In theory, if the circuit you tapped into has the capacity for the additional load, you're OK. That means you have to have a wiring diagram and figure out the load on that circuit. The other problem is that these connectors don't always get a reliable connection when you snap them in and it may not keep one, especially in the underhood environment where water and dirt have free access.

If you are looking for a single source of battery power, find an empty *fused* terminal on the fusebox for a power supply, making sure that the circuit has the capacity for the item you want to add. You will probably need to uprate the fuse. The next easy idea is to find an empty *unfused* terminal off the fusebox, and add an inline fuse for the accessory.

When multiple accessories will be added, the best idea is to get your power from a source that has a large capacity (such as the solenoid or a bulkhead connection) and deliver it to a separate, new fusebox, from which all the new accessories are wired. Avoid attaching a power lead directly to the battery if you can, as corrosion will kill a smaller wire much more quickly.

A separate accessory circuit leaves the Jeep's original wiring to work as designed and allows accessories to be cleanly and reliably wired. Mount the new fusebox in a protected location or use one that is waterproof. Some folks have salvaged wiring harnesses from wrecked Jeeps, complete with fusebox, and adapted them as an auxiliary circuit. Others simply dialed a company like

Painless Wiring and bought their accessory wiring harness to make the job easy.

The connectors you use can mean the difference between light and no light, smoke or no smoke. For anything under the hood or in an area where weather, water, or dirt has access, sealed connectors should be used. Most crimp-on connectors are unsealed, meaning that when they are exposed to the weather, they will corrode and the connection will be lost. There are several ways to solve this potential problem, and the steps are best taken before they become problems.

To start with, electrical tape is unreliable in the long run, so let's leave that off the list. Eastwood's liquid electrical tape can be painted on open terminals. Shrink tubing, when carefully applied, can work well. Some shrink tubing is complete with a silicone sealer inside to further waterproof the connection. Sealed connectors can be purchased that have both silicone and shrink tubing attached. In short, all the trick means to build a reliable auxiliary electrical system, as good as OE, are available to you. Some of the connectors cost more, but any savings you might get from going the el-cheapo route will be nullified if you have to go back in a year and redo your wiring.

## Complete Rewire Tips

If you are building a Jeep from the ground up, you may want to completely rewire it. You can do this on your own from bits and pieces by first making a wiring

Relays are better for accessories than running the circuits through switches. Relays have amp ratings, so make sure the relay is a bit oversized for the load you intend. These relays from PIAA are weather resistant and would not be affected by much less than total immersion.

This backup light is worth its weight in gold if you've ever experienced a practically blind nighttime backing up scenario. This kit comes from IPF and can be set up to come on automatically when triggered by the tranny backup light switch, or independently by the driver. These lights are best mounted low and should have a wide beam. In this position, the lamp is fairly well protected.

diagram, planning the routing of circuits in the body with string, and carefully assembling everything on the floor or table. Or, you can buy a complete new harness from a company like Painless Wiring.

If you have added a multitude of new items and radically changed the electrical needs of your Jeep, you will likely do the former. If your Jeep will remain fairly stock, the best idea is to do the latter and add an accessory circuit for goodies.

## Lighting

You've seen the rigs with 10 lights on top. In some cases, they might be necessary for that individual, other times they are for looks. Consider moderation in this area and spend your money wisely. A good set of halogen headlamp replacements, one pair of auxiliary lights, and a good, bright backup light are usually enough for most circumstances.

A set of auxiliary lights can be a valuable accessory for trail use and also on the highway. Mounted here, these lights would give the driver significant and probably unbearable glare on the hood. This position may also be above some state mounting height restrictions.

We'll start this section by saying that lighting output is regulated by both the Feds and most state governments. Those burn-the-paint-off-the-car-ahead lights are likely illegal for use anywhere. The Feds regulate certain aspects but each state has its own interpretation of how much wattage, how many lights, what type of lights, and how high (or low) they can be mounted. It's up to you to find this stuff out in your area. The laws change constantly, usually getting more restrictive as some folks abuse their privileges.

### Light Constriction and Specifications

Lights are rated by wattage and candlepower. Wattage, we have discussed, but candlepower is a rating of brightness. It's only useful in some respects, because how the lens and the reflector of the light are constructed have more to do with lighting performance than the candlepower.

Lenses are fluted, or given reflective prisms, to make a specifically designed pattern of light. The lenses are usually constructed of various qualities of glass, but sometimes lead crystal is used. The reflectors are constructed of various materials but the important points are how it is shaped and the reflective coating used. Both of these factors combine with the candlepower of the bulb to produce a pattern and intensity of light.

Bulbs can be anything from an ordinary incandescent bulb to the quartz halogen bulb. quartz halogen (QH) lights have all but taken over the automotive lighting game. The QH bulb produces more than three times the light for the same wattage and lasts longer to boot. The bulb consists of a filament inside a quartz envelope that is filled with bromine gas (a member of the halogen family of gases, hence quartz-halogen).

QH bulbs come in four standard configurations, H1, H2, H3, and H4. H1–3 are all single filament bulbs designed for use as auxiliary lamps or in some multi-headlamp systems, while the H4 is a dual filament bulb intended for use as a headlamp. QH bulbs are even being made to replace ordinary small lamp bulbs, such as the 1157, commonly used as turn signal or brake light bulbs. The very newest aerodynamic OE head-lamps use a 9004, 9005, 9006, or 9007 type bulb.

The QH bulbs are commonly rated by watts. For headlamps, 55/60 watts are mandated by law but 80/100, 90/130, and 100/165 watt combos are avail-able. In the H1–e. Remember that watts ÷ volts = amps and calculate the draw on your electrical system before installing any high output light.

### Selecting a Light

The lights you need vary according to the situation. Going slowly up a trail, you need a wide beam that fully covers the area to the front and as far to the sides as pos-sible. A wide beam off-road or fog light will accomplish this very well, as will a set of QH replacement headlights (especially the more expensive H4 variety). Standard headlights produce a "cone" of light approximately 60 degrees wide. Many auxiliary lights can cover 100, 110, 120 degrees, giving an exceptional spread of light.

Those fast movers in the crowd will want driving or spot light to reach farther out. These are often combined with wide beam lights to light up the countryside like a UFO.

Since backing up is as much a part of Jeeping as going ahead, it makes sense to have good lighting available for those times. A set of fog lamps does wonders. You can wire them to a separate switch or get more elaborate and hook them up to a relay triggered by your OE backup lights. IPF went so far as to build a backup light kit with a three-position switch that allows you to operate as OE, have the auxiliary light come on only in reverse, or switch the light on independently.

### Mounting Lights

Where you mount a light can have a large effect on its efficiency. Wide beam lights are best mounted low. Since terrain and clearance will dictate how low you can put a light, the top of the bumper usually becomes the low point. A guard of brush screen can keep your lights intact longer.

Driving, or spot lamps, like to be higher so they can reach out farther. These can be mounted to the bumper or even to the windshield frame. Often, they are mounted on the roof or roll cage. Bear in mind that lights up high have a tendency to produce glare on the hood. There are various fixes for this, which include keeping them on the bumper, painting the hood flat black, reflector plates under the lights, and mounting the lights farther toward the rear and allowing the top to shade the hood.

## Electrical Waterproofing

With the exception of sensitive items such as ECUs, stereos, CBs, electronic ignition modules, and the like, the wiring in your Jeep is not immediately vulnerable to water. Get the fusebox wet and things usually keep working. When you fill the ECU with water, you get an immediate sign. The engine stops! The troubles with the less sensitive stuff come later. Water will often go into tight-fitting areas quite easily, but does not drain and is slow to evaporate. The water stays in a connector and slowly corrodes the contacts. Pretty soon, some-thing quits working.

How much you need to worry about this stuff depends on how much you play in the water and how much "deep diving" you do. Very few of us need a true submarine. We need stuff that's resistant to water, not a Jeep that can explore the Titanic.

Stage one, the basic easy stuff everyone can do, starts with spraying electrical connections, ignition pieces, and ignition wires with silicone spray. This helps repel water, but is a temporary measure. You'll need to touch up reg-ularly. Dielectric silicone grease inside of connectors (sin-gle and multipin) helps keep water out. Also, Accel sells a product called Pro-Tape, which is a silicone type tape that is useful for ignition systems and other places that need sealing. You could paint open connections, such as grounds, with Eastwood's liquid electrical tape. Painless Wiring's waterproof terminals on any new wiring you install add to the water resistance of these items. Shrink tubing is also useful for sealing all sorts of connectors.

Stage two involves using vented waterproof boxes for the sensitive stuff. This usually means a certain amount of rewiring and relocating. The boxes can be anything from ammo cans to Tupperware. Remember to vent everything with a hose to a higher location.

Relays are sensitive to water ingress, so they should be relocated to a higher place or inside a box. They are pretty resistant to a splash but not immersion. Switches are also vulnerable to water and corrosion. Marine type switches can be used in many locations and nonre-placeable switches should be protected with dielectric silicone grease and silicone spray.

## How Many Amps

If you want to upgrade your battery and charging system or redesign your electrical system, the first thing you'll need to do is to figure out your total amperage load. Basically, you add up the amp draw from all the accessories and sort them into two lists. Continuous items such as lights, AC, and mega-stereo, go on one list, and momentary items like power windows and seats on the other. Very heavy draw items such as an electric winch or an invertor might go onto a third list.

Add the continuous draw items up and add at least 20 percent to cover the momentary stuff. If your momentary stuff is a long list, add extra capacity. Items such as winches and invertors require the biggest unit you can fit, though with the winch, you still may not be able to equal the draw.

When rewiring, use this list, or the wattage spec from the item, and the chart on page 176, to select the correct wire for the job. If the wattage is close to the max spec for the wire, bump up to the next larger wire.

### Typical Amp Draw for Selected Items, in Amps

| Item | Amps |
|---|---|
| Air Conditioner | 12–25 |
| Backup Lights | 4 |
| Brake Lights | 4 |
| Dome Light | 2 |
| Fuel Injection System | 6 |
| Headlights, Low-Beam | 9–10 |
| Headlights, Hi-Beam | 14–16 |
| Heated Windshield | 30–50 |
| Heater | 12 |
| Invertor | 400w–33.3 |
| Ignition | 4 |
| Gauges | 2 |
| Marker Lights | 2–4 |
| Power Door Locks | 3–5 |
| Power Seats | 20–55 |
| Power Windows | 15–25 |
| Winch, 8000-pound | 150–500 |
| Windshield Wipers | 4–6 |
| 100w Aux. Light | 8.3 |
| 150w Aux. Light | 12.5 |
| 800w Stereo Amp. | 66.6 |

WATTS ÷ VOLTS = AMPS

## Electrical System—Definitions and Formulas

*Volts*

Volts provide the movement of electrical current and you can think of them as the water pressure. The higher the volts (pressure), the faster the flow. Most Jeep electrical systems are 12 volts, although some of the old rigs are 6 volt.

*Amps*

Amperes to be exact. Amps are the volume of the current, the water itself. Amps do the work.

*Watts*

This is a measurement of the total amount of electrical work being done. Volts times amps equal watts.

When adding accessories, it becomes necessary to evaluate the draw of the devices being added. Any modern electrical device will have a rating. Usually it will be stamped into the body or printed on an attached tag. It will list the voltage requirements and the draw in amps or watts. You may find certain items rated in amps (batteries, motors, alternators) and others in watts (lights, stereos). You can convert using the following formulas.

$$\text{Watts} = \text{volts} \times \text{amps}$$
$$\text{Amps} = \text{watts} \div \text{volts}$$

If you want to find out the amp draw for a pair of 100-watt lights, simply divide 100 by 12 to get 8.3 amps per light, or 16.6 amps.

## CALCULATING ALTERNATOR SPEED

Crankshaft Pulley Diameter in Inches—Input 800 Engine rpm

| | Pulley Size | | | | |
|---|---|---|---|---|---|
| **Alternator** | **4-in.** | **5-in.** | **6-in.** | **7-in.** | **8-in.** |
| 1.9-in | 1,684 rpm | 2,105 rpm | 2,526 rpm | 2,947 rpm | 3,368 rpm |
| 2.2-in | 1,455 rpm | 1,818 rpm | 2,182 rpm | 2,545 rpm | 2,909 rpm |
| 2.4-in | 1,333 rpm | 1,667 rpm | 2,000 rpm | 2,333 rpm | 2,667 rpm |
| 2.7-in | 1,185 rpm | 1,481 rpm | 1,777 rpm | 2,074 rpm | 2,370 rpm |
| 3.3-in | 969 rpm | 1,212 rpm | 1,454 rpm | 1,696 rpm | 1,939 rpm |

crank pulley dia. (in.) ÷ alt. pulley dia. (in.) x eng. rpm= alt. rpm

## 12-VOLT WIRE SELECTION GUIDE

**Gauge**

| Amps | Watts | 0–4 ft. | 4–7 ft. | 7–10 ft. | 10–13 ft. | 13–16 ft. |
|---|---|---|---|---|---|---|
| 1–20 | 12–240 | 14 | 12 | 12 | 10 | 10 |
| 21–35 | 252–420 | 12 | 10 | 8 | 8 | 6 |
| 36–50 | 432–600 | 10 | 8 | 8 | 6 | 6 |
| 51–65 | 612–780 | 8 | 8 | 6 | 6 | 4 |
| 66–85 | 792–1,020 | 6 | 6 | 4 | 4 | 2 |
| 86–105 | 1,032–1,260 | 6 | 6 | 4 | 2 | 2 |
| 106–125 | 1,272–1,500 | 4 | 4 | 4 | 2 | 2 |
| 126–150 | 1,512–1,800 | 2 | 2 | 2 | 2 | 0 |
| 151–200 | 1,812–2,400 | 2 | 2 | 2 | 0 | 0 |

# Chapter 12

# SAFETY ITEMS

## Stayin' Alive

Four-wheeling, even extreme four-wheeling, may be safer by far than the rush hour commute. For one, you are most often moving at a snail's pace (much like rush hour, but without the road rage) but the main difference is that you don't have other people to worry about. No drunken, nose-picking, bebopping, glazed over, nodding off, or incompetent drivers to worry about. That leaves 99 percent of the control of nearly every off-highway situation in the driver's hands. The control freak's dream!

The very first items on the safety equipment list are your attitude, judgment, and skill. With most of what happens in your hands, you become like the pilot of an airplane. You are responsible for the safety of your passengers, your vehicle, and yourself. In the heat of an adrenaline-charged moment, you may be faced with a decision to abort takeoff in the face of some ribbing from your buddies on the trail.

Once past the human equation, we can look at the equipment requirements for a safe and well-prepared Jeep. A well-equipped Jeep has more than trick suspension parts and big tires.

Here is a selection of dry chemical extinguishers from Ansul. From right to left, a 2 1/2-pound unit, a 5-pound unit, and two 10-pound units. The smallest unit is adequate for most Jeeps, but a 5-pound unit is a safe overkill. The differences in performance are, with the 2 1/2-pound first and 5-pound second, weight: 5 pounds/9 pounds 14 ounces; range 11 feet/14 feet, discharge time: 9 seconds/14 seconds; discharge rate: .31 pounds per second/.38 pounds per second. The 10-pound units are probably too big for most applications, but they double the performance of the 2 1/2-pound and nearly double the 5-pounder.

### Fire Extinguisher

You're out on the trail. A fuel line splits and sprays gas all over the engine. As soon as it hits the hot engine, it vaporizes. A spark from the multitude of electrical devices under the hood ignites the mixture and suddenly your vehicle is ablaze. If you or someone in your group has a fire extinguisher, this can be dealt with before the vehicle is damaged beyond repair. If not, then you can throw dirt at it and watch the Jeep slowly melt to the ground. Every Jeeper should have a fire extinguisher. From mild to wild buildups, this should be one of your first expenses.

There are many types of fire extinguishers, the most common and inexpensive being the dry chemical vari-

ety. These are divided into two general categories, the standard being the stored pressure types. In this case, the dry chemical is stored in a pressurized container. The chief advantages of this type are low cost and compact size. Disadvantages are chiefly in the relatively vulnerable container and the possibility of the unit losing pressure over time.

In the cartridge-operated extinguisher, the chemical is stored in one container and a small, separate, nitrogen-charged container provides the pressure when actuated. These extinguishers are very efficient but expensive to buy and maintain. They are bulky but you can get by with a smaller unit than you could with a

Here's a decent spot to mount an extinguisher. It's up above the general cargo clutter in back and reachable from both the front and back seats. Unfortunately, it's a plastic-valved "el cheapo" model with no pressure gauge. If you want to buy cheap extinguishers like this, throw them away every couple of years and buy a new one to ensure that it will work when you need it. A good extinguisher can be serviced and maintained for many years.

stored pressure extinguisher. They are also more durable in harsh environments.

Fire extinguishers are rated for different types of fires, Classes A, B, C, and D. Class A fires are of combustible materials such as wood, paper, and such, which can be extinguished by either cooling with water or smothering with certain (but not all) dry chemicals. Class B fires are from flammable liquids or vapors that require smothering. Class C fires are electrical in nature, and so smothering is necessary by agents that are nonconducting (using water on electrical fires can get you electrocuted). Class D fires occur in materials like magnesium, titanium, sodium, and zirconium. Putting these difficult fires out requires very specialized equipment that is beyond the scope of our discussion.

Looking at the classifications, Class B and C come to mind for vehicles, but consider that you may need fire suppression for other things, such as a campfire that gets out of control or a brush fire started by a catalytic converter. In this overall situation, an ABC extinguisher has you covered for everything. The difference is in the chemicals used. The B and C rated units use plain old sodium bicarbonate (baking soda), which is white in color. The ABC units use monoammonium phosphate, which is a good smother agent, and is yellow in color.

Mount your extinguishers in a place that is easily accessible and readily visible. Check the gauges regularly and service them every couple of years. Not only can the pressurized charge leak slowly, but the powder inside can get compacted and you may not get a full charge when you need it.

The last words concern the quality of the extinguisher. You can go to the discount stores and buy a

cheap, nonserviceable, one-shot extinguisher. These units are better than throwing dirt, certainly, but since the vital parts are made of plastic, they may not hold up well in a rough and tumble Jeep. For a few dollars more, you can get an extinguisher with metal parts. These can be serviced over and over and are essentially lifetime units, as long as the containers are not dented.

## Roll Bars

Rollovers are a very real possibility on the trail, with the possibility increasing as the terrain gets tougher. Good driving and judgment put the odds in your favor, but you never know what surprises await. A rock moves at an inopportune moment. A dirt ledge gives way. It doesn't always take much to put you rubber side up and in such a situation, you want more than a hat between you and the ground.

First off, anything open-topped needs minimal protection. Simple as that. A hardtopped vehicle has some built-in protection but they come in two categories. Older rigs or Jeeps with bolted-on hardtops are often at risk even in minor rollovers, because in many cases the tops offer little crush protection. Newer rigs, from the late 1980s up, are better due to more stringent federal standards in that area.

In general, a full cage with legs up front is an ideal and cost-effective safety item in an open-topped Jeep. This cage is a custom-fabricated unit that's tied in to the chassis via polyurethane bushings. This owner took the more expensive route with his cage.

This custom CJ cage built by Stage West provides major protection for all passengers in this family-operated rig. It's costly, but in this case safety was adjudged the No. 1 concern. This Jeep goes in harm's way but carries precious cargo—kids.

How you drive your Jeep, whatever type, may have more to do with the need for a roll bar than anything. If you are a hard-core Jeeper, you need extra protection. Ditto if you like to drive fast, on or off the pavement. If you are in this latter category, you definitely need more than just the basic protection.

### Mounting Systems

Roll bars come in many styles and types, some production pieces and some custom. Those built to racing standards are the best but they cost serious bucks. The most basic are the single tube bars. These come as standard equipment in newer open-topped 4x4s and Jeeps. The single overhead bar is braced by rearward angled braces. This setup is adequate for mild rides but in a bad rollover, the windshield can collapse into your face. This setup is inexpensive and kits are available for nearly every Jeep, hard or soft top, and pickups. This is your minimum situation, Jeepers!

Next up is a full cage that combines the rear hoop with a front hoop and connecting tubes that run fore and aft. This is the most commonly seen trail Jeep setup. Even the basic variations of this are pretty effective and relatively inexpensive. Many Jeepers will have the front hoop added to their existing rear piece via custom fabrication or an add-on kit (welding usually required). This setup is tricky to install in pickup cabs.

Variations of the setups mentioned above are common. These include diagonal bracing, a third hoop over the passenger area, the halo design, and even cages that extend around the outside of the body. In many cases, valid engineering concepts are being utilized. In other cases it's simply the look. Let your pocketbook be your guide, but the simple cage type of roll bar is adequate for most serious Jeeps, unless high speeds or cliffhanging exploits are expected.

Roll bars and cages are available from a variety of manufacturers, in a variety of price ranges. Application is usually for the more common and popular Jeep models. If you have a less common Jeep or you want to be different, you can have a custom cage built. Count on this being expensive.

### Materials and Construction

You will see roll bars made out of everything from plumbing pipes to exhaust pipe. Don't trust your life to substandard material. Good roll bars are made from HREW (Hot Rolled Electric Weld) tubing of about .120 wall thickness. You can get thicker material but it's considered overkill by many. Tubing diameter is commonly 2-inch I.D. (inside diameter), but in some cases 1 3/4-inch is used for tight areas. Sometimes larger tubing is used.

Better roll cages are built of DOM (drawn-over mandrill) tubing, which is used in similar sizes as HREW but the material is inherently stronger. It's also about twice as expensive and not necessary except in extreme cases. This material is a good choice for pedal-to-the-metal rigs that are more at risk.

The hands-down best tubing is chrome-moly, because it's so much stronger than DOM or HREW that the material can be made much thinner with equivalent strength. This pricey stuff is almost exclusive to spare-no-expense race rigs, in which every ounce of weight counts. It requires special Heli-Arc welding and is difficult to form.

This front hoop set from M.O.R.E. is a cost-effective way to add protection to an existing cage. It fits 1987–95 YJs and does not require welding. Because it uses 13/4 inch tubing, it is not quite the knee-knocker that 2- or 3-inch tubing becomes.

When adding a hoop kit, the front legs are commonly bolted to the sheet-metal floor. This is not the strongest spot, so it makes sense to add some chassis support. This kit is available from M.O.R.E. to do just that. It requires welding to the chassis and uses a polyurethane body puck for insulation between the mount, the floor, and the roll bar foot.

Some detail items to look for in a roll cage include the location of the seam in the tubing. Ideally, it is put in compression, so the force of impact doesn't split it apart. Also, the places where one tube is welded to another should be fish-mouthed, or contoured to fit tightly against the other tube before welding. Lastly, gusseting adds strength, whether it's a simple triangular piece of plate, or an elegant, fish-mouthed piece of smaller tubing, which may also be strategically placed as a handle/gusset.

Mounting the seats to a custom roll cage is probably the ultimate safety protection. If the belts are also mounted to the cage, the passengers are contained by a stout assembly that will essentially remain intact as the vehicle falls apart around them.

Finally, roll bars should be padded in all areas where human brain-cases might be delivered a blow. There are documented deaths due to impact with roll bars. Pad it or wear a helmet.

### Mounting

As mentioned above, the body-mounted cage is the most common setup. Jeep CJs have had roll cages available since 1969 but it wasn't until 1979 that they were mounted to a structurally solid point where the body and chassis meet. Ditto for the Wranglers. This mounting point is adequate but often, when a front hoop is added, it's mounted to the floor. Depending on the severity of the roll, this may or may not be adequate.

The problem with this, and with any other Jeep in which the roll bar is mounted to mere sheet metal, is that it may punch through or tear away. Building a chassis mounting bracket for the a roll bar is a worthwhile endeavor. Mountain Off-Road Enterprises builds such mounts for Wranglers.

The next step up is a chassis-mounted roll cage. This is a bit controversial on several levels. On one side of the argument, you are mounting to the strongest part of the vehicle and creating a sturdy, protective cage that only a trip off the top of Everest could break. The other side is that it makes the chassis very rigid. With CJs and YJs, chassis flex provides some extra articulation. Many Jeepers are reluctant to lose this extra stretch.

If you decide to mount the cage to the chassis, how you go about this is important. Welding is usually a no-no because some chassis are best not welded upon.

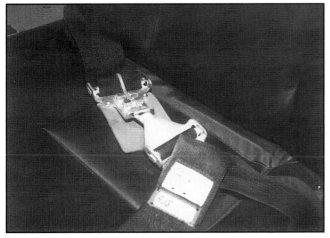

A lap belt, such as this stout racing-style belt, is the bare minimum. An OE lap and shoulder harness may be adequate but bear in mind that you can slip out of the upper part in a severe roll. Racing supply outfits can fix you up with a variety of styles, including the preferred four-point-style harness.

This is the OE type of seatbelt mount. If you install belt mounts onto sheet metal, emulate this method by reinforcing the spot with a piece of plate and a stout Grade 10 bolt.

Many experts prefer to build brackets that bolt up. Some folks emulate racing cages and mount the bars in polyurethane. This has several good effects, the main one being that it allows for some chassis flex. The main downfall is that the bushings tend to squeak, though it's possible to use greaseable bushings in some cases.

### Seat Belts

If there is someone out there who doesn't know about the value of seat belts, please come out from your cave! The ordinary set of lap belts is the bare minimum setup for a Jeep, with the ordinary shoulder harness being a few steps up and much preferred. A four-point H- harness is much better still. Add a crotch strap to that (making it a five-point harness) and you have the ideal. A racing-type harness is a pain in the wazoo to put on and take off, but it might just save your life when the lesser setups might not.

How seat belts are mounted is important. Your factory-installed belts should be OK, but if you intend to install a racing harness, bear a few items in mind. First, if you can, use the roll cage mounts as seat belts, as did the factory. Second, if you have to mount a seat belt to sheet metal, use a large plate for strength so it won't tear away.

When installing a racing harness, many folks anchor the upper half of the harness to the floor. Unfortunately, in a severe impact, this can break collarbones. Ideally, this anchor point should be level with, or no more than 4 inches below, the shoulder level. This may mean adding an extra (and inconvenient) bar to the cage, just behind the seats. Some custom Jeep builders mount the seats and seat belts to the cage. This allows the body to essentially fall apart while minimally affecting the occupants.

Seat belts have been mandated for so long that those of us who remember new vehicles without them are starting to get a bit gray. Odds are that most of the folks reading this book have a Jeep with belts installed. At least, use what you have. At best, improve what you have. It's your head!

### First Aid

Depending on your outlook, the solitude that comes with getting out in the boondocks is either the main reason for four-wheeling, or a darn nice side effect. Many times you are completely on your own. This is good, healthy stuff but it makes you more dependent on yourself to solve any problems that might arise. Medical problems certainly fit in that category.

A first aid kit of some type is a must for a well-equipped Jeeper. How elaborate you go depends a lot on your planned destinations. Obviously a desert crossing of the Sahara will require more preparation than a day in the hills, but there are some basics that should be in every first aid kit.

The first items would fall under the heading of prescription drugs. If there is anyone in your party with special needs in that area, it's appropriate to find out whether that person has sufficient medication for the time on the trail.

Most medical situations on the trail are minor. A headache, diarrhea, indigestion, or altitude sickness

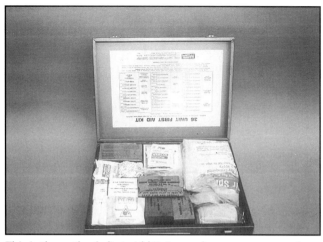

This is the author's first aid kit, in use for many years and updated many times. While major trauma is covered by such things as an air splint and military style compresses, the everyday stuff such as aspirin, stomach remedies, and sunscreen are just as important. Once a year, the dated materials are replaced with fresh stuff. This metal box, found at a long-forgotten yard sale, has seals and is weather resistant.

can take the fun out of a trip, so it makes sense to have some remedies around for these minor ailments. Too much fun can also result in minor cuts and abrasions, so antiseptic and small bandages are in order. Turned ankles and such are not unusual in outdoor frolicking, so ace bandages can be handy. Skin lotions, sunblock, and a poison oak or ivy protection (in the areas where it abounds) are all commonsense items.

When you get into more major injuries or illnesses, your knowledge of first aid becomes important. Whether you are trained in this area or not, there may be someone else who is, and having the right stuff on hand could mean life or death for the person in trouble.

You can buy first aid kits in any form from just a few Band-Aids in a box to something that beats many Third World hospitals. You need not go to elaborate extremes if you are an occasional day tripper, but if you like the really offbeat locales, think about a high-end kit. Look at page 184 for some ideas on what to carry.

## Cargo Tie Downs

Yep, this is a safety item. Have you ever been beaned in the back of the head on a steep downhill by some small bit of cargo that came adrift. Imagine your overloaded toolbox hitting you in the head. It might be the last thing you imagine!

You can buy nifty, flush-mounted tie downs for the cargo area. You can also head down to the wrecking

yard or surplus store and find something that works. The main thing is to get your heavy gear secured. Sometimes the storage boxes highlighted in Chapter 8 are the answer, but however you do it, tie down your gear!

## Radios and Cell Phones

Citizen Band (CB) radios are a fun way to pass the time with trail buddies. They may also be the closest thing to a 911 call you can make on the trail, though the range is very limited on most common CB units. Other communications options exist, including cell phones. With each passing year, cellular phones are reaching farther out. I once ordered emergency repair parts from a mountaintop in a remote part of Colorado.

CB radios can be anything from a cheap handheld that can get you to the end of the block, to a big linear boosted unit that can reach to South America. By law, CBs of any type are limited to a four-watt output. Range is often limited to line of sight (a mile or less). Sometimes you can get out 10 to 15 miles with a good antenna and perfect conditions. Weather conditions, mountains, trees, interference from power lines, and even your engine all play a part in how well the unit transmits or receives.

There are add-on devices called linears that can boost your output signal from 4 to 400 watts, or more. This increases the range by several orders of magnitude. Some are so powerful that they can fry a receiving radio at close range. Sound great? Well, they're illegal. Some people use them anyway.

Legal steps up include the Single Side Band, which is a close cousin to the CB. They can legally run 12 watts and reach farther out. There are FM radios of various types as well as Amateur Radio (ham radio) that have a very long range, but these require licenses.

Going back to cellular phones, if you have one, bring it along. A 12-volt recharging jack couldn't hurt either. I am hesitant to advise getting a cell phone for trail emergencies alone, because you never know if it will work or not. Still, it is surprising how many places get coverage and this may be the best method to get help quickly if the unit does work.

## CB Radio Choices

At the beginning of your range of choices are the handheld units. Though they will have the maximum four-watts output, their short antennas and low and short-term battery power put them at a disadvantage. A

12-volt jack becomes an important accessory for them in vehicular use. They can be handy on a slow trail for helping guide vehicles through tough obstacles or where people are walking around.

A mounted transceiver is the best overall choice. There are many out there, from under a hundred bucks to into the thousands of dollars. It all comes down to the quality of the components and the features. We could get very technical here, but let's not. Some of the common desirable features are a built in SWR meter and a built-in weather channel feature. Some units will allow your CB to be used as a mini PA system. There are also upgrades you can make to microphones. The best bet is to see your local CB radio shop or stop in at a Radio Shack for details.

### Antennas

With your output limited to four watts, the choice of antenna becomes of paramount importance to good range. All types of CBs rely on good antennas. Handhelds are at the bottom of the food chain in this area and are usually limited to a mile or so with their tiny antennas. Many can be temporarily converted to work on an outside antenna. This makes a worthwhile supplemental purchase.

Bear in mind that the radio and antenna must be matched, or tuned, to the vehicle via an SWR (Standing Wave Radio) meter. Each vehicle is slightly different, so getting a professional to set you up after installation is akin to a performance tune-up on your engine. In some cases, a severely out-of-tune radio can suffer damage.

There are many types of antennas, from 108-inch whips to short, loaded antennas. Obviously the loaded units are easiest to deal with. A loaded antenna mimics a long whip by containing extra coils of wire inside. Fiberglass or carbon fiber antenna bodies are used with the wire inside. Some are metal.

The antenna is connected to the radio via coaxial cable. There is a definite quality difference between department store cable and professional quality stuff. This material can mean the difference between really good range and being able to shout farther than your CB can transmit.

The best place to mount a CB antenna is dead center of a metal roof. Of course, you may not want to put it there. The person who tunes your radio might be able to find the next best spot. It varies from vehicle to vehicle. One specialist told me that two identical vehicles can be completely different in this regard. Magnetic mounts on the hoods are popular, as are clamp-on mounts on the side view mirrors, bumper mounts, and windshield frame mounts. Some folks don't even mind the hole in the side of the body and mount a bracket there.

### External Speakers

In a loud, or open-topped vehicle, hearing your CB may be difficult. The units have a small built-in speaker, but often an external speaker is necessary. These are specially designed to make the human voice sound louder and clearer. Almost all CBs have a jack for this speaker. Many also have a jack for a low power PA-type speaker. This can be very useful for the trail, but take care using it in street traffic, as they are illegal in some locales.

## A First Aid Kit

Here is a commonsense kit that has most of what may be needed. It does not cover every eventuality but is usable within the realm of most people's first aid knowledge. If you have any medical training, add to the list as your experience dictates. I strongly suggest that Jeepers take a Red Cross CPR and First Aid class. Many serious health threats can be averted with a little training.

*Pain Medication*
   aspirin
   ibuprofin

*Stomach Medication*
   antidiarrheals (Immodium, Pepto Bismol, etc.)
   antacids (Tagamet, Rolaids, Tums)
   Ipecac (for inducing vomiting)

*Antiseptics*
   alcohol swabs
   alcohol (liquid, in plastic bottle)
   hydrogen peroxide

*Bandages*
   selection of Band-Aids
   sterile pads, non-stick (Telfa) assorted sizes
   tape
   sterile gauze roll
   sterislips (for closing wounds)
   large sterile dressings

*Tools*
   fine tweezers
   scissors
   splint (inflatable)
   cervical collar
   cold pack (for sprains and burns)
   face shield or mask (for rescue breathing)
   a compact first aid manual
   tourniquet
   sterile latex gloves
   sturdy case for first aid kit

*Skin Medication*
   sunblock
   calamine lotion
   hand cleaner
   poison ivy/oak lotion (for appropriate areas)
   hydrocortisone creme
   antibacterial ointment

# APPENDIX 1

## A Source for Jeep Performance Parts

If you can't find what you need here, it probably doesn't exist. By no means is this the entire list, either. These sources are as accurate and timely as can be at the time of publication, unless marked with an *. Addresses so marked have not been checked and may be stale.

### I. Axles, Gearing, and Driveshafts

*A. Axle Shafts*
(See also Summers I-B-9 )
1. Dura Blue*
   1450 N. Hundley
   Anaheim, CA 92806
   (714) 632-6803
   Custom axle shaft and drivetrain parts
2. Dutchman Motorsports
   PO Box 20505
   Portland, OR 97220
   (503) 257-6604
   Custom axle shafts and drivetrain parts
3. Moser Engineering
   102 Performance Drive
   Portland, IN 47371
   (219) 726-6689
   Custom axle shafts and drivetrain parts
4. Strange Engineering
   1611 Church St.
   Evanston, IL 60201
   (847) 869-7010
   Custom axle shafts and drivetrain parts

*B. General Axle Service or Parts*
(See also Moser I-A-3)
1. Boyce Equipment
   226 West 20th Street
   Ogden, UT 84401
   (800) 748-4269
   New, used, and rebuilt axles and drivetrain parts
2. Currie Enterprises
   1480 N. Tustin Ave.
   Anaheim, CA 92807
   (714) 528-6957
   Complete custom axle assemblies, custom axle shafts, and floater kits
3. Dynatrac Products
   7236 Garden Grove Blvd.
   Westminster, CA 92683
   (714) 898-5228
   Complete custom axle assemblies, custom axle shafts, and floater kits
4. 4-Wheel Parts Wholesalers/Genuine Gear
   14100 S. Kingsley Dr.
   Gardena, CA 90247
   (800) 421-1050
   Replacement drivetrain parts

5. Hicks 4x4
   1321 S. Garey
   Pomona, CA 91767
   (800) 999-POSI
   Custom axles and general drivetrain
6. RandP 4WD Parts
   11889 S. New Era Rd.
   Oregon City, OR 97045
   (503) 557-8911
   Complete custom axle assemblies, floater kits, and custom adapters
7. Sam's Off-Road Equipment
   4345 S.W. Blvd.
   Tulsa, OK 74107
   (918) 446-5535
   Complete custom axle assemblies, drivetrain and engine swaps
8. Stage West 4-Wheel Drive Center
   7920 Hwy. 82
   Glenwood Springs, CO 81601
   (800) 240-5227
   Custom axle assemblies, fabrication, general drivetrain, swaps
9. Summers Brothers
   530 S. Mountain Ave.
   Ontario, CA 91762
   (714) 986-2041
   Complete custom axle assemblies, custom axle shafts, and floater kits
10. Tri-County Gear
    1143 W. Second St.
    Pomona, CA 91766
    (909) 623-3373
    Custom axles, gear swaps, trans /T-case swaps, steering mods

*C. Driveshafts and Related Equipment*
(See also Moser I-A-3)
1. Denny's Driveshaft Service
   1189 Military Rd.
   Kenmore, NY 14217
   (800) 955-1872
   Custom drivelines and related gear
2. Six States Distributors
   1112 W. 33rd South
   Ogden, UT 84401
   (800) 453-2022
   Custom drivelines and related gear

*D. Locker and Limited Slip Manufacturers*
1. ARB Air Locker
   1425 Elliot Avenue
   W. Seattle, WA 98119
   (206) 284-6171
   ARB air locker, on demand locker
2. Auburn Gear Inc.
   400 E. Auburn Dr.
   Auburn, IN 46706-3499
   (219) 925-3200
   Cone clutch type automatic locker

3. Power Trax
   245 Fischer Ave., Bldg. B-4
   Costa Mesa, CA 92626
   (714) 545-7400
   Lock-Rite automatic locker
4. Precision Gear
   12351 Universal Drive
   Taylor, MI 48180
   (734) 946-0524
   Powr-Lok limited slip (Dana 44 and 60)
5. Tractech
   11445 Stephens Dr.
   Warren, MI 48090
   (800) 328-3850
   Detroit Locker automatic locker, EZ locker, and TrueTrac limited slip

*E. Ring and Pinion, General Drivetrain Parts and Service*
(See also Dynatrac I-B-3, Mile-Hi VI-F, Precision Gear I-D-4, RandP I-B-6, Tri-County Gear I-B-10)
1. Dana/Spicer Axle Division
   PO Box 1209
   Fort Wayne, IN 46801
   (219) 483-7174
   Manufactures axle assemblies, axle, ring and pinions, U-joints, and more
2. Drivetrain Specialists
   26400 Groesbeck Hwy.
   Warren, MI 48089
   (800) 521-0628
   Manufactures ring and pinions and carries general drivetrain parts
3. Motive Gear
   4200 S. Morgan
   Chicago, IL 60609
   (800) 934-2727
   Ring and pinions and general drivetrain parts
4. Reider Racing
   12351 Universal Drive
   Taylor, MI 48180
   (734) 946-1330
   Ring and pinions and high performance differential parts
5. Richmond Gear
   PO Box 238
   Liberty, SC 29657
   (803) 843-9231
   Ring and pinions
6. Ring and Pinion Service
   11630 Airport Rd.
   Everett, WA 98204-3752
   (800) 347-1199
   Differential parts and service

## II. Body, Chassis, and Interior

### A. Body Coatings

1. Arma Coatings
   1551 Pearl Street
   Eugene, OR 97401
   (504) 484-5915
   www.armacoatings.com
   Urethane coatings, local dealers in
   many areas

2. Duraback Bedliner
   Cote-L Distribution Co.
   4064 S. Atcheson Way, Ste. 301
   Aurora, CO 80014
   (303) 690-7190
   DIY polyurethane coating

3. Eastwood Company
   PO Box 3014
   Malvern, PA 19355-0714
   (800) 345-1178
   Equipment for powder coating at home
   and restoration supplies

4. Rhino Linings
   (800) 447-1471 for the nearest dealer
   Spray on bed liners and body coating

### B. Body Hardware
(See also Four Wheel Drive Hardware VI-
D, Steel Horse II-C-5)

1. Con-Ferr
   123 S. Front St.
   Burbank, CA 91502
   (818) 848-2025
   A variety of body hardware and
   accessories

2. Kentrol
   PO Box 3304
   Youngstown, OH 44512-0304
   (216) 549-2235
   Stainless-steel accessories

3. Pierce Sales
   Expressway 287
   Henrietta, TX 76365
   (800) 658-6301
   Stainless-steel body hardware

### C. Bumpers, Brushguards, Nerfs, Carriers, Racks, etc.
(See also ARB I-D-1, Con-Ferr II-B-1,
Four X Doctor VII-F-1, M.O.R.E. VII-C-1,
Ramsey Winch X-A-3, Rubicon Express
VII-G-7, Tomken VII-G-11, Warn X-A-5)

1. Bulletproof Mfg.
   581 Lorraine Ave.
   Santa Barbara, CA 93110
   (805) 967-2005
   Custom bumpers for Jeeps

2. Get Serious*
   644 Keagle Rd.
   El Paso, TX 79927
   (915) 859-2161
   Custom bumper and roll cages

3. Grizzly Products*
   1802 Santo Domingo Ave.
   Duarte, CA 91010
   (800) 253-2859
   Custom body products and bolt-ons

4. Smittybilt
   2090 Corona Avenue
   Corona, CA 91719
   (909) 272-3176
   All sorts of bolt-on body goodies

5. Steel Horse Automotive
   601 W. Walnut Street
   Compton, CA 90220
   (800) 533-7704
   All sorts of body and interior accessories

### D. Chassis, Chassis Modification, and Repair
(See also M.O.R.E. VII-C-1)

1. Matkins
   2715 1st Ave.
   S. Billings, MT 58181
   (406) 248-3797
   Box tube replacement Jeep chassis and
   fiberglass bodies

### E. Fiberglass Bodies
(See also Matkins II-D-1)

1. AJ's Sales and Mfg.
   Rd 3 Box 284A
   Jersey Shore, PA 17740
   (717) 398-7520
   www.csrlink.net/ajs/
   Replacement fiberglass bodies and parts

2. Malotte
   PO Box 305
   Lincoln, CA 95648
   (916) 645-8111
   Replacement fiberglass bodies and parts

3. Shell Valley Fiberglass
   Rt. 69-PFW
   Platte Center, NE 68653
   (402) 246-2355
   www.shellvalley.com
   Replacement fiberglass bodies and parts

4. U.S. Body Source
   9009 C.R. 325
   Hampton, FL 32044
   (352) 468-2203
   Replacement fiberglass bodies and parts

### F. Floor Products

1. Fox Ent. Inc.
   PO Box 1126
   St. Charles, IL 60174-1126
   (630) 513-9010
   www.dwinc.com/fox
   Weatherboot footwell liners

2. Winfield Consumer Products
   PO Box 839
   Winfield, KS 67156
   (800) 344-8759
   Husky waterproof floor liners

### G. Fuel Tanks

1. Aero Tanks
   1780 Pomona Road
   Corona, CA 91720
   (909) 737-7878
   Replacement and oversize fuel tanks

2. Northwest Metal Products
   3801 24th Avenue
   Forest Grove, OR 97116
   (503) 359-4427
   Replacement and oversize fuel tanks

### H. Interior Storage
(See also Bestop II-J-2)

1. Tuffy Security Products
   12540 W. Cedar Dr.
   Lakewood, CO 80228
   (800) 348-8339
   Locking steel storage boxes.

### I. Seats
(See also Bestop II-K-2, Steel Horse
II-C-5)

1. Corbeau USA
   9503 S. 560 W
   Sandy, UT 84070
   (801) 255-3737
   High performance seating

2. Flowfit
   127 Business Center Drive, Unit B
   Corona, CA 91720
   (800) FLOFITS
   High performance seating

3. Wet Okole
   1727 Superior
   Costa Mesa, CA 92627
   (714) 548-1543
   Waterproof seat covers

### J. Steel Replacement Body Parts and Bodies

1. Archer Brothers
   19745 Meekland Ave.
   Hayward, CA 94541
   (415) 537-9587
   Repro flatfender bodies and parts

2. Classic Enterprise
   Box 92
   Barron, WI 54812
   (715) 537-5422
   Body repair pieces for Jeeps

3. I Luv Trucks
   18121 Napa St.
   Northridge, CA 91325
   (800) 367-8725
   Replacement body parts

4. Raybuck Auto Body Parts
   RD4
   Punxsutawney, PA 15767
   (814) 938-5248
   Replacement body parts

### K. Tops

1. Beachwood Canvas
   PO Box 137
   Island Heights, NJ 08732
   (908) 929-3168
   Custom and reproduction canvas parts
   for vintage Jeeps

2. Bestop
   PO Box 307
   Broomfield, CO 80038
   (303) 465-1755
   Tops, seats, interior, and storage

3. Kayline Mfg.
   200 E. 64th Ave.
   Denver, CO 80221
   (800) 525-8118
   Tops, interior parts, and racks

4. Rock Gear
   2221 E. River Rd.
   Farmington, NM 87401
   (888) 765-4327
   www.thejeep.com
   Windbreaker bikini top and emergency
   top

## III. Brakes

### A. Brake Boosters and Pedal Parts
(See also Tri-County Gear I-B-10)

1. Off-Again
   Farmington, NM
   (505) 325-5761
   Dual diaphragm brake booster for Jeeps

### B. Brake Pads, Shoes
(See also Rancho Suspension VII-G-5)

1. Performance Friction
   PO Box 819
   Clover, SC 29710
   (803) 222-2141
   Composite high performance brakes
   and brake products

2. Praise Dyno Brake
   1061 S. Munson Rd.
   Royse, TX 75189
   (972) 636-2722
   Composite high performance brakes
   and brake products

C. *Brake Lines, Hoses, Fluid*
   (See also Explorer Pro Comp VII-G-2,
   Skyjacker VII-G-8)

1. Classic Tubes
   80 Rotech Drive
   Lancaster, NY 14086
   (716) 759-1800
   Replacement brake lines, custom and
   OE fit

2. Earl's Performance Products
   189 W. Victoria St.
   Long Beach, CA 90805
   (310) 609-1602
   Steel braided brake lines

3. Wilwood Engineering
   461 Calle San Pablo
   Camarillo, CA 93012
   (805) 388-1188
   High temp brake fluid and other brake
   supplies

D. *Disc Brake Conversions*
   (See also Currie I-B-2, Dynatrac I-B-3)

1. Foothill 4 Wheel Drive
   1472 Grass Valley Hwy.
   Auburn, CA 95603
   (916) 889-2021
   www.foothill4x4.com
   Front disc brake conversions for Dana
   25, 27, 30, or 44 axles

2. Stainless Steel Brakes
   11470 Main Rd.
   Clarence, NY 14031
   (800) 448-7722
   Rear Disc Brake conversions

3. TSM
   4321 Willow Creek Rd #4
   Castle Rock, CO 80104-9766
   (303) 688-6882
   Rear disc brake conversions

## IV. Electrical

A. *Alternators*
   (See also MG IV-E-1, Phoenix Gold IV-F-
   4)

1. Premier Power Welder
   PO Box 639
   Carbondale, CO 81623
   (800) 541-1817
   FAX/TECH line (970) 963-8875
   Mega power alternators, underhood
   welders, and electrical products

2. Wrangler Power Products*
   PO Box 12109
   Prescott, AZ 86304-2109
   (800) 962-2616
   Mega power alternators, plus wiring and
   electrical products

B. *Batteries*

1. Crishell Automotive Products
   PO Box 260965
   Highlands Ranch, CO 80126
   (800) 44-CRANK
   Black Panther battery and electrical
   products

2. Optima Batteries
   17500 E. 22nd Ave.
   Aurora, CO 80011
   (303) 340-7440
   Optima batteries and electrical products

3. Trojan Battery Company
   12380 Clark St.
   Santa Fe Springs, CA 90670
   (800) 423-6569
   Deep cycle and marine batteries

C. *Ignition*
   (See also Crane V-C-1)

1. Accel
   8700 Brookpark Rd.
   Cleveland, OH 44129
   (216) 398-8300
   Performance ignitions and performance
   products

2. Jacobs Electronics
   500 N. Baird St.
   Midland, TX 79701
   (800) 627-8800
   Performance ignitions and electrical
   systems

3. MSD Ignition
   1490 Henry Brennan Dr.
   El Paso, TX 79936
   (915) 857-5200
   Performance distributors and ignition

4. Performance Distributors D.U.I
   2699 Barris Dr.
   Memphis, TN 38132
   (901) 396-5782
   Performance and water-resistant distributors and ignition stuff

D. *Lights*

1. Hella Inc.
   201 Kelly Dr.
   Peachtree City, GA 30269
   (800) 247-5924
   Assorted performance lights and lighting products

2. IPF
   1425 Elliot Ave. W.
   Seattle, WA 98119
   (206) 284-5906
   Assorted performance lights and lighting products

3. PIAA
   15370 S.W. Millikan Way
   Beaverton, OR 97006
   (503) 643-PIAA
   Assorted performance lights and lighting products

E. *Starters*

1. MG Industries (Mean Green)
   PO Drawer 336
   Laughlintown, PA 15655-0336
   (412) 532-3090
   High-torque starters and high-output
   alternators

F. *Wiring Kits and Accessories*

1. Centech Wiring
   7 Colonial Dr.
   Perkiomenville, PA 18074
   (610) 287-5730
   www.centechwire.com
   Replacement wiring harnesses and
   power steering kits

2. M.A.D. Enterprises*
   15180 Raymer St.
   Van Nuys, CA 91405
   (818) 786-5725
   Wiring kits and electrical products

3. Painless Wiring
   9505 Santa Paula
   Ft. Worth, TX 76116
   (817) 244-6898
   www.painlesswiring.com
   Wiring kits and electrical products

4. Phoenix Gold International
   PO Box 83189
   Portland, OR 97283
   (503) 288-2008
   Power flow products, mega alternators,
   isolators, etc.

5. Sure Power Industries
   10189 S.W. Avery
   Tualatin, OR 97062
   (503) 692-5360
   Battery controlling devices, isolators,
   and cable

## V. Engines and Engine Adaptors

A. *Adapters*
   (See also RandP I-B-6)

1. Advance Adapters
   PO Box 247
   335 Santa Bella Ave.
   Paso Robles, CA 93446-0247
   (800) 350-2223
   Adapters for a variety of engine, trans,
   and T-case swaps.

2. Novak Enterprises
   13321-A Alondra Blvd., Dept. P
   Santa Fe Springs, CA 90670-5520
   (562) 921-3202
   Adapters for a variety of engine, trans,
   and T-case swaps.

B. *Air Filters*

1. Amsoil
   Amsoil Building
   Superior, WI 54880
   (715) 392-7101
   Foam filters and lubrication products

2. K&N Engineering
   PO Box 1329
   Riverside, CA 92502
   (909) 684-9762
   Performance oiled cotton gauze filter
   and intake products

C. *Camshafts and Valvegear*
   (See also Edelbrock V-D-5)

1. Crane Cams
   530 Fentress Blvd.
   Daytona Beach, FL 32114
   (904) 258-6174
   Cams, valvegear, and performance
   products

2. Crower Cams and Equipment
   3333 Main St.
   Chula Vista, CA 91911-5899
   (619) 422-1191
   Cams, valvegear, custom crankshafts,
   and engine performance

D. *Carburetion and Fuel Injection*

1. Accel
   8700 Brookpark Rd.
   Cleveland, OH 44129
   (216) 398-8300
   Bolt-on TBI kit, intake manifolds, and
   fuel system products

2. BG Fuel Systems
   Rt. 1, Box 1900
   Dahlonega, GA 30533
   (706) 864-8544
   Builder of VFI (venturi fuel injection)
   systems

3. Brad Urban's Carb Shop
   8460 Red Oak St.
   Rancho Cucamonga, CA 91730
   (909) 481-5816
   Performance carburetor rebuilds. Q-Jet
   Specialists

4. Clifford Inline Performance Products
   2330 Pamona Rincon Rd.
   Corona, CA 91720
   (909) 734-3310
   Performance products for inline
   engines, 4 and 6 cylinder

5. Edelbrock Corp.
   2700 California St.
   Torrance, CA 90503
   (310) 782-2900
   TBI and MPI systems, carbs, manifolds,
   cams, and performance parts

6. Electromotive Inc.
   14004-J Willard Rd.
   Chantilly, VA 22021
   (703) 378-2444
   Bolt-on fuel injection and ignitions for
   Jeep and other engines

7. Holley
   PO Box 10360
   Bowling Green, KY 42102-7360
   (502) 781-9741
   TBI, MPI, carbs, manifolds, exhaust, and
   engine performance

8. Howell Engine Developments
   6201 Industrial Way
   Marine City, MI 48039
   (810) 765-5100
   TBI kits for Jeep and other engines

9. Weiand Automotive Ind.
   PO Box 65301
   Los Angeles, CA 90065
   (213) 225-4138
   Intake manifolds and performance
   products

E. Engines/Kits/Parts
   (See also Clifford V-D-4)
1. Jegs*
   751 East 11th Ave.
   Columbus, OH 43211
   (800) 345-4545
   Performance engine parts

2. PAW
   21001 Nordhoff St.
   Chatsworth, CA 91311-5911
   (818) 678-3000
   Performance engine kits and parts

3. Summit Racing
   PO Box 909
   Akron, OH 44309-0909
   (330) 630-3030

F. Engine Swaps
   (See also Sam's I-B-7)
1. Big Boys Toy Store
   564 25 Road
   Grand Junction, CO 81505
   (800) 556-6040
   Engine Swaps and Drivetrain Repairs

2. Farmington Motors
   2508 East Main
   Farmington, NM 87401
   (505) 327-4424
   AMC V-8 engine swaps

3. Mepco 4X4 Warehouse
   7250 South 620 West
   Midvale, UT 84047
   (801) 561-3299
   Jeep Parts from A to Z, plus AMC engine
   swaps

G. Exhaust
   (See also Clifford V-D-4, Edelbrock
   V-D-5, Mopar Performance VI-G)
1. Borla Performance Industries
   5901 Edison Dr.
   Oxnard, CA 93033
   (805) 986-8600
   Performance stainless exhaust systems
   and headers

2. Dynomax
   Walker Manufacturing
   1201 Michigan Blvd.
   Racine, WI
   (800) 767-DYNO
   Manufactures performance mufflers,
   exhaust systems and cat converters

3. Flowmaster
   2975 Dutton Ave., Unit 3
   Santa Rosa, CA 95407
   (707) 544-4761
   Performance mufflers

4. Gibson Performance
   3910-B Prospect Ave.
   Yorba Linda, CA 92686
   (714) 528-3044
   Performance exhaust products

5. Hedman Headers
   9599 W. Jefferson Blvd.
   Culver City, CA 90232
   (310) 839-7501
   Headers and exhaust system products

6. Hooker Industries
   1024 W. Brooks St.
   Ontario, CA 91762
   (909) 983-5871
   Headers and performance exhaust
   products

7. Performance Exhaust and Undercar
   1087 Valentine SE
   Pacific, WA 98047
   (800) 437-2969
   www.performanceexhaust.com
   Performance exhaust systems

H. Fans
1. Flex-a-Lite
   PO Box 9047
   Tacoma, WA 98409-9037
   (800) 851-1510
   Electric and mechanical cooling fans

2. Hayden Inc.*
   1531 Pomona Rd.
   Corona, CA 91720
   (800) 854-4757
   Fans, oil coolers, and cooling accessories

I. Forced Induction
   (See also B&M IX-A-3)
1. Rimmer Engineering
   940 Motor City Drive
   Colorado Springs, CO 80906
   (800) 500-3480
   (719) 636-9100 fax
   www.rimmerengine.com
   Supercharger kits

J. High Flow Water Pumps
   (See also Edelbrock V-D-5, Weiand
   V-D-9)

1. Flowcooler
   289 Prado Rd.
   San Luis Obispo, CA 93401
   (800) 342-6759
   High flow water pumps and thermostats

K. Radiators
   (See also Mepco V-F-3)
1. Modine Manufacturing*
   1500 De Coven Ave.
   Racine, WI 53403
   (414) 636-1641
   Replacement and high efficiency
   radiators

2. Griffin Racing Radiators
   100 Hurricane Creek Rd.
   Piedmont, SC 29673
   (864) 845-5000
   Custom and high performance radiators

3. U.S. Radiator Corp.*
   6710 S. Avalon Blvd.
   Los Angeles, CA 90003
   (213) 778-5525
   Replacement and high efficiency
   radiators

## VI. General
(See also Mepco V-F-3, Off-Road General
Store VII-G-3, Sam's I-B-7, Stage West I-B-8)

A. Clemson 4-Wheel Center
   PO Box 1006
   Clemson, SC 29633
   (864) 882-0277
   Big parts, fabrication and repair outlet

B. Dick Cepek
   17000 Kingsview Ave.
   Carson, CA 90746-1230
   (800) 992-3735
   Performance products, with several
   stores around the country

C. Don-a-Vee Motorsports
   17308 Bellflower
   Bellflower, CA 90706
   (800) 533-7696
   Claims to be world's biggest supplier of
   Jeep parts

D. Four Wheel Drive Hardware
   44488 State Route 14
   Columbiana, OH 44408
   (330) 482-4924
   A huge supplier of Jeep parts and
   accessories

E. Leon Rosser Jeep
   1724 1st Ave. N.
   Bessemer, AL 35201
   (800) 633-4724
   Claims to be world's biggest Jeep parts
   and accessories specialist

F. Mile-Hi Jeep Rebuilders
   724 Federal Blvd.
   Denver, CO 80204
   (303) 629-0278
   Lots of new, used, aftermarket, and NOS
   Jeep parts.

G. Mopar Performance
   See your local jeep dealer
   (810) 853-7290 tech line
   A variety of Jeep performance products

H. *Quadratec*
5125 W. Chester Pike
Newtown Sq., PA 19073
(800) 745-5337
A wide variety of Jeep parts and
accessories

I. *Warrior Products*
17317 SE McLoughlin
Milwaukie, OR 97267
(800) 233-1238
Builds a variety of Jeep products

## VII. Suspension and Steering

A. *Custom Springs*
1. Alcan Spring
2242 Hwys. 6 and 50
Grand Junction, CO 81505
(970) 241-2655
Custom springs
2. Eaton Detroit Springs
1555 Michigan Ave.
Detroit, MI 48216
(313) 963-3839
Manufactures custom and OEM springs
and suspension parts back to 1902
3. Flex-A-Form Inc.
2060 Frontage Road
Anderson, SC 29621
(803) 261-7006
Custom fiberglass springs
4. National Spring
1402 N. Magnolia
El Cajon, CA 92026
(619) 441-1901
Specializes in thin leaf springs. Also has
suspension kits

B. *Power Steering Improvements*
(See also Advance Adapters V-A-1,
Centech IV-F-1)
1. AGR Inc.
2610 Aviation Parkway
Grand Prairie, TX 75052
(800) 662-3649
Super Saginaw steering boxes and high
volume pumps
2. Lee Mfg. Power Steering Systems
11661 Pendelton St.
Sun Valley, CA 91352
(818) 768-0371
Custom power steering hoses, power
steering boxes, and pumps

C. *Shackle Reversal Kits*
(See also Rough Country VII-G-6,
Warrior VI-I)
1. M.O.R.E.
Mountain Off-Road Enterprises
PO Box 843
Rifle, CO 81650
(970) 625-0500
Shackle reversal kits, suspension
upgrades, and performance
equipment

D. *Shocks*
(See also Edelbrock V-D-5, Old Man
Emu VII-G-4, Rancho VII-G-5, Trailmas-
ter VII-G-12, Warn X-A-5)
1. Bilstein Corp.
8845 Rehco
San Diego, CA 92121
(619) 453-7723

2. Doetsch Tech
340 Vernon Way, Ste. H
El Cajon, CA 92020
(619) 593-1800
3. Fox Shox*
3641 Charter Park Dr.
San Jose, CA 95136
(408) 269-9200

E. *Suspension Bushings*
(See also suspension kit mfrs.)
1. Daystar
841 South 71st Ave.
Phoenix, AZ 85043
(800) 595-7659
Polyurethane bushings, shock boots,
and poly engine mounts
2. Energy Suspension
1131 Via Callejon
San Clemente, CA 92673
(714) 361-3935
Polyurethane bushings, shock boots,
and poly engine mounts

F. *Suspension Hardware*
(See also Currie I-B-2, MORE VII-C-1,
Rubicon VII-G-7, Tomken VII-G-11, Tri-
County I-B-10)
1. Four X Doctor
1033 N. Victory Pl.
Burbank, CA
(818) 845-2194
U-bolt reversal kit and bumpers

G. *Suspension Kit Manufacturers*
(See also National Spring VII-A-4)
1. Dick Cepek
17000 Kingsview Ave.
Carson, CA 90746
(310) 217-1805
2. Explorer ProComp
2758 Via Orange Way
Spring Valley, CA 91978
(800) 670-5222
3. Off-Road General Store
23052 Lake Forest Dr. B-4
Laguna Hills, CA 92653
(714) 770-9300
Specializing in coil spring Jeeps and
more
4. Old Man Emu
ARB
1425 Elliot Avenue
W. Seattle, WA 98119
(206) 284-6171
Old Man Emu suspensions and shocks
5. Rancho Suspension
6925 Atlantic Ave.
Long Beach, CA 90805
(310) 259-6221
6. Rough Country Suspension Systems
1445 Hwy. 51 Bypass E.
Dyersburg, TN 38025
(800) 222-7023
7. Rubicon Express
3315 Monier Circle
Rancho Cordova, CA 95742
(916) 858-8575
8. Skyjacker
PO Box 1678
West Monroe, LA 71294
(800) 763-8743
9. Superlift
211 Horne Ln.
West Monroe, LA 71292-9421
(800) 551-4955

10. Teraflex
Tera Mfg.
7241 S. 700 W.
Salt Lake City, UT 84047
(801) 256-9897
11. Tomken Machine
36580 U.S. Hwy 24 N.
Buena Vista, CA 81211
(719) 395-2526
www.tomken.com
12. Trail Master
420 Jay St.
Coldwater, MI 49036
(800) 832-4847

H. *Sway Bar and Track Bar Improvements*
(See also M.O.R.E. VII-C-1)
1. JKS Manufacturing
PO Box 98
Alliance, NE 69301
(308) 762-6949
Sway bar and track bar disconnects, sus-
pension hardware, tie rods

## VIII. Tires and Wheels

A. *Compressors, Tire Tools, and Tire
Accessories*
1. Advanced Air System
5901 Southview Dr.
San Jose, CA 95138
(800) 641-3206
CO-2 tanks for tire inflation
2. Automatic Controls Technology
480 N. Main St.
Brewer, ME 04412
(800) 982-0409 X 002
High output 12-volt compressors
3. Oasis Off-Road Manufacturing
PO Box 674
Lake Forest, CA 92630
(888) 966-2747
Fast air down accessories
4. Safety Seal*
North Shore Laboratories Corp
PO Box 568
Peabody, MA
(800) 888-9021
Tubeless tire repair kits
5. Sun Performance
17 Musick
Irvine, CA 92618
(714) 588-8567
A variety of compressors, tanks and
inflation devices

B. *Custom Wheels and Repairs*
1. Stockton Wheel
648 W. Fremont St.
Stockton, CA 95203
(800) 395-WHEEL
Steel wheel fabrication and repair

C. *Tires*
1. B.F. Goodrich
PO Box 19001
Greenville, SC 29602-19001
(803) 458-5000
2. Big O Tires
11755 E. Peakview Ave.
Englewood, CO 80111
(303) 790-2800
3. Bridgestone
1 Bridgestone Park
Nashville, TN 37214-0991
(615) 391-0088

4. Continental General Tire
1800 Continental Blvd.
Charlotte, NC 28273
(800) 847-3349
5. Cooper Tire
PO Box 550
Findlay, OH 45839
(800) 854-6288
(800) 822-8686 dealer info.
6. Dayton Tire
1 Bridgestone Park
Nashville, TN 37214-0991
(615) 391-0088
www.dayton-tire.com
7. Denman Tire Corp.
400 Diehl S. Rd.
Leavittsburg, OH 44430
(800) 334-5543
(216) 675-4242
8. Dick Cepek
17000 Kingsview Ave.
Carson, CA 90746
(310) 217-1314
(310) 527-5888
9. Dunlop Tire Co.
PO Box 1109
Buffalo, NY 14240-1109
(716) 639-5200
10. Falken Tire Corp.
10404 6th St.
Rancho Cucamonga, CA 91730
(909) 466-1116
(800) 723-2553
11. Firestone
1 Bridgestone Park
Nashville, TN 37214-0991
(615) 391-0088
12. Goodyear Tire and Rubber
1144 E. Market St.
Akron, OH 44316
13. Interco Tire Company
PO Box 486
Rayne, LA 70578
(800) 299-8000
14. Kelly Springfield Tire Company
12501 Willow Brook Rd. S.E.
Cumberland, MD 21502
(800) 638-5112
15. Michelin
PO Box 19001
Greenville, SC 29602
(803) 458-5000
16. Mickey Thompson Performance Tires
4670 Allen Rd.
Stow, OH 44224
(800) 222-9092
17. Pirelli Armstrong Tire Co.
500 Sargent Dr.
New Haven, CT 06536-0201
(203) 784-2200
(800) 243-5105
18. Pos-A-Traction
PO Box 8010
Compton, CA 90224-8010
(800) GET-POSI
19. Sumitomo Tire Co.
601 Gateway Blvd., Ste. 650
South San Francisco, CA 94080
(415) 583-5555
20. Uniroyal
600 S. Main St.
Akron, OH 44397-0001

21. Yokohama Tire Corp.
601 S. Acadia Ave.
Fullerton, CA 92631
(800) 423-4544

D. *Wheels*
1. Alcoa Wheels
1600 Harvard Ave.
Cleveland, OH 44105
(800) 668-1150
2. Alpha/McLean
1340 W. Gladstone St.
Azusa, CA 91702
(818) 969-3200
3. American Racing Equipment
19067 S. Reyes Ave.
Rancho Dominguez, CA 90221
(310) 635-7806
4. Boyds Wheels
8380 Cerritos Ave.
Stanton, CA 90680
(714) 952-4038
5. Center Line Performance Wheels
13521 Freeway Dr.
Santa Fe Springs, CA 90670
(310) 921-9637
6. Cragar Industries
4636 N. 43rd Ave.
Phoenix, AZ 85031
(602) 247-1300
7. Colorado Custom Wheels
363 Jefferson St.
Fort Collins, CO 80524
(303) 224-5750
8. Freedom Design
750 Eisenhower Ave.
Alexandria, VA 22304
(703) 823-5606
9. Mickey Thompson Performance Tires
4670 Allen Rd.
Stow, OH 44224
(800) 222-9092
10. Prime Wheel
17705 S. Main St.
Gardena, CA 90248
(310) 516-9126
11. Progressive
3400 Jefferson St.
Riverside, CA 92504
(909) 785-4700
(800) 726-5335
12. Ronal Intl.
15692 Computer Lane
Huntington Beach, CA 92649
(714) 891-4853
13. Superior Industries
7800 Woodley Ave.
Van Nuys, CA 91406-1788
(818) 781-4973
14. TSW Alloy Wheels
311 E. Alton Ave.
Santa Ana, CA 92707
(800) 578-4879
15. Ultra Wheel Co.
6300 Valley View Ave.
Buena Park, CA 90620
(714) 994-1111
16. Weld Racing
933 Mulberry St.
Kansas City, MO 64101
(816) 421-8040

17. ZZ Wheels
1215 Commerce Dr.
Richardson, TX 75081
(214) 480-9997

## IX. Transmission and Transfer Case

A. *Automatics and Parts*
(See also Hayden V-H-2)
1. A-1 Automatic Transmissions
7359 Canoga Ave.
Canoga Park, CA 91333
(818) 884-6222
Low gear sets, performance built automatics, and parts
2. Art Carr Transmissions
10575 Bechler River Ave.
Fountain Valley, CA 92708
(714) 962-6655
Performance built automatics, converters, and parts
3. B&M Racing and Performance
9142 Independence Ave.
Chatsworth, CA 91311
(818) 882-6422
Performance automatics, shifters, and parts
4. Premier Performance Transmissions
1020 S. Melrose St., Unit B
Placentia, CA 92670
(714) 630-3235
Performance built automatics and parts
5. TCI Automotive
1 TCI Drive
Ashland, MS 38603
(601) 244-8972
Performance built automatics, converters, and parts
6. TransGo Performance
2621 Merced Ave.
El Monte, CA 91733
(818) 443-4953
Performance automatic parts

B. *Clutches*
1. Centerforce Performance Clutches
2266 Crosswind Dr.
Prescott, AZ 86301
(520) 771-8422
Extreme duty and performance clutches and related gear
2. Hayes Clutches
8700 Brookpark Rd.
Cleveland, OH 44129
(216) 398-8300
Standard and performance clutches

C. *Overdrives and Splitters*
(See also Advance Adapters V-A-1, 4 to 1 IX-D-6)
1. Gear Vendors
1717 N. Magnolia Ave.
El Cajon, CA 92020
(619) 562-0060

D. *Transfer Case Gearing Changes and Modifications*
(See also Currie I-B-2, Mile-Marker X-A-2, Rubicon Express VII-G-7)
1. Hicks 4x4 Specialists
1321 S. Garey Ave.
Pomona, CA 91766
(909) 865-7170
Extra-low range kit for Dana 20

2. JB Conversions
PO Box 2683
Sulpher, LA 70664-2683
(318) 921-3202
Short tailshaft kits, 2-lo kits, and various beefing parts

3. M.I.T.
1112 Pioneer Way
El Cajon, CA 92020
(619) 579-7727
Short tailshaft kits, service, and parts

4. O'Brien's 4-Wheel West
1302 Hidden Ct.
Roseville, CA 95661
(916) 773-3278
Extra-low low range gears for Dana 18 and 20

5. Tera-Low
Tera Mfg.
7241 S. 700 W.
Salt Lake City, UT 84047
(801) 256-9897

6. 4 to 1 Manufacturing
PO Box 1365
Sandy, UT 84091
(801) 641-1421
3.5:1, 4:1 low range kits and splitters

## X. Winches and Recovery Gear

### A. Electric, Hydraulic Winches

1. MegaWinch Corp.
7911 N.E. 33rd Dr., Ste 310
Portland, OR 97211
(503) 288-1245

2. Mile-Marker
1450 SW 13th Ct.
Pompano Beach, FL 33069
(305) 782-0604

3. Ramsey Winch
1600 N. Garrett Road
Tulsa, OK 74116
(918) 438-2760

4. Superwinch Inc.
45 Danco Rd.
Putnam, CT 06260
(203) 928-7787

5. Warn Industries
12900 S.E. Capps Road
Clackamas, OR 97015-8903
(800) 543-9276

### B. Ground Anchors

1. Pull Pal
PO Box 639
Carbondale, CO 81623
(800) 541-1817
www.truckworld.com/pullpal/
Foldable, portable ground anchor

2. SureClaw Wheel Anchor
Mesa Industries
2687 Orange Ave., Ste. A
Costa Mesa, CA 92627
(714) 548-8616
Wheel anchors

### C. Manual Winches, Come-Alongs, and Recovery Gear

1. MAX
Forrest Tool Company
PO Box 768
Mendicino, CA 95460
(707) 937-1817
Multi-purpose ax, 7 tools in one

2. More Power Puller
Avenir
PO Box 1176
Newark, OH 43055
(800) 626-0095
Two-ton come along

## XI. Safety

### A. Fire Extinguishers

1. Ansul Inc.
1 Stanton Street
Marinette, WI 54143-2542
(800) TO-ANSUL
Fire fighting products

### B. Roll Bars
(See also M.O.R.E. VII-C-1, Smittybilt II-C-4, Stage West I-B-8)

# APPENDIX 2

## Bibliography

Adler, Ulrich (Editor). *Bosch Automotive Handbook*. Robert Bosch GmbH, 1993. 3-1-419115-X.

Horner, Jim. *Automotive Electrical Handbook*. HP Books, 1986. 0-89586-238-7.

Jacobs, David H. *How to Restore Bodywork*. Motorbooks International, 1991. 0-87938-514-6.

King/Worthy. *Jeep Bible*. The Quellen Company, 1997. 0-9618473.

Lawler, John. *Auto Math Handbook*. HP Books, 1992. 1-55788-020-4.

Ludel, Moses. *Jeep Owners Bible*. Robert Bentley, Inc., 1992. 0-8376-0154.

Mopar Performance. *Jeep Engines*. Chrysler Corporation. Available from Mopar Performance.

Oberg/Jones/Horton. *Machinery's Handbook* 75-1962. Industrial Press, 1978.

Puhn, Fred. *Brake Handbook*. HP Books, 1985. 0-89586-232-8.

Remus/Overholser. *Hot Rod Wiring*. Wolfgang Publications, 1997. 0-9641358-6-8.

Rundle, Randy. *Wired for Success*. Krause Publications, 1995. ISBN: 0-87341-402-0.

Smith/Wenner. *The Design and Tuning of Competition Engines*. Robert Bentley, Inc., 1977. 0-8376-140-1

Urich/Fisher. *Holley Carburetors, Manifolds and Fuel Injection*. S-A Design, 1994. 1-55788-052-2.

Vizard, David. *How to Build Horsepower, V1*. S-A Design, 1990. 0-931472-24-5.

Vizard, David. *How to Build Horsepower, V2*. S-A Design, 1996.

Vizard, David. *Performance With Economy*. S-A Design, 1981. 0-931472-09-1.

Voegelin, Rick. *Engine Blueprinting*. S-A Design, 1988. 0-931472-21-0.

Yunick, Smokey. *Power Secrets*. S-A Design, 1989. 0-931472-06-7.

## Magazine Subscription Info

*Four Wheeler*
PO Box 420235
Palm Coast, FL 32142-01235
(800) 777-0555

*Jp*
PO Box 56249
Boulder, CO 80322-6249
(800) 800-4294

*Off-Road*
PO Box 68033
Anaheim, CA 92817-0833
(714) 693-1866

*Open Road*
PO Box 51922
Boulder, CO 80323-1922

*4-Wheel Drive and Sport Utility*
PO Box 68033
Anaheim, CA 92817-0833
(714) 693-1866

*4-Wheel and Off-Road*
PO Box 56249
Boulder, CO 80322-6249
(800) 800-4294

# INDEX

Air filters, 147–149
  capacity and flow, 148, 149
  choosing, 149
  efficiency, 148
  open vs. closed element, 149
  size formulas, 164
Air intake system, waterproofing, 150
Airflow, through radiator, 160
Alternator, 168–170
Alternator, mega-amp, mounting, 169
Alternator speed, calculating, 176
Amps, calculating total, 175
Antennas, 183
Automatic gearing changes, 97
Available aftermarket gear ratios, 81
Axes and saws, 105
Axles
  aftermarket, 68–70
  assembly swaps, 68, 79
  front, 60, 61
  front, universal joint guide, 78
  list of all factory, 78
  rear, 61–63
  shafts, 65, 66
Batteries, 166–168
  cables and connections, 170, 171
  choosing, 167
  deep-cycle, 166
  dual, 167, 168
  marine, 166, 167
  starting, 166
Beadlocks, 20
Body, 119–127
  defense strategies, 119, 120
  fiberglass, 121, 122
  replacement steel, 120, 121
Body armor, off-highway, 122, 123
Body hardware, 123, 124
Body lifts, 45, 46
Brakes
  disc brake calipers, 134, 135
  disc vs. drum, 129, 130
  drum, 131
  drums and rotors, 136, 137
  front disc brake conversions, 131, 132
  hydraulic, 132–137
  lines and hoses, 135
  list of all OE brakes, 138
  parking, 137
  rear disc brake conversions, 132
Brake bias, 135
Brake boosters, 136
Brake fluid, 135, 136
Brake linings, 130, 131
  hard vs. soft, 131
  riveted vs. bonded, 131
Brake master cylinder, 134
Brush bars, 123, 124
Bumpers, 123, 124
Camshaft, 140–143
Camshaft dictionary, 162
Carburetor, 140–143
Carburetor capacity, calculating, 163
Carburetors and angles, 146, 147
Cargo tie downs, 182
CB radios, 182, 183
Cell phones, 182
Chassis, 115–119
  armor, 118, 119

failure, 116, 117
  specifications, 128
  protecting, 117, 118
  unibody, 118
Clutches, 98–100
  OE specs, 103
  release mechanism, 99, 100
  selection, 99
Clutch discs, 98, 99
Clutch linkage, upgrading, 100
Coil springs, 40, 41
Coil spring lifts, 41–43
Common steel groups, 81
Compressors, onboard, 14
Converters, choosing, 95
Cooling system tips, 158–161
Crawl ratio, 83
CV joints, 77
Dipsticks and breathers, waterproofing, 151
Driveshafts, 43–45, 74–77
  custom, 44, 45
Driveshaft and low gear torque, calculating, 80
Driveshaft clearance, 76, 77
Electrical systems
  definitions and formulas, 175
  waterproofing, 174
  rewiring, completely, 172, 173
Electricity, flow of, 165
Electronic fuel injection (EFI), 140–143
Emissions regulations, 161, 162
Engines
  swapping, 154–158
  waterproofing, 150, 151
Engines, popular swaps
  90-degree GM V-6, 157
  AMC V-8s, 157
  Buick V-6, 157
  Chevy small-block V-8, 155, 156
  Factory Jeep, 151–154
  Ford small-block, 156, 157
Exhaust system, 143–145
Fuel tank capacities, 128
Fenderwell clearance, 12, 13
Fire extinguisher, 177, 178
First aid kit, 181, 182, 184
Forced induction, 145, 146
Fuel cans, 127
Fuel injection, waterproofing, 151
Fuel tanks, 126, 127
Gear ratio, effective, 25
Gearing change options for assorted automatics, 102
High-pinion differentials, 70, 71
Horsepower and torque, 139
Hubs, 66–68
Hydraulic formulas, 138
Ignition systems, waterproofing, 150, 151
Interior, 124
Jacks, 106
Jeep model abbreviations, 5
Leaf spring lift, 36
Leaf spring lift complications, 38, 39
Leaf spring rate, 28, 29
Leaf spring trucks, 35
Lift kit, selecting, 38
Light, constriction and specifications, 173, 174

Lights, choosing and mounting, 173, 174
Limited slip, 71, 72
Lockers, 71–74
  automatic, 72
  choices, 73, 74
  on-demand, 72, 73
Max multipurpose tool, 105
No-load line speed comparison, 114
Oil coolers, 161
Open differential, 71
Overdrive, 89
Picks, 105
Pinion angles, 43–45
Power steering, 54, 55
  conversions, 55
  coolers, 54, 55
  more power, 55
  temps, 59
Pressure plates, 99
Radiator, 159, 160
Ramp travel index, 58
Ring and pinions, 63, 64
Roll bars, 178–181
Seat belts, 181
Select low-range crawl ratio combinations, 92
Shackle angles and choices, 32–34
Shackle position, 31, 32
Shock absorbers, 46–51
  choosing, 50, 51
  multiple, 48, 49
Shock boots, 48
Shovels, 104, 105
Snorkels, 149, 150
Soft tops, 124, 125
Speakers, external, 183
Speedometer correction, 15
Splines, 64, 65
Spline strength graph, 79
Splitters, 89, 90
Sprags, 96
Springs
  composite, 30
  dictionary, 57
  factory specs, 56
  innovative steel, 30
  long vs. short, 29
  selecting, 35, 36
  wide vs. narrow, 29
Spring and chassis bushings, 36
Spring over, 37
Spring rate, calculating, 56, 57
Stall speed, 95
Starters, 171
Starters and alternators, waterproofing, 151
Steering dampers, 52, 53
Steering linkage mods, 52
Steering, 51–55
  camber, 53, 54
  caster, 53, 54
  common problems, 52
  toe-in, 53, 54
Storage, 125, 126
Straps, 105, 106
Suspension
  add-a-leaf, 37
  camber, 30
  coil spring, 40–43

hardware, 39, 40
  leaf-spring, 28–40
  lift blocks, 37
  longer shackles, 37, 38
Sway bar disconnects, 45
Tailshaft conversions, 87
Tailshaft kits, 44
Tires, 11–18
  and gearing, 13, 15
  chains, 17, 18
  fitment guide, 24
  glossary, 21–23
  load vs. inflation, 26
  pressure, street, 15, 16
  pressure, suggested, 26
  pressure, trail, 16, 17
  radial vs. bias ply, 11
  repairs, 17
  sizes, maximum recommended for Jeep axles, 77
Torque converter, 94, 95
Torque, building for, 139–146
Torque-to-weight ratios, 162
Towing points, 104–106
Track bar disconnects, 45
Transfer case and differential yoke availability, 80
Transfer cases, 82–88
  factory, 83–86
  gearing, extra low, 86, 87
  list of all factory, 90
  swapping and beefing, 88
Transfer case/Trans adapter availability chart, 90, 91
Transmissions
  automatic, 93–97, 102
  manual, 97, 98
  ratings, 103
  specs, 101
  temp control, 96
Transmission coolers
  OE, 96
  external, 97
Universal joint dimensions and torque ratings, 80
Water pump, 160, 161
Welders, underhood, 169
Wheels, 18–21
  choosing, 20, 21
  size and offset, 19, 20
Winches, 106–112
  accessories, 111, 112
  capstan, 107
  choosing, 109, 110
  electric, 108, 109
  hand 106, 107
  hydraulic, 107, 108
  mounting system, choosing, 110, 111
  prepping your Jeep for, 112
  PTO Drum, 107
  specs, 6000 pounds and up, 113
Winch pull, how it is affected by terrain, 113, 114
Wire, 12-volt, selection guide, 176
Wires and cables, 170, 171
Wiring accessories, 171, 172
Yokes, upgrading, 75